THE EVOLUTION
OF
WEAPONS AND WARFARE

THE EVOLUTION
OF
WEAPONS AND WARFARE

by
Colonel Trevor N. Dupuy
U.S. Army, Ret.

The Bobbs-Merrill Company, Inc.
Indianapolis/New York

To my princess

Preface

The origins of this book are many and are, to some extent, complex.

Its principal source was a study that I directed, which was done for the U.S. Army by the Historical Evaluation and Research Organization (usually identified by its modest acronym, HERO) in 1964 and 1965, entitled: "Historical Trends Related to Weapon Lethality." But the book also reflects many other ideas about the relationship of military history to modern military affairs, which coalesced in my mind during the 1970s.

I have become increasingly concerned by the lack of attention to historical experience in military analysis, and in the formulation of military policy, doctrine and plans in the United States, a concern that has been intensified by realization that our most likely opponent in a future war — the armed forces of the Soviet Union — have been, and continue to be, greatly influenced by their intensive study of modern military history. If this book in any way contributes to increased recognition on the part of senior Pentagon officials in and out of uniform of the essentially evolutionary nature of warfare (no matter how revolutionary new weapons and technology may be), recognition that modern warfare always will be an extrapolation from past warfare, and realization that some aspects of war never change, then it will have accomplished its purpose.

I am indebted to a number of people for their contribution to this book. First, I am grateful to Tom Gervasi for suggesting that I write it. I am grateful to the several colleagues who worked with me in 1964 and 1965 in the preparation of the study, "Historical Trends Related to Weapon Lethality." I am indebted to my current colleagues on the HERO staff who have contributed ideas, or who have stimulated my own thinking of these. I am particularly grateful to Paul Martell.

Unquestionably my greatest debt of gratitude must be to my former and greatly respected colleague, Billie P. Davis, who (at my request, and with my guidance) took the confused mass of things I had written for the various chapters of this book, and pulled them together into a coherent manuscript — and in the process added some very relevant thoughts of her own. While the concept, most of the ideas, and most of the words in this book are mine, and mine alone, their structure and presentation owe much to Billie. Had it not been for her devotion to the task, it is doubtful if the book would ever have been finished.

Only slightly less important is the contribution of Grace P. Hayes, Vice President of HERO, and my colleague for longer than she or I care to remember. Her careful, thoughtful, repeated editorial reviews of the manuscript forced me to sharpen my ideas and tighten my wording from start to end. If the book has merit, Grace is responsible to a very large degree.

I received some very valuable suggestions from four respected historian colleagues to whom I sent the manuscript for comment. I am extremely grateful to Professor Martin Blumenson, Dr. Hugh M. Cole, Mr. Brereton Greenhous of the Canadian Directorate of History, and Professor Theodore Ropp.

Several members of HERO's administrative staff typed the various drafts of the manuscript, including Blanche Griffin, Virginia Rufner, Laura Fentin, and Vicki Stumpf. The person most responsible for the production of the manuscript, however, was HERO's Administrative Director, Marie A. Tysinger. I am most grateful to her and her assistants for their help.

I hope it is clear from these expressions of gratitude that, if the book is good, many other people are in large part responsible. But if it has shortcomings, then I alone am responsible.

T. N. Dupuy

Dunn Loring, Virginia
May, 1980

Contents

Part Three: The Age of Technological Change

Part One: The Age of Muscle

I. Pike, Bow, Sword, Shield, and Chariot 2000–500 B.C.

War and History

The first battle described in recorded history took place at Megiddo in Palestine. In 1469 B.C. tribes of Palestine and Syria revolted against the young Egyptian pharaoh Thutmosis III. The rebels assembled at Megiddo, north of Mount Carmel, with outposts assigned to hold the Megiddo Pass. Thutmosis, in his chariot, led his army in a bold thrust through the pass. Quickly arranging his army into a crescent formation, the pharaoh advanced against the rebels, who were previously unaware of the proximity of the Egyptians. While his right wing contained the surprised enemy in a holding attack, Thutmosis led his left wing in an envelopment of the enemy flank to the north, achieving an overwhelming victory.

Armed conflict was a fact of life long before this first recorded engagement. *Homo sapiens* probably first recognized the value of stones or sticks as implements while using these "weapons" in the search for food, a mate, a place to live, or in satisfying his inherent desire to dominate. He later discovered that a stone with a sharp edge or a stick with a pointed end could be more lethal than the ordinary round stone or blunt club. This primitive man also learned that it was tactically expedient to attack his enemy or prey from concealment in the grass or by jumping unexpectedly from a tree or a ledge. And so the pattern was set for discovery, improvement, adoption, and use of weapons with tactics especially devised to suit their capabilities. This pattern has been followed throughout history.

The Early Implements of War

The origins of many weapons in the arsenal of fighting men are lost in thousands of years of unrecorded history. The first use of metal, the invention of the sword, of the bow, and of the spear had revolutionary effects on the development of combat practices and, ultimately, tactics, but these events were not recorded. In later ages evolutionary changes in these basic weapons and their uses continued to affect what men did in battle.

From the beginning, weapons fell into two major categories: shock and missile. The original shock weapon was the prehistoric man's club; the first missile weapon was the rock that he hurled at his enemy or prey.

From prehistoric times leather slings were used to hurl small, smooth rocks with greater force and for longer distances than was possible by arm power alone. Clay balls baked into bullets were also used with slings. Later pellets were made of lead; samples in an acorn shape have been found at Pompeii and other ancient sites. Balearic Island slingers, particularly famous for their skill, were equipped with three slings, one each for long, medium, and short range. David used a sling to kill Goliath. Slingers played an important role in the military lineup for many centuries.

In some regions the hurled rock gradually was displaced by throwing sticks which, in turn, evolved into darts, javelins, and the boomerang. Homer's heroes each apparently carried two javelins to be hurled at the enemy before closing with a sword. The shock-action counterpart of the javelin was the heavy pike, or thrusting spear. In many ancient societies the spear was the symbol of military prowess and a sacred symbol of majesty as well. The spear was venerated in the shrine of Mars at Rome and at various holy places in Greece.

Greek spears were commonly six to nine feet long but, being handmade, were of many varieties and lengths. The spear or pike was the standard weapon of the Greek *hoplite* — a heavily armed and armored soldier — who was the basic element of the fighting formation known as the phalanx.

Over time the basic Stone Age club took on a variety of forms, of which the American Indian tomahawk is an axlike example. Clubs with sharpened edges became prototypes of the sword. The long thin blade that characterizes the sword could not be created until metallurgy developed to permit the working of hard, malleable metal. Bronze was the first such metal used by man; since it exists in nature, it is impossible to say when bronze was first made artificially. Bronze implements were used as early as 3000 B.C. in Crete, 2800 B.C. in Egypt and Mesopotamia, and 2000 B.C. in Troy. Comparable developments occurred in the Indus Valley some time before 2500 B.C. and in the Yellow River valley of China probably several centuries later. Bronze was hard, tough, and durable, and could be made into excellent pointed and edged weapons.

As metalworkers became more expert through the centuries, and as they discovered new techniques for making and molding their products, the reliability of the sword changed, as did its shape. Bronze swords were at first pointed, often enlarged at the point, and from the beginning seem to have been used both for thrusting (like rapiers) and cutting (like sabers); because of the relative softness of bronze, the use for thrusting at first predominated.

Iron implements were first made around 1500 B.C. About a century later the Chalybes tribe in the Armenian mountains had learned to harden wrought iron through a process of alternately heating it in a charcoal fire, quenching, reheating, and hammering. (In fact, the first steel was made by the accidental absorption of charcoal particles into the surface of the metal during this process.) This new technology became known throughout the eastern Mediterranean world before 1200 B.C.

The discovery of iron had tremendous impact on ancient weapons and warfare, but despite its potential iron was at first costly and rare. By 1200 B.C. the slashing sword began to appear in Asia Minor, Syria, and Egypt. With this stronger, less brittle metal came changes in the shape of the sword.

By 1000 B.C. there were two principal types of swords. One was a long, saberlike weapon for slashing, often made without a point, such as was used later by the Gauls or Celts. A relatively short sword rather akin to a dagger was carried by the Greek hoplite. This Greek short sword had a blade about 16 to 18 inches long, was 2 to 2½ inches broad, and had a handle 4 or 5 inches in length. It was the prototype of the slightly longer and broader Roman short sword. Although still a cut-and-thrust weapon, the pre-Roman sword was used mainly for cutting.

The advent of the use of metal also brought developments in the manufacture of armor. The most important protective armor devised by primitive man had been the shield, at first an animal skin held almost invariably in the left hand or on the left arm, leaving the right arm free to wield a weapon. Later, shields usually were made of leather or hide covering a simple wooden framework, although some ancient ones were made entirely of wood, and in Asia wicker shields were common. Originally, protective covering for head, torso, and legs was made of leather, wicker, padded or quilted cloth, or wood.

Even after the introduction of metal in weaponry, leather remained the basic and most common material for shields, although it was often reinforced with metal. To hammer out plate armor and helmets needed skill and long hours of labor. A less expensive, practical alternative was a kind of scale armor of small forged plates. The Assyrian warrior, benefitting from the new metallic technology, carried a long iron cutting sword, and armor of iron scales sewed to a leather base. After the introduction of iron, the spear of the Greek hoplite was iron-tipped, and the short iron sword on his belt was also made of iron, but his armor, shield, and helmet were of bronze. The Roman legionary soldier wore a cuirass of overlapping jointed plates of bronze or iron on leather.

The bow appeared late in the Stone Age. It was the basic missile weapon until the advent of gunpowder. The bow was in use at the dawn of recorded history in the Middle East, India, and China. From earliest times until the sixteenth century A.D. the Chinese appear to have relied on it as their principal hand weapon. It was also a major weapon in the Assyrian armies, which included heavy and light archers. The bow was also important to the Greek, Macedonian, Hellenistic, and Roman forces, but was an auxiliary weapon.

In India the bow was four to five feet long and remained essentially unchanged for twenty-two hundred years. Bamboo was usually the preferred material, though other materials, including metal, were tried. Arrows were two to three feet long, made of bamboo or of cane, and usually tipped with metal. Bowmen did not usually carry shields, but were protected by a front rank of shield-bearing javelin throwers. Both Indian archers and javelin men were also armed with fairly long, broad-bladed swords.

Effective use of the bow required constant practice as well as suitable, open terrain. It therefore became the weapon of professionals, like the Assyrian archers, or later the Cretan mercenary archers (highly regarded by the Macedonians and Romans), or of nomadic hunting people.

Early bows were "self-bows," that is, made of one kind of wood. In the Near East and Asia composite bows, sometimes called horn bows, made their appearance by about 1500 B.C. Available materials determined their composition. These horn bows became standard equipment of all Asian and some European people, and they are still in use in some remote areas of the world.

A composite bow is built of layers of different material. For most historical periods a flat wooden stave usually formed the central frame; on the side toward the archer a layer of split horn was attached; on the side away from him there was a layer of animal sinews. Most composite bows were reflex, that is, when unstrung they bent in the direction opposite to the way they were bent when the bowstring was tight. Composite bows usually were under four feet long, but the Turkish or Mongol bow was more than five feet in length.

The numerous types of horn bows varied in range and penetration ability. The Turkish horn bow shot well over 300 yards and had considerable penetration potential. Not until about the fifteenth century A.D., however, could an improved Turkish bow penetrate mail armor. A significant increase in the lethality of the horn bow took place when it was used by mounted troops, creating a formidable combination of mobility and firepower.

The chariot, a small cart drawn by one or more armored horses, was developed in very early times. In the Trojan Wars (ca. 1200 B.C.), chariots were used as mobile platforms for archers and spearmen, and until late in the Greek period they served primarily as a means of transporting officers to the battlefield, where they would descend to fight hand to hand. In India and China they were large and seem to have been used as mobile command posts by kings or nobles, who were usually accompanied by a drummer-signaler, a driver, and one or more archers. But as time went on chariots became the principal shock-action weapons of most Asian armies, being used to knock down or run over the opposing forces. In this role their deadliness was increased by attaching scythes and other blades to axle and wheels, and in some varieties a kind of armor protection was provided by hanging shields on the side. The Bible tells that the Hebrews fleeing out of Egypt were particularly afraid of Pharaoh's chariots. Assyrian war chariots much impressed contemporary and later chroniclers.

On the whole, however, chariots were of limited use because of the vulnerability of the horses, and they were effective only on flat and open terrain. Nevertheless, as weapons of opportunity, used at the right time and place, chariots won many a battle.

Cavalry appeared about 1000 B.C. and was composed of lesser nobles who had enough wealth to own horses and to supply themselves with armor and good weapons. The elite striking force of most armies, however, remained a contingent of chariots in which the great nobles or members of royal families rode to battle.

Since it was difficult to breed good horses in the Indian climate, and since the best animals were used with chariots, cavalry was rarely employed in ancient India. Partly because of this, about 600 B.C. elephants began to appear on the field of battle. The unexpected appearance of a contingent of these great animals could be most terrifying, though their presence often proved of little more than psychological value. After the initial shock of seeing them, disciplined troops could find effective means of dealing with elephants, and not infrequently the beasts stampeded and caused much disorder in their own ranks. For this reason, the war elephant's mahout (driver) carried a steel spike to hammer into the beast's brain should he stampede. In India antielephant measures included the use of heavy iron arrows and fire arrows. Some unidentified Greek genius evolved the prototype of an antitank mine field: iron spikes, chained and anchored in place, to rip the tender feet of the pachyderms.

Despite their limitations and vulnerabilities, elephants were never scorned by their opponents, and their use spread across much of the Near East and North Africa. One of the earliest arms limitations in recorded history was the Roman prohibition of war elephants in the peace imposed on Carthage after the Second Punic War.

Mobility, or the lack of it, played an important role in the composition of early armies, in the use of their weapons, and in the tactics employed. These armies invariably consisted of large masses of infantry, probably carrying pikes and shields, with additional foot troops — slingers and archers — armed with missile weapons. This infantry component provided a solid base around which the better-armed contingents of chariots, horsemen, or war elephants could operate.

When armies met, the infantry spearmen stayed together in large groups, with swarms of lightly armed archers and slingers out in front. The nobles on horses or in chariots took position in front and on the flanks. As the armies approached each other the archers and slingers maintained harassing fire until the chariots or horsemen started to charge. The light troops then drifted to flank and rear through intervals in the heavy infantry masses. With a few exceptions, such as we have seen in Thutmosis's performance at Megiddo, maneuver was more a matter of chance than plan. Usually the two masses converged to sway back and forth over the growing numbers of dead and wounded. Or, if the initial charge of chariots and horsemen by one side struck terror into their opponents, the battle became a chase.

From the beginning of recorded history, military tactics, organization, and doctrine were much more likely to be affected by new ideas or new concepts of employing men and weapons than they were by the appearance of new weapons alone. More often than not the great developments in military affairs resulted from the application of sound, imaginative thinking to existing weapons.

The Assyrian War Machine

An illustration of this was the adoption of a new organizational concept in Assyria. About 700 B.C. Tiglath-Pileser III abolished the then-existing militia organization of Assyria and organized the state around a permanent regular army. The soldiers, of course, had to be paid and fed, and the army could be most easily sustained on foreign soil. Thus the principal business of the nation became war; its wealth and prosperity were sustained by booty and by what seems to have been the first truly military society of history. No effort was spared that would contribute to the efficiency of the army, and with it Tiglath-Pileser extended the empire far beyond the area already conquered by a series of warrior kings before him.

The Assyrians were apparently the first soldiers to recognize fully the advantage of iron over bronze, and their army was completely equipped with weapons, chariots, and armor made of iron. Technical superiority was maintained by constant and systematic improvement of weapons and by the careful training of soldiers in the use of their arms.

The bulk of an Assyrian army was comprised of large masses of spearmen, slow-moving and cumbersome, but relatively better trained and more maneuverable than similar infantry formations of other peoples of the time. Their irresistible advance was the culminating phase of a typical Assyrian battle plan.

Assyrian archers were also more highly organized than their counterparts elsewhere, and evidently had stronger bows, from which they shot iron-tipped arrows with deadly accuracy. They created confusion in the enemy ranks in preparation for a closely coordinated chariot and cavalry charge.

The main striking force of the Assyrian army was the corps of horse-drawn, two-wheeled chariots. Their mission was to smash their way through the ranks of enemy infantry. Like their contemporaries, the Assyrians used chariots in simple, brute force, but employed them in larger numbers, with more determination, and in closer coordination with archers, spearmen, and cavalry.

The cavalry was the smallest element of the army, but probably was the best trained and equipped. The nobles all rode to battle on horses. Some dismounted to fight on foot, or on chariots. But many served as horsemen in battle, and fought with a combination of discipline, skill, and ingenuity not achievable in the other elements of the army. Only the cavalry could be employed in the occasional maneuvers attempted in battle.

The high degree of organization of the Assyrian army is clearly evidenced by its ability to fight successfully over all kinds of terrain. The organizational details are not known, but Assyrian field armies may occasionally have approached a strength of 50,000 men. Forces of such size would have required large supply trains for desert or mountain operations, and could have functioned only with smoothly operating staff and logistical systems.

Terror was another factor contributing greatly to the Assyrians' success. Cruelty and ferocity were characteristic of most armies of the period, but theirs was also a calculated policy of terror — possibly the earliest example of organized psychological warfare. It was not unusual for the Assyrians to kill every man, woman, and child in a captured city, or to carry away entire populations into captivity. This policy was employed with callous vigor and proved an invaluable contribution to security.

Beginning of Naval Warfare

About the same time that the Assyrians developed a standing army, the Phoenicians seem to have introduced the first naval vessels designed essentially for fighting. The use of boats for warlike purposes had long been a common practice of the seafaring peoples living along the shores of the Mediterranean and Aegean seas, but this had been largely limited to employing merchant vessels as troop and supply transports. These short, broad-beamed craft, combining sails and oars, were essentially adjuncts of land power. The new warships made by the Phoenicians, however, were oar-propelled galleys, longer, narrower, and speedier than the typical merchant craft.

The Greeks, particularly the Athenians, improved the design of Phoenician galleys, and brought to naval warfare a skill and perfection in technique hitherto unknown in fighting on either land or sea. The Athenian trireme was long, low, and narrow, deriving its name from the fact that its oars were ranged in groups of three on each side of the vessel. Seaworthiness, comfort, cargo capacity, and range were sacrificed to achieve speed, power, and maneuverability in these fighting vessels. In addition to its oars, the trireme carried sails on its two masts as a means of auxiliary power; in battle, however, it was propelled exclusively by its oarsmen, who numbered anywhere from 75 to more than 150.

The principal weapon of the trireme was a metal beak projecting some ten feet in front of the prow at the waterline. When this beak was rammed into the side of another vessel, the results were deadly. The difficulties of accomplishing this, however, were such that most Greeks usually preferred to rely upon the older tactics of pulling alongside a foe and boarding, and for that purpose they carried boarding troops.

Athenian sailors relied upon superior seamanship, speed, and maneuverability to bring victory. When there was not an immediate opportunity to smash directly into the side of an opponent, Athenian vessels would swerve unexpectedly beside their foes, shipping their oars at the last moment, and breaking those of the surprised enemy. The disabled foe was then a sitting duck, to be rammed at leisure by one of the Athenian vessels.

Although the influence of the ancient Phoenicians, and their "heirs" at Carthage and Syracuse, cannot be discounted, for hundreds of years the war galleys and tactics of the Athenians were the models for the navies of the world. There were, of course, modifications: The number of oars was increased or decreased or their placement was changed; vessels became lower and longer; turrets were added to mount war engines; grappling hooks and boarding bridges were used. But for two thousand years the long, low war galley continued to be the basic fighting vessel of the western world, and ramming or capture by boarding continued to be the fundamental naval tactics. This changed only in the fifteenth century A.D. when sailors from Portugal, Spain, and England broke out of the Mediterranean and away from coastal waters and began overseas expansion and conquests across the Atlantic and Indian oceans.

Concepts of Combat in Early Antiquity

From what we know of the Assyrians, in addition to scattered accounts of early battles such as Megiddo, it is evident that military men of antiquity had well-developed concepts of what we would today call doctrine and tactics. There must also have been some glimmerings of strategic thought among the kings and pharaohs of the ancient empires, but we do not know enough about this to do more than speculate.

Clearly, however, there was doctrine, as we understand the term today.

Elsewhere* I have defined doctrine as "Principles, policies, and concepts which are combined into an integrated system for the purpose of governing all components of a military force in combat, and assuring consistent, coordinated employment of these components. The origin of doctrine can be experience, or theory, or both. Doctrine represents the best available thought on the employment of forces that can be defended by reason. Doctrine is methodology and, if it is to work, all military elements must know, understand, and respect it."

Doctrine is implemented by tactics, which I define as: The technique of marshaling, distributing, and manipulating a discrete

---

*Historical Evaluation and Research Organization, *Strategic Concepts and the Changing Nature of Modern War*, (Washington, 1966), vol. 1, p. 239.

element of available resources in order to contribute toward achievement of defined goals.

Although few ancient battles are described in detail in surviving records, enough is known to make it evident that the military leaders of ancient times (well before 500 B.C.) had developed basic doctrine for combat, and tactics for best using the men and weapons available to them. They were organizing and deploying their forces to good advantage, calling upon the various types of fighting men for specific contributions to the whole. The advantage to be gained by surprise was well understood. And classical maneuvers that would continue until modern times, foremost among them envelopment, had already been recognized. So, too, had missile firepower. Launched at ranges beyond the reach of hand-to-hand weapons, missiles created disruption in opposing ranks that could be exploited by a well-coordinated assault.

One other feature of ancient combat worth noting is the fact that, allowing space for employment of weapons, and additional space between major components of an army, each man, on the average, occupied an area of one square meter. Thus a typical Assyrian army of 50,000 men, with its 45,000 infantrymen in masses 20 men deep, and its cavalry and chariots perhaps 5 deep, and with interior space between units perhaps the equivalent of the ground occupied, took up less than one quarter of a square kilometer — about 2500 meters in length by about 100 meters in depth.

II. Phalanx and Sarissa
500–200 B.C.

The phalanx — a massed body of infantry spearmen — was known as a tactical formation in Sumeria as early as the third millenium B.C. It was used by the Greeks probably from the seventh century B.C. Except in the northern, flatter regions of Thessaly and Macedonia, Greece with its mountains was unfavorable to cavalry movements. The Greeks in general, therefore, neglected that arm and relied chiefly on the steadily improved infantry phalanx.

This disciplined body of heavy infantry formed itself for battle in long lines that varied in depth from eight to twelve men. The individual well-trained, disciplined soldier of the Greek phalanx — the hoplite — was kept in excellent physical condition by sport or frequent combat. His major weapon was a pike, usually 6 to 9 feet long. The hoplite's short sword was usually sheathed and attached to his belt while he was in the phalanx formation. He also wore a helmet, breastplate, and greaves (armor to protect the legs from knees to ankles), and carried a round shield. In battle the hoplites in the front two or three ranks pointed their spears toward the foe; those further in the rear rested theirs on the shoulders of the men in front, forming a sort of hedge to break up flights of enemy arrows.

The phalanx and its individual units were capable of limited maneuvers in combat formation. In battle the invariable deployment was a long, solid line with narrow intervals through which the *psiloi* — light troops — could pass. Battle was waged — usually by mutual accord — on the flattest ground available, since movement over rough ground created gaps that could be fatal to the cohesion of the formation.

The hoplites came from the upper and middle classes of the free citizens of the Greek states. The psiloi generally were neither so well armed, trained, nor disciplined as the hoplites, and for the most part came from the lower classes of society. Many of the psiloi, particularly those with special weapons and skills, like bowmen or slingers, were mercenaries. Along with the generally inferior cavalry, the psiloi protected the flanks of the phalanx on the march and provided a skirmish-line screen in front at the outset of battle.

In addition to rigorous training and excellent physical condition, the Greek hoplite possessed the military advantages and disadvantages of alert, intelligent, literate free citizens of proud and independent city-states. These qualities made the Greeks suspicious of regimentation, even though intellect clearly accepted the need for a tactical organization and order that depended on discipline.

By the fifth century B.C. the expansion of Greek civilization and culture had completely Hellenized formerly barbarian Macedonia. But the military development was *sui generis*. While the Macedonian kings of the fifth and early fourth centuries B.C. had had some infantry, their military strength was based principally upon the nobles of the kingdom, who commonly fought on horseback. When Philip II came to power (359 B.C.) he completely reorganized the Macedonian army. While he made improvements in his cavalry, he devoted particular attention to the infantry. Philip's army was composed of native Macedonian professional soldiers, rather than the mercenaries found in most other Greek armies of that period. They were recruited from the Macedonian peasantry and organized within the phalanx in companies (*taxiarchia*) on a territorial basis. This resulted in a degree of unit *esprit* that was unusual at that time. Philip also took all possible measures to inspire the army's loyalty to himself.

The result of this reorganization was the finest fighting force the world had yet seen: a cohesive army, combining the disciplined skill of Greek mercenaries with the patriotic devotion of Greek citizen-soldiers. For the first time in history, scientific design, based on exhaustive analysis of the capabilities and limitations of the men, weapons, and equipment of the time, evolved into a clear concept of the coordinated tactical action of combined arms. Careful organization and training programs welded the mass into a military machine which, under the personal command of Philip, and later Alexander, probably could have been successful against any other army raised during the next eighteen centuries; in other words, until gunpowder weapons became predominant.

The basic weapon of the Macedonian army was the spear or pike, as it had been for the Greeks before them, and for the Mesopotamian people since the third millenium B.C. Philip, however, introduced the *sarissa*, a longer spear, probably about 13 to 14 feet long. The added pike length gave the Macedonian phalanx an immediate and important advantage over the Greeks — with their shorter pikes — by enabling it to engage the enemy before coming within range of his spears. This is one of the few examples in antiquity of a deliberate, intentional change of weapons by a known agent to achieve an advantage in combat — an early example of research and development. After the time of Alexander, and possibly during his reign, the sarissa was lengthened still further to 15 to 18 feet, and held with both hands. Some authorities assert that the war sarissa was 21 feet long, the training sarissa 24 feet long, but this is doubtful.

The backbone of Philip's army was its infantry. The Macedonian phalanx was based on the Greek model, but sixteen men deep instead of eight to twelve. Also there was somewhat more space between men, instead of the shoulder-to-shoulder mass of the Greek phalanx. The first three men and the last man in each file were selected for these critical posts on the basis of proven courage and skill. The formation advanced in a solid mass, normally at a run, acting as a battering ram against the enemy's line. In this compact formation individual retreat was impossible.

There were two types of hoplites: *pezetaeri* and *hypaspists*. The more numerous pezetaeri carried sarissas; the hypaspists were armed with the standard Greek pike. In addition each man carried a shield, slung over his shoulder. The pezetaeri's was only about two feet in diameter; but the hypaspist's shield was large enough to cover his body when kneeling. The sarissa was held three to six feet from its butt, with the points of the first four or five ranks projecting forward while those behind were held either at an angle or vertical. Aemilius Paullus reported that at the battle of Pydna on seeing "the bristling rampart of outstretched pikes" he "was smitten at once with astonishment and terror."

The solid mass of the phalanx was hardly an easily maneuverable arrangement. Despite this bulk and their heavier armament, however, constant training made pezetaeri units more maneuverable than the normal Greek phalanx. Both the taxiarchiai and entire phalanxes were capable of performing a variety of movements and maneuvers in perfect formation, as was demonstrated by Philip and Alexander in their many battles. It is likely, however, that in rough terrain the pezetaeri left their sarissas with the baggage, and fought with the shorter Greek pike.

The hypaspist was more adaptable to any form of combat. He was the cream of the infantry, distinguished from the pezetaeri only by his shorter pike, larger shield, and possibly by slightly lighter armor. Formations and evolutions of the hypaspist phalangeal units were identical to those of the pezetaeri. They were at least equally well trained, but the hypaspists were possibly more highly motivated, and certainly faster and more agile. Since Alexander usually used an oblique order of battle, the hypaspists were echeloned back from the right-flank cavalry to provide a flexible hinge between them and the relatively slow pezetaeri in the center of the line. The hypaspists were used also for rapid night marches, to storm walled places, and to follow up the cavalry in exploitation and pursuit.

Although Philip designed his heavy infantry phalanx of pezetaeri as a base of maneuver for the shock action of his cavalry, it was a highly mobile base, which, completing a perfectly aligned charge at a dead run, would add its powerful impact upon an enemy not yet recovered from a cavalry blow. To facilitate these aggressive tactics, Philip and Alexander tried to choose flat battlefields; but the concept was also applicable, and was applied, on rough terrain.

The Macedonian heavy cavalryman was armed and equipped much like the pezetaeri. He usually carried a sarissa even though it was difficult to wield on horseback. In anticipation of combat the rider normally rested it on his shoulder, point slightly depressed. When charging, the horseman normally used the sarissa with a downward thrust, although it could be carried underhand. The sarissa was usually abandoned in the impaled body of the first victim; the trooper then drew his sword for use in the remainder of the battle. He would recover his sarissa after almost invariable victory.

The elite formation of the Macedonian army was the heavy

cavalry formation made up of young noblemen, called the *Companions*, because they accompanied the king into battle. In many respects the Companions were the prototype of the knights of medieval chivalry.

To protect flanks and rear, and to keep contact with the cavalry even on the most extended battlefields, there were two additional types of lighter infantry. For every four hoplites the organization called for two *peltasts* and one *psilos*. In normal prebattle formation, the peltasts — light pikemen — were drawn up in a line approximately eight men deep, behind the phalanx. The psiloi, most of whom were servants and foragers for the heavy infantry, formed a skirmish line in front; their armament was the normal ancient mixture of bows, javelins, darts, and slings.

The organization of the phalanx was remarkably like that of a modern army: a platoon (tetrarchia) of 64 hoplites; company (taxiarchia) of 128; battalion (syntagma) of 256; regiment (chiliarchia) of 1,024; division (simple phalanx) of 4,096 hoplites. Like the modern division, the simple phalanx was a self-contained fighting unit of combined arms; in addition to the heavy infantry, it included (at theoretical full strength) 2,048 peltasts, 1,024 psiloi, and a cavalry regiment (epihipparchy) of 1,024, for a total of 8,192 men. The grand phalanx, composed of four simple phalanxes, could be likened to a small modern army corps or field army, and had a strength of about 32,000 men. This was the typical expeditionary force of Alexander the Great.

How the Macedonian army operated, and in particular how the phalanx was used, can be illustrated by brief descriptions of two battles.

At Chaeronea in 338 B.C Philip decisively defeated the Thebans and the Athenians to gain military and political supremacy in Greece. No detailed description of the battle has survived. However, it is clear that Alexander, then eighteen years of age, commanded the left wing, and Philip the right. After the initial encounter Philip feigned retreat, drawing the Athenians after him, while Alexander pressed forward against the Thebans. As Alexander's forces broke through the Thebans, Philip suddenly halted his withdrawal, charged into and through the Athenians, then wheeled to his left as Alexander wheeled to the right. The converging Macedonian wings crushed the enemy center between them. This complex maneuver of retreat, advance, and coordinated double envelopment could have been executed only by a phalanx highly trained not only in the use of its own weapons but in close cooperation with the cavalry to its flanks.

At Arbela, 331 B.C., the action was even more complicated. In brief, Alexander on the right advanced obliquely and rapidly against the left center of Darius's army, preceded by a thin screen of light cavalry and light infantry. While the Macedonian light cavalry engaged elements of the Persian cavalry, opening a gap in the massive Persian line, the light infantry shot down the drivers of the scythed chariots which Darius had thrust forward to meet them, widening the gap. Alexander, seeing this breach in the Persian line, shifted his direction of advance slightly to his left front and then — with his Companion cavalry, closely supported by four hypaspist divisions of the phalanx, to his left — charged through the gap directly toward Darius. The Persian emperor fled the field in terror.

Because of the speed of Alexander's advance, however, a gap was also opened in the Macedonian line between the pezetaeri and hypaspists sections of the phalanx, and several formations of Indian and Persian cavalry dashed through this gap. But instead of capitalizing on this advantage to attack the phalanx from the rear, the Persian horsemen headed for the Macedonian baggage train still farther in the rear, where members of the Persian royal family were known to be held prisoner.* But Alexander had anticipated such a possibility and had held out a strong reserve. While this reserve engaged the penetrating Persian cavalry, some elements of the phalanx also turned to attack them, driving them off the field to the flanks.

Meanwhile, the left wing of the Macedonian army had been hard pressed by other Persian cavalry elements. Alexander, victorious in the center, turned to help his left, which was slowly gaining the upper hand. The Persians fought stubbornly, but ultimately were crushed and routed by the Macedonian wings.

As is the case with all ancient battles there are no reliable figures available as to numbers involved and numbers of casualties. However, the operational details are described realistically in apparently reliable accounts. This victory, like many other successes, was won by a combination of effective weapons, sound organization, and the superb tactics of Alexander.

---

*They had been captured at the Battle of Issus, 333 B.C.

III. Gladius, Pilum and Legion
400 B.C. – A.D. 300

At the time the Macedonian phalanx reached its peak of proficiency, Rome was becoming a military power to be reckoned with. In the early days of the Roman kingdom and republic, armies were mobilized from the citizenry. Since the soldiers provided their own weapons, the cavalry and best-armed heavy infantry were drawn from the wealthiest class. But, as in Greek and Macedonian armies, there were also less well equipped infantry contingents: javelin men, slingers, and other unarmored auxiliaries. Each class of troops was organized in units of 100 men, called centuries. The combat formation of these early Romans was the phalanx, with the better-armored heavy infantrymen in the front. The light troops operated ahead of the main body and covered the flanks.

Through the years the lessons of combat influenced Roman doctrine, and many modifications in organization and tactics were introduced. Some changes were the result of, or were accompanied by, changes in weapons; some were due to factors of a political or social nature.

By about 300 B.C. the manipular legion evolved, and for the first time in military history the individual warrior was liberated from the limitations of mass formations, while he still was provided with the necessary assurance of support for flanks and rear. This was accompanied — and made possible — largely by the introduction and perfection of the *gladius* and the *pilum*.

Hitherto the sword had been used generally as a secondary weapon for horsemen and foot soldiers who relied primarily upon pike or bow. In the late third century B.C. the Romans gave up their cutting swords and converted to a slightly shorter thrusting sword known as the *gladius*. According to Polybius and Livy the style was adopted from the swords of Spanish mercenaries. The gladius was about two feet long, with a heavy, sharply pointed blade about two inches wide. The hilt was of wood, bone, ivory, or metal.

The Roman sword was more maneuverable and versatile than a spear. It could be used as a cutting weapon to lop off the heads of phalanx spears, and it provided more ways of wounding an enemy than the pure slashing sword. This was important in an era when wounds of any intensity (especially incision) were likely to be fatal. Livy tells how horrified the Macedonians were "when they [saw] bodies chopped to pieces by the Spanish sword, arms torn away, shoulders and all, or heads separated from bodies, with the necks completely severed, or vitals laid open."

On the other hand, as a very short-range weapon, the gladius provided less protection to a soldier than did the spear, which kept an enemy at a distance. But this was offset by a much improved shield. The Macedonians had enlarged the small, circular Greek shield, but the Romans also changed its shape to a sturdy convex design, about four feet high and two feet wide, which covered much of the body. The shield, which resembled a slightly flattened quarter section of a barrel, was made of wood, covered with hide, and strengthened by narrow strips of metal. With this protection the body armor of the Roman soldier could be lighter than that of the Macedonian hoplite.

To wield the gladius, the Roman soldier needed about six feet of cleared space to his right front. To inflict a wound he had to close with his enemy, so that battle was hand to hand in a very real sense. Such direct combat required unprecedented motivation. Not until the time of the Roman Republic were political and psychological conditions ripe for a warrior using a weapon essentially by himself; the Roman of the republic was a citizen rather than a subject.

The other significant Roman development in weapons was the *pilum*, a type of javelin which, like the gladius, appeared in the third century B.C. Javelins had been known since Paleolithic times, and in the Greek and Macedonian armies had been used by auxiliary troops in the initial phases of battle to shake the enemy's morale, to open gaps, and to worry flanks. The Romans used and experimented with many variations of the pilum, but by the second century there seems to have been basic standardization of a light javelin, easily handled and with great penetration capability. The weapon was half metal, half wood — a four-and-a-half-foot wooden shaft into which was inlaid a four-and-a-half-foot iron rod, so that the total length of the weapon was about seven feet. Beginning in the time of Marius, one of the two pins that held the two parts of the pilum together was usually made of wood so that it would break off in the enemy's shield or body. A later variation, possibly introduced by Julius Caesar, was to make the rod of soft metal with a hard tip instead of solid iron, so that it would penetrate and then bend, adding to the difficulty of withdrawing it from a wound or a shield.

The pilum was thrown with one hand from a maximum distance of about 60 feet, usually much less, normally by the legionaries in volley in order to secure maximum psychological effect. To improve accuracy, and sometimes distance, a cord was at times wound around the shaft and jerked upon launching to give the weapon a spin. It would render an enemy shield useless if well stuck in, leaving its owner open to a thrust from the Roman gladius. It could penetrate a breastplate or a helmet if the angle of incidence was forty-five degrees or greater. Held in the hand, it could and did also serve as an effective short thrusting pike. At first secondary to the sword, by the first century B.C. the pilum became valued as a weapon of equal importance. The legionary usually carried two of these weapons, one heavy and one light.

The legion's most significant period of combat effectiveness began with the introduction of the gladius and the development of the highly mobile manipular legion, which replaced the earlier phalangeal formations. With the manipular legion the Romans moved out of Italy and conquered the entire Mediterranean world in a blaze of wars in which they were very rarely defeated.

In this army there were four classes of soldiers — all free citizens with an intense feeling of civic loyalty to the state. The youngest, most agile, and least trained men were the *velites*, or light infantry. Next in age and experience came the *hastati*, who comprised the first line of the legion heavy infantry. The *principes* were veterans, averaging about thirty years of age; the backbone of the army, mature, tough, and experienced, they made up the second line of the legion. The oldest group, the *triarii*, who contributed steadiness to offset the vigor of the more youthful classifications, comprised the third line of heavy infantry.

The basic tactical organization was the *maniple*, roughly the equivalent of a modern company. Each maniple was composed of two centuries, or platoons, originally of 100 men, later of 60 to 80 men each; however, the maniple of the triarii was one century only. A unit of 100 men was too large to be readily controlled by a single officer — the centurion — but though strength was decreased, the designation "century" was retained. The *cohort*, comparable to a modern battalion, consisted of 450 to 570 men: 120 to 160 velites, the same number of hastati and principes, 60 to 80 triarii, and a *turma* of 30 cavalrymen. The cavalry component of the cohort rarely fought with it; the horsemen were usually consolidated into larger cavalry formations.

The legion itself — the tactical equivalent of a modern division — comprised 10 cohorts, some 4,500 to 5,000 men, including 300 cavalrymen. For each Roman legion there was (during the republic) one allied legion, organized identically, except that its cavalry component was usually 600 men. Some authorities suggest that allied contingents were not organized in this formal manner, but that it was merely Roman policy to support each legion with an approximately equal number of allied troops, whose largest formal organization was the cohort. But in Julius Caesar's time at least, the allied legions appear to have been organized just as formally as the Roman legion.

A Roman legion combined with its allied counterpart was the equivalent of a modern army corps, a force of some 9,000 to 10,000 men, of whom about 900 were cavalry. Two Roman and two allied legions comprised a field army, known as a consular army, commanded by one of Rome's two consuls. A consular army was usually 18,000 to 20,000 men, with a combat front of about 2,500 meters; the combat formation covered an area of about 600,000 square meters, an area nearly triple that of a phalangeal army of comparable size.

The flexibility of the legion lay in the tactical relationship of the maniples within each line, and the relationship between the lines of heavy infantry. Each maniple was like a tiny phalanx, with a front of about 20 men, 6 deep, but with the space between men somewhat greater than in the phalanx. Each man occupied a space about one and one-half meters square. Between the maniples in each line were intervals of the same frontage as that of a maniple, about 30 meters. The maniples in each line were staggered, with those of the second and third lines each covering intervals in the line to their front, providing a kind of checkerboard or *quincunx* pattern. There were approximately 100 meters between each two lines of heavy infantry maniples.

This cellular, checkerboard formation had a number of inherent advantages over the phalanx. It could maneuver more easily in rough country, without fear of losing alignment and without need for concern about gaps appearing in the line — the gaps were built in. If desired, the first line could withdraw through the second, or the second could advance through the first. With its triarii line, the legion had an organic reserve, whether or not the commander consciously used it as such. The intervals were, of course, a potential source of danger, but one that was kept limited by the stationing of other troops immediately behind those of the first two lines. In battle it appears that the first two lines would close up to form a virtual phalanx, but they could quickly resume their flexible relationship when maneuver became necessary once more.

The hastati and principes each were armed with two sturdy pilum javelins and with the broad-bladed gladius short sword. Each man carried the rectangular, convex Roman shield. Each soldier of the triarii carried a pike 12 feet in length, instead of the pilum, as well as the gladius. The velites were armed with javelins and darts.

To obtain a greater diversity in effective long-range missile weapons, the Romans sometimes employed foreign mercenaries, such as Balearic slingers and Aegean bowmen, with the velites.

In battle the advancing hastati — and possibly the principes also — fired their pila in a volley just before contact. Then the hastati closed with the enemy using their swords. When they tired, the principes moved up to replace them, and the hastati retired. The attack was made on a broad front and usually in a series of waves as one line replaced the other. The men were armed and trained for the offensive, and if at all possible their leaders always sought to take the initiative.

Against barbarians, the legionaries checked the usual enemy assault with a volley of pila, then closed with the gladius. The battle became one of swordplay in which the civilized, trained, and organized endurance of the Romans carried the day.

Against the Macedonian phalanx, a single Roman legionary faced two spear-bearers of the phalanx front line as well as the spears of the men in the four lines behind them. With his pila he could neutralize one or two of these. Then with the gladius he had to hack and break and push aside enemy spears while advancing, retreating and maneuvering until gaps could be opened in the hostile ranks. Then the legionaries and their gladii could play havoc in the massed ranks of the phalanx.

The Macedonian phalanx and Roman legion met in two major battles — Cynoscephalae in the Second Macedonian War and Pydna in the Third Macedonian War. In both the legion was victorious. At the battle of Cynoscephalae in northeastern Greece in 197 B.C. the two armies — each of about 26,000 men — met unexpectedly in hill country, in a fog. The Macedonians were led by their king, Philip V. The Romans — supporting independent Greek states attempting to resist Macedonian efforts to reconquer the peninsula — were under a brilliant young general, Titus Quinctius Flamininus. Philip, encouraged by initial success, brought on a general engagement on terrain unfavorable to the phalanx. His right wing drove back the Roman left, but while the Macedonian left was deploying from march column on even ground, it was struck by the Roman right — led by Flamininus — and routed. Part of the advancing Roman right then swung around, hitting the Macedonian right and driving it from the field in confusion and with great loss. The greater flexibility of the legion had been demonstrated.

The Third Macedonian War resulted from renewed efforts by King Perseus of Macedonia (son of Philip V) to dominate Greece. Again the Romans intervened against Macedonia. The war culminated at Pydna, where the army of Perseus — 32,000 strong — was opposed across the Aeson River by a slightly smaller army under Lucius Aemilius Paulus. On June 22, 168 B.C., a battle was started by accident while the opposing sides were watering horses on opposite banks of the river. Perseus, seizing the initiative, formed his phalanx and attacked across the fordable river. Despite the efforts of Aemilius to rally his men, the phalanx swept forward irresistibly on the flat ground near the river, but it was unable to keep alignment in rolling ground farther south. Aemilius counterattacked, taking advantage of gaps in the phalanx, which, once penetrated, again fell apart. The result of this battle was to give Rome control of Greece, Macedonia, and the eastern Mediterranean.

Not only was the manipular legion composed of independently maneuverable units, which could take advantage of gaps in the enemy defenses, the individual legionary was trained to operate, on a smaller scale, in much the same manner. He was the first soldier in history to be placed on the battlefield in a tactical formation in which he could so operate, and he was the first to rely primarily upon the sword rather than the spear. His relative independence and his high degree of training reflected the rise of a unified Roman state, with troops paid to serve throughout the year. The Roman soldiers were citizens who felt their own importance, and they fought accordingly.

The expansion of Rome into a Mediterranean empire brought the development of the cohortal legion, which was in some respects a retrogression from the manipular legion. It was developing during the second century, but it was consolidated by General Gaius Marius in the last years of the century. The needs of the expanding Roman Empire and many foreign threats to this vast region made considerable military reorganization necessary, just as they were to lead to a reorganization of the government from republic to empire.

With the tremendous expansion of year-round military commitments due to the steady growth of imperial dominion, the militia concept of annual levies of citizens was no longer capable of meeting the manpower requirements of the army. It became necessary to maintain, in effect, a standing army of professional soldiers. More and more these were recruited from the less reliable elements of the society, and discipline, training, and trustworthiness declined. An increasing lack of confidence between commander and troops created a tendency to reduce the intervals between the maniples of the legion, which began to approach the old Greek phalanx in battle order. This in turn decreased the inherent superiority of the Roman formation over those of its enemies, and contributed to a number of defeats along the fringes of the empire.

These developments influenced the consul Marius, about 100

B.C., to adapt the Roman military system to the realities of the time, a process that would be repeated a number of times in subsequent centuries by highly pragmatic Roman leaders. During his terms as consul, Marius established a new system of organization that would continue to be effective through the early years of the Christian era. The old aristocratic distinctions between militia classes were eliminated, as were also the distinctions of age and experience. This permitted interchange of units and individual soldiers, greater operational flexibility and maneuverability, and increased efficiency in recruitment and replacement. A complete and revised manual of drill regulations was produced, and, though later refined, these were the regulations in effect in Julius Caesar's time. In this respect, as in others, the trend to professionalism in the army tended to offset the decline in martial spirit and in civic responsibility to the state.

Accepting the trend toward a phalanx formation, Marius made the cohort his basic tactical organization. The maniple remained, but merely as an administrative element within the cohort, and 10 cohorts, 400 to 500 men each, continued to comprise a legion.

The cohort formed for battle in a line of ten or eight ranks, with a frontage of about 50 men. In close order, which was used for maneuvering and for massed javelin launching — but rarely for hand-to-hand combat — there was an interval of about three feet between men. This did not leave adequate room for wielding a sword, so the open formation, with six feet between men, was used for close combat. To permit rapid extension from close to open formation, it was necessary to keep an interval of one cohort's width between cohorts prior to actual engagement. Thus, with a legion formed in two or three lines, Marius was able to retain the traditional flexibility and maneuverability of the legion by a cellular, checkerboard arrangement of cohorts, to keep the traditional sword-length interval between legionaries engaged in combat, and yet at the same time to adapt this flexibility to the natural tendency of soldiers to crowd together in phalangeal formation by permitting a continuous front when engaged in close combat. It was a simple, brilliant, practical development, perpetuating the inherent flexible virtues of the old legion.

The cohort formed battle line from marching column in fours or fives simply by closing up to massed double columns, then facing right or left. The marching evolutions to achieve this and various changes of front and direction were comparable to those of modern close-order drill.

The usual formation of the legion was three lines, with four cohorts in the first line, and three each in the second and third lines, alternately covering the intervals of the lines to the front in the traditional checkerboard concept. In two-line formation, obviously, there were five cohorts to the line. On rare occasions the legion would be drawn up in one line and even more rarely in four. The front of a cohort, about 120 to 150 feet, with an equal interval between cohorts, meant that in the normal three-line formation the legion covered a front of about 1,000 feet. The distance between lines was usually about 150 feet, giving the legion in normal formation a depth of about 350 feet.

An army of eight legions, then, with an average strength of 4,500 men per legion, would in the normal three-line formation take up a front of about 2,500 meters, like the old manipular legion, but with somewhat less depth. Even so, the Marian legion, with some 13 men per meter of front, still had about half the density of the Macedonian phalanx, which had about 25 men per meter.

The major defensive formations of the legion were the line, square, and circle. The line was usually a single line of ten cohorts when formed behind fortifications or entrenchments. The square was formed from a normal three-line formation by simple facing movements of seven of the cohorts, leaving three facing front, while three faced the rear, and two to each flank. This, or its modification, the circle, was employed in defense against cavalry. Usually, however, if the flanks were protected by friendly horsemen or light auxiliary troops, the legion preferred to face the cavalry in its normal linear formation; the combination of pilum, shield, and gladius was usually too much for even the shock of the most desperate cavalry charge.

Militarily the cohortal legion was the most versatile unit of ancient times. Julius Caesar, its greatest commander, made no major tactical innovations but used the legion deftly. Thanks in part to the reorganization of the train so that troops carried their own basic necessities, he and others could march swiftly. Scouts and cavalry units reconnoitered up to 20 miles ahead of the main body. This was remarkable, for ancient armies previously had often blundered into an encounter.

Roman generals preferred to operate on the offensive and when possible sought to attack the enemy's wings or reach his flanks. Like their enemies, they tried to obtain the important advantage of being on higher ground than the foe. This enhanced the range of missiles, increased the shock effect of a charge while reducing the physical effort in making it, and even made it slightly easier to wield sword and spear. Usually Caesar had his best cohorts in the first line, to get the maximum results from the initial shock of battle.

After the skirmishing and missile harassment by light troops had ended, the main opposing battle lines approached each other. The legion either advanced deliberately or awaited the enemy until the lines were about 20 yards apart. Then the first two ranks of the Roman front lines hurled their javelins. Usually by this time the legion had adopted the open-order semiphalangeal formation, though sometimes this maneuver would be delayed until the javelins had been thrown.

The legion almost always charged just before the actual hand-to-hand contact of the main battle lines. The first line of 8 or 10 ranks dashed violently against the foe, with only the first 2 ranks able to employ their swords. The ranks behind would then throw their javelins over the top of the melee. After a few minutes, the second set of two ranks would move forward to relieve the men already engaged, and so on, for as long as the fight lasted. Meanwhile, the rear-rank men would be resupplied with javelins by the light troops, who, in addition to protecting the rear and flanks, had the mission of salvaging all usable javelins or darts they could find on the field.

If the first line was unable to prevail, or was hard-pressed, the second line would advance through the six-foot intervals in the first line, whose exhausted soldiers would fall back to recuperate and reorganize. Finally, the third line was available as the reserve. Throughout the battle, therefore, there was incessant movement by ranks within lines and between two or three main lines themselves. Discipline and organization were essential for such movement and commitment of replacements, and were the main reasons that the Roman forces, under good leadership, were consistently able to defeat vastly larger aggregations of barbarians and troops of other civilized states.

No new weapons were introduced in the Marian legion, but those already known were increased in effectiveness by training and the use of gladiatorial techniques, as well as virtual professionalization of soldiers. The long-service soldiers were grouped in permanent units, each with its silver eagle as an emblem. Unit loyalty was basic. The large *scutum* was probably the most efficient shield of antiquity, and its dexterous employment combined with helmet, breastplate, leather or sometimes metal jerkin, and greave (right leg only), gave the legionary excellent protection. There was growing use of small missile engines. By Caesar's time each legion apparently had a complement of 30 small catapults and *ballistae*, each served by ten men. In addition to use in sieges, defense of field fortifications, and coverage of river crossings, these machines were sometimes used on open battlefields during the preliminary phase and before the actual shock of heavy infantry lines.

The fact that there were no fundamental changes in the Roman military system from about 50 B.C. to A.D. 300 reflects both the lack of technological change in these centuries and the thoroughness with which Rome, at the peak of its power, had adapted existing technology to the art and science of warfare.

Augustus, in trying to relate the security of the empire to economic stability, formulated military policy on a "cost effectiveness" basis. Under him, except for the 10,000 Praetorians, who were intended to maintain internal tranquillity, the armed force of 25 legions was scattered along the frontiers. A superb road network was built to enable detachments to move from region to region to meet threats.

To support the 25 legions, Augustus maintained an approximately equal force of auxiliaries: archers, slingers, light infantry, and cavalry. Most were recruited from barbarian or semibarbarian tribes outside the empire. Originally auxiliary units were permitted to retain their tribal organization and leadership. This, however, was found likely to lead to revolt or mutinies, and so it became the principle to shift barbarian auxiliary units from their homelands to other frontier regions, where the tribal organization was adapted to standard Roman procedures, and further diluted by reinforcements from other tribes.

Hadrian modified the mobile defensive concept of Augustus to one of rigid frontier defense. He established man-made obstacles designed to supplement natural barriers — rivers and mountains. The Limes in Germany and Hadrian's Wall in Britain were high ridges of earth topped by wooden palisades. This fortified line provided protection and concealment for Roman border patrols and made it more difficult for barbarian raiders to cross frontiers secretly.

Later emperors tried modifications of the system of sending units from one portion of the frontier to reinforce other units engaged in warfare. Finally, it was decided that this expedient — which caused confusion and disruption among units, sometimes for years — was not satisfactory and that a mobile reserve was the answer. In other words, a compromise was reached between the concepts of Augustus and Hadrian. To provide this the army was divided into two major portions: permanently garrisoned frontier troops and mobile field forces. Approximately two thirds of the army strength was in the frontier garrisons. The remainder was composed of the mobile units, which were kept centrally located in several regions.

As early as the time of Augustus the organization, training, and equipment provided the barbarian auxiliaries by the Romans were sometimes used against Rome. Discharged auxiliaries or deserters served in the barbarian ranks during raids across the frontier. At the same time the barbarians learned much by experience from their battles against Roman formations. Certainly this continual improvement in barbarian methods of war contributed to the final overthrow of Rome. That this did not happen earlier is a tribute to Roman political skill, to the societal discipline of Rome, and to the organizational and leadership abilities of the outstanding Roman generals.

IV. Ancient Fortifications and Siegecraft
1000 B.C. – A.D. 300

Even before ancient military leaders demonstrated a grasp of the strategic fundamentals of warfare there was a general awareness of and emphasis on economic warfare. Pitched battles were relatively infrequent; rather, opposing generals concentrated on raiding each other's resources while at the same time protecting their own. This led directly to the organized consolidation of the first crude individual and family security measures in fortresses and walled towns.

The first permanent fortifications worth noting were walls of earth or stone built around places to be protected. Such a wall was often surmounted by a timber stockade, which was usually permanent, but sometimes was erected during a period of attack and removed in times of peace. Such crude fortification gave the defenders protection from the thrown missiles of the enemy and provided height from which to command the surrounding ground. It was quite naturally discovered that when the earth to construct the walls was taken from immediately in front of the wall, the resulting ditch formed a further obstacle to the approach of the enemy. Simple ditches, and ramparts made of the dirt dug out of them, are still among the most important and effective defensive obstacles.

As attackers developed or improved weapons, techniques, and material with which to breach walls and stockades, defenders automatically strengthened their fortifications. The principal result of this evolutionary process of escalation was a high masonry wall studded with still higher towers at frequent intervals; from the towers, flanking fire could be brought to bear against attackers attempting to breach or scale the wall. The ditch in front of the wall was retained and its effectiveness further enhanced by filling it with water to make a moat. The most effective walls were made of double masonry curtains, with an earth fill between the outer and inner curtains.

The art of fortification was well developed in the Middle East* long before 1000 B.C. The great walls of the large cities were almost invulnerable to the means of attack available within the limited technology of the times. Nineveh, the ancient Assyrian capital, is reputed to have had a massive stone wall that stretched two and a half miles along the Tigris River, with a total circumference of eight miles around the inner walls of the city.

An extreme example of a long-term attempt at defensive fortification is the Great Wall of China (started about 200 B.C., with the greater part being built in the fourteenth century A.D.). It averages 22 feet in height and forms a barrier more than 1,200 miles long, with branches that extend it to 2,000 miles.

By the beginning of the Christian era permanent fortification had in fact progressed about as far as available means would permit.

One of the great Roman military innovations was castramentation, or camp building. At least until the third century A.D., no Roman military force, whatever its size or whatever the circumstances, ever halted overnight without building a fortified camp. No matter how far they might be from Rome, the troops were provided with a secure base and the commander with a choice of offensive or defensive combat. The construction of the camp was a relatively quick process in which every man had a specific job. To build a palisade, each man carried two long stakes as part of his marching equipment. A ditch was dug completely around the camp, with the earth thrown against the palisade to add thickness and sturdiness. Beginning about 200 B.C., the Romans also employed field fortifications in battle to a degree previously unknown. On numerous occasions they were able to wield their shovels and axes in such a way as to integrate field fortifications into aggressive, offensive battle plans.

While converting their militia to a standing army and becoming

*For the purpose of this book the Middle East (a modern regional appellation) is considered to be the area from the Nile to the Khyber Pass, south and east of the Mediterranean, Caspian, and Black seas, including Egypt and the lands bordering the Red Sea and the Persian Gulf.

a true military state (*ca.* 1000– 700 B.C.) the Assyrians were masters of both permanent fortification and siegecraft. The Assyrians achieved their conquests mainly because they applied organization, ingenuity, and skill to the development or refinement of methods and engines that enabled them to overcome the fortifications of their neighbors, thus creating the first important system of siegecraft. Accompanying their armies were siege trains and various forms of specialized equipment, including materials for building large movable wooden towers (protected from the flaming arrows of defenders by dampened hides), and heavy battering rams. From the tops of the wooden towers, skilled archers would sweep the walls of the defenders, to prevent interference with the work of demolition while nearby, other archers, sheltered by the shields of spearmen, would fire arrows — some of them flaming — in a high trajectory over the walls, to harass the defenders and to terrify the population.

The basic siegecraft weapons of the Assyrians were the battering ram and the movable tower, often used in combination with an earthen ramp built up against a defensive wall. Also used were mines, countermines, protective shields, grappling hooks, tongs, levers, ladders, lifts, flaming arrows, liquid fire, and various engines of attack and defense. But the successes of the Assyrians led to ever-stronger fortifications. For several centuries the art of siegecraft failed to keep pace with that of fortification. There were, of course, instances of surprise, ruse, or betrayal, but generally, during the period from the eighth to the fourth centuries B.C., walled cities or fortresses were impervious to everything but starvation.

The Hindus were able to make effective use of elephants in battering the gates of besieged forts or cities. However, the usual battering ram was a large pole, often a complete tree trunk tipped with an iron head. Such rams could either be mounted on wheels or suspended within huge wooden assault towers. These towers were so constructed as to overlook the fortress walls and thus give the attackers the benefit of commanding height. Usually the fortress towers were equipped with ramps that could be lowered to act as bridges to the defending parapet. The towers were rolled into position for attack on logs or crude wheels by hundreds or thousands of men, working levers and using brawn. The largest battering rams in these towers could be as long as 200 feet and were operated by as many as 1000 men.

The use of fire in combat goes back to very early times. Since the science of chemistry, except for metallurgy, was undeveloped, no true chemical formulas for fire weapons were developed to be passed from army to army or to succeeding generations. Each army used the materials at hand in whatever manner it found successful. The Assyrians used burning pitch or crude petroleum — even then abundant in Mesopotamia — in defending the walls of besieged cities. Using both bows and ballistae, the Romans employed incendiary arrows. The incendiary materials consisted of various combinations of sulphur, pitch, naphtha, bitumen, and quicklime and were used throughout most of the ancient world, both East and West.

Mantelets, great wicker or wooden shields, sometimes mounted on wheels, were used to shelter outpost guards and the operators of siege engines and assault towers within range of weapons on the city walls. Movable gallery sections, like roofed huts, were placed together and covered with dampened skins, providing fire-resistant and missile-proof corridors through which troops and workmen could walk to the most advanced works and entrenchments.

Alexander's engineer, Diades, invented a mural hook, consisting of a long, heavy bar or lever suspended from a high vertical frame to knock down the upper parapets of a wall. He also invented the *telenon*, a box or basket large enough to contain a number of armed men, slung from a boom, which the Romans called "the crow." This boom was in turn suspended from a tall mast or vertical frame on which it could be raised or lowered by tackle. By this elevator a group of infantrymen could be hoisted above parapet height, swung over any intervening obstacle, such as a moat, and deposited directly upon the enemy's battlements.

Archimedes was partial to the use of huge grappling devices, or tongs, to be used against battering rams or to seize hostile warships approaching the seawall of Syracuse.

Although various throwing machines were known to the Assyrians and employed by them against fortifications, the great improvements or developments in the catapult and ballista family of weapons occurred several hundred years later, when the knowledge of mathematics and the mechanics of engineering were applied. Most historians attribute to Dionysius of Syracuse the beginning of the development of these progenitors of artillery in 399 B.C. Refined by the Macedonians, these weapons were further improved by the Romans. They were in continued use during the Middle Ages, particularly in the East Roman Empire.

Weapons of this family applied the principles of tension and/or torsion to propel various kinds of projectiles in flat, curved, or parabolic trajectories. In some instances the principle of the sling was added. Varying designations and nontechnical descriptions resulted in considerable confusion in nomenclature, particularly in the Middle Ages.

Without question the original catapult was a flat trajectory weapon from which shafted missiles, like large arrows, were launched. Ballistae probably were initially used for throwing stones or similar objects along curved or parabolic trajectories. Some modern authorities insist that machines based on the principle of tension — force created by the bending of the arms of a bow or a long plank — should be called ballistae, while those based upon the force of torsion, created by twisting ropes and fibers, should be designated catapults. Others, perhaps more realistically, lump them all together as catapult-type weapons. But the essential characteristics of these missile-propelling machines remained the same, although the engines varied greatly in size and in tactical employment.

The *euthytonon*, usually considered a ballista (indicating how meanings changed over the years), was a tension-driven flat-trajectory weapon. Its essential parts were a frame, the propelling gear, a trough (comparable to the barrel of a modern cannon) and a pedestal. The frame, firmly mounted on the pedestal, consisted of two horizontal beams separated by four strong uprights. Thus the frame created three windows. The trough passed through the middle window. Fixed firmly on the outer support of each side window was a lightly twisted vertical skein of rope — composed of human hair and animal tendons. Two stiff wooden arms were inserted into the rope and joined with an extra stout bow cord. This cord was pulled back mechanically and secured under great tension behind a missile — usually a dart — in the trough and released by a triggering device.

Ballistae and catapults varied greatly in size. The smallest type used extensively in the armies of the Roman Empire weighed some 85 pounds and shot darts about 26 inches long, weighing up to one pound, to ranges of approximately 275 yards. This was primarily an antipersonnel weapon. Slightly enlarged and mounted on a wheeled frame, it was called a *carroballista* by the Romans and was in common use in this enlarged form after A.D. 200. Crews were 2 to 4 men for the smaller versions, 10 to 15 for the larger.

A somewhat modified version of this weapon was the *lithobol*, which shot stone or lead pellets through the trough.

A Greek weapon similar to the ballista was the *palintonon*. This worked on the same principle except that the guide beams were on an inclined plane along which the cord joining the two arms pushed a stone ball in a sliding trough. Palintonons were large weapons, up to 10 yards in length, 5 yards high, and 4 yards wide. Essentially this was a siege or garrison weapon, hurling stone projectiles up to eight pounds in weight to ranges of 300 or more yards.

A typical torsion-driven catapult consisted of a stout heavy rectangular frame placed on the ground, one upright throwing bar, and two solidly braced uprights with a heavy crossbeam on top. The base of the throwing arm was inserted in a single, tightly twisted horizontal skein of heavy cord stretched between the two sides of the frame just behind the uprights. At rest, this cord held the throwing arm tightly against the crossbeam. The top, or end, of the throwing arm was usually in the form of a spoon-shaped ladle, or sometimes a leather pouch was attached to the end of the arm. For firing, the arm was cranked back to a near-horizontal position by a windlass, and a rock or other missile was inserted into the "spoon" or the leather pouch. When a trigger mechanism released the throwing arm from the windlass rope, it returned with great force to a vertical position to hit the crossbeam, and the force of inertia hurled the missile in an arc in the general direction of its target. Roman soldiers called this engine an *onager* (wild ass), reflecting the tendency of the rear end of the frame to lift or "buck" when the throwing arm hit the crossbeam. This type of catapult was a very powerful siege weapon and could, at best, fling a 40- to 60-pound stone for about 450 yards.

The capabilities of these weapons were limited either by strength or by mobility. The small ballistae were strictly antipersonnel and essentially defensive weapons, but by themselves they could not fire fast enough to stop a charge. However, integrated into the defensive deployments of the later Roman legions along the imperial frontiers, they were undoubtedly very effective. The heavier siege engines were even more specialized in their utility. Even the strongest catapult had very little impact energy beyond that generated by the weight of its missile falling free, and this would hardly breach the solid walls of the more powerful cities and fortifications of antiquity and medieval times. Against personnel and opposing machines, however, they could be very effective in both offense and defense. In the attack, ballistae and catapults interdicted the defender's wall space so that rams, siege towers, and ladders could be brought up under covering fire. Alternatively their use by defenders could seriously interfere with the operations of the besiegers, and they contributed greatly to the relative invulnerability of the most powerful fortifications during most of antiquity.

Before 400 B.C. neither Persians, Greeks, Romans, nor Chinese had achieved any marked improvement over the engineering techniques that had been developed by the Assyrians. About this time, however, the separate efforts of a handful of inspired military leaders and great mathematicians began to bring about important changes in siege-weapon design and tactical use.

Philip of Macedonia was apparently the first to carry lightweight prefabricated catapults and ballistae in a siege train. His attempts to make them still lighter, however, were not completely successful, and it is not clear whether Philip actually used these weapons except in sieges. But his son Alexander succeeded in reducing the weight of effective catapults to about 85 pounds, and he had about 150 euthytonons and about 25 palintonons in his field train. He habitually used these weapons in tactical situations where rapid movement was not of prime importance, such as mountain-and river-crossing operations. Alexander was truly the father of field artillery.

Philip's engines had been so designed that the essential parts could be carried on a mule or pack horse, with the bulky wooden elements hewn on the spot from tree trunks. This, of course, delayed their employment in field operations, so Alexander always carried a number of the assembled weapons in wagons, ready for quick commitment.

Philip, Alexander, and their engineers introduced several innovations in siege warfare, and were far more successful in their sieges than their Asian or Greek predecessors. Alexander was undoubtedly the greatest master of siege warfare in the eras before gunpowder, and — as in other respects — only Genghis Khan can be compared to him. The highly organized and efficient Macedonian corps of engineers was responsible for the siege train and the technical tasks of siege operations.

Two very different illustrations of the success of the Alexander siege technique are his operations against Tyre and Gaza. A less successful, but perhaps more typical, effort was made against Rhodes by Demetrius, one of the successors to Alexander.

In 332 B.C. a key element of Alexander's strategy for conquering Persia was the capture of the Phoenician city of Tyre, the main base of the Persian navy in the Mediterranean. Tyre was situated on an island about half a mile off the Phoenician mainland. To get at the city, Alexander built a mole — a long solid pier of rock and earth 200 feet wide — from the mainland out to the island. Tyrian opposition was vigorous. Using fire ships, the defenders several times interrupted the work, burning down wooden scaffolding holding the rocks together, and also destroying or damaging the wooden besieging towers being erected on the mole. Alexander scraped together a naval force and defeated the Tyrians in a tough sea fight, then blockaded the island, cooping up the remaining Tyrian ships in their harbors. Finally, as the mole approached the island city's walls, a breach in the wall was made by shipborne engines on the side *away* from the mole. The city was then taken by storm from two directions.

Immediately after this victory Alexander marched south into Palestine toward Egypt. His advance was blocked, however, by the fortress of Gaza. The most remarkable feature of the ensuing siege operation was Alexander's construction of a great earthen mound, close to the city walls. This mound was 250 feet high and a quarter of a mile in circumference at its base. He mounted catapults and a ballista with which to bombard the defenders, and to cover the expansion of the mound toward the city wall. When the mound finally abutted the wall, a simple assault took the city. The mound technique was an old one, but Alexander was a master of it. He frequently used it, or adaptations, in subsequent sieges in Persia, India, and central Asia.

When Demetrius attacked Ptolemy's garrison at Rhodes in 305 B.C., a two-year siege ensued. All the devices known to the times were tried by both sides: rams, attacking towers, liquid fire, mines and countermines, all the engines of attack and defense, raids and assaults in both directions. Ptolemy's sea power, however, assured adequate logistical support to the garrison, and Demetrius finally had to withdraw and return to Greece, leaving Rhodes in the hands of Ptolemy.

Early Roman armies were deficient in siegecraft, and their sieges were usually drawn-out affairs of attrition. Only after the lessons learned from Hannibal in the Second Punic War (219–201 B.C.) did this situation improve. Finally, Caesar became, next to Alexander, the outstanding director of siege operations of the ancient world. After his time every Roman army had an engineer detachment, skilled in the construction of bridges as well as in the specialized structures of siege operations. They carried with them, in a special baggage train, tools and equipment needed for their missions, though they relied on materials and lumber found at or near the scene of operations. By this time small-missile engines were in common use in Roman armies. Each legion apparently had a complement of 30 small catapults and ballistae, each served by 10 men. They were primarily used in sieges, and for defense of field fortifications, but they were also employed as artillery in special field operations, for instance to cover river crossings.

Caesar — a typical logical, methodical Roman — brought systematic procedure to siege operations. While the sequence of the details of operational and engineering actions naturally varied as required by local circumstances and the reactions of the besieged, a clear picture of ancient siegecraft can be found in a summary description of a typical application of the Roman system of siege operations.*

a. The establishment of a fortified camp was routine whenever a Roman army was in the field; thus the camp became the base of operations for the siege.

b. At the outset the commander, assisted by subordinates and staff, conducted a thorough reconnaissance of the fortifications, and also of the surrounding region, in order to assess local resources in lumber, stones, animals, food, and fodder. This became the basis of a comprehensive estimate of the situation.

c. The decision to besiege having been taken, the enemy fortifications were blockaded by part of the army while the remaining troops collected materials needed for construction and for siege engines.

d. Mantelets and movable gallery sections were constructed, and frames for siege engines were built.

e. A line of redoubts was erected around the circumference of the fortified place; then these individual forts were connected by lines of contravallation, thus completely surrounding the defenders. This was usually begun at the same time as the two previous steps. Sometimes a wall of circumvallation (facing outward) would also be built to protect the siege operations against raids or attacks by relief forces. Caesar almost invariably built such double walls.

f. By use of mantelets, galleries, and entrenchments, a system of covered field fortifications was advanced toward the enemy walls, usually in several places; these would lead to mine heads, subterranean passages, and the emplacement of advanced siege engines, which soon began to harass the besieged troops and civilian population. Use of heavy and light machines, catapults and ballistae and their variants, became constant on both sides.

g. A terraced mount (like that of Alexander at Gaza) was very often built, starting at extreme range from the enemy ramparts, then raised one level at a time, and advanced gradually toward the walls, under the cover of a rampart of mantelets along its forward crest.

h. Several towers were erected (usually on the mount) overlooking the wall of the besieged place. These towers would

---

*With modifications, this is based upon the discussion in *Julius Caesar* by T. A. Dodge (Boston: Houghton Mifflin, 1892), pp. 387–399.

be placed on great logs, then rolled gradually forward toward the besieged walls. The fronts of these towers were covered with dampened skins to prevent them from being burned by incendiary arrows; the bases of the towers were guarded by alert infantry units, in turn protected by mantelets, to prevent a destructive sortie by the defenders.

i.   If the town or fort was surrounded by a moat, this would usually be filled in front of the mound, and at any other point where a breach was desired or was threatened.

Breaches were achieved in two principal ways: (1) by use of rams, under protected galleries; or (2) by mine galleries advanced underground toward the walls, which would then be collapsed in order to cause the wall to crumple. Determined garrisons would usually build new interior walls behind the threatened sections, and this breaching operation might have to be repeated several times. Defenders could also interfere with mining operations by construction of countermines.

The final assault was usually a charge through a breach in the defending wall. Sometimes an assault would be attempted without a breach, the attackers rushing onto the ramparts from movable towers, up scaling ladders, or by telenons, or by a combination of these methods. Sometimes an advance party would be sent secretly into the interior of the defended place through a mine shaft, thence to open the city gates and/or attack the defenders from the rear. One typically Roman innovation in the assault phase was the advance of a cohort to the walls under the protection of a *testudo* (turtle back) made by raising and interlocking the men's shields over their heads.

The Romans were particularly adept at using field fortifications to achieve local economy of forces in offensive operations, demonstrating their understanding of a basic truth later expressed by Clausewitz: "Defense is the stronger form of combat." Fortifications, which could be manned by a few men, were "multipliers" by means of which the Romans could extend a combat front, and served as a base of maneuver for mobile field forces. Here was a classic demonstration of the concept, usually considered a principle of war, of economy of forces.

Septimus Severus (A.D. 193–211), perhaps the most able Roman soldier since Caesar, made exceptionally skillful use of field fortifications, combined with increased reliance upon portable, battlefield war machines—catapults and ballistae. During his reign, at the beginning of the third century, the standing army of

Rome increased to 40 legions, and he kept 34 munitions factories busy making arms — particularly small war machines.

Under Septimus Severus and his successors the use of hastily erected fortifications, thrust out provocatively toward the enemy, was not just a siege technique. Such fortifications in field operations, particularly when they threatened hostile flanks or communications, almost automatically attracted an enemy assault. Small Roman forces, amply equipped with light war machines, their strength further multiplied by field works, could engage and exhaust much larger forces, which were then struck by counterattack, or were enveloped by other Roman forces held in reserve for this purpose. These tactics, of course, brought the Romans fully back to a phalangeal formation, since the fortifications were of necessity linear, and linear deployment also maximized the fields of fire of the war machines.

These concepts and tactics optimizing the value of available weapons and techniques were every bit as effective as had been the old quincunx methods. The new concepts and tactics, incidentally, are as applicable to the twentieth century as they were to the third century.

V. Stirrup and Lance: The Rise of Cavalry
A.D. 300 – 500

As early as 1000 B.C. horsemen were used in conjunction with troops on foot, but cavalry was the smallest element of the army and generally limited to the royalty and nobility, who rode into battle on horseback if not on chariots. By about 600 B.C., however, cavalry played a major role on the wide plains of central and southwest Asia, and both the Persians and Chinese were forced to adapt themselves to the use of the horse to neutralize the effectiveness of the horsemen on whom their barbarian foes mainly depended. By the time of Cyrus the Persian heavy cavalry and mounted archers had become by far the best in the world. By the beginning of the Christian era the horse archer dominated warfare in central and southwest Asia. But Asian cavalry was never able to defeat the disciplined infantry of Greece, Macedonia, and Rome consistently.

Under Philip and Alexander, cavalry was a decisive arm of the Macedonian army, as well trained and as well equipped as the infantry. The elite were the Macedonian aristocrats of the "Companion Cavalry," so called because Philip, and later Alexander, habitually led them personally in battle. Hardly less skilled were the mercenary Thessalian horsemen. When formed for battle the Companions usually held the place of honor on the right of the infantry phalanx, the Thessalians on the left. The principal weapon of the Thessalian heavy cavalryman was a pike about 10 feet long, light enough to be thrown, heavy enough to be used as a lance to unhorse an opposing cavalryman, or to skewer an infantry foe. The Companion horseman carried a sarissa identical to that of the pezetaeri heavy infantryman. Each Companion and Thessalian carried a short sword at his belt and wore a scale-armor breastplate, shield, helmet, and greaves. His horse had a scale-armor headpiece and breastplate.

The Macedonian army also included intermediate and light cavalry formations that were armed with lances, javelins, or bows. Their functions were screening, reconnaissance, and flank protection. The Companions and Thessalians were used for shock action.

The Roman legion, at the time of its greatest success, used cavalry in much the same manner as the Macedonians, but generally less effectively. The Marian legion, with its allied counterpart, was a force of some 10,000 men, of whom about 900 were cavalry. In battle the cavalry was generally formed on the flanks of the infantry in checkerboard fashion similar to that of the cohorts of the legion. But the Romans never achieved the balance of combined arms so important to the successes of Alexander of Macedon, and their triumphs were mainly those of the legionary infantrymen.

One of the most significant portents of future military developments was the Battle of Carrhae (53 B.C.), where the horse archers of the Parthian leader Surenas gained an overwhelming victory over the infantry legions of the Roman consul Crassus. Alexander had had little trouble with similar foes, but no leader of genius comparable to Alexander appeared for centuries who could meet the irregular horse archer with truly balanced forces of well-trained infantry and cavalry working together as an integrated team. In the decades after Carrhae the Parthians were rightly more fearful and respectful of the military power of Rome than vice versa. Nevertheless, Carrhae pointed to a trend. A few centuries later the horse archer would replace the legionary as the principal guardian of the eastern frontiers of Rome and Byzantium.

The period from the middle of the third century to the middle of the fifth may be considered a period of organizational and doctrinal transition in the military history of the Roman Empire. During this time the heavily armed infantry, which for centuries had formed the core of the Roman battle order, gradually lost its importance and ceded its place to the cavalry, which finally became the supreme arm not only of the Roman army but also of other western armies.

This conversion to cavalry can be attributed in part to political and social developments, although military considerations predominated. The Romans found that they needed greater mobility, speed, and maneuverability when operating over the great distances and flat spaces of eastern deserts and East European steppes. At the same time the increased use of missile weapons (ballistae, catapults, and onagers) on the battlefield created a tendency to extend and thin out the formations of the infantry, making them more vulnerable to cavalry charges, while also reducing the prevalence of hand-to-hand infantry fighting. Simultaneously a slow but perceptible weakening of Roman discipline made it more difficult for legionaries to stand up against the terror of a cavalry charge. Finally, the pressure of the barbarian peoples, especially barbarian horsemen on the Roman borders, and the new requirements of extensive border defense, induced the Romans to increase the proportion of cavalry and light infantry at the expense of the heavy legion.

But the greatest impetus to the employment of cavalry, particularly for shock action, came through developments in Asia. First, and most important, was what was essentially a technological invention, the invention of the saddle with stirrups. Before the stirrup was invented, the horseman was seated on a pad or saddle blanket, or he rode bareback, and wielded the lance with an overhead thrust. The time and place of the invention of the stirrup is not certain, but Hindu cavalrymen apparently used them as early as the first century B.C. Use of the stirrup gave the horse soldier a firm base from which a stout lance, couched under the upper arm, could brutally apply the force resulting from the speed of the horse multiplied by the weight of horse and rider.

Second, in Persia and on the steppes of central Asia new breeds of heavy horses appeared, particularly suitable for such shock action. By the fourth century A.D. these had been adopted by the Romans, who, like the Persians, covered man and horse with coats of chain mail to make them relatively invulnerable to small missiles and light hand weapons.

By the beginning of that century cavalry made up one fourth of the strength of the average Roman army, instead of less than 10 percent as in the time of Marius and Caesar. The percentage was even higher in the eastern deserts in combat with Persians and Arabians.

The first great victory of heavy cavalry over Roman infantry came in the Battle of Adrianople (A.D. 378). Emperor Valens of the East Roman Empire had assembled a large army for a showdown with the Ostrogoths and Visigoths. These barbarian tribes, after having separately and thoroughly devastated his trans-Danubian provinces, had joined forces, crossed the Danube and invaded the Balkan peninsula. The Visigoths were led by Fritigern; the Ostrogoths were under Alatheus and Saphrax.

About noon on August 9, 378 A.D., Valens reached Adrianople; his scouts had discovered the Gothic camp of barricaded wagons nearby, and Valens also learned that most of the Gothic horsemen were out on a foraging expedition. He immediately advanced on the camp. As the Romans approached, Fritigern, the only major leader in the camp, sent for Alatheus and Saphrax, who were leading the foragers. Meanwhile he tried to gain time by seeking a parley with Valens.

Although his troops were tired and sluggish after a long morning's march in the midsummer sun, Valens began at once to deploy them for an attack, even while ostensibly agreeing to negotiate with Fritigern. However, Roman auxiliaries opened fire on the Visigothic negotiating party, precipitating battle before either side was ready. Though the legions were still only partially deployed from their march columns, the cavalry was ready on the flanks; so Valens ordered a general attack.

As the two forces became locked in fierce fighting, the main force of the Gothic cavalry under Alatheus and Saphrax arrived on high ground overlooking the valley where the battle had just started. The Gothic horsemen fell like a thunderbolt on the Roman right wing cavalry just as they were reaching the wagon camp, and swept them from the field. The impact of the cavalry charge was so violent and powerful that it threw the whole Roman army into confusion. The Gothic horsemen then moved to attack the Roman left-flank cavalry, some streaming through the camp, others sweeping around behind the Roman army. At the same time Fritigern ordered a Visigothic counterattack from behind the wagon ramparts. The Roman cavalry was routed, and the Goths then attacked and rolled up the infantry of the Roman left wing and drove it upon the Roman center. The infantry, wedged together and still partly in march column, was unable to deploy. In the crush the legionaries could not use their spears and swords, and were unable to flee. They were slaughtered on flanks and rear by Gothic horsemen armed with lances and swords, and by Gothic infantry who charged down from their camp against the Roman front.

The Roman losses were tremendous: Emperor Valens, all his chief officers, and perhaps as many as forty thousand men were killed. By the end of the fighting only a few thousand men of the right wing and the center, and the Roman cavalry that did not participate in the battle, succeeded in breaking out and escaping death. The Roman army was practically annihilated.

The lance and the sword used by the victorious Goths were not new weapons. However, their employment in combination with full use of the mobility of the horse increased their lethality enormously. The four elements which decided the outcome of the battle were: maneuver (which brought the mass of cavalry from a distance toward the enemy's flank), surprise, a flank attack, and the violence of the lancers' charge. These elements were brought into coordinated action partly by accident and partly by the genius of Fritigern and his colleagues; but the realization of their potential required the mobility of the horse and the courage of the horsemen. These four elements would form the basis of cavalry tactics during the next ten centuries.

Rightly or wrongly, as far as the Romans were concerned, the lesson of Adrianople meant that the legion was finished as an offensive instrument. It was to be replaced by heavy cavalry — horse archers and lancers — as the main elements of the Roman army. Horsemen would remain predominant in Europe for a thousand years.

This shift to cavalry necessarily involved changes in weapons, and over the next thousand years a great variety of weapons were used. The majority were adaptations of types that had long been known.

One of the main cavalry weapons was the spear or lance. Greek, Macedonian, and Roman cavalry had all used it in variant forms. By the fourth century A.D. it was generally a stout shaft, 9 to 11 feet long, of equal thickness (two to three inches in diameter) throughout its length, with a small spike at the end. A large variation, the Carolingian winged spear, had a crosspiece behind the spike which made it easier for the rider to withdraw the weapon after impaling the enemy.

The next most important weapon for the cavalryman was the sword. The various Germanic tribes had swords, but they were poor weapons made of unhardened iron. They were two-edged cut-and-thrust swords, with a pointed blade about 25 to 32 inches in length. By the time of Charlemagne a greatly improved weapon had been developed. It had a hard blade and was nearly 40 inches long, including its simple cross-guarded hilt. It was wielded dismounted as well as mounted. The effective use of this sword required skill and training, and further set aside the well-trained, disciplined cavalry from barbarians.

The Romans and their enemies discovered that heavy lancers

and swordsmen did not displace the light and heavy archers which the Parthian, Chinese, and central Asian peoples had long used so effectively. These two types of horsemen complemented each other: The horse archers prepared a foe for the charge of the lancers, while the threat of the lancers forced an enemy to remain in close order, thus becoming vulnerable to the archers. Therefore, from late Roman times the bow became increasingly important in military use in Europe.

Effective use of the bow required constant practice as well as suitable, open terrain. It therefore became the weapon of professionals like the Assyrian archers, or later the Cretan mercenary archers.

To an ever-increasing degree the East and West Roman empires of the fifth century made use of barbarian mercenaries in their armies. Quite naturally, with the growing importance of cavalry, men from tribes who were natural horsemen were favored. Thus the tribes of Asian origin — Huns, Alans, Avars, and Bulgars — were enlisted as light cavalry bowmen. The German tribes inhabiting the plains between the Danube and Black Sea — mainly Goths, Heruli, Vandals, Gepidae, and Lombards — provided heavier cavalry who relied upon shock action with lance or pike.

Experience against the effective Hun horse archers and against the Persians influenced the development of Roman cavalry in the late decades of the empire. At first this was mainly light cavalry, distinguished from the barbarian mercenaries only by better organization and discipline. Gradually, however, Roman cavalrymen became more heavily armored, and carried lance, sword, and shield as well as bow. Thus emerged (by the beginning of the sixth century) the *cataphract*, who, as the mainstay of the Byzantine army of future centuries, would be the most reliable soldier of the Middle Ages. This heavy Roman horse archer combined firepower, discipline, mobility, and shock-action capability, and was the true descendant of the Roman legionary.

VI. Squalid Butchery
A.D. 500 – 1000

The dissolution of the decaying western elements of the divided Roman Empire was accompanied by a parallel decline in military leadership, ingenuity, sophistication, and discipline. The crumbling of the West ushered in a new military era; armed force was applied vigorously and violently, but with no thought of systematic doctrine, with little spark of imagination, and consequently with no interaction of system and ingenuity.

The frantic Roman search for a new answer to the combined threats of missile weapons and cavalry shock action had been relatively successful in the cavalry arm, but had failed utterly in the infantry. There was no infantry organization anywhere in the world that combined both the strength and the flexibility of the old legion.

In consequence infantry became completely subsidiary to cavalry. Ponderous masses of footmen (sometimes combined with missile engines) could provide a base of maneuver for mobile cavalry. The light skirmishers (bowmen, javelin throwers, or both) could confuse, distract, and soften up a foe for the climactic shock of a cavalry charge. But the western military leaders of this period found it difficult to coordinate such combinations of missile and shock, steadiness and mobility. The results were stereotyped tactics and a general reversion to methods of warfare antedating the first organization of infantry into the phalanx.

The one important exception to reliance upon cavalry in the early Middle Ages was found among the northern Teutons, particularly the Franks, who in the fifth and sixth centuries still fought almost entirely on foot. They had crudely combined infantry mass with mobility, missile power, and shock action. Lightly armored, or almost completely unarmored before the sixth century, the Franks rushed into action in dense, disorganized masses, tactics comparable to those their ancestors used against the early Romans. Just before contact with the enemy they would hurl a francisca (a single-bladed ax with a heavy head that could shear through the stoutest Roman shield or helmet) or a javelin, then dash in with sword to take advantage of the confusion thus created. The fearless barbarians awaited cavalry charges in their dense masses, then swarmed around and under the stalled horsemen, cutting down mount and rider.

The success of the Franks during this period was due in large part to their extraordinary vitality as well as to the degeneration of the military art among their enemies. How much they had learned about weapons, discipline, or tactics from their centuries of contact with the Romans is not certain. There is evidence that Clovis was able to instill some discipline in his fierce warriors, and that he was an admirer of the Roman military system. Certainly he could not have been consistently victorious over other Teutonic tribes without a degree of organization and tactical control of his small armies, which were outnumbered by foes in many campaigns.

The Angles, Saxons, and Jutes, in their migratory invasion of

Britain, employed the same kind of disorganized infantry tactics as the Franks. Nowhere in the western world did the art of war sink lower than in Britain during the period A.D. 600–800. Savage ardor had overcome all vestiges of the Roman system. Strategy and discipline were unknown; tactics simply consisted of the disorderly alignment of opposing warriors in roughly parallel orders of battle, followed by dull, uninspired butchery until one side or the other fled. Fortifications were crude, rudimentary wooden palisades, or simple ditches. Armor was scarce and poor. Infantry remained predominant in Britain simply because there was no challenge from an enemy possessing good cavalry. Near the end of the eighth century, Norse raiders began to appear along the coast of Britain and Ireland to find lands ripe for conquest.

Frankish experiences against Ostrogoths, Visigoths, Lombards, Avars, and East Romans gave them a healthy respect for cavalry, and beginning in the seventh century Frankish armies included increasing proportions of cavalry. They, too, came to rely upon the shock action of heavy, lance-carrying horsemen, and during the reign of Charlemagne a large proportion of the Frankish levy consisted of mounted men.

No new weapons were introduced in western Europe during this period, though there were some modifications of old weapons. The sword achieved its final medieval form and was used mainly as a cutting weapon. It was broad near the hilt, tapering to the point, double edged, about 44 inches from pommel to point. Because its use required skill and training, it was a weapon largely limited to the aristocracy, who were equally adept at wielding it dismounted and on horseback.

Charlemagne brought the bow back into the arsenals of western Europe, but it was soon discarded by most armies after his death. The Normans occasionally used the bow, but usually for hunting rather than warfare.

Defensive armor became more common and more effective. The ancient crested helmet disappeared, to be replaced by an iron conical headpiece, to which was attached a protective nosepiece. The mail shirt was universally the basic item of armor, and was increased in length so that its flaps would cover the knees of a mounted man. One of the most important innovations of western Europeans in the early Middle Ages was the evolution of the kite-shaped shield, which may have been the result of a conscious effort to combine the best features of the ancient Roman scutum and the more common round targe. The medieval shield was a much more sensible item of equipment for mounted men, providing more protection with less area than a round shield, without the unwieldy bulk of the scutum. Another useful innovation was the hauberk, to protect the neck between helmet and mail shirt.

Stimulated by the barbarian invasions, there was a great revival of fortification throughout most of Europe, which naturally put a premium on siegecraft. In the attack and defense of fortified places and, indeed, in tactics in general, the western Europeans tried to follow Roman example as best they could understand it and could adapt it to their own form of ponderous, heavy shock cavalry. However, weapons and technique were both crude in comparison with those the Romans had employed a thousand years earlier.

The military system during Charlemagne's reign (A.D. 771–814) was a revolutionary departure from the military anarchy that had prevailed in western Europe for more than three centuries, and which generally returned after his death. Before Charlemagne, the principal military characteristics of the Franks had been exceptional vigor and exceptional indiscipline. Frankish armies were unreliable, their conquests impermanent.

Charlemagne, however, was able to harness Frankish vigor in a disciplined, efficient organization, while at the same time providing a high order of personal leadership. In large part this was attributable to the emerging feudal system, based upon vassalage and enfiefment. In a sense Charlemagne was reestablishing a kind of social discipline that had disappeared with the collapse of the Roman Empire.

Charlemagne had relatively little trouble in defeating the Lombards in two brief campaigns, but recognized an intrinsic superiority of the Lombard cavalry to his own Frankish horsemen. He worked successfully to improve his cavalry while also making use of the Lombards, who provided the major component of the Frankish armies that defeated the Avars. These same Lombards had been nearly helpless against Avar raids into north Italy prior to their reorganization and disciplining under Charlemagne.

Frankish armies had also lacked logistical organization and had subsisted on foraging and plunder. In friendly areas this antagonized the inhabitants and contributed to internal unrest. In hostile territory the dispersal of forces on plundering missions often led to disaster at the hands of an alert, concentrated foe. Supply shortages almost always caused the dissolution of Frankish armies after a few weeks in the field. Charlemagne established a logistical organization, including supply trains with food and equipment sufficient to maintain his troops for several weeks. Replenishment of supplies was done on an orderly basis, both by systematic foraging and by convoying additional supply trains to the armies in the field. This permitted Charlemagne to carry war a thousand miles from the heart of Gaul and to maintain armies in the field on campaign, or in sieges, throughout the winter.

Charlemagne also revived the Roman and Macedonian practice of maintaining a siege train to deal with hostile fortifications. The supply and siege trains slowed down the advance of his main armies, but assured reliable progress. Furthermore, by increasing reliance upon cavalry, accompanied by mule pack trains, he was still able to project substantial strength quickly and forcefully.

A key element of Charlemagne's military system was his use of fortified frontier posts, or burgs, along the frontiers of every conquered province. A road network was built to connect the burgs along the new frontier with each other and with the burgs of the old frontier. Stocked with supplies, these forts became bases for maneuver of the Frankish cavalry.

Charlemagne established a system of calling men to service through his noble vassals, which enabled him to maintain standing armies in the field indefinitely without placing an undue strain on the economy, without being forced to employ unreliable riffraff, and without denuding the provinces of local resources for preserving law and order. He demanded high military standards of the contingents the nobles furnished to his armies.

This policy of levying men through his nobles provided a basis for subsequent acceleration of the feudalizing process. The immediate stimuli for this acceleration in western Europe were the Viking and Magyar invasions. Kings and nobles took frantic measures to protect their people, livestock, and commercial centers from the raiders.

After the death of Charlemagne the chaotic dynastic disputes among his successors precluded centralized effort against the devastations of the Vikings and Magyars. There was no leader with the ability to re-create centralized military and administrative machinery. Therefore, defensive and protective measures became local, and largely uncoordinated. This led to construction of more fortifications to protect rural populations as well as commercial and communications centers, and creation by each landowner of permanent military forces to man his fortifications and to harass the raiders whenever possible. The trend toward cavalry continued. The standing forces were entirely mounted men, knights, and men-at-arms. The nobles would on rare occasions call up levies of all their able-bodied men who had had some training as foot soldiers, but these were generally inadequately armed, protected, and organized. The role of such infantry was always passive and defensive.

Each great lord was prepared to lead his men on royal expeditions at the call of the king for a given period each year. The military result of this system was that when royal armies were assembled and employed for offensive operations, they lacked homogeneity; there was no bond of loyalty to king and nation; they had no cohesive discipline based on common organization and integrated training; and there was no effective unity of command.

Meanwhile in northern Europe a different system was developing. The Vikings were essentially raiders, more interested in plunder and the spoils of victory than in any kind of permanent conquest. On the other hand they were skillful and eager warriors with a high standard of discipline and loyalty to their immediate chieftain. They were foot soldiers, usually armed with spears, swords, and axes, and they sometimes carried bows. Defensive armor consisted of helmet, round shield, and leather jacket. Later, many adopted the mail shirt.

The Vikings found defensive-offensive tactics effective against the more numerous, but poorly armed, poorly trained, poorly led militia levies with whom they first had to deal in western Europe. The same tactics were obviously the best against the new professional class of cavalrymen developed to meet their threat. As opposition to their invasions became more effective, the individual marauding Viking bands of 100 to 200 men would join together sometimes forming large armies. The force that besieged Paris in 885–886 was described in contemporary accounts as approaching 30,000 men, but was probably much smaller than that.

The Europeans, from their standpoint, found that cavalry professionalization combined with fortification was an effective answer to the Norse raids. The heavy cavalrymen with their shock power could fight the Vikings on equal or better terms if not outnumbered. If the Vikings were too strong, then fast-moving cavalrymen could operate from a secure, fortified base, keep up with the Viking foot columns, and frequently harass them effectively. They could also concentrate rapidly with other contingents to force battle on the raiders.

This led the Norsemen to take countermeasures. Wherever they went ashore they would seize all horses in the vicinity, mounting as many men as possible to permit rapid movement. At first they used such horses for transportation. Later, as their cavalry opposition became more formidable, they maintained large, permanent, well-defended bases on coastal or river peninsulas and islands, and developed their own cavalry units. To the end, however, the bulk of the Viking force was infantry.

The Magyars fought and raided as Scythians and other central Asian horsemen had since the dawn of history. They were light horsemen, usually unarmored, whose principal weapon was the bow, and whose most important characteristic was mobility. They could not stand up and fight the heavy West European cavalry, and they avoided hand-to-hand combat if it was at all possible. Using their superior mobility and exploiting their missile weapon, the bow, they would try to encircle their more ponderous foes, harassing them from all sides for hours until the combination of casualties, exhaustion, and frustration led to gaps in the European formations. They would exploit such gaps, usually by attacking from the rear, endeavoring to cut off and overwhelm any isolated groups.

On their long raids the Magyars relied mainly on speed and rapid changes of direction to avoid large concentrations of West European cavalry. However, the steady improvement in effectiveness and mobility of European heavy cavalry, combined with the growing number of fortifications, gradually reduced the returns from these raids.

By the end of the ninth century the old military organization of Rome had completely disappeared, replaced in the west by comparatively small bands of mailed, mounted knights, a professional class of fighting men who enrolled in the service of the king or a wealthy nobleman. It was this class of mail-clad horsemen who eventually succeeded in repulsing the Vikings and the Magyars and checking their invasions of western Europe. These victories assured the supremacy of the feudal cavalry, which was maintained for the next four hundred years.

The feudal era was a period of complete stagnation of strategy and tactics. With the development of the feudal order, each man of noble blood received military training; but the only aim of this training was to enable the future knight to control his horse, to handle lance and sword with skill, and to show courage and determination in charging the enemy.

Most feudal armies, when assembled, were characterized by a general lack of discipline, insubordination, and the ever-present danger of a willful act by some subordinate commander, which could precipitate a general engagement at an inopportune time or break a formation at a critical moment. The hierarchy of command was based on social status, not on professional capability or experience. Under these circumstances skillful tactics were superseded by shock action, by a blind frontal attack when the enemy came into sight, usually without reconnaissance and with no effort to conduct enveloping or flanking maneuvers.

VII. The Islamic Explosion
A.D. 630 – 1000

While the armies of the West were at their lowest ebb, having forgotten the Roman art of war, and relying upon the primitive tactics of brute force, the explosive rise of Islam started the sweep of Moslem conquest across nearly half of the civilized world.

The meteoric expansion of Islam was due not to the development of new weapons, strategy, or tactics, but to an *esprit* — dubbed fanaticism by westerners — engendered by the charismatic leadership of Mohammed, and by specific tenets of his teachings that promised everlasting pleasure in heaven to those who died in holy war against the infidel. Also contributing was the consolidation of political, military, and religious authority in the person or name of the caliph. No other religion has ever been able to inspire so many men, so consistently and so enthusiastically, to be heedless of death and of personal danger in battle.

Thus it was energy more than skill (although there *was* a measure of skill), religious fervor rather than a superior military system, and missionary zeal instead of an organized scheme of recruitment that accounted for Moslem victories. There were other important circumstances that contributed to this success. The disintegration of the Western Roman Empire and the absence of strong political or military institutions or leaders left western Europe apparently ripe for the taking by any vigorous invader. In southwest Asia the Byzantine and Persian empires had exhausted each other in prolonged wars, and both were plagued by serious internal political and religious unrest that left their outlying provinces rebellious and easy marks for conquest. Without the impetus derived from their early, relatively easy victories against these Byzantine and Persian fringe regions, it is doubtful if the Moslems would have been able to expand so fast or so far.

The Moslem armies were at first made up almost entirely of unarmored horsemen wielding sword and lance. As the bow became the prominent weapon on a worldwide basis during this period, the Arab leaders recognized its general effectiveness and utility, and adopted it for their own use. It was a weapon particularly suited to their light-cavalry organization. They also later recognized the wisdom of wearing defensive armor and began to supply their horsemen with mail shirts. However, they never allowed the weight of armor to reach the point where it inhibited mobility of the soldier or his mount.

Tactics for Moslems consisted of heedless light-cavalry charges, constantly harassing the opposing force, and waiting for an opening in the enemy line in order to attack small elements of the enemy ranks piecemeal; in other words, light-cavalry tactics since time immemorial. Later Moslem efforts to imitate the tactics of the Byzantine army were not completely successful since they lacked the necessary training, discipline, organization, and control.

Before the death of Mohammed (632 A.D.) and even before the complete consolidation of his control over Arabia, the new religious tide of Islam began to sweep northwestward and northeastward against the Byzantine and Persian empires. The eastern provinces of the Byzantine Empire — particularly Syria and Egypt — were estranged from Constantinople by a sectarian Christian dispute. So bitter was this schism that the Syrians and Egyptians for the most part welcomed the Moslems as deliverers from tyranny; they gave no support to the imperial armies, and in some instances actually aided the invaders. At the same time Persia was prostrated by defeat and in a state of political anarchy. In a little more than a decade the Byzantines were ejected from Syria and Egypt, to be thrown back across the Taurus Mountains of Anatolia. Simultaneously the Sassanid power was completely destroyed, and the vast Persian Empire fell to the Arabs.

After a brief pause caused by internal Arab disputes, the amazing vitality of Islam was demonstrated by a centrifugal push in all directions. The main thrust was against the Byzantines in Anatolia, but simultaneous advances were made westward along the North African coast, eastward toward India, northward against the Khazars through the Caucasus, and northeastward across the Oxus into central Asia.

The Moslems were twice repulsed at Constantinople by the Byzantines. They were also stopped along the line of the Caucasus Mountains by the fierce resistance of the Khazars. But they continued a slow advance into south and central Asia, while sweeping across North Africa and through Spain.

The Moslem conquest of Spain was completed quickly. The Ibero-Roman inhabitants were glad to be rid of the Visigothic monarchy, and the Moslems were lenient in allowing Christians and Jews to continue to practice their faiths. The Visigothic refugees, meanwhile, established themselves in a narrow strip of mountains in the northwest of Spain. Centralized Arab control was established in Spain by Prince Abd er-Rahman ibn Mu'awiya.

After these spectacular successes, the initial Moslem tide was halted early in the eighth century by several factors. Most important of these was the resilience of the Byzantine Empire (see Chapter

VIII). Next, perhaps, was the vitality of the Franks, demonstrated under the leadership of Charles Martel (the grandfather of Charlemagne) at the battle of Tours (or Poitiers). This battle serves as a good example of the strengths and weaknesses of the Arab military system and demonstrates the effectiveness of the inspired leadership shown by Martel, which was rare in that day of unimaginative tactics.

From Spain Abd er-Rahman led a Moslem army into Aquitaine (a feudal province comprising southwest France; the nobility was largely Visigothic, but the Visigoths owed allegiance to the Frankish Merovingian kings), slipping past the western flank of the Pyrenees. The Moslem army, almost entirely cavalry, consisted mostly of Berbers and other Moors, with a leavening of Arab leadership. It was probably less than 20,000 strong. Abd er-Rahman met and defeated a Frankish army at Bordeaux. Charles Martel, vigorous Mayor of the Palace at the decadent Merovingian court, and the most gifted leader of the Franks before the time of Charlemagne, hastily returned from a campaign along the upper Danube upon hearing of the Moslem invasion.

The invaders were halted temporarily by the fortified city of Poitiers. Leaving a part of his army to invest the city, Abd er-Rahman advanced to the Loire, near Tours, plundering en route. The Moslems had just laid siege to Tours when they became aware of the secret and rapid approach of Charles from the east, south of the Loire, threatening their line of communications. Abd er-Rahman hastily dispatched a great train of booty to the south, following in a slow withdrawal toward Poitiers.

The Franks evidently made contact with the Moslems somewhere south of Tours. It appears that for the next six days Abd er-Rahman endeavored to cover the retreat of his train of booty in a classical delaying action marked by frequent but indecisive skirmishes. It would seem also that Charles maintained strong pressure on the Moslems and forced them back steadily toward Poitiers. Accordingly, Abd er-Rahman decided to fight a major battle somewhere between Tours and Poitiers, probably near Cenon, on the Vienne River.

Though the respective strengths are unknown, the Frankish army was probably larger than that of the Moslems. Charles had both infantry and cavalry, probably in nearly equal proportions, consistent with the increasing trend toward cavalry in Frankish armies. His rapid and secret march into Touraine, and the nature of the skirmishing during the week prior to the battle, support the assumption that he had a substantial cavalry contingent, which he used skillfully against the Moslem horsemen.

The Franks had engaged in more or less constant warfare against the Moslems near the Pyrenees and the Mediterranean coast for nearly two decades. Thus Charles was undoubtedly aware of the respective strengths and weaknesses of his own and Abd er-Rahman's forces. He evidently realized that the heavy Frankish cavalry was undisciplined, sluggish in comparison with the mobile, light Moslem cavalry, and extremely difficult to control in mounted combat. He also realized that the Moslems were effective only in attacking, that they were deadly in taking advantage of a gap in a battle line, but that they had no defensive staying power and that they lacked the weight to deliver an effective blow by shock action against well-prepared defenders. These considerations seem to have led him to dismount his cavalry when he saw the Moslems preparing for a decisive encounter. Apparently he formed his army into a solid phalanx of footmen, presumably on the most commanding terrain available in the rolling country of west-central France.

All accounts indicate that repeated and violent Moslem cavalry attacks were repulsed by the Frankish phalanx in desperate fighting that lasted until nightfall. Yet Charles apparently retained a capability to maneuver, since one report implies that the Franks' right wing enveloped the Moslems' left and forced them to withdraw to protect their threatened camp. At any rate, by nightfall the disheartened and exhausted Moslems had withdrawn to their camp. It was apparently at this time that they discovered that Abd er-Rahman had been killed during the fight. The Moslems seem to have panicked; they abandoned their train and fled south in the darkness.

At dawn next morning Charles formed his army again to meet a renewed assault. When cautious reconnaissance revealed the flight of the enemy, he rightly refused to pursue. In pursuit his own undisciplined troops were at their weakest, and not amenable to control. He knew that it was a favorite Arab tactic to entice the cumbersome Frankish cavalry to such pursuit, and then to turn and slaughter them when they were spread out.

The Battle of Tours is generally considered by historians to have been one of the decisive battles of history. The hitherto irresistible tide of Moslem expansion had been thrown back. Christian Europe was thereby assured of several centuries of growth and development.

Once their initial headlong rush of conquest had run its course, the Moslems began to realize that even their own religious élan could not afford the appalling loss of life resulting from their reckless light-cavalry charges against the skilled bowmen of China and Byzantium, and the solid masses of the Franks. Having by this time come into contact with practically every important military system in the world, the Mohammedans recognized the superiority of the Byzantine military system, and sensibly attempted to adopt many Byzantine practices. However, they were never so well disciplined as the East Romans nor so well organized. They relied primarily upon tribal levies rather than upon a standing military force. Their continuing fervor, nevertheless, combined with astute adaptation of Byzantine tactics and strategic methods to their own system, made them still the most formidable offensive force in the world at the close of the eighth century.

Overextension unquestionably drained Moslem resources, despite remarkable ability to inspire converts to a religious zeal matching that of the original Arab disciples of Mohammed. Violent internal religious and dynastic struggles also tore at the early caliphate and its successors. These forces led to the rise of numerous, largely independent, great and small Moslem principalities and heretical religious communities. The rivalries among these independent Moslem groups, and between them and central authority, combined with raids by Byzantines, Khazars, Turks, and Spanish Christians, led the Moslems to adopt the same kind of local defensive fortification and protective measures that appeared about the same time in western Europe. This growth of local defensive capability contributed to the rise of feudalism within the Islamic empire and compounded its fragmentation.

VIII. Byzantine Guile and Skill
A.D. 630–1000

Early in the fourth century, old Byzantium had been rebuilt by Emperor Constantine, and it became the capital city of the Eastern Roman Empire. When the Western Empire fell, and Rome was lost, the Eastern Empire survived, and — despite vicissitudes — it flourished for nearly a millenium. Life in Constantinople continued much as it had in Rome — but with a distinctly Greek flavor and accent.

During the latter decades of the fifth century and throughout the sixth century, the supremacy of the Byzantine armored cavalry was clear-cut over the entire Mediterranean Basin. This was due not to greater numbers or new arms, since the Byzantines were greatly outnumbered by most of their enemies. It was the result of superior and flexible tactics based on precise knowledge of strong and weak points of their opponents, as well as the imaginative employment of combined arms, all integrated into a military system and organization fully as effective as those of Rome at its zenith. The Byzantine art of war attained a particularly high level during the reign of Emperor Justinian (527–565) in the hands of two celebrated commanders, Belisarius and Narses, who reconquered Italy, northern Africa, and southern Spain, thus halting both the Germanic expansion and the decline of the Roman Empire.

In the first half of the seventh century a long and initially disastrous war with Persia ended in an overwhelming victory achieved by the brilliant genius of Emperor Heraclius. At this juncture Islam swept out of Arabia to strike the Persian and Byzantine empires, which, in their exhausted condition, were unable to cope with the Moslems. Persia was quickly overwhelmed. The Byzantines lost all their provinces east of the Taurus Mountains; only the Anatolian and Thracian heart of the empire survived. For the next century Byzantine rulers devoted most of their attention to desperate defense against repeated Arab assaults. Frequently close to disaster, and battered by numerous Moslem raids deep into Anatolia, the Byzantines nevertheless maintained the frontier generally along the line of the eastern Taurus Mountains.

The remarkable longevity of the Byzantine Empire was due primarily to the fact that its military body was the most efficient in the world for several centuries. This army was characterized by discipline, organization, armament, and tactical methods, combined with an unsurpassed *esprit de corps* — all heritages from Rome. These superiorities were achieved and maintained by emphasis on analysis: analysis of themselves, of their enemies, and of the geophysical factors of combat.

Through the famous work on military art, *Strategikon*, which appeared by the end of the sixth century and is attributed to Emperor Maurice (582–602), we know much about the organization, armament, and tactics of the Byzantine cavalry in the second half of the sixth century. It is noteworthy that, despite some changes in details, all Byzantine institutions described in *Strategikon* remained fundamentally unchanged during the next three hundred years, as confirmed by another celebrated work, the *Tactica* — attributed to Emperor Leo VI (886–912) — that appeared in 900. (Both the *Strategikon* and the *Tactica* were probably the work of several authors, compiled during the reigns of these emperors; their specific doctrines may represent ideas and theories as much as they do actual facts.)

The organization and doctrine discussed in the books are those that emerged in the centuries following the challenge of Islam. The system was not universally successful, but despite some defeats and occasional disasters, the superior bases on which the system rested reasserted themselves under thoughtful and energetic leadership. For an incredible five centuries such leadership always appeared in time to reestablish Byzantine military supremacy over encroaching neighbors; and for almost four centuries after that, the vestiges of the system helped to postpone the final demise of the empire.

The *Strategikon* was a comprehensive manual on all aspects of warfare and military leadership, not unlike the field regulations of modern armies. It covered training, tactical operations, administration, logistics, and discussions of the major military problems to be encountered in operations against any of the many foes of the empire.

The basic administrative and tactical unit of the Byzantine army, for infantry as well as cavalry, was the *numerus*, or *banda*, of 300 to 400 men; roughly the equivalent of a modern battalion. The numerus was commanded by a tribune, or count, or (later) a *drungarios*. Five to eight numeri were combined to form a *turma* — or division — under a *turmarch*, or duke. Two or three turmae comprised a *thema* — or corps — under a *strategos*. A deliberate effort was made to avoid uniform organization of the larger formations, so as to make it difficult for opponents to estimate the exact strength of any Byzantine army.

The field organization of the Byzantine army was integrated into a geographical military district system, and local governmental authority was exercised by the military commanders responsible for defense of each region. Each district, or *theme*, was commanded by a strategos; his thema was the garrison of the district. In the more critical frontier regions the garrisons were maintained in an especially high state of readiness against attack.

By the end of the seventh century there were thirteen themes; seven in Anatolia, three in the Balkans, and three in island and coastal possessions in the Mediterranean and Aegean seas. By the tenth century the number of themes had grown to about 30. The size of the army had not grown comparably; there were simply smaller forces in each theme. The standing army during this period was about equally divided between horse and foot.

Themes closer to the frontier usually had larger standing forces than those in the interior. On the average each strategos could take to the field on short notice with two to four turmae of heavy cavalry. He also had available an approximately equal force of infantry. The role of the infantry was far less important than that of the cavalry. Thus, depending upon the situation (such as the nature of the foe, or the area of expected operations) he could leave some or all of his foot soldiers for local garrisons.

Theoretically maintained by universal military service, in practice the standing forces of each theme were kept up by selective recruitment from the most promising of the local inhabitants. No longer was the empire dependent upon the barbarians for its soldiers, though some barbarian units were usually maintained in the army. The theme system included a militia concept of home-guard local defense. This was satisfactory in such regions as eastern Anatolia, where the local inhabitants were hardy and warlike, and the guerrilla tactics of the local militia greatly assisted the regular forces of the empire in repelling or destroying invading forces. During the revival of the tenth and eleventh centuries, Byzantine wealth permitted the hiring of substantial mercenary forces.

During most of its existence the Byzantine Empire had no incentive for conquest or aggression. At the same time, Byzantine leaders recognized that their wealth was a constant attraction to predatory barbarian neighbors. The essentially defensive Byzantine military policy is thus easily understood. The objective was the preservation of territory and resources. Strategy was based on a sophisticated medieval concept of deterrence, and upon the desire to avoid war if possible — but when fighting was necessary, to react by repelling, punishing, and harassing aggressors with the minimum possible expenditure of wealth and manpower. The method was usually that of elastic defensive-offensive, in which the Byzantines would endeavor to throw the invaders back against their own defended mountain passes or river crossings, then to destroy them in a coordinated, concentric drive of two or more themas.

Economic, political, and psychological warfare assisted, and often obviated, the use of brute force. Dissension among troublesome neighbors was craftily fomented. Alliances were contracted from time to time to reduce danger from formidable foes. Subsidies to allies and to semi-independent barbarian chieftains along disputed frontiers also helped to reduce the burden on the armed forces. In all of this, imperial action was facilitated by an efficient, widespread intelligence network comprised mainly of merchants and of trusted, well-paid agents in key positions in hostile and friendly courts. Nor were the emperors against using religion for temporal ends. They found that missionaries could exert subtle and helpful influence at the courts of converted rulers — and that common adherence to the Christian faith automatically created a bond against pagan and Moslem.

The basic military strength of the empire lay in its disciplined heavy cavalry. The cataphract of the Byzantine Empire symbolized the power of Constantinople in the same way that the legionary had represented the might of Rome.

The individual horseman wore a casque or conical helmet topped with a colored tuft of horsehair. His chain-mail shirt covered him from neck to thighs. On his feet were steel shoes, usually topped with leather boots or greaves to protect the lower leg. Hands and wrists were protected by gauntlets. He carried a small round shield strapped to his left arm, which left both hands free to control the horse's reins and to use his weapons, yet was available to provide protection to his vulnerable left side in hand-to-hand fighting. Over his armored shirt he wore a lightweight cotton cloak or surcoat, dyed a distinctive color for each unit; helmet tuft and shield also were of this same color for uniform purposes. A heavy cloak for cool weather, which served also as a blanket, was strapped to the saddle. Horses normally deployed in front-rank positions wore armor on their heads, necks, and chests. Saddles, solid and well stuffed, had large iron stirrups. (The stirrup was introduced into the Byzantine army before the beginning of the sixth century.)

The cataphract's weapons usually included bow, quiver of arrows, long lance, broadsword, dagger, and sometimes an ax strapped to the saddle. Apparently a proportion of the heavy cavalry were lancers only, but most seem to have carried both bow and lance. Presumably, when he was using the bow, the soldier's lance rested in a stirrup or saddle boot, like the carbine of more modern cavalrymen. In turn, the bow was evidently slung from the saddle when he was using lance, sword, or ax. Attached to the lance was a pennon of the same distinguishing color as helmet tuft, surcoat, and shield.

Men and horses were superbly trained and capable of complex evolutions on drillground and battlefield. There was great emphasis on archery marksmanship and on constant practice in the use of other weapons.

Although it was not at all unusual for Byzantine armies to be composed entirely of cavalry, more frequently the two arms were combined on campaign in about equal proportions. The infantry, in turn, was usually divided equally between heavy and light.

The heavy infantrymen, known as *scutati* from the round shields they carried, were equipped much like the cataphracts. They wore helmet, mail shirts, gauntlets, greaves (or knee-length boots), and surcoats. They carried lance, shield, sword, and sometimes ax. Uniform appearance was achieved by color of surcoat, helmet tuft, and shield.

Most of the light infantrymen were archers; some were javelin throwers. To permit maximum mobility they carried little in the way of armor or additional weapons, though apparently there was some leeway allowed to individual desires. Most wore leather jackets, some may have worn helmets, and apparently they usually carried short swords in addition to either bows and quivers or javelins.

Surprisingly, there seems to have been less use of war engines — ballistae and catapults — than during the second to fourth centuries in Roman armies. Such weapons were employed, but mostly in defensive combat.

One major new weapon appeared during this period. Greek fire was introduced to warfare by the Byzantines during the first Moslem siege of Constantinople in A.D. 717, and seems to have played a great part in repulsing the attackers. But we know little in detail about this weapon. Knowledge of the exact composition of this explosive-flammable material has not survived to modern times. Apparently this prototype of the modern flamethrower was based upon a mixture of sulphur, naphtha, and quicklime that burst explosively into flames when wetted.

The combustible mixture was evidently packed into brass-bound wooden tubes or siphons. Water was then pumped from a hose at high pressure into the tube. The material burst into flames and was projected a considerable distance by its own explosion as well as by the force of water pressure. The deadly effect of this weapon upon wooden ships and upon the flesh of opposing soldiers can well be imagined. Greek fire retained Byzantine maritime supremacy against a strong Moslem challenge. It also helped to keep the walls of Constantinople inviolate for six centuries.

Byzantine doctrine was based upon offensive, or defensive-offensive action, and envisioned a number of successive coordinated blows against the enemy. The basic tactical formation, which could be varied greatly depending upon circumstances, comprised five major elements. There were: (1) a central front line; (2) a central second line; (3) a reserve/rear security, usually in two groups behind each flank; (4) close-in envelopment/security flank units; (5) distant envelopment/screening units. In a force of combined arms, with infantry and cavalry present in about equal numbers, the first two of these elements were infantry, with the scutati in the center and the light troops to their flanks; the last three elements were always cavalry. If the infantry contingent was small, it might compose only the central second line or be placed as an additional reserve behind two cavalry central lines.

When the opposing army was mainly cavalry, and the Byzantine army included substantial infantry, the infantry front line would await enemy attack. Byzantine scutati, confident of flank and rear protection by their cavalry, were as effective against horsemen as the Roman legionaries had been. The enemy's first attack would be struck on the flanks by the close-in envelopment/ security flank units. Soon thereafter would come a heavier blow to the hostile flank and rear from the distant envelopment/screening units. If these counterpunching tactics failed to achieve their objective, and if the Byzantine front line should be forced to fall back, it could do so through the intervals in the second line — left there in the traditional Roman manner for this purpose. The enveloping units would withdraw, regroup, and return to the attack. Finally, if the second Byzantine line should fail, and the former front line had not yet had time to rally, the day could still be saved by a smashing coordinated counterattack by the fresh reserve units, almost always conducted as a double envelopment rather than a frontal attack.

Obviously there was room for many variants in such a set-piece battle, and innumerable combinations were possible against different enemies and different kinds of forces. The important thing to note is the existence of a standard tactical doctrine and oft-rehearsed battle drill. Note also the emphasis on envelopment, on coordinated action (including coordination between missiles and shock action, between the two basic arms, and among all elements of the force), and on retaining a fresh reserve with which ultimately to gain the day in a hard-fought action.

Though subsidiary to the cavalry, Byzantine infantry doctrine was far from passive. Whenever opposed by infantry, either in a combined-arms battle or in essentially infantry operations in rough terrain, the scutati, in close coordination with archers and missile throwers, were wont to seize the initiative and to carry the attack to the foe. The normal formation of the scutati was 16 deep, and separate numeri were capable of individual evolutions, extending and closing ranks like the old Roman cohort. In the attack they would rush on the foe, throwing their lances just before contact, again like the cohort of the legion. Thus the numerus of the scutati combined the attributes of legion and phalanx.

The numeri of the cavalry usually formed in lines 8 to 10 horsemen in depth. The Byzantines recognized that this was more cumbersome than a line of two or three ranks, but they were willing to accept the slight decrease in flexibility in exchange for the greater feeling of security the men derived from the deep formation.

Byzantine military theoreticians spent as much time in study of the characteristics of their various foes as they did in elaboration of their own tactical formations. Whenever possible, campaigns were undertaken during seasons and circumstances in which the various and diverse neighbors were least prepared to fight. Mid-

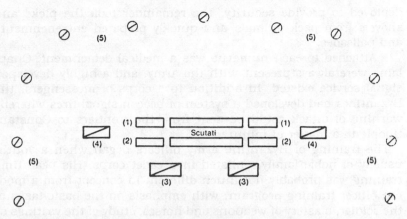

FIGURE 1.
Standard Byzantine Battle Formation*

winter was best against the Slavic marsh dwellers, since the Byzantine troops could cross the ice to their hideouts, and the defenders would be unable to take refuge in water and reeds. In February and March the horses of the Huns and Scythians would be suffering from a lack of forage. Snow would reveal the enemy's tracks, and lack of foliage would reduce the concealment of mountain tribes in fall, winter, and spring. And cold or rainy weather was good for campaigning against the Persians or Arabs, since they were depressed and less effective at such times.[†]

Constant reevaluation of these different studies and analyses was an important aspect of the consistent Byzantine military superiority.

Although each soldier carried his weapons, elementary necessities of life, and food for several days, each army was always accompanied by a supply-and-baggage train with sufficient additional supplies and equipment to permit sustained operations and to undertake siegework if necessary. This baggage train was composed partly of wagons and partly of pack animals.

Basic equipment included picks and shovels, necessary for the practice of castramentation, observed by the Byzantines as faithfully as by the early Romans. A camp site was selected and marked out in advance by the army's engineer unit. While part of the army

---

*R. E. Dupuy and T. N. Dupuy. *Encyclopedia of Military History.* New York: Harper & Row, 1977.

†Recent research and analysis of modern warfare has revealed that there is a direct and measurable decline in combat effectiveness when troops are uncomfortable due to weather conditions.

deployed to provide security, the remainder took the picks and shovels from pack animals and quickly prepared entrenchments and palisades.

Attached to each numerus was a medical detachment. Chaplains were always present with the army, and a highly developed signal service existed. In addition to a corps of messengers, the Byzantines had developed a system of beacon signal fires whereby warning of attack could be sent from the frontiers to Constantinople in a matter of minutes.

The training of Byzantine army officers began when a youth, usually of noble family, enlisted in a cadet corps. His peacetime training was probably not much different in concept from a modern officer training program, with emphasis on the basic tasks of the soldier, mastery of weapons and horses, study of the writings of military experts, and exercises in which theoretical knowledge was put to practice. During war the cadet corps served on the staffs of the various strategi, acting as clerks and messengers, possibly occasionally assisting staff officers in the simpler aspects of writing orders and preparing plans.

The young officer was apparently advanced through a variety of staff and command duties arranged to give him experience and to give his superiors an opportunity to observe him in action. During these formative years conscious emphasis seems to have been given to encouragement of objective analysis, since the Byzantines were convinced that this provided the basis of their success and that it was essential to the development of good commanders and staff officers.

Guile and fraud were admired by the Byzantines and used whenever possible. They scorned the often hypocritical honor of western chivalry; their objective was to win with minimum losses and the least possible expenditure of resources — if possible without fighting. Bribery and trickery were common, and considered respectable. The Byzantines were masters of forms of psychological warfare that caused dissension in hostile ranks, and they did not hesitate to use false propaganda to raise the morale of their own men.

In the light of some modern practices of warfare one cannot be too critical of the amoral pragmatism of the Byzantines. Theirs was a practical, no-nonsense, alert approach to the basic issues of national survival. Furthermore, they did have a moral code of conduct for war — although they did not always adhere to it. Signed treaties were inviolate — *usually*. Captured male and female noncombatants were *usually* treated with as much consideration as the realities of field operations would permit. A brave, defeated foe was *usually* treated with generosity and respect.

Such was the Byzantine military system that held back the Slavs and Saracens who increasingly nibbled at and eroded the borders of the empire from 700 to 1000. Toward the end of the period the imperial frontiers were deliberately expanded in the Balkans, Asia Minor, Syria, Armenia, Italy, and the Mediterranean islands. This was not a reversal of the traditionally defensive strategic policy of the empire, but was rather a logical implementation of that policy, in consonance with objective assessment of their military capabilities in comparison to the gradual weakening of the Moslem threat. Expansion was limited to areas which, in previous centuries, had been traditionally Byzantine.

Although the internal conditions and administration of the Byzantine Empire steadily deteriorated during the eleventh century, the army showed no decline until the battle of Manzikert (1071). There were several reasons why this purely cavalry battle between the Byzantines and the Seljuk Turks was lost by Emperor Romanus Diogenes. In the first place, his army was not adequately prepared for battle. Second, he persisted in attacking with heavy horsemen a volatile swarm of Turkish horse archers in open, rolling country, with insufficient protection for his exposed flanks and rear. The Byzantine situation was finally compromised by the treacherous retreat of the reserve, which uncovered the rear of the main body of the imperial army. The Byzantine army was destroyed and the wounded emperor taken prisoner. Almost overnight practically all of the Asian dominions of the empire were lost to the Turks.

In the chaos of civil wars which followed this disaster, and with the loss of the Anatolian provinces — which were the main recruiting ground for the army, especially the cavalry — the empire never fully recovered from Manzikert.

IX. The Crusades: Interaction of East and West 1100– 1300

The forces that brought about the Crusades were set in motion by the victory of the Moslem Seljuk Turks over the Byzantines at Manzikert and the Seljuk conquest of Jerusalem that same year over the more tolerant Fatimid caliphs of Cairo. The subsequent Seljuk conquest of practically all of Anatolia from the Byzantines, combined with persecution of Christian pilgrims to Jerusalem, aroused Christendom.

The result was two centuries of nearly constant religious warfare in that part of western Asia that became known as the Near East, punctuated by several great Christian expeditions, the Crusades. The first three of these were the most important historically and militarily. Extending over a century, they were undertaken by armies led by French, German, and English kings and nobles in the years 1096–1099, 1147–1149, and 1189–1192.

The Crusades were military expeditions undertaken by West Europeans for purposes primarily religious but in which political considerations frequently played an important part. The immediate direct or ostensible object of the Crusades was the liberation or preservation of the Holy Land, particularly the holy places of Jerusalem, from Moslem control.

Although the military skills of Europeans—particularly the heavy European cavalry—were undoubtedly superior to those of the Moslem Turks, warmaking methods of the West were relatively crude. The First Crusade would therefore almost certainly have failed had not the Moslems of the Near East been hopelessly divided by internal squabbling. There had been almost constant strife among minor potentates in the Moslem Near East throughout the eleventh century. The appearance of the Crusaders, and their continuing presence, shaped events in the region during the entire twelfth century.

The main enemies of the Crusaders, the Seljuk Turks, were numerous and formidable opponents. They fought on horseback, and their primary weapon was the bow. Their method of warfare was typical of the wild, evasive, irregular, hit-and-run tactics of Asian horsemen that had frustrated more formal western armies since the time of the Persian Empire. Only Alexander had been able to deal with them successfully. His successors among the Diadochi and the Romans tried and failed—most spectacularly and significantly at Carrhae in 55 B.C. and Manzikert in A.D. 1071. Even the victory of Aetius over Attila at Chalons in 451 and that of Charles Martel over Abd er-Rahman at Tours in 732 had been essentially defensive successes. In those battles, the western commanders, understanding the strengths and weaknesses of their heavily armed but undisciplined soldiers better than most of their contemporaries, had been able to hold their men in formation, resisting the temptation to charge after their taunting, elusive foe.

So it was in the Crusader encounters with the Seljuks. Lightly armed and mounted on fleet horses, the Turkish cavalrymen evaded direct attack from the heavy, ponderous Crusader horsemen, while luring them deep into open plains by feigned flight. Once the Crusader formation was broken during such pursuit, the Seljuks would turn to attack their enemy from all sides, especially to strike at his flanks and rear, continuously discharging arrows.

It was during the battle of Dorylaeum (1097) that the warriors of the First Crusade made their acquaintance with these Turkish tactics. The engagement was a good illustration of the strengths and weaknesses of western feudal cavalry in the Middle Ages.

After a successful siege of Nicaea the Crusaders advanced southeastward, marching in two parallel columns separated by a distance of about ten kilometers, and keeping generally in touch with each other. One column was jointly commanded by Duke Godfrey de Bouillon of Romaine and Count Raymond of Toulouse; the other, to the north, or left, was led by Norman Duke Bohemund of Taranto. The Turks attacked Bohemund's column when it was advancing through rolling country well suited to Turkish tactics. Swarms of them suddenly appeared from all directions, closing in on the flanks, the rear, and the front of the Crusaders, discharging showers of arrows into the massed, heavily armed cavalry, but presenting no main body against which the knights could charge. The Turkish arrows at first did little harm to mail-clad men, but they killed a number of their horses. The situation of the Crusaders, surrounded on all sides by great numbers of Turkish archers and exposed for hours to their intensive arrow fire, was becoming critical, when suddenly the cavalry of the right column (under Godfrey de Bouillon), warned by messengers of the plight of Bohemund's corps, appeared on the battlefield and charged with all their usual vigor into the flank and rear of the Turks, massed around Bohemund's Crusaders. The effect of this unexpected attack was tremendous and decisive; the whole Turkish army was routed and fled in wild panic, pursued by the knights.

In view of the substantial numbers involved in the engagement (the exact figures are unknown), the losses on both sides seem extremely light. The Turks suffered serious losses (amounting to about 3,000 men) only during the last minutes of the battle, when their left wing was caught between the two Crusader corps. Godfrey's column suffered practically no loss, and Bohemund's column, subjected for five hours to the Turkish arrow-fire, lost about 4,000, about half of whom were infantry massacred by the Turks in their camp. The knights' armor protected them, but the loss in horses was very high.

During the centuries of the crusading era there were several important modifications of weapons and armor. The first and most important of the weapons was the crossbow. Actually this was the reintroduction of an older weapon, for crossbows were widely used in China about 200 B.C., and a small form, the *manuballista*, had been used by the Romans as early as the first century A.D. However, the weapon then disappeared from sight, and even the Byzantines, who kept many of the Roman engines for siege warfare, did not use it. It reappeared in western Europe early in the eleventh century but remained a novelty until the Crusades, when it was used in tactical configurations with heavy cavalry. Perfected and made more powerful, the crossbow remained in use in continental Europe into the sixteenth century.

The crossbow consisted of a small, very stiff bow set crosswise at the end of a stock. The bow was at first made of pliant wood or horn, and after about 1560 was usually made of steel. There was a notch to hold the bowstring, usually with a trigger release. To gain elasticity some crossbows were composite bows (see Chapter I, page 4).

This short, powerful bow could fire a missile with great initial speed and thus had greater range and penetration capabilities than standard bows. The tension required for this high initial velocity could not be achieved by ordinary hand or arm strength. So various mechanical devices were used. The simplest of these was a small stirrup at the front in which the archer placed his foot, bending over to attach the bowstring to a hook from his belt; by simply straightening up he pulled the bowstring into a trigger-release notch. He then raised the bow, aimed, and fired at his target. A cranked windlass for spanning heavy bows was introduced in Europe in the late fourteenth century, although such devices were known by the thirteenth century in East Asia.

By the beginning of the fifteenth century an improved windlass fitted with a set of pulleys was used. The most frequent device, however, was the lever and cogwheel. The cogwheel was turned by a lever or handle which moved an iron-toothed rod with a hook in the end; this caught and stretched the cord. This mechanism combined simplicity with speed, and could even be used by mounted archers.

At first the missiles were arrows with short wooden shafts and leaf-shaped arrowheads. By 1100, however, quarrels (bolts with square armor-piercing heads) were in common use.

Although loading was much slower than with a conventional bow, crossbowmen could maintain a high rate of fire. As many as 500 quarrels per archer were provided for one campaign. The crossbow penetrated mail and dealt a large, disabling wound, but its range was short, that of the best crossbows being something like 150 yards. Although it was a powerful weapon, the ballistics of the crossbow were fundamentally poor, because the heavy cord, often weighing as much as the projectile, absorbed much of the energy that was generated.

An indirect testimonial to the effectiveness of the crossbow was the ruling by a Vatican edict in 1139 that outlawed its use in warfare between Christians. Its employment against Moslems, or other infidels, however, was deemed perfectly appropriate. This, incidentally, is one of the first examples of arms control.

Another new weapon in western Europe was the infantry halberd. This was a pike modified by the addition of an axhead near the point so that the weapon could be used for cutting as well as thrusting. The focus of attention on new infantry weapons like the halberd and the crossbow manifested a revival of the importance of foot troops.

Another example of weapons improvement was the perfection of the Moslem scimitar. The significance of this light, curve-bladed sword lay more in the quality of metallurgy than in any radical change of design. The craftsmen of Damascus and Toledo, particularly, became known for the magnificent steel blades they created: amazingly supple, yet tough and sturdy and capable of being honed to razor keenness.

European defensive armor continued to improve, but also became increasingly heavy. The mail shirt was shortened, its long skirts replaced by mail breeches. Sleeves were lengthened to the wrists, and a coif, or mailed hood, was often added, replacing a helmet. Such a suit of chain mail weighed between 30 and 50 pounds. To enhance protection and to prevent bruises from blows against its hard surface, mail armor was worn over a coat of heavy leather or felt. Such leather or felt jackets were usually the only body protection of the foot soldier. But even this was enough to stop most arrows; Turkish chroniclers describe unharmed Crusader infantrymen in battle as often looking like pincushions.

The fit of the helmet was improved. The nosepiece was lengthened and strengthened. Complete facial coverage was provided by many armorers, who produced flat-topped casques covering the entire head and neck, with slits in the front for vision and breathing. These were so heavy and suffocating, however, that they were usually carried on the saddle pommel until action was about to begin. The most common pot helmet of the period weighed 15 or 20 pounds. During the thirteenth century armorers also began experimenting with pointed helmet fronts designed to deflect frontal blows and to reduce the unpleasant possibility of having the helmet smashed back into the wearer's face.

The steadily improving metallurgical skill of medieval European armorers led to the introduction of plate armor in the thirteenth century. At first these iron plates, covering vital and vulnerable areas such as shoulders and thighs, were worn under chain mail. By the middle of the century they were being worn over the mail, or in its place, covering shoulders, elbows, kneecaps, shins, and thighs. Late in the century, plate cuirasses or breastplates began to replace chain shirts.

Early combinations of plate and mail sometimes resulted in inadequate protection at the junction of the two, and on the inside of elbow, shoulder, and knee joints. This led armorers in the fourteenth century to develop cleverly constructed complete suits of plate armor that began to replace mail.

Skillful European smiths introduced mail mittens early in the thirteenth century, and these were soon followed by mail gloves.

These innovations increased the weight of the knight's armor to such an extent that if knocked down, or unhorsed, he could rarely rise without assistance. This put a premium upon disabling the enemy's heavy mounts, which in turn led to increasing the armor protection of horses. By the end of the fourteenth century the heavy-cavalry horse was usually carrying a total weight of at least 150 pounds of armor and equipment — its own and its rider's — in addition to the man's basic weight. This meant that only ponderous, slow horses could be used for heavy-cavalry work, and even these could charge only at a trot or a slow canter.

Mobility was sacrificed for protection,. yet mobility was the essential inherent characteristic of cavalry. Thus relative invulnerability was purchased at the expense of the quality that had made cavalry ascendant in warfare.

These improvements in armor kept casualties low in most European battles, but on occasion they could also result in massacres of unhorsed, immobile defeated armies. In general there was great disproportion in the losses of Crusaders and more vulnerable Moslems in their battles in the Near East. When the Crusaders won, their casualties were always relatively light; but when they were defeated, they suffered heavily in the final phases of the battle, since they were unable to escape from their more mobile foes.

Around A.D. 1000 a new siege engine made its appearance in China. It consisted of a large sling beam, pivoted on an upright frame and actuated by a team of men who, in unison, pulled ropes attached to the beam end away from the sling. This weapon appeared in European operations by 1147. A more complex version of this machine, the trebuchet or mangonel, was developed in Persia and quickly adopted in Europe for siege operations. The men pulling ropes were replaced by a sliding counterweight.

This trebuchet was a missile-hurling machine for battering fortifications or for throwing rocks or other projectiles over walls. Unlike the ballista and catapult, which obtained their power from tension or torsion, the propelling force of the trebuchet was provided by the counterweight.

The trebuchet was a siege weapon *par excellence.* Modern experiments show that a trebuchet with a 50-foot arm and a 10-ton counterweight could throw rocks weighing 200 to 300 pounds about 300 yards. By the second quarter of the fourteenth century projectiles of nearly 1,000 pounds were thrown on occasion. For instance, there are many accounts of putrefying horse carcasses being heaved into besieged towns and castles to spread disease and cause discomfort.

The Crusaders learned lessons from the Byzantines about fortification that completely changed then-current West European concepts of the protection and defense of cities. But in one important respect the Europeans differed from the Byzantines in their application of these lessons. To the Byzantines, fortresses were essentially bases for defensive-offensive operations in the field, and thus they were usually located on commanding but accessible ground. The Europeans, more defensive-minded, and still limited by their feudal concepts of short-time, small-scale military operations, sited their new forts or castles in the most inaccessible spots possible. Thus it was extremely difficult for an attacker to reach and to assault such forts. But it was almost as difficult for the defenders to debouch rapidly, and so they had little opportunity to seize the initiative from a besieging or blockading force.

Even prior to the Crusades western Europeans had discovered that an army that included a reliable foot element had an advantage over a completely cavalry force. The infantry provided a base of maneuver for the cavalry, and could seize and hold commanding or vital ground. For this reason, many European leaders would habitually dismount a portion of their knights and men-at-arms to obtain a reliable nucleus for the less trustworthy footmen of the feudal levies. Sometimes the only foot element of an army would be its dismounted knights. This was obviously an uneconomical use of expensive cavalry; so a kind of intuitive medieval cost effectiveness led to development of standing forces of well-equipped, disciplined infantry.

This phenomenon was accelerated by Crusade experience. In fighting the mobile Moslems, the Crusaders found it essential to maintain a solid infantry base from which to launch their overwhelming cavalry charges. By the Third Crusade, therefore, the standard Crusade battle formation had foot crossbowmen deployed in line to form a screen in front of the cavalry, a screen that would open when necessary to let the heavy-cavalry charge out. The significance of this infantry-cavalry cooperation was soon realized by the Moslems, who then made it one of their important objectives to separate the Crusader cavalry from the infantry, then to defeat each in detail. This Moslem tactic, in turn, taught the Crusaders to devote more attention to close coordination of the actions and movements of both infantry and cavalry, leading to some really effective operations of combined arms.

Another influence on the increasing Crusader use of infantry was the decline in numbers of heavy horses from Europe due to battle and natural attrition. Thus many men-at-arms and knights were forced to fight on foot, or serve as light cavalrymen. However, even when they had only a few hundred present, the Crusaders relied upon their heavy cavalry as the crucial battle-winning element of their armies.

Part of the coordination of foot and horse elements was centered around the related concept of fire and movement. There was a steadily increasing emphasis upon the use and improvement of the crossbow as a result of the Crusaders' recognition that they needed firepower to offset that of the Turkish horse archers. Whenever possible the Crusaders would launch their battle-winning heavy-cavalry charges immediately after a crossbow volley had shaken the opposing force.

The Turks, in turn, found that they needed combined arms against the formidable Crusaders. Saladin was apparently the first who effectively combined aggressive Arab and Egyptian foot soldiers with Mameluke (originally Turkish slaves) horse archers. But in such a contest the more lightly armed Moslems had little chance of success against well-coordinated European combined arms.

There were three distinct cavalry types during this period. First was the horse archer of the Byzantine and Turkish armies, with the Byzantines being far better disciplined, more heavily armored, and capable of functioning also as the second type: heavy shock-action cavalry. The West Europeans were supreme in this type. No other military force in the world could stand up against equal numbers of European mailed knights and men-at-arms. The third type was light cavalry, usually lightly armored and equipped with lance and sword. Only the Arabs, Egyptians, and North Africans attempted shock tactics with such horsemen, and these could not stand up against the Crusaders, who, prior to the time of Saladin, were invariably successful in cavalry combat against much more numerous Moslem opponents.

The Crusaders, learning from both Byzantines and Moslems,

did make use of light cavalry themselves for screening and reconnaissance purposes. They also used light horse archers. Later, in addition to using Moslem mercenaries in these light-cavalry roles, they also had units of lightly armed European horse bowmen who were usually second-generation Europeans born in Syria. Efforts to introduce horse archers in western Europe were generally unsuccessful.

The Crusaders also experimented with mounted crossbowmen, but discovered that the added mobility was more than offset by the decrease in accuracy and in rate of fire. (Interestingly, the Chams of Southeast Asia apparently used mounted crossbowmen at about this same time.)

The initial success of the First Crusade, and the consequent creation of the Kingdom of Jerusalem and the other Crusader Latin states of the East, had far-reaching results. In the Levant, to an extent unmatched elsewhere, three distinct civilizations met and mingled. The sophisticated, cultured, cynical, and resilient Byzantine civilization had already had fruitful interactions with the equally cultured and intellectual civilization of the Moslem East, which had been revitalized by recent Turkish migrations. Both eastern societies looked with a mixture of awe, amusement, and disgust at the rough, brutal, crude European society whose military spearhead literally bludgeoned its way into their midst.

Though there was never real peace among these three societies during the two centuries of the Crusading era, nonetheless there was considerable social contact, facilitated by frequently shifting alliances in their wars against one another and in the inevitable meddling of neighbors in the incessant internal disorders of each.

From these contacts the Crusaders profited most, since they had the most to learn. The basically vigorous home societies of Europe became the beneficiaries of the lessons learned in the Near East. The military lessons were also as important to the West as were those in culture, science, and economics.

Among the tactical lessons learned by the Crusaders were the use of maneuver in the form of envelopment and ambuscade, the employment of light cavalry for reconnaissance and for screening, the use of mounted firepower in the form of horse archers, and above all the importance of the coordinated employment of the combined arms of infantry and cavalry, and of missiles and shock action, when dealing with a resourceful, mobile foe.

The most obvious military effect of the Crusaders' eastern experience was seen in European fortifications. The westerners were particularly impressed with the powerful Byzantine walled cities and fortresses, with double or triple concentric lines of massive turreted walls. There was nothing like this in the West at the time. The result was a complete revolution in castle construction and city defense in western Europe in the twelfth century. The most impressive single manifestation was Château Gaillard, built by Richard the Lion-Hearted in Normandy after his return from the Third Crusade.

The Crusaders learned little new about siegecraft, but improved the methods and machines that they already used. Nor did they learn much about weapons, except for increased emphasis on the bow. The one aspect of military activity in which they probably taught more than they learned was in arms and armor. Yet even here they profited, learning better methods of manufacture and construction so as to obtain comparable protection, or equal striking power, with lighter equipment.

One of the important lessons was a regained recognition of the importance of logistics, an art that had practically disappeared in the West after the fall of Rome. European armies lived off the countryside, or they evaporated. Because obligatory feudal service was for short periods, campaigns were rarely long, except for sieges and for small-scale operations and raids by the relatively small mercenary standing forces of kings and nobles. But in protracted campaigns in the Near East, with long marches over barren country, the Crusaders had to learn logistical organization or perish. In the First and Second crusades, in fact, more men perished from starvation, or from lack of fodder for their horses, than from any other single cause, including Turkish swords and arrows.

Richard I of England, in particular, showed how well he had learned this lesson by establishing an intermediate supply base at Cyprus, by exploiting the logistical potentialities of sea power, by the excellent logistical arrangements of his march from Acre to Ascalon, and by his refusal to embark on a protracted siege of Jerusalem with inadequate logistical facilities. This campaign, distinguished by Richard's brilliant tactical victory at Arsouf, and by his pragmatic, successful diplomacy in dealing with Saladin, reveals Richard to have been the first resourceful, imaginative western general of the Middle Ages, and the first of an exceptional line of English royal generals that included Edward I (probably the greatest of the line), Edward III, the Black Prince, and Henry V.

X. Whirlwind from Mongolia
1200 – 1300

A unique type of mounted force was developed in north central Asia in the late twelfth and early thirteenth centuries by Genghis* Khan and maintained by his successors. Unfettered by preconceptions of European military traditions, the Mongol cavalry became a system that won for its commanders control of the largest contiguous empire the world has ever known.

Credit for creation of this force belongs to Temuchin, son of Yekutai, who in 1206 was given by his admiring vassals the title of Genghis Khan, or Mightiest Leader. It was he who developed — from a people divided into numerous separate clans rent by jealousies and constant fighting among themselves — a military organization that proved almost invincible. In 1211, having gained control of most of Mongolia, he set out upon the conquest of China. For five years the Mongols swarmed over northern China and Korea, plundering, killing, and devastating the towns and villages. It was during this period that, having found it impossible to capture walled cities with only cavalry forces, Genghis learned from Chinese engineers the use of siege engines, mangonels, and catapults.

It finally became apparent that so large a territory as China would take years to conquer, and, disturbed by reports of unrest in Mongolia, Genghis Khan left China, leaving a small force behind. He next turned against the Khwarismian Empire of Persia, which he conquered in 1221. He continued south, west, and east, his armies swarming across Asia, destroying villages and towns and laying waste whole areas, ruthlessly slaughtering inhabitants who had no value to the Mongols.

Pushing still farther northwest from Persia, in an extensive reconnaissance in force, an army of about 20,000 men under the generals Subotai and Jabei crossed the Caucasus into Russia and sent scouts to explore the land in all directions. After defeating a force of Russians and Kumans (the latter having fled before the Mongol advance through the Caucasus) on the banks of the river Kalka in 1223, the Mongols met and defeated an army of the Kama Bulgarians and then turned back eastward. On the basis of the intelligence gathered on that expedition, Genghis Khan's successors

---

*There are many variations in the western spelling of the name, such as, for instance, Jenghis, Jenghiz, Ghingis.

fifteen years later were able to make detailed plans for the conquest of Europe.

The word *horde*, denoting a Mongol tribe or a field army, has become synonymous with vast numbers, because the Mongols' western foes refused to believe that they had been overwhelmed by small forces. Half to excuse their defeats, half because they never had the opportunity to understand the marvelous system that permitted the Mongols to strike with the speed and force of a hurricane, thirteenth century Europeans sincerely but wrongly believed the Mongol armies to be tremendous, relatively undisciplined mobs that achieved their objectives solely by superior numbers.

Genghis Khan and his successors accomplished feats that would be hard, if not impossible, for modern armies to duplicate, principally because they had one of the best-organized, best-trained, and most thoroughly disciplined armies ever created. The Mongol army was usually much smaller than those of its principal opponents. The largest force Genghis Khan ever assembled was that with which he conquered Persia; fewer than 240,000 men. The Mongol armies that later conquered Russia and all of eastern and central Europe never exceeded 150,000 men.

Quality, not quantity, was the basis of the Mongols' success. The simplicity of their organization was its chief characteristic. The standard Mongol field army was organized in three units called *toumans*, each of 10,000 horsemen, and roughly corresponding to a modern cavalry division. Each touman contained 10 regiments of 1,000, each regiment 10 squadrons of 100, each squadron 10 troops of 10. All normally fought mounted. If, however, a large number of horses were in poor shape, the men were trained to shoot standing behind the horses, supported always by mounted troops.

There were no significant innovations in weaponry made by the Mongols. The significance lay in the use they made of those weapons they had.

About 40 percent of a typical Mongol army consisted of heavy cavalry, for shock action. These men wore complete armor, usually of leather, or mail armor secured from defeated enemies. They wore a simple casque helmet such as was normally used by contemporary Chinese and Byzantines. The heavy-cavalry horses also usually carried some leather armor protection. The main heavy-cavalry weapon was the lance, but each man also carried a scimitar or mace either on his belt or attached to the saddle.

Light-cavalry troopers, comprising about 60 percent of the army, wore no armor except usually a helmet. The mission of the light cavalry included reconnaissance, screening, provision of firepower support to the heavy cavalry, mopping-up operations, and pursuit.

The primary weapon of the light cavalryman was the bow, a very large one, with a pull of at least 166 pounds, somewhat heavier than the English longbow, and with a range of 200 to 300 yards. He carried with him arrows of two classes — light ones with small, sharp points for use at long range, and heavy ones with large, broad heads, which he used at close quarters. Like the heavy cavalryman he also carried a heavy scimitar or a mace, as well as a kind of lasso, and sometimes a javelin or a lance with a hook at the end.

Each man also had a shirt of strong, raw, tightly woven silk to be donned just before action. Genghis found that an arrow would rarely penetrate such silk, but rather would drive the cloth into the wound. Then conscript Chinese surgeons were able to extract arrowheads from wounded soldiers merely by pulling out the silk.

To assure and to enhance mobility, each Mongol trooper had one or more spare horses. These were herded along behind the columns, and were available for quick change of mounts on the march, or even during battle. Changes were made in relays, to maintain security and to assure minimum interference with accomplishment of assigned missions.

The individual Mongol troopers were the best-trained soldiers of the time. Brought up in the harsh school of the Gobi Desert, from the age of three or four the Mongol was trained to ride and to shoot, and he had astonishing control of both horse and weapon. He was able, for example, to turn and shoot behind him while in rapid retreat. Inured to hardships and extremes of weather, lacking luxuries and rich food, these men had strong bodies and needed little or no medical attention to keep fit for operations. Instant obedience to orders was demanded and received. Discipline was of an order unknown elsewhere during the medieval period.

The horses, too, were very highly trained. Unlike those in Europe, they could live off the land, summer or winter, go for days without food if necessary, and, in short, sustain themselves. They could travel almost incredible distances over the worst kind of terrain in a very short time. A noteworthy example was the march in 1241 by Subotai's advanced guard from the Ruska Pass through the Carpathians to the Danube River near Gran, over 180 miles, much of it in deep snow, across a hostile country in three days.

With no necessity of carrying food for the horses and with each man responsible for his own food and equipment, and accustomed to a minimum of both, there was no need for the Mongols to have a large supply train or to maintain a base camp. (The food supply problem was eased by the Mongol practice of drinking mare's milk;

most of their horses were mares.) Even the siege artillery, which they learned to use in China — after failing with their accustomed assault tactics to take the walled Chinese cities — was kept to a minimum that was easily transportable by yak and camel. Like Alexander's, Mongol engineers could quickly construct engines on the spot from local materials. Thus the Mongol armies were mobile to a degree that no other army has ever attained. And they were able to make the most of that mobility through a remarkable intelligence system and a scouting screen that ranged at times well over a hundred miles in advance of the fighting force.

At the outset of a campaign, the Mongol toumans usually advanced rapidly on an extremely broad front, maintaining only courier contact between major elements. When an enemy force was found, it became the objective of all nearby Mongol units. Complete information regarding enemy location, strength, and direction of movement was transmitted to central headquarters, and in turn disseminated to all field units. If the enemy force was small, it was dealt with promptly by the nearest commanders. If it was too large to be disposed of so rapidly, the main Mongol army would promptly gather behind an active cavalry screen. A rapid advance would then overwhelm the enemy army, usually in detail before its concentration was complete.

Genghis and his able subordinates avoided stereotyped patterns when moving to combat. If the enemy's location was definitely determined, they might lead the bulk of their forces to strike him in the rear, or to turn his flank. Sometimes they would feign a retreat, only to return at the charge on fresh horses.

Most frequently, however, the Mongols would advance behind their screen of light horsemen in several roughly parallel columns spread across a wide front. The column encountering the enemy's main force would then hold or retire, depending upon the situation. Meanwhile others would continue to advance, occupying the country to the enemy's flank and rear. This would usually require the opponent to fall back to protect his lines of communication. The Mongols would then close in to take advantage of any confusion or disorder in the enemy's retirement. This was usually followed by his eventual encirclement and destruction.

The standard Mongol battle formation was composed of five lines, each of a single rank, with large intervals between lines. Heavy cavalry comprised the first two lines; the other three were light horsemen. Reconnaissance and screening were carried out in front of these lines by other light-cavalry units.

As the opposing forces drew nearer to each other, the three rear ranks of light cavalry advanced through intervals in the two heavy lines to shower the enemy with a withering fire of well-aimed javelins and deadly arrows. Then, rather than becoming embroiled, the first of the lines would retreat, to be followed by the next rank of light cavalry. The intensive firepower preparation would shake even the staunchest of foes. Sometimes this harassment would scatter the enemy, and there would be no need for shock action. When the touman commander felt that the enemy had been sufficiently disrupted by the preparation, the light horsemen would be ordered to retire, and synchronized signals would start the heavy-cavalry charge if needed. Orders were transmitted by flags and pennants by day and by lamp and fire signals at night.

The individual Mongol squadrons were in tight formation, but the wings of the army would spread out when the center became engaged, moving around the flanks and to the rear of the enemy, concealing their movements with smoke screens or clouds of dust or behind hills or valleys. Then, attacking from all sides, they created confusion and chaos that usually culminated in disastrous defeat and a rout. This encircling movement was standard procedure, and the Mongols were adept at using trickery to accomplish it.

Unlike the chivalrous knights of western Europe, the Mongols disdained no trick or ruse that might give them an advantage, or that would reduce their own losses or increase those of their foes. Some examples are worth noting.

The Mongols liked to operate in the winter, when their mobility was enhanced by frozen marshes and ice-covered rivers. A favorite way of finding out when the river ice was thick enough to support the weight of their horses was to encourage the local population to test it for them. In late 1241, in Hungary, Mongols left untended cattle on the east bank of the Danube, in sight of the famished refugees they had driven across the river earlier in the year. When the Hungarians were able to cross the river and bring the cattle back with them, the Mongols decided to start their next advance.

Another stratagem, which might more properly be called a tactical technique, was their use of smoke screens. It was common practice to send out small detachments to start great prairie fires, or fires in inhabited regions, both to deceive the enemy as to their intentions and to hide movement.

Frequently Mongol commanders would send an advance guard to make contact with the enemy. After a brief encounter this unit would retreat, luring the hostile force behind it. Such a retreat might go on for days, but ultimately the enemy would find himself in a trap, surrounded and ambushed on all sides by Mongol cavalrymen.

In Genghis Khan's early campaigns in China, his cavalry armies were frequently frustrated by the strong walls of Chinese cities. After intensive analytical study, and the adoption of Chinese weapons, equipment, and techniques, the Mongol leader in a few years developed a system for assaulting fortifications that was well-nigh irresistible. Important components of this system were a well-equipped siege train and the best Chinese engineers, who had been conscripted to comprise the manpower of his siege train.

In the later campaigns of Genghis and his brilliant subordinate Subotai no fortification could long stop the march of a Mongol army. Those of importance, and those that contained large garrisons, would usually be invested by a touman, which was supported by all or part of the engineer train, while the main force marched onward. Frequently an enemy city would be quickly stormed as a result of stratagem, ruse, or audacious assault. The leading Mongol light horsemen always attempted to pursue defeated enemies so closely and so vigorously as to ride through the gates before they could be closed. If the enemy was sufficiently alert to prevent this, the besieging touman and the engineers speedily and efficiently began regular siege operations, while the main army sought out the principal field forces of the enemy. Once the inevitable victory had been achieved in the field, besieged towns and cities usually surrendered without further resistance. In such cases, the inhabitants were treated with only moderate severity.

But if the defenders of a city or fort were foolish enough to attempt to defy the besiegers, Genghis's amazingly efficient engineers would soon create a breach in the walls, or otherwise prepare for a successful assault by the dismounted toumans. To add to the difficulties and confusion of the enemy, often the assault was preceded by light cavalrymen dashing in front of the walls, firing flaming arrows to start fires in the besieged camp or city. When they were prepared to make their final major assault through a breach or over the opposing fortifications, the Mongols frequently made use of a ruthless but generally effective method of approach. Herding great numbers of captives in front of them, the dismounted troopers would advance to the walls, forcing the defenders to kill their own countrymen in order to bring fire against the attackers. Finally the conquered city, its garrison, and its inhabitants would be subjected to the pillaging and destruction that made the name of Genghis Khan one of the most feared in history.

We know little of the staff system of Genghis Khan, probably because the history of his operations was mostly written by his enemies, who rarely understood how he accomplished his victories. Strategy and tactics for every campaign were obviously prepared in painstaking detail in advance. An essential element of Mongol planning was its intelligence system. Operations plans were based on study and evaluation of amazingly complete and accurate information. The Mongol intelligence network spread throughout Europe and Asia; its thoroughness excelled all others of the Middle Ages. Spies generally operated under the guise of merchants or traders.

Once intelligence had been evaluated, lines of operation were decided upon in advance for the entire campaign, and toumans were assigned to follow these lines, each with its own objective. Wide latitude was given to each subordinate commander to accomplish the specific objective assigned to him. He was at liberty to maneuver and to meet the enemy at his discretion as long as he maintained general conformance with the overall plan. Swift mounted couriers expedited the exchange of orders and combat intelligence between headquarters and subordinate units, assuring flexible unity of command at all levels and yet retaining for the khan close personal control over the most extensive operations.

Intelligence gathering, planning, training, trickery, stratagem, all were brought to bear when in December 1237, under the leadership of Subotai and Genghis Khan's grandson, Batu, the Mongols advanced again into Europe, crossing the Volga. They laid waste virtually everything in their path and, defeating all the forces whom they encountered, spread terror before them. They rode on across Russia, destroying the north Russian principalities in a few months. By the end of 1238 most of Russia had been overrun. The next two years Subotai spent resting his army, consolidating control over central and southern Russia, and gathering detailed information about Europe to his west. Early in 1241, having established a base in the regions southeast of the Carpathian Mountains and northwest of the Black Sea, Subotai was ready to start his next campaign. His field army was probably between 100,000 and 120,000 in strength.

The main body consisted of two hordes, advancing in parallel columns under Subotai and Batu, with the mission of forcing the passes over the central Carpathians. They would meet on the Hungarian plains in front of the city of Pest, on the east bank of the Danube opposite the capital, Buda. Two other columns, each composed of a horde, had the missions of protecting the northern and southern flanks of the main body.

The flank column in the north swept through Poland, Silesia, and East Prussia as planned, defeating large armies as it went, and diverting the attention of west central European princes from the main objective. The column covering the southern flank was equally effective; resistance collapsed in Transylvania after three pitched battles, and the column passed between the Danube and the Carpathians at the Iron Gates, then drove northward into the Hungarian plain to meet Subotai near Pest.

Meanwhile, on March 12, the two columns of the main body broke through the Hungarian defenses at the Carpathian passes. King Bela of Hungary, learning of this, called a council of war in Buda, 200 miles away. While this council was in progress, on March 15, he received word that the Mongol advance guard had already arrived at the opposite bank of the river.

Within two weeks Bela gathered nearly 100,000 men, while the Mongol advance was held up by the broad Danube River and the formidable fortifications of the city of Pest. At the beginning of April Bela marched eastward from Pest, cautiously seeking battle with the Mongols, who slowly withdrew in front of the Hungarian host. Contact was made on April 10 near the Sajo River, almost 100 miles northeast of the twin cities of Buda and Pest. Bela surprised Subotai by promptly and vigorously seizing a bridge over the Sajo and establishing a strong bridgehead beyond the river. He encamped with the remainder of his army in a fortified camp of wagons chained together on the west bank. He was confident of victory, knowing that his army of more than 90,000 men was considerably more numerous than the Mongols, probably about 60,000 strong.

Just before dawn the Hungarian bridgehead defenders found themselves under a hail of stones and arrows, which was followed closely by fierce assault. The defenders were quickly overwhelmed, and the Mongols streamed across the bridge. Bela's main army hastily sallied out of its fortified camp. A bitter battle ensued. Suddenly it became evident, however, that this was only a Mongol holding attack.

The main effort was made by three toumans, some 30,000 men, under the personal command of Subotai. In the predawn darkness he had led his troops through the cold waters of the Sajo River, far south of the bridgehead, then turned northward to strike the Hungarians' right flank and rear. Unable to resist this devastating charge, the Europeans hastily fell back into their camp, which was quickly invested by the Mongols. For several hours they bombarded it with stones, arrows, and burning naphtha.

A few desperate Hungarians discovered an apparent gap to the west and galloped out safely. As the intensity of the Mongol assault mounted elsewhere, more and more men slipped out. Soon a stream of men was pouring westward through the gap. As the defense collapsed, the survivors rushed to join those who had already escaped. Many of the fugitives threw away weapons and armor in order to flee more quickly. Suddenly they discovered that they had fallen into another Mongol trap. Mounted on swift fresh horses, the Mongols appeared on all sides, cutting down the exhausted men, hunting them into marshes, storming the villages in which some attempted to take refuge. In a few hours of horrible butchery the Hungarian army was completely destroyed. A handful of survivors brought their tale of terror to Pest.

All Europe was fearful of which way the Mongols would move next. But even as their armies were approaching Vienna, early in 1242, word came from distant Mongolia that Ogatai, Genghis Khan's successor, was dead, and that Batu and Subotai must return to Karakorum to help elect a new ruler. So, to the surprise and relief of all western Europe, the Mongols disappeared into the mysterious regions whence they had come. They left an occupation army in Russia, however.

After the departure of the Mongols the extent of the devastation they had wrought in Hungary, Silesia, and Poland became apparent. Whole provinces had been depopulated and laid waste. In the city of Pest, for example, 100,000 had died, while at the battle of the Sajo River about 70,000 men had been killed. The area was in economic chaos. Its former inhabitants had fled, or perished at the hands of the invaders.

By thorough training and discipline the Mongols developed a military machine based on the bow and the horse that proved to be virtually unbeatable. They understood and exploited to the utmost the military principles of surprise and of maneuverability, as well as the psychological concepts of treachery and ruthlessness. The armies they encountered in Europe in the thirteenth century were cumbersome and slow to maneuver and unable to cope with the highly mobile Mongols on their lively little horses. Were adequate and reliable figures available they would undoubtedly indicate that the casualty rates of European forces opposing the Mongols in battle were among the highest — if not the highest — in all history. In addition to, and in large part because of, this tremendous lethality potential, Mongol campaigns had a great and lasting effect on the social and economic life of the lands they invaded. But the European armies that were unable to stand long against the Mongols never learned how to cope with them. Nor did they learn much from them. The brief Mongol incursion west of the Carpathians made no direct impression on military tactics and tradition in central or western Europe.

There is no question, however, that the Russians learned much from Mongol cavalry doctrine and tactics. Dr. Hugh Cole, a respected military historian, said in a recent letter to the author that "Russian light-cavalry tactics as late as the Carpathian campaigns of 1914 were based on the Mongol example."

Mongol influence has indeed been felt in modern times, as their campaigns, tactics, and techniques have been widely studied in the West. As Hugh Cole further writes, "Liddell Hart used the Mongol prototype to sell cavalrymen on the tank. And note that [Douglas] MacArthur, as Chief of Staff of the U.S. Army made an appeal in one Annual Report to the Congress using the Mongol experience to substantiate his plea for funds for mechanization of the Army."

Why did the Mongol experience not have more effect on contemporary warfare in Europe? A tantalizing question that has never been fully or satisfactorily answered. But there are some partial answers that probably, in combination, can provide insights.

In the first place the Mongols encountered a number of local forces, none of which was able to cope with the invaders; most of the military elites of the overrun countries were destroyed, and before the survivors could even think about further resistance, the foe was gone, or — in Russia — so firmly entrenched that resistance was unthinkable for nearly a century. It was a bad dream, a nightmare that could happily be forgotten. The only comparable historical parallels were the destruction of the military societies of Mexico and Peru three centuries later.

There were substantial differences in the circumstances when, barely two decades after the Battle of the Sajo River, Mongols began a similar sweep into the Levant. Mongol power had unquestionably passed its peak, and the invaders were facing a substantially more sophisticated military system. This was the Turkish system, which had learned much and incorporated much from the Byzantines and the Crusaders in the two previous centuries. It is doubtful if Babers or his Mamelukes could have stopped either Genghis Khan or Subotai when the Mongols were in their prime. But at Ain Jalut (1260), tough Mameluke-Turk resistance combined with enormous logistical problems were more than their successors could handle.

The Mongols were not badly defeated at Ain Jalut. But they had reached the limit of their capabilities. And as the Mongol flood receded, it left behind in the Middle East a new military society — that of the Ottoman Turks — with a combined Mongol-Saracen-Byzantine-Crusader heritage. This was the military society that (unlike the Mongols) was to succeed in pushing deep into the Mediterranean Basin and far up the Danube Valley — and staying there for centuries.

XI. The Revival of Infantry:
English Longbow and Swiss Pike
1200 – 1500

Although cavalry domination of warfare reached its zenith in the Mongol conquests, the swing back to predominance of the infantry soldier on western European battlefields had already begun. Medieval heavy cavalry began to decline from about the middle of the thirteenth century. Three old infantry weapons, improved and used in different ways, were chiefly responsible for depriving the medieval cavalry, armed with the lance, of its supremacy. These were the crossbow, which had been modified to become a more effective and powerful weapon; the longbow developed in England; and the pike, which in Swiss hands had become formidable indeed.

Two other technical developments that had a major influence were, first, the dilution and dwindling of the fine breeds of horses that the Crusaders had created by blending European with Arabian stock, and second, the shift from chain mail to plate armor. In combination these developments had the effect of destroying the tactical flexibility that had made heavy cavalry so effective an instrument on thirteenth century battlefields. Encumbered by full plate armor and similar protection for his charger (perhaps 140 to 150 pounds in all), plus sword and shield and a larger and heavier lance, the fourteenth century man-at-arms became a kind of lumbering armored mass capable only of charging straight forward — not very fast — and unable to make sudden stops or starts. Faced by longbow or crossbow fire — and by gunfire, toward the end of the fourteenth century — such cavalry could be thrown into confusion, since even armored horses could not be wholly shielded from arrow-fire, and they became unmanageable if wounded. Against more agile opponents, mounted or dismounted, the fully plated man-at-arms was helpless. Nevertheless, since the urge to self-protection was fundamental, the trend toward ever heavier armor had proved irreversible.

The thirteenth century saw the development in England of the longbow, which was to hasten the downfall of cavalry as the predominant arm. English monarchs from Edward I (1272 – 1307) to Henry VIII (1509 – 1547) made determined efforts to encourage archery and to increase the power of the bow, and thus was developed a weapon whose effectiveness and flexibility ultimately caused the abandonment of the crossbow.

The longbow was made of elm, hazel, basil, and later primarily of yew. The best yew was not native to England but imported from Italy and Spain. The longbow was six feet long, propelling a three-foot arrow. The bow shaft tapered from an inch and a half wide in the middle, where the hand grasped it, toward the ends, which were horn-capped. The staff was round toward the front and flat toward the rear. It not only had twice the range of the crossbow — up to 400 yards maximum, and an effective range approaching 250 yards — but also a far more rapid rate of fire — 10 to 12 arrows a minute. In the hands of English professional soldiers it was more accurate than the crossbow, it was lighter, more easily handled, and it was adaptable for skirmishing or for volley fire. It was the most effective and most versatile individual weapon yet to appear on the battlefield.

The longbow had one drawback. The strength, coordination, and skill necessary for its successful use could be acquired only by years of training and practice. To encourage youths to devote themselves to such practice, football was outlawed in Britain early in the fourteenth century. Crossbowmen, on the other hand, could be trained to operate their machines rather quickly.

The return of infantry to predominance in warfare as the principal element of a balanced combined-arms infantry-cavalry team became unquestioned at the battle of Crecy, which took place on August 26, 1346. There the English bowmen were the critical ingredient of a dismounted army that defeated and bled white the most formidable French cavalry.

In July of that year Edward III had sailed from Portsmouth to northern France to assist hard-pressed allies in Flanders and Brittany. For about a month he moved across northwestern France toward the Low Countries, followed by a much stronger army belonging to the French king, Philip VI. Having crossed the Seine, and thus not having to worry about a major obstacle should a further retreat into Flanders be necessary, Edward decided to fight. He discovered a suitable battleground near the village of Crecy-en-Ponthieu, where a gentle slope overlooked the route the French army would have to take.

The English organized their position carefully. The right flank, near Crecy, was protected by a river. The left flank, in front of the village of Wadicourt, was covered by trees and by ditches dug by the English infantry. The army was formed in three main divisions, or "battles," each of about equal strength. Two divisions were deployed in line, that on the right under Edward, the Prince of Wales (the Black Prince), the other commanded by the Earl of Northampton. The third division, behind the other two, was under the king's personal command. The total English strength was probably about

20,000. The king took position in a windmill, from which he could observe all of the action and send orders to his subordinate commanders.

The core of each division was a phalanx of some 1,000 dismounted men-at-arms, probably six ranks deep and about 250 yards long. There were two reasons for dismounting the bulk of the English cavalry. First there was the military desirability of providing a solid base of maneuver and operations for the bowmen, and also for the small cavalry reserve held out for counterattack. Second was the psychological necessity for assuring the bowmen that they could stand firm against French cavalry charges and would not be abandoned.

The archers were ranged on the outer flanks of each division and echeloned forward so as to obtain clear, converging fields of fire. In front of the center of the army, the flank archers of the two front divisions met in an inverted V pointed toward the enemy. Behind the center of each division was the small mounted heavy-cavalry reserve, prepared to counterattack if any French assault should break through the front lines. During the day it appears that the English and Welsh infantrymen dug a number of small holes in the rolling fields to their immediate front as traps for the French cavalry horses.

The French army, estimated at nearly 60,000 fighting men, was composed of approximately 12,000 heavy cavalry — knights and men-at-arms — about 6,000 Genoese mercenary crossbowmen, 17,000 additional light cavalry, and some 25,000 communal levies — an undisciplined rabble of footmen straggling along in the rear.

This force, strung in an interminably long march column without any reconnoitering screen, bumped unexpectedly into the English line of battle about six o'clock in the late afternoon. Philip endeavored to halt the mass and concentrate. He was apparently able to get his crossbowmen into the lead, but the impetuous knights, filled with pride and the valor of ignorance, could not be controlled; so the French vanguard began to pile forward in a confused mass behind the Genoese.

The disciplined Genoese, deployed in firm alignment, crossed the valley and started up the slope. Halting about 150 yards from the English front, they fired their bolts, most of which fell short. Then they moved on again to meet the full blast of cloth-yard English arrows sheeting like a snowstorm on their line. Shattered, the Genoese reeled away from this devastating fire. The French van, impatient, put spurs to their mounts and rolled through and over the Genoese in a ponderous, disorganized avalanche. In a moment the slope was covered by a churning mass of mailed men and horses, pounding and stumbling through the unfortunate Genoese, while English arrows rained down on all. The impetus of the assault carried some of the French as far as the English line, where a sharp fight developed for a few moments. Then, repulsed by the stout English line, French survivors were driven back by the English mounted detachments.

Without rhyme or reason, each successive element of the French column came rushing into this horrible welter, to be caught in turn by the devastating arrows. The slaughter continued into the night; some 15 or 16 separate French waves dashed themselves to fragments in that ghastly valley. Then the French gave up.

In dreadful piles across the little valley lay 1,542 dead lords and knights; about 15,000 men-at-arms, crossbowmen, and infantrymen; and thousands of horses. The English loss was probably about 200 dead and wounded; the killed included 2 English knights, 40 men-at-arms and archers, and 100 or so Welsh infantrymen.

The full significance of this English victory over a force nearly three times its size was not appreciated even by the English. As for other fourteenth century leaders, they sought in vain for the elusive key to victory by following the English example of dismounting their heavy cavalry in battle. They failed to realize that the secret of English success was not merely their dismounted knights and their archers, but the judicious combination of these two with one another and with mounted cavalrymen to obtain a flexible combination of missile firepower, defensive staying power, and mobile shock action.

In the course of the fourteenth and fifteenth centuries, apart from the unsolved threat of the English longbow, the prestige of heavy cavalry suffered other violent shocks, even more ominous for the future. These were the repeated defeats administered to first Austrian, then Burgundian, cavalry over a period of a century and a half by the pike phalanx of the Swiss mountaineers. And as gunpowder weapons became more effective, cavalry became ever more vulnerable to well-trained infantry.

From the early part of the fourteenth century, starting with their struggle for independence against the dukes of Austria, the Swiss developed the pike as a national weapon, much as the English had done with the longbow. One crucial difference was, of course, that the longbow was essentially an individual weapon, and the skill of the archer an individual skill, whereas the Swiss pikeman with his long unwieldy weapon, if detached from his formation, was both useless and helpless. Like the English bowman, the whole training of the Swiss pikeman began in childhood, but was aimed at making him a smoothly functioning, anonymous member of the phalanx. It is significant that no single mastermind seems to be associated with the creation of this remarkable instrument.

The Swiss pikeman was a sturdy mountaineer — burgher or peasant — a freeman who, in the earlier heyday of the Swiss phalanx, was motivated primarily by patriotic determination to defend his small country (or canton) against invasion. His pike, the key weapon of the phalanx, had been progressively lengthened over a century until by the fifteenth century it was as long as 20 feet. This included a three-foot iron shank to prevent its being lopped off by sword or ax. The front of the phalanx thus bristled with the serried pikes of four to six ranks of men, impenetrable except to similar and longer weapons. Swiss pikemen wore very little, if any, armor; those in the front ranks sometimes wore steel breastplates.

In the attack the pike was held a little above shoulder height with the point slightly lowered. This posture permitted a vigorous downward thrust (though the Swiss were little given to fencing, relying rather on mass impact); it also made it harder for an adversary to force the point harmlessly upward, and protected the man behind from a rearward recoil of the butt. In defense the front rank dropped pike butts to the ground, braced against the right foot and steadied by the left knee, with left hand thrust forward on the shaft and the point elevated to breast height. Rear ranks retained the attack posture, those behind the first four or six holding their pikes vertically, ready to step forward into the places of the fallen.

The principal auxiliary weapon of the phalanx was the halberd, which had an older and perhaps equal claim to being the national weapon and had dominated some of the early battles with the Austrians. This was probably the most lethal individual weapon in the whole medieval arsenal.

The halberd was a pike 6 to 10 feet in length, with a heavy axhead, an opposing (sometimes curved) spike or hook, and a spike or spearhead at the top. Its use was revived by the Swiss in the early fourteenth century. It could cleave through helmet and armor, sever a sword blade, or fell a horse with a blow. It could also be used as a short pike, and, finally, the hook could be used to drag mounted men off their horses.

The early Swiss columns used halberds predominantly. But for all of its deadliness, this weapon had severe limitations in a mass formation, especially against an armored enemy in unbroken formation. At Sempach (1386), where they were equipped almost exclusively with halberds, the Swiss sustained heavy losses — although the final outcome of the battle was a Swiss victory.

Thereafter, they combined the long pike, which gave them reach, with the halberd. The halberdiers, on the flanks of the column, charged in when the enemy line or square was shaken by the charge of the pikemen.

In the days before Sempach the Swiss arsenal had also included a number of other weapons — two-handed swords, morning stars (iron-spiked clubs), Lucerne hammers (a sort of halberd, with curved prongs instead of ax blade), and of course the crossbow, made famous by Wilhelm Tell. By 1500 all these weapons, except the crossbow, had disappeared or dwindled to insignificance in the standard Swiss formation of pikemen and halberdiers.

In the process of their fight for independence the Swiss had discovered the benefits of mobility, which they gained through lack of encumbrances, and had also rediscovered the ancient Greek concept of the massed shock effect of a body of pikemen charging downhill. They recognized, furthermore, that this same principle of momentum would work on level ground if the pikemen could maintain their massed formation without gaps. To exploit this principle required excellent organization, rigorous training, and iron discipline of a sort unseen since Roman times. The determined Swiss met these challenges, and produced forces comparable to the Macedonian phalanxes in weapons, maneuverability, cohesiveness, and shock power. As a result, by the middle of the fourteenth century they were universally recognized as incomparably the finest troops in the world.

The Swiss phalanx was essentially an offensive weapon system, possessing also the defensive capabilities traditional in pike-bearing infantry. The advancing wall of bristling pike points struck an opposing line with a momentum and speed that no other infantry of its day could equal. Indeed, the tough, agile, and unarmored Swiss could move in formation at a pace only slightly less than that of the overweighted, mailed cavalry against which they were often pitted. This was where training paid off. Incessant drill was required to enable the close-ordered ranks to maintain their alignment in a rapid advance even over smooth terrain. The Swiss drilled, marched, and even advanced to the attack to the sound of the drum — marching, according to some authorities, in cadence. (If so, this seems to have been the earliest example of a military formation that marched in step.*) The phalanx could quickly change direction, flow over or around obstacles, form a square (the

---

*It is surprising that cadenced marching was not tried before this, and possibly it had been. But there is no clear earlier evidence of troops marching in step, though the Spartans may have done so.

"hedgehog") for defense, and retire in good order with its wounded. Like all massed infantry, it was limited by terrain, but less so than most. The Swiss gained the reputation of being able to surmount almost any physical obstacle, and they did not hesitate to attack across ditches, up steep hills, or against field fortifications — although sometimes with disastrous results.

The basic Swiss unit was a company of about 300 men, of which about 250 were pikemen arrayed in a square of 16 ranks and 16 files; the remaining men were halberdiers or crossbowmen. A typical Swiss column consisted of two or three companies in line, with at least equal depth.

The effects of speed and mobility were the essence of Swiss tactics. A Swiss army (as opposed to a Swiss contingent in a multi-national army) normally was grouped in two or three "battles" or columns. The battle plan was usually established in a council of the cantonal leaders, by majority vote, a few hours before the attack. The troops were formed for combat out of sight of the enemy and then rolled swiftly forward without the traditional time-consuming ritual of marshaling in line of battle on the field. In this way the Swiss were sometimes able to strike their enemy before his lines were formed. The Swiss battles normally advanced in echelon, rather than abreast or one behind the other, and sometimes the second or third would be held back, or would execute a wide turning movement, while the van battle held the enemy pinned down. Sometimes the flanks were refused and the center battle or, alternatively, the two wings made the initial attack. Another attack formation was the "wedge," actually a single deep, massed column, rather than a triangle. In defense, the phalanx ordinarily formed into a hollow square, with all pikes facing outward, a formation that was virtually impregnable to attack by other infantry or cavalry.

Both in attack and in defense, the Swiss fought with a ferocity that appalled their adversaries even in that ferocious age. It was their rule that quarter should be neither asked for nor given, and this was seldom broken, even long after the struggle for national independence had been won and Swiss soldiers were fighting solely for hire outside the homeland in the employ of foreign princes whose causes did not interest them. The patriotic fervor that animated the Swiss in their battles against the Austrians, and to a considerable degree against the Burgundians, became, in this later mercenary period, a professional pride in their unique prowess that provided an almost equally strong motivation.

Poverty was an historic circumstance of mountaineers which, to some degree, originally shaped the Swiss choice of weaponry and tactics. It also led them, from the late fifteenth century on, to make soldiering for hire (with cantonal and municipal governments acting as contractors) virtually the national occupation—a pursuit imitated, on a smaller scale, by German princelings and (for different basic reasons) the Irish and the Scots. As mercenaries, the Swiss pursued their calling with a dedication to pecuniary gain that matched their intensity and tenacity in combat. *Pas d'argent, pas de Suisses* (No money, no Swiss) became a rule that no employer dared ignore. Indeed, the Swiss had no compunction about abandoning one employer, contractual terms notwithstanding, in favor of another who offered higher pay.

The success of the English with the longbow in the fourteenth and fifteenth centuries had given to the defense a substantial tactical superiority over the offense in European warfare. This had complemented and reinforced the inherent combat superiority of the defense, particularly when enhanced by fortifications. It was the Swiss who again made infantry an element of offensive warfare for the first time since the decline of the Roman legion.

Even though no real solution had been found to the frustration experienced at the hands of the English longbowmen and the Swiss pikemen—frustrations multiplied by new gunpowder weapons— heavy cavalry lingered on as a major component of all of the West European armies. Class pride and feudal prejudice did not permit the knight to accept tactics and weapons he considered beneath his dignity.

As a compromise, however, more lightly armed and armored horsemen began to appear in western Europe. Some westerners who had participated in the Turkish wars of eastern Europe had noted the effectiveness of the relatively lightly armed and armored Hungarian, Turkish, and Albanian cavalry, who combined discipline and some shock power, on the one hand, with the mobility and flexibility of unarmored light cavalry on the other. These were mixed horse archers and lancers, quite similar in organization, armament, and tactics to the old Byzantine cataphract, though less heavily armored.

This was the first step in a series of major transformations in European cavalry, which did not really regain effectiveness until the seventeenth century.

The more immediate effect of the military decline of cavalry and the renaissance of infantry—during an era known to history for other reasons as the Renaissance—was a recognition among thoughtful soldiers of the complementary nature and characteristics of the two arms. The result was the creation of combined arms teams such as those used so effectively by Alexander and Hannibal. In an era of intellectual and artistic revival, intellect and imagination again became important determinants of battle outcomes. At the same time the introduction of gunpowder weapons and the increasing complexity of war, and the requirements for training, drill, and practice in inter-arms coordination, established a requirement for full-time professionals to replace part-time feudal dilettantes.

PART TWO: THE AGE OF GUNPOWDER

XII. Bombard, Hackbut, Petard, and Howitzer 1400–1600

The Appearance of Gunpowder

Gunpowder by itself was merely a mildly dangerous explosive known in Europe by 1250. Fifty to seventy-five years passed before someone discovered how to make it lethal by confining and igniting it in an open-ended tube.

With the introduction of gunpowder weapons into European warfare in the fourteenth century, a new phenomenon appeared in military history. The use of the explosive power of burning gases in an enclosed space, produced by igniting a mixture of potassium nitrate (saltpeter), sulphur, and wood charcoal, provided a basis for weapons and weapon systems of potentially greater lethality than any hitherto known. The earliest firearms, however, were inaccurate, short of range, slow to fire, heavy, and awkward. As shown in Table I, in which the relative lethality capability of weapons is compared over the course of history, they were substantially less effective than contemporary longbows and crossbows. However, infantry levies could be trained to use the weapons very quickly, in contrast to the months of training required to use the crossbow effectively, and the years of practice necessary for real proficiency with the longbow. Thus, the transition was a slow and painful process. It was only after a long period of development that firearms replaced the pike, crossbow, and longbow and became the preeminent weapons of the battlefield.

Crossbows were not discarded in France until 1566, and firearms were not officially adopted as infantry weapons in England until 1596. In the Ottoman forces, too, the bow was most reluctantly discarded, especially in the cavalry. In the sixteenth century the elite Turkish spahis refused to exchange their bows for

TABLE 1
Theoretical Lethality Index*

Weapons	TLI
Hand-to-hand (sword, pike, etc.)	23
Javelin	19
Ordinary bow	21
Longbow	36
Crossbow	33
Arquebus	10
17th century musket	19
18th century flintlock	43
Early 19th century rifle	36
Mid-19th century rifle/conoidal bullet	102
Late 19th century breech-loading rifle	153
Springfield Model 1903 rifle (magazine)	495
World War I machine gun	3,463
World War II machine gun	4,973
16th century 12-pdr cannon	43
17th century 12-pdr cannon	224
Gribeauval 18th century 12-pdr cannon	940
French 75mm gun	386,530
155mm GPF	912,428
105mm howitzer, M-1	657,215
155mm "Long Tom"	1,180,681
World War I tank	6,926
World War II medium tank	575,000
World War I fighter-bomber	6,926
World War II fighter-bomber (P-47)	135,000
V-2 ballistic missile	3,338,370
20-KT nuclear airburst	49,086,000
One-megaton nuclear airburst	695,385,000

*Relative effectiveness capability of historical weapons, based upon such considerations as range, rate of fire, accuracy, reliability, radius of damage, etc.

firearms, though they were, in the opinion of contemporary observers, thereby handicapped. The crossbow and longbow finally disappeared from military operations only in the late seventeenth century.

The confused history of the emergence of explosives and firearms as the arbiters of the battlefield must be seen as a complex of parallel regional developments. While gunpowder and rockets were international developments, and the first crude guns were introduced in China almost simultaneously with their appearance in Europe, development of guns was much more rapid in the West. By 1350 guns of very large caliber as well as rudimentary handguns were common in Europe. The earliest evidence of guns in China dates from about the same time, although a century earlier the Chinese had used crude bamboo rockets to frighten the enemy or for incendiary purposes.

The most significant single technological advance making possible the development of gunpowder weapons was the invention of the technique of casting iron. Throughout the Middle Ages the older techniques of smelting iron continued to be used. But the appearance of new methods — such as the use of water-driven hammers for the crushing of ore, and the application of water power to the forging process and to operate larger and more powerful bellows — made possible the high temperatures needed to cause absorption of the carbon into the iron and liquefaction so that the molten iron could be released from the bottom of the furnace through clay-sealed holes to flow into previously prepared molds of sand and clay. Beginning in the fourteenth century blast furnaces in the Rhineland were casting iron in a variety of shapes. Since iron was relatively cheap, the products of casting found a rapidly growing market. The casting of copper and bronze also expanded after the discovery, in the mid-fifteenth century, of a process for separating silver from common argentiferous copper through the use of lead.

The Evolution of Firearms

The production and development of small handguns commenced at the same time as the production of larger pieces, since it was easier to forge or cast a barrel when the measurements were small. The earliest handguns were merely short barrels, tubes of iron or brass, commonly less than 10 inches long, with a caliber between 25 and 45 millimeters, held in one hand and fired with the other. The touchhole was usually on top. Such small guns were extremely difficult to control or aim, and the barrel would soon get too hot to hold. For this reason they were sometimes mounted on wooden boards, and apparently such weapons were used at Crecy. From these rudimentary hand cannon developed the various forms of hand firearms that soon appeared.

About the middle of the fourteenth century a stock or tiller had been invented to control the barrel of the handgun. At first the barrels were clamped to simple poles, usually about four to five feet in length. Even with a stock, accuracy was poor.

The effectiveness of the weapon was further compromised by the quality of the powder. During transport the heavier saltpeter settled to the bottom while the lighter charcoal drifted to the top. Thus powder had to be mixed shortly before an engagement. In addition, the lack of sufficient airspace between the fine powder particles retarded the explosion. Because of this gunpowder weakness, large quantities were used, often as much as three quarters of the volume of the barrel. This was rammed down, then a wooden plug (sabot) was placed on top, followed finally by the ball, which was practically at the muzzle. Slow and inefficient combustion also impelled users to pack in the shot with rags or clay to obtain space for pressure to build up. At first, therefore, handguns were essentially psychological weapons, not very lethal, but the noise, smoke, and fire of the explosion were useful in frightening cavalry horses.

The problem of the pressure in handguns was solved in the fifteenth century with the invention of corned powder. By holding the three components in steady relationship and by providing equal distribution of airspace, corned powder made explosion more uniform and nearly instantaneous.

With the new powder, the early handguns had a potential range of nearly 200 yards, although their effective range was barely 50. However, they now delivered a much heavier punch than the longbow, although the bow was for a long time superior in speed, volume of fire, accuracy, and mobility. One reason for the relative immobility of handguns was the need for access to fire. The weapons were ignited by a red-hot coal or a piece of red-hot iron thrust into the touchhole. Thus the gunner was forced to stay near a fire and pick up his coal or iron at the last minute.

The inaccuracy of the earliest handguns was due in part to the difficulty of holding the stock. Usually it was held in the left hand, directly behind the barrel, with the butt clamped between the left arm and the body; ignition was applied with the other hand. Sometimes the gunner braced the gunstock on the ground or used a forked rest. In any event, the gunner had to keep his eye on the touchhole so he would not miss it or burn his hand. Consequently he could not look where he was shooting, and could not take effective aim.

In the fifteenth century devices were invented to make ignition more secure and aiming more accurate, increasing the lethality of the weapon. The touchhole was moved from the top to the right side of the barrel and a little ledge or "pan" was added to hold priming powder to make ignition more certain. Barrels were lengthened and stocks shortened. But the most important development was the introduction of a glowing "match" and a device for holding it. The match was a cord or tightly twisted rag that had been soaked in saltpeter and then dried out. This would smolder (unless extinguished by rain) and would ignite priming powder sprinkled in the pan.

The earliest device for holding the match was a simple pivoting serpentine to be lowered and raised by hand, but this was soon connected with a trigger, to become the matchlock. When the gunner pulled the trigger he raised the lower end of the serpentine while the upper end holding the match in its clamp was lowered into the pan. The gunner could now look where he was pointing his piece while firing.

The shortened stocks, curved to be brought up against the cheek, shoulder, or breast, also aided in taking aim. This new type of weapon was commonly called a *hackbut* (in German) or *arquebus* (in French) — words which literally mean "hookgun."

The hackbut weighed about 10 to 15 pounds and fired a ball weighing somewhat less than an ounce with a muzzle velocity of about 800 feet per second and a range of about 100 to 200 yards. Its firing speed was still slow; about two shots in three minutes was considered exceptionally good by the 1570s. In spite of its limitations, here, for the first time, was a truly usable small-arms gunpowder weapon. It remained the standard weapon for the next century. But it was limited by its relatively low power of penetration, and as infantry body armor came into increasing use there arose the need for a weapon capable of both piercing plate armor and stopping heavy cavalry.

The matchlock musket, a heavier weapon with improved ballistic properties, was developed by the Spaniards and first used in the Italian wars in the 1530s as a defensive-position weapon. It had a longer barrel and fired a heavier ball, which could pierce armor and stop a cavalry charge. The longer barrel and improved powder gave somewhat higher velocities and further range. On the other hand, because of its weight, it was really a small cannon, and relatively immobile.

In its earliest form the musket was six or seven feet long, weighed 25 pounds or more, and fired bullets with a weight of 10 to 14 to the pound. Although its proponents claimed that the matchlock could kill at 600 paces if the powder was good, its effective range was well under 200 yards. Although gradually modified and improved until it replaced the hackbut, the musket remained heavy, 14 pounds or more, and had to be fired from a forked rest.

Matchlocks functioned only in dry weather and consumed great quantities of match. Moreover, the need to have the match smoldering during and before action created hazards. It gave away night operations, sometimes exploded the ammunition carried by individuals, and always presented a great danger to the powder supply of the artillery. The necessity of lighting matches before action sometimes prevented troops from firing when attacked by surprise.

In the sixteenth century there appeared mechanical devices in which pyrite or flint was struck against steel, producing sparks to ignite the priming powder in the pan. One such device, the wheellock, had important influence on cavalry arms and tactics, but it was too expensive and delicate a device for general issue. Cavalry and special infantry units employed it, but it never supplanted the matchlock as the principal infantry weapon.

A second system utilizing flint and steel was the snaphance lock. A carefully sharpened piece of flint was held in the jaws of a cock mounted on the side of the barrel, which, when released by trigger action, was forced by a heavy V-shaped spring to strike against a hinged piece of steel called a battery or frizzen. The frizzen was arched over the priming pan, and the shower of sparks discharged the weapon. A cover protecting the pan from rain and spilling was opened mechanically before firing and closed by hand after each reloading.

In the sixteenth century, when the use of firearms in battle became practical, battlefields were still dominated by the two rival shock systems — the pike phalanx and heavy, armored cavalry. It was to the defensive armament of the pike phalanx and, independently, to the defense of entrenchments and fortifications, that firearms made their main battlefield contribution.

Because of their inaccuracy, short range, slow rate of fire, weight, and unhandiness, early firearms left the soldiers using them more vulnerable than did the longbow and crossbow. Like those weapons the early firearms were not generally employed individually. They were fired in volleys from massed formations, normally at a massed hostile formation, with the hope that some of the balls would hit someone. When used thus in mass at short ranges the difference in accuracy was of less importance, and they attained greater lethality through impact and penetrating power than did the earlier missile weapons. Because of their vulnerability, troops using firearms in massed fire in the fifteenth century required the protection of pike formations or entrenchments. For harassing fire at maximum ranges and for skirmishing preliminary to the main action, their usefulness was limited.

Unable to wield both a firearm and a weapon useful in melee fighting, the arquebusier, musketeer, and artilleryman remained auxiliaries of the dominant shock formations, separate but not independent, and organized mostly in small formations attached to heavy masses of pikemen. Yet the early clashes between arquebus and crossbow in the wars in Italy left little doubt as to the superiority of the former in all the qualities that counted on the battlefield. Competition between the arquebus and the English longbow, on the other hand, was less direct, since the latter had virtually disappeared from the Continent with the expulsion of the English in the middle of the preceding century. The record of performance of the two weapons, however, suggests on the whole that before the middle of the sixteenth century hand firearms did not surpass the lethality of the longbow. The longbow had obvious advantages over the crude firearms of the period — in accuracy, range, rapidity of fire, handiness, lightness, simplicity of construction. Firearms had advantages in the heavier and more disabling impact (including penetrability) of a one- or two-ounce ball as contrasted with the arrow; the lack of need for long training, since they could not be precisely aimed in any event; and the nasty tendency of gunshot wounds to cause blood poisoning. With little to choose between the weapons, it is not surprising that the longbow was slow to decline in English armament, that there were persistent pleas, as late as the eighteenth century, for its revival.

The lethality of firearms on the battlefields of the sixteenth century was limited by their subordinate and auxiliary role in the armament and tactics of the period. Throughout the century, despite the slowly growing ratio of "shot" to "pike" and the gradual improvement of firearms, most battles were decided in the clash of hand-to-hand combat. By this measure, the most lethal weapons of the age were not the newfangled firearms but the old-fashioned pike, lance, and sword. Yet gunfire power, even in its still primitive state of development, was indispensable; lacking it, no sixteenth century army dared engage one that possessed it. How to combine shot with pike in a single weapon system was the main unsolved tactical and technical problem of warfare at the end of the century.

The Evolution of Artillery

It is uncertain when long cannon were first made by casting. Cast bronze guns came first, though cast iron pieces are recorded at Dijon before the middle of the fifteenth century—evidently isolated and not very successful products of a technology still in its infancy. The new techniques were brought to England by the early Tudors, laying the basis for the Sussex iron industry that dominated European gun metallurgy until the rise of the Swedish iron industry in the seventeenth century. The advantage of cast iron lay in its cheapness, not its superiority over other metals; both brass and bronze, though expensive, were tougher and less prone to bursting.

The technique of casting large guns was adapted from that of bell founding. This involved pouring the metal into a clay mold consisting of a core and an outside cope. The clay mold was lowered into a pit; the furnace was tapped and the molten metal poured into the mold; after the metal had cooled, the mold had to be broken. Thus each gun was an individual product, like a piece of sculpture, which indeed it also resembled in its elaborate decoration. Quality of cannon depended upon the skill of the workmen that made each individual casting. Not for two hundred years was an effort made to cast cannon in series from a single mold.

After the mold had been broken, the rough casting had to be bored out by a bit mounted on a long shaft powered by a water wheel. Since the shaft was supported on one end only, the boring was frequently inaccurate. Furthermore, the boring process could not remedy inaccuracies in the original mold. A gun was fit for service if it could pass proof tests, which consisted of visual examination, hammer blows, and the firing of charges of increased amounts, the last of which was equal to the weight of the shot. By the eighteenth century the Dutch had achieved a reputation as the leaders in boring out solid-cast barrels.

Until the middle of the nineteenth century, bronze and brass held their own against cast iron in the manufacture of artillery except in heavy naval ordnance. Bronze gun barrels, being relatively soft, had a tendency to deform under the repeated pounding of round shot bounding eccentrically through the tube, and thus proved unsuitable for heavier guns.

By the late fourteenth century, cannon had begun to transform warfare. As the new techniques for making both wrought and cast metal were introduced, the changes became progressively more significant.

The trebuchet, which had appeared in China in the eleventh century and quickly spread into Europe where it largely replaced the older Greek and Roman tension and torsion siege engines, continued in use long after the introduction of gunpowder. It was inexpensive, simple to construct, could hurl heavy loads, and was dependable. But the new guns began to take their place beside the older engines. From the introduction of gunpowder, cannon were easier to use and more effective than handguns, and so it was that gunpowder had its first significant impact in siege artillery. It was not until the second half of the fifteenth century, however, that cannon became sufficiently efficient to replace the trebuchet as siege artillery.

The most important of the various types of heavy cannon appearing in the fourteenth century were enormous guns called bombards. They were short-barrelled and usually cast from bronze or iron, although copper and brass were also used. Since their stone shot weighed as much as 300 pounds, enormous quantities of powder, almost filling the entire barrel, had to be used. The shot often protruded from the barrel and thus could attain almost no accuracy and little velocity. To be effective, bombards had to be moved virtually within stone's throw of the walls that were to be battered.

Cast iron bombards are alleged to have been used at the siege of Terni in 1340, and tiny versions were probably employed by the English — inconclusively — at Crecy in 1346.* By the end of the century longer pieces were being made from forged iron bars welded together and bound with hoops. Richard II had some of these constructed for the defense of the Tower of London. The famous Mons Meg gun at Edinburgh was made of several cast sections screwed together, the whole piece being strengthened by welded hoops.

The effectiveness of siege cannon improved greatly when barrels lengthened and the art of iron casting improved. Around 1450, stone shot was replaced by cast iron balls, which had less "windage" (space between projectile and interior of bore) and therefore attained greater muzzle velocity and impact energy. From 1470 on, siege artillery was able to reduce medieval walled fortifications in short order. Because of limitations of weight and trajectory, it was impossible to emplace large cannon suitable for counterbattery within the confines of castles and walled cities, and by the end of the century artillery had made medieval fortifications obsolete (see Chapter XIII).

---

*There may have been bombards at the siege of Metz in 1324, and that of Algeciras in 1342.

The impact of the new artillery on siege warfare was immediate and pronounced, precisely because its role and its potential effects were, from the beginning, hardly open to question. On the battlefield, however, despite its formidable possibilities, the role of artillery was for a long time somewhat ambiguous.

Few new weapons in history had achieved such spectacular success and devastating impact in battle as did the miscellaneous collection of primitive pieces that John Ziska's embattled Hussites mounted in their *Wagenburgen* in the 1420s and 1430s. The Hussites moved in columns of horse-drawn carts or wagons, most of which were armor-plated, the sides pierced with loopholes. Inside these protected wagons, or on other open four-wheeled carts, were carried a number of small bombards. The troops were mostly footmen, some armed with handguns, but most with pikes. In addition there was a small force of lightly armored cavalrymen used for reconnaissance and for counterattack. Ziska always avoided an offensive battle in the open. His strategy was to penetrate as far as possible into enemy territory and then to select a good defensive position upon which to establish a wagon fort. Raids from the wagon base were designed to force the foe to disastrous attack.

The wagons were formed into a laager and linked together by chains. In front of this wall of wagons a ditch was dug. The bombards were placed in the intervals between wagons, possibly on their four-wheeled carts, but more likely on earthen mounds or heavy wooden platforms. Also in these intervals, and firing from the wagon loopholes, were handgun operators and crossbowmen. Pikemen were available to protect the bombards and to prevent enemy infantry from cutting the chains holding the wagons together. They rarely had to perform these missions, however, since the attackers were more often than not repulsed by the firepower of the wagenburg. As soon as an attack was repulsed, Ziska's pikemen and cavalry charged to counterattack, sealing the victory.

Though Ziska did not introduce true field artillery, and did not use gunpowder in a tactically offensive role, his was a most imaginative and offensive-minded use of field fortifications, and his battles were classics of defensive-offensive tactics. The wagenburg, however, could not be properly established if the enemy army was alert and aggressive; nor could it bring victory if the enemy was not drawn into attack after it was established. Furthermore, the wagon fort was extremely vulnerable to true field artillery and to efficient small arms; thus it was soon outmoded.

The first effective use of field artillery in western Europe was in the final stages of the Hundred Years' War. The new French artillery designed for Charles VII by the brothers Jean and Gaspard Bureau was sufficiently mobile to play a leading role in several battles. At Formigny (1450) a small English force, well positioned for defense, was so plagued by French artillery fire that it attacked under unfavorable conditions and was annihilated. Three years later, at Castillon, the English frontally attacked a French camp, defended by emplaced guns, with similar results. In neither case was true field artillery involved. It should be noted that the culverins (relatively light long-range cannon) and bombards that facilitated the French victories had in each instance been previously emplaced for siege operations and were merely shifted in direction to repulse English relieving armies. They could not be maneuvered on the field.

True field artillery made a sudden and dramatic appearance in the final decade of the fifteenth century when the French mounted new and relatively light cast bronze cannon on two-wheeled carriages pulled by horses. The new mobile French field artillery could be quickly unharnessed and unlimbered on the battlefield. It was during this decade that the French also introduced the concept of the trunnion, which facilitated the mounting of cannon on permanent wheeled carriages and permitted relatively accurate aiming and ranging — in sharp distinction to the earlier awkward methods of raising and lowering the weapon's bore by digging holes under the trail or putting the wheels on blocks.

The improved French artillery proved its worth and achieved a decisive success over the Swiss at the two-day, bitterly contested Battle of Marignano, September 13 – 14, 1515. The Swiss, shocked by this first serious setback in over a century of dominance of European battlefields, quickly negotiated peace with France, a peace that was to endure until the French Revolution, two and two-thirds centuries later.

Development of artillery weapons in the sixteenth century, however, failed to keep up with the progress of small arms mainly because artillerymen had not yet been able to solve the problem of combining mobility with reliable long-range firepower. It had long been realized that long range, accuracy, and destructiveness (or lethality) were best achieved by guns that were 20 or more calibers in length (bore length 20 times the bore diameter), and with thick walls, which could withstand the pressures built up by detonation of a large powder charge. Pieces with thinner walls and lighter powder charges could fire equally heavy projectiles, but with significant reduction in accuracy and range. But even the lightest of these weapons was still clumsy, difficult to move, and took a long time to prepare for action.

Because of these limitations, the artillery supremacy achieved by the French at the end of the previous century was soon reversed by dramatic Spanish improvements in infantry small arms and the tactics of their employment. As a result, artillery declined in importance during this century, save in the attack and defense of fortifications and in naval warfare. Few major battles were fought without artillery being employed, but in general, after the bloody Battle of Ravenna, small arms were the more decisive factor.

At about the same time the French also lost their superiority in artillery construction and techniques to more imaginative German gunmakers and artillerymen. These in turn were soon excelled by the Spanish, who enjoyed a clear-cut superiority in this, as in most other aspects of military science, for most of the century.

Gunmakers experimented constantly with new designs and combinations of bore diameter, wall thickness, powder charges, and projectile weights. As a result there were almost as many types of artillery pieces as there were weapons. Ammunition supply became an impossible task, contributing to the decline of artillery's importance in field operations. To correct this situation, shortly before the middle of the sixteenth century, Emperor Charles V ordered standardization of all imperial artillery weapons into seven types. Soon afterward Henry II of France followed suit by establishing six standard models for French artillery. Experimentation continued, and many additional types were added to these basic standard models, but in a more orderly and systematic manner than previously. (See Table 2.) Weapon types continued to vary from nation to nation, although many were produced in imitation of Spanish designs.

By the seventeenth century the art of gunmaking had progressed to the point where range, power, and major types of guns were to change little for nearly two centuries. Further artillery modification would be mainly limited to improved mobility, organization, tactics, and field gunnery techniques.

By this time artillery weapons were beginning to coalesce into three principal classes, prototypes of modern artillery: first was the culverin type, comparable to the modern gun; second was the cannon, prototype of the howitzer; finally there was a thin-walled, high-trajectory weapon (called variously a pedrero or mortar, depending upon its characteristics), the genesis of the modern mortar.

The culverin, counterpart to the modern field gun, had a relatively long barrel (about 30 calibers) and a high muzzle velocity, which, in turn, resulted in a flat trajectory, long range, and a relatively high order of accuracy. In order to achieve the necessary muzzle velocities without danger of the tube exploding and killing or injuring the gun crew, the barrels of the cannon were made

TABLE 2

SIXTEENTH-CENTURY ARTILLERY PIECES*
(Characteristics are indicative and approximate; records are incomplete, confusing, and contradictory)

Name	Piece Weight (lbs.)	Pro- jectile Weight (lbs.)	Bore (in.)	Length (ft.)	Point- blank or Effective Range (yds.)	Maxi- mum Range (yds.)
Class I: Culverin Types (25–44 calibers in length)						
Esmeril (or rabinet)	200	.3	1.0	2.5	200	750
Serpentine	400	.5	1.5	3.0	250	1,000
Falconet	500	1.0	2.0	3.7	280	1,500
Falcon	800	3.0	2.5	6.0	400	2,500
Minion (or demi- saker)	1,000	6.0	3.3	6.5	450	3,500
Pasavolante	3,000	6.0	3.3	10.0	1,000	4,500
Saker	1,600	9.0	4.0	6.9	500	4,000
Culverin bastard	3,000	12.0	4.6	8.5	600	4,000
Demiculverin	3,400	10.0	4.2	8.5	850	5,000
Culverin	4,800	18.0	5.2	11.0	1,700	6,700
Culverin royal	7,000	32.0	6.5	16.0	2,000	7,000
Class II: Cannon Types (15–28 calibers in length)						
Quarto-cannon	2,000	12.0	4.6	7.0	400	2,000
Demicannon	4,000	32.0	6.5	11.0	450	2,500
Bastard cannon	4,500	42.0	7.0	10.0	400	2,000
Cannon serpentine	6,000	42.0	7.0	12.0	500	3,000
Cannon	7,000	50.0	8.0	13.0	600	3,500
Cannon royal	8,000	60.0	8.5	12.0	750	4,000
Basilisk	12,000	90.0	10.0	10.0	750	4,000
Class III: Pedrero and Mortar Types†						
Pedrero (medium)	3,000	30.0	10.0	9.0	500	2,500
Mortar (medium)	1,500	30.0	6.3	2.0	300	750
Mortar (heavy)	10,000	200.0	15.0	6.0	1,000	2,000

*R. E. Dupuy and T. N. Dupuy, *Encyclopedia of Military History*, (New York: Harper & Row, 1977).

†Though variations were great, pedreros were usually 10–15 calibers in length, and fired projectiles up to 50 pounds in weight. Mortars were 3 to 5 calibers in length, and fired projectiles up to 200 pounds.

thick, resulting in heavy, relatively immobile weapons. Thus heavy-caliber culverins were used almost exclusively for siegecraft.

The second class consisted of lighter, shorter pieces designed to fire relatively heavier projectiles shorter distances, sacrificing range and accuracy in order to achieve more mobility without loss of smashing power. This was the so-called cannon type of weapon, about 20 calibers in length and roughly comparable to the modern howitzer. Most early cannon, however, were not much more mobile than culverins, and some, in fact, were bigger and heavier than the largest culverin.

Small cannon could be moved readily to the battlefield on wagons, as was done by the Hussites and the French in the fifteenth century. At first the guns had to be placed on stands or scaffolding constructed on the spot, and could not be moved once the battle began. The introduction of two-wheeled carriages with trails (and soon after this of trunnions, allowing elevation and depression of the barrel without having to raise the whole gun) was the beginning of the modern fieldpiece.

The invention of corned powder (page 94), combined with lengthened barrels, resulted in higher velocities and improved accuracy. But lengthening the barrels still further increased the weight of cannon, thus continuing to preclude the use of large pieces on the battlefield.

By the beginning of the seventeenth century it was obvious to thoughtful soldiers that there was a need for a fieldpiece that would have range and accuracy comparable to a cannon, with the battlefield mobility of the fourteenth- and fifteenth-century pedrero (see Table 2). The Dutch led the way in the development of such a new weapon, which became known as the howitzer, and by the end of the century it was a standard artillery type of all European armies.

A howitzer combined a relatively short, large-bore barrel with the two-wheeled carriage of the field gun. The trail of the weapon was rather short to permit higher elevation. The barrel was shorter and lighter than that of the culverin or gun, but longer than that of the mortar, thus permitting a somewhat flatter trajectory and greater accuracy. The importance of the howitzer lay in its combination of striking power and relatively light weight, and therefore greater mobility. Where shells could be used and obstacles had to be cleared, the howitzer (like the mortar) had advantages over cannon because of its trajectory.

Mortars, short-barrelled weapons throwing projectiles with parabolic trajectories, were known from the very beginning of the gunpowder period. They were important in siege warfare largely because they could fire explosive shells, and their trajectories permitted them to fire over the walls of fortifications and to reach such targets as magazines, barracks, and reserve formations. A major advantage of the mortar was that its short barrel and thin tube (possible because of small powder charges) permitted light weight and high mobility. Offsetting these advantages were short range and low accuracy.

Mortars came in all sizes, some very large, and some so small that they were used to hurl hand grenades. The mortar usually was a wide-mouthed, short-barrelled piece fixed to a square bed, sometimes at a fixed angle of forty-five degrees, sometimes adjustable. A popular small weapon of the seventeenth and eighteenth centuries was the coehorn, a weapon invented by Baron Coehorn in 1673. This type threw shells weighing up to 24 pounds. There also were monstrous siege pieces weighing several tons and hurling 10- and even 12-inch shells.

XIII. New Fortifications and Siegecraft 1400–1700

The Crusaders learned lessons from the Byzantines that completely changed western European concepts of fortifications and of defense of cities. The westerners were particularly impressed with the powerful Byzantine walled cities and fortresses, with double or triple concentric lines of massive turreted walls. There was nothing like this in the West at the time. The result was a complete revolution in castle construction and city defense in western Europe in the twelfth century.

During the next two centuries, however, the only important refinement in fortifications was the general adoption of stone machicolation on the upper ramparts of the permanent walls of castles and fortified towns. Extending out over the tops of the walls, these permitted the defenders to fire down (or pour boiling oil, or the like) through narrow slits directly onto attackers at the base of a wall or tower without incurring much danger in the process. Prior to this, machicolation had been in the form of wooden galleries or "hoardings" hung over the tops of walls. But these had been vulnerable to incendiary missiles and to pulverizing blows from siege engines and bombards.

Following a familiar historical cycle, the technique of siegecraft lagged far behind the art of fortification. Human ingenuity and mechanical skill had seemingly exhausted themselves. Few monarchs were skillful, powerful, or wealthy enough to be able and willing to devote sufficient resources to the task of overcoming the most powerful defenses. Feudal armies could seldom be maintained in the field long enough to undertake the prolonged sieges necessary to capture such powerful forts; feudal levies could be called to action for only a few weeks of the year, and mercenary armies were extremely expensive to maintain in the field indefinitely. At this time the success or failure of a siege very much depended on the availability of basic supplies of food and water within the fortification and the determination of the defender to hold out.

The introduction of gunpowder weapons in the early fifteenth century soon changed this situation. The impact of the new artillery on the science of siegecraft and defense of fortifications was literally shattering. Even the crude bombards, mortars, and cannon available early in the century were more potent than pregunpowder siege weapons. The most solid medieval masonry crumbled before crude cannon firing stone balls.

However, this did not happen overnight. Siege artillery using gunpowder was at first more a morale booster than a lethal instrument. Edward III used some 20 guns in the siege of Calais (1356), but even though the city was cut off from all help, it held out for more than eleven months. And when the Bohemian Hussites besieged Castle Karlstein in 1422 they emplaced 46 small cannon, 5 large cannon, including a medium quickfirer (a quickfirer could fire 30 times a day, while others could fire only 5 or 6 times), and 5 trebuchets. After about 11,000 cannonballs, 932 stone missiles, 13 fire barrels, and some 32 tons of rotting carcasses had been fired, the castle still held out, and the Hussites lifted the siege.

Thirty years later the breaching of the massive defenses of Constantinople in 1453, after less than two months of concentrated fire by Turkish guns, dramatized the end of a military as well as an historical era. No longer were well-fortified places all but impervious to capture except by prolonged engineering operations or starvation.

Probably the most famous and formidable bombards were the monsters used by the Turks during that siege of Constantinople. Twelve of these, including one superbombard called "Basilica," were designed for the sultan by a Hungarian engineer, Urban, who had defected from the employ of the Byzantine emperor. Basilica was built of wrought iron bars and hoops; it measured 36 inches in bore diameter, and fired stone balls weighing 1,600 pounds; its range was more than a mile, and 200 men and 60 oxen were required to move it. It was designed to fire at the rate of about seven shots a day, but after the first few shots it blew up. The smaller pieces in the sultan's siege train proved more effective. Some of them were used 354 years later with good effect against a British squadron attacking Constantinople by sea.

The final stages of the expulsion of the English from northern France in the mid-fifteenth century were in large part a series of sieges in which the newly acquired artillery of the French king rapidly demolished the English-held strongholds. When Charles VIII invaded Italy in 1494 his up-to-date mobile siege train knocked over the Italian fortresses so rapidly that his advance down the peninsula was virtually a procession, described by Machiavelli as executed with "chalk in hand" — that is, simply by marking on the map the route to be followed. A few years later Pedro Navarro, Gonzalo de Córdoba's famous engineer, developed techniques for using gunpowder in mining beneath the walls of besieged fortresses.

By the end of the fifteenth century, artillery had made medieval fortifications obsolete. To a degree, as already noted, this was because castles and walled cities had found no way to emplace large cannon suitable for counterbattery. Light guns mounted on high walls could not reach long-range attacking guns. Heavier weapons, when they could be laboriously lifted to the tops of the ramparts, soon became counterproductive; the force of recoil shook the foundation, dangerously weakening the walls and making them easier to breach.

In the following century a revolution in the science of fortification went far to restore the balance between defense and offense in siege operations, and in this revolution firepower was again the key.

The old vulnerable, high, curtain walls and towers were replaced by a lower, thicker wall that not only provided adequate emplacements for defending artillery but also made the breaching process more difficult for siege guns. New fortifications were built with broad, low walls from which triangular bastions extended to permit defending artillery to sweep all approaches to the fort. Existing fortifications were modernized by the erection of new walls and bastions of this type; older walls were lowered and broadened where possible. The ideal design surrounded the fortress proper with a wide ditch or moat, and beyond that with a low counterscarp fringed by a sloping glacis or earthwork, with a covered way along its top to permit rapid movement of defending forces from one point to another. Light artillery pieces could be emplaced on the counterscarp wall to keep the great siege guns at a distance.

Instead of confronting the besieger with physical obstacles, which he could batter down at his leisure, the new theory of fortifications was to provide a low but massive screen as a basis for a murderous counterfire that would stop an assault before it began. The slope of the glacis was swept by fire from guns mounted within or behind broad parapets on the fortress ramparts inside the ditch. These ramparts were only slightly higher than the counterscarp, and were carefully designed with projecting, sharply angled bastions at regular intervals at the corners, to ensure that every point along the walls could be covered by flanking fire from guns in protected emplacements on the wall.

The increasing complexity of combat with gunpowder weapons, and the growing significance of economic and political considerations of waging war attracted the attention of more and more men of intellectual bent. All aspects of military affairs were subjected to analysis in this revival of interest in the theory of warfare. In the design of the new fortifications it became a matter of crucial importance to calculate angles and fields of fire precisely so as to eliminate the blind spots which, in medieval fortresses, had often enabled an attacker to find protection from defending fire under the defenses themselves. It was, therefore, no accident that two of the more specialized theoreticians of the time were mathematicians: Niccolò Tartaglia (1500– 1557), who published a number of works on the science of gunnery, ballistics, and fortifications; and Simon Stevin (1548– 1620), who served as advisor to Maurice of Nassau at the end of the century, and who placed particular stress on the use of defensive firepower to destroy a besieger's own protecting works.

Since practice lagged behind fortification theory in the sixteenth century, much of the military writing of the period, including Machiavelli's *Arte della Guerra*, was devoted to the problem of improvising internal defenses after a besieger had breached the main ramparts. Few cities could afford to raze their old defenses and rebuild from the ground. The usual compromise was to mount artillery on the old ramparts (which often necessitated strengthening the walls), improvise bastions from existing towers, and build additional bastioned outworks and defenses for particularly vital points. Before the end of the century, however, a few cities, including Antwerp (1540), Hesdin (1554), Verona (after 1520), Havre, and Marseilles, completely redesigned their defenses in the new manner.

The new fortification designs had another incidental, but important, advantage. Mining became difficult, since tunnels had to be too long to permit fresh air to reach the diggers. Another deterrent to mining was the costliness of gunpowder. When an opportunity for mining could be exploited, it was usually by collapse rather than explosion, a reversion to the ancient technique of burning the tunnel support timbers.

The problems posed by the new fortifications naturally stimulated new and serious efforts to improve siegecraft. In both offense and defense, siege methodology was refined and systematized to keep pace with the new scientific methods of fortification. These methods had, at least for a time, outstripped gunnery development, although the balance was extremely delicate. It was necessary to find a relatively safe method of getting attacking artillery and small arms close enough to the defenses to bring effective fire to bear. The old mantelets and siege towers were ineffective against defending gunpowder weapons. Attackers, accordingly, resorted to digging. Under the cover of long-range culverin-type guns, attacking engineers and infantry dug trenches toward a presumably vulnerable point in the defenses. When these trenches were within artillery battering range of the fortification's counterscarp, thick earthen walls were thrown up in front of wide, shallow trenches that became protected emplacements for siege guns. Under cover of darkness the heavy weapons would be trundled into the emplacements and would then begin the painstaking battering process. Under cover of this fire, new trenches would be pushed still further forward until a combined artillery and infantry attack could overwhelm the counterscarp defenders. Again the big guns would be moved forward, this time to concentrate against the main fortifications.

Before the end of the century the concept of approach entrenchments was quite well developed, though crude in comparison with the refinements that would be introduced by Vauban in the seventeenth century. But it was a long, laborious, costly, and bloody process — almost prohibitive against active and alert defenders. A sixteenth-century fortress, if provided with adequate stocks of food and ammunition, was as impregnable as the thirteenth-century castle had been in its day. By the latter part of the sixteenth century sieges had again become the slow, elaborate undertakings they had been two centuries earlier. Warfare once more became a series of sieges, punctuated by battles only when some combination of maneuvering skill, confidence, or logistical pressures brought two armies face to face in the open.

The new fortifications, and the siege processes to deal with them, greatly stimulated the long-lost art of field fortifications, largely dormant in Europe since Roman times. The principal stimulus, however, had already been provided by farsighted Spanish soldiers led by Gonzalo de Córdoba, who was apparently the first to realize the potentialities of field fortification in combination with the new firepower of gunpowder small arms. Following his example, Pedro Navarro and Alexander of Parma kept Spanish engineering and field fortification techniques preeminent as a major element of Spanish military supremacy throughout the sixteenth century.

Maurice of Nassau (see Chapter XVI) made a real and lasting contribution to siege warfare. He sought to bring order into the confusing array of guns by standardizing his artillery with regard to caliber. He adopted the practice of concentrating massive barrages against small sections of the enceinte, following this by creating practicable breaches in the fortification. He used long approach trenches, and protected his guns effectively when they were brought up to do their battering task. He also employed mines when he could, although the wet soil of Holland was not favorable for such work. He usually offered liberal terms to besieged towns, and his strict discipline paid off by reducing plunder and rapine, thus encouraging the citizens of the places he besieged to lay down their arms. His methods generally shortened the duration of the siege.

The French engineer Sebastian de Vauban dominated the culminating developments of the two opposed functions of siegecraft and fortification. Through his efforts both opposed functions approached the ultimate capabilities of military forces limited to muzzle-loading weapons and black powder. Under the direction of François Louvois, minister of war for Louis XIV, a chain of fortresses, fully equipped and stored with all the supplies needed by an army, was maintained along the northern frontier of France. The Vauban-Louvois system was intended partly for defense, but mainly to provide a base for combined arms offense — a sort of fortified depot system. Altogether Vauban built 33 new fortresses and remodeled 300 others. Any one of these posts could be used by an army on the march as a base where it was certain of finding everything it needed, including heavy artillery. An enemy, on the other hand, would find the task of breaching these forts, one after the other, an overwhelming job.

It was also Vauban, more than any other, who made siege warfare an art as well as a science, with his system of approaches by parallels. The ultimate objective of the approach was either to permit the siege artillery to blast a breach in the defensive wall and the covering obstacles through which an infantry column could make an assault, or to allow the infantry to assault over the walls, under cover of fire from the approach trenches, without waiting for the artillery to breach the walls. In the latter case, fascines (bundles of twigs or brushwood) were usually used to fill ditches and the moat before the assault; then the attackers would cross the moat and climb the wall under the cover of artillery and small-arms fire.

In the Vauban system the method of approach was standardized. A first parallel was dug some 600 to 700 yards from the fortification. This trench was parallel to the line of defenses at the selected point of assault, precluding enfilade fire by the defenders down the length of the trench. The distance was fixed because it was close to the maximum effective range of the defending and attacking artillery of the time. After this first parallel was dug, additional earthworks were thrown up in front of it as protection for siege-artillery emplacements. Under cover of fire from these guns the attacking engineers began to dig "saps," or approach trenches, toward the fort (thus the origin of the word "sapper" for a military engineer). These saps were always dug at an angle to the defensive works, and zig-zagged back and forth, again to reduce the defender's opportunity for enfilade fire. The sappers were protected from direct fire by movable shelters called gabions, wicker baskets filled with earth and frequently put on wheels so they could be pushed in front of the sap.

When the approaches progressed to a point about 300 yards from the defenses, a second parallel was dug, and new artillery emplacements prepared. From these positions the siege guns could begin an intensified bombardment to drive the defenders from the ramparts, to silence their artillery, and to begin to batter a breach. The defenders would, if possible, sortie in limited counterattacks to prevent the completion of the second parallel and to try to destroy or to "spike" the attacking guns. (Guns were spiked by driving spikes, nails, or bayonets down their touchholes, thus rendering them useless until the spike could be removed.) The attackers had to be ready for such sorties, and strong forces of infantry were maintained constantly in the parallels to protect the guns and the cannoneers.

If the defenders persisted, and if the attackers did not believe they could assault successfully from the second parallel, approach saps were again pushed forward, this time in the face of small-arms fire from the defenders, but under the cover of fire from the second parallel. These new approaches continued to within a few yards of the ditch or moat at the base of the walls. There a third parallel was constructed. While fire from attacking infantry prevented the defenders from manning the ramparts, the breaching batteries were emplaced to batter the walls at point-blank range. Sometimes improved mining techniques were also used, either to help knock down the wall or to permit small groups of attackers to debouch inside the fortification. The defenders, of course, would normally drive countermines.

A day or two of siege-gun pounding from the third parallel would usually smash a breach in the wall. The assault followed, if the garrison had not already surrendered.*

During the eighteenth century, wars of position were the rule. Fortresses sprang up all over Europe, and operations took place mostly against fortified positions, magazines, and key points. There were precise rules for attacking a fortress and just as precise rules on when and how it could be surrendered with honor.

From the invention of the cast bronze cannon in the late fifteenth century to the disappearance of smoothbore muzzle-loading guns in the nineteenth century there was no radical change in the design of artillery. And Vauban's methods of fortification and of siegecraft continued to be used until the middle of that century.

XIV. Spanish Square and Spanish Galleon 1500–1600

The Spanish in general, and their *gran capitan*, Fernández Gonzalo de Córdoba in particular, were the first to appreciate the potentialities of the arquebus, which was a principal weapon in the brilliant campaigns that drove the French from southern Italy early in the sixteenth century. Their eager adoption of small arms weapons, their constant efforts to improve them, and their attempt to establish a tactical organization to enhance the value of the new weapons initiated a century of Spanish military supremacy in Europe and, indeed, in the world.

During this period of development of firearms, the effectiveness of the weapons, offset by the vulnerability of arquebusiers and musketeers when reloading their clumsy weapons, posed to generals an ever-present challenge in coordination of combined arms. To get the maximum advantage from infantry small-arms fire, commanders experimented with a variety of techniques, including cavalry shock action, cavalry small-arms attacks, artillery fire, pike assaults, and field fortifications.

The medieval combat formation of three massive "battles," or dense blocks of mounted men and infantry, which lingered on into the early years of the sixteenth century, was particularly vulnerable

---

*This description of approaches by parallels is based on Dupuy and Dupuy, *Encyclopedia of Military History*, pp 454-455.

'to firearms and artillery. The Spanish took the lead in efforts to solve the problem by thoughtful experimentation and improvisation.

The ambitions of Spanish monarchs in exploring, conquering, and settling most of the Western Hemisphere, endeavoring to establish command of the seas, fighting interminable wars against France and Turkey, and in supporting the cause of the imperial Hapsburgs elsewhere in Europe, all constituted an intolerable strain on Spain's slender manpower resources. Yet this relatively small nation had an impact on the rest of the world, in a similarly short period of time, comparable to that of earlier Macedonia and Mongolia. The result was the same: a brilliant burst of glory, lasting less than a century, followed by a long, slow decline.

Infantry Tactics

In his campaigns at the end of the fifteenth century in support of the king of Naples against the French, Gonzalo de Córdoba led the way in recognizing and exploiting the potentialities of small-arms fire. He probably discovered one of the most significant tactical effects of gunpowder weapons: that firepower is a "multiplier" greatly enhancing defensive strength. In any event, he was the first to exploit the discovery, and through the economy of force permitted by holding extensive frontages with arquebusiers behind entrenchments, he was able to meet, outmaneuver, and defeat much larger French forces. He also devised a solution to the basic infantry tactical problem of the century: protection for arquebusiers in the open while they were reloading. He combined them in mixed units with pikemen, who provided steadiness in the defense, and who could exploit small-arms firepower by offensive shock action.

Based upon the experience of Gonzalo de Córdoba in Naples in 1505, Ferdinand II of Aragon authorized the creation of 20 units called *colunelas* (columns), each consisting of some 1,000 to 1,250 men (mixed pikemen, halberdiers, arquebusiers, and sword-and-buckler men) organized into five companies. This was the first clear-cut tactical formation based upon a coherent theory of weapons employment to be seen in western Europe since the decline of the Roman cohort. The colunela was, for all practical purposes, the genesis of the modern battalion and regiment. It was commanded by a *cabo de colunela* (chief of column), or colonel.

Over the next thirty years the Spanish gradually replaced the old medieval "battles" with an organization called a *tercio*, which consisted of several colunelas, finally standardized at three, giving the tercio a total strength of slightly more than 3,000 men. By the time this formation became standardized the sword-and-buckler soldiers and halberdiers had been eliminated, leaving pikemen and arquebusiers as the components of the tercio, or "Spanish square," which dominated European battlefields for the remainder of the century. It is significant of the new trends in weaponry that the tercio contained an equal number of companies of arquebusiers and pikemen, and that an expert arquebusier might draw up to four escudos per month, whereas no pikeman drew more than three escudos.

The fame of Spanish arms in the latter half of the sixteenth century is usually associated with the Spanish square. On the battlefield the pikes were massed in a formation of three lines, probably each with a front of 50 to 60 men, 20 files deep. There were square clumps of arquebusiers at the four corners. This solid but maneuverable mass was about 150 meters broad, and about 100 meters deep. A fringe of arquebusiers was ranged outside each face of the square; a separate detail of arquebusiers was thrown forward to skirmish.

The French soon copied the successful colunela concept and organized permanent regional units, at first called legions and later regiments. Each legion consisted of six bands of 1,000 men each: 600 pikemen, 300 arquebusiers, and 100 halberdiers.

The increasing proportion of shot to pike reflected in the emergence of the legion and tercio was accompanied by a tactical development of major significance: the countermarch. This was a maneuver in which successive ranks of arquebusiers or musketeers each fired a volley and then retired between the files to reload. After the introduction of the musket a minimum of ten ranks was needed to maintain continuous fire. How early this device was generally adopted is not clear, but it remained the basic means of compensating for the slow rate of fire characteristic of contemporary firearms until the appearance and perfection of the flintlock musket more than a century later. By permitting continuous, rolling fire, the countermarch made it both feasible and profitable to use arquebusiers in larger numbers, along with pikemen, in the open field both in offense and defense. The countermarch also tended to perpetuate the columnar tactics already characteristic of pike formations.

It was the steadiness and training of the Spanish soldier, whether pikeman, arquebusier, or musketeer, that, more than any other factor, enabled Spanish infantry to dominate the battlefields of Europe in the latter part of the sixteenth century and the early years of the seventeenth. The tercio, unlike the Swiss phalanx in the century before, was a representative rather than a distinctive tactical system, even though it was the most efficient in its day. It embodied no novel weaponry of greater lethality than those against which it was pitted, and the tactical innovations that markedly increased the lethality of existing weapons were used or quickly adopted by its adversaries. The sources of the tercio's success lay essentially beneath the surface of technological advance and tactical forms, in the slow refinement of the routine mechanisms of individual and group action in battle, and in the growth of a body of established procedures for command and administration. The Spanish Army of the second half of the sixteenth century was the most homogeneous and professional force in Europe, forged by years of campaigning under the same flag and in the same cause, but far from home and from the domestic decay that was already sapping the foundations of Spanish power. The Spanish veterans were as tough and well drilled as the Swiss, and far more versatile. Their self-confident *esprit de corps* was probably as good, and their command (or control) system was much superior.

During the latter part of the century the Spanish endeavored to enhance the solidarity of their infantry tactics by the introduction of a heavier small arm, the musket, with a range up to 300 yards. Although the matchlock musket was a simple mechanism, actual operation was complex, and loading required some ninety different steps. The appearance of the musket, which had to be fired from a fork rest, and which took longer than the arquebus to load and fire, added complexity to already complicated maneuver and loading drills. The existence of the fork to support the weight of the musket made necessary elaborate drill arrangements, and resulted in a very slow rate of fire. After the piece had been fired it took the musketeer some fifteen movements just to shift the fork rest, before he could even begin to reload. The exact number of movements required to reload depended of course on how the actions were counted. Removing the bullet from its pouch could be described as one movement or four: open pouch, remove bullet, place in mouth, close pouch. To assure regularity in training and in drill, and particularly in the stress of battle, each simple movement was discrete and became a matter of note. Speed of fire was at best two shots in three minutes, until reforms by Gustavus Adolphus lightened the musket and sped up fire considerably (see Chapter XVI). The sacrifice of slow rate of fire was accepted, however, because the range, accuracy, and striking power of the musket were so much greater than those of the arquebus. By the end of the century the musket had largely replaced the old arquebus as the basic infantry weapon of Europe.

Adapting Firearms to Cavalry

Heavy cavalry, which had been so much altered in the previous century by the pikes of the Swiss phalanx, the English longbow, and the bombards of the Hussite wagenburg, was further out-moded by the increased use of small firearms. Among the many experiments made to retain combined mobility and shock power of cavalry were increased proportions of light horsemen, and attempts to adapt gunpowder firearms to cavalry.

These efforts resulted early in the century in the development of a small, light, horse arquebus. This prototype of the pistol was theoretically a one-hand weapon, but because of the complexities of handling the clumsy matchlock, two hands were really necessary. Thus horse arquebusiers usually had to choose between firepower and horsemanship; both were generally inadequate and the combi-nation was chaotic. The invention about 1515 of the wheellock, which was more expensive and more delicate, did not replace the reliable matchlock for infantry, but it did allow the cavalryman to fire with one hand. To assure a modicum of sustained fire, the horse pistoleer carried three weapons: two in holsters and one in the right boot. After all three pistols had been fired, the cavalryman either had to drop the last pistol and draw his sword or retire to reload the pistols — an operation requiring both hands.

During this period of experimentation the Germans developed a new species of heavy cavalry armed with the new wheellock pis-tols. The man at first wore mail armor; later this became open hel-met, breastplate, and heavy thigh-length leather boots. This cavalry "charged" at a trot in a line of small, dense columns, each several ranks deep, and with intervals of about two horses' width between files. As they approached a foe, the front-rank horsemen each emptied their three pistols, then swung away sharply to the rear in a 180-degree turn — a tactic called the "caracole." While they were reloading and joining the rear of their respective files, the succeed-ing ranks continued the process of deliberate advance, pistol fire, and peeling off. Usually the caracole tactic was employed prior to a general advance. It was a very difficult operation to carry out smoothly, and could easily be disrupted by a cavalry countercharge.

German mercenaries led the way in this adaptation of gun-powder to cavalry. Since they usually wore black armor and accou-terments, these horsemen were at first called *schwarzreiters*, or "black riders." In time this was shortened to *reiters*, the term usu-ally used for the German horse mercenaries of this century.

Despite the initial German leadership in the trend to cavalry firearms during the latter part of the century, French cavalry soon regained its preeminence in Europe. Charging at the gallop in long lines two or three ranks deep, the French heavy cavalry fired their pistols as a prelude to shock action with the sword. By the end of the century most European cavalry had been equipped with some kind of firearms. The only significant exceptions were Spanish and Polish lancers. The Spanish lancers were light cavalry of the Arab-Moorish type, and adjuncts to the heavy pistoleers. The Poles, however, eschewed firearms for their horsemen, relying solely — and essentially successfully — on the shock effect of horse and lance for both heavy and light cavalry.

Decline of the Galley

The sixteenth century witnessed an unprecedented revolution in naval warfare. The era of the galley, which had lasted for more than two thousand years, ended as the potentialities of naval gunfire were realized and exploited. War galleys continued to operate in the Mediterranean for more than a century, but merely as auxiliaries to the broadside-battery sailing ship whose era had begun.

Naval vessels and tactics changed little between the battles of Salamis (450 B.C.) and Lepanto (A.D. 1571). The objective of combat was either to ram or to board an opponent. The fragile galleys at Lepanto were not much different from those that had been used in the Punic Wars. They were long, narrow, single-decked vessels, about 150 feet long and 20 feet in beam, propelled by about 54 oars, 27 to a side. In addition they had two or three lateen-rigged masts, useful to rest the oarsmen and to give added speed when the wind was favorable. There were four to six oarsmen — usually slaves — on each oar. In Christian vessels they were usually protected by mantelets; the Turks did not bother with such consideration for galley slaves. The total crew consisted of some 400 men, including oarsmen, sailors, and a contingent of soldiers. Most Christian galleys at Lepanto had five small cannon mounted in the bow; the slightly smaller Turkish galleys had only three guns. Projecting forward from the bow, just above the waterline, was a metal beak, some 10 to 20 feet long, for the purpose of ramming.

There were two important variants of these galleys at the time of Lepanto. The first was the Turkish galiot, a smaller, faster vessel, modeled after an earlier Byzantine type, with 18 to 24 oars and a crew of about 100. The other variant, in the other direction, was the galleass, introduced by the Venetians. This was a double-sized galley, slower but stronger, more seaworthy, and carrying more soldiers. It was not a very successful compromise between the fast

Mediterranean war galley and the new multi-cannoned sailing vessels of northern Europe. The galleass carried 50 to 70 guns, but most of these were falcons or smaller, designed for man-killing rather than ship-smashing.

Gunpowder and the Sailing Warship

Until the middle of the century, the northern European sailing warship, like the Mediterranean galley, was a floating fort or platform, carrying soldiers whose mission was to engage other soldiers on hostile ships. Naval battles were essentially fought like ground combat as soon as the vessels came within archer or light-cannon range of each other, with the conflict culminating in the boarding and capturing of one ship by the soldiers of the opponent. The vessels were still essentially transformed merchant "round" ships, barely twice as long as they were wide. The advent of gunpowder merely added to the range of the fighting by the incorporation of small cannon on fore and after superstructures — called castles — and along the railings of the upper deck. Heavy cannon could not be mounted on the castles or upper decks without risk of capsizing the vessel.

Appearance of the Galleon

At the beginning of the sixteenth century the "port" was invented: an opening in the ship's side with a hinged cover, facilitating the stowage of cargo in the hull without hoisting overside. English shipbuilders seized on the idea as a way to permit a cannon to be fired from the lower decks of a ship. Thus the broadside battery — its weight safely distributed below the center of gravity — came into existence. The Spanish soon followed this example. The resulting warship, barely 100 feet long and about 30 feet in beam, was called a galleon — probably because, like the galley, it was a vessel designed specifically for war, tended toward a slimmer shape, and had a low beak just above the waterline that facilitated ramming. This three-masted, square-rigged sailing ship still carried castles fore and aft, with large numbers of small cannon mounted on the upper works. But its row of larger cannon in the main hull gave the galleon the ability to extend the initial phase of naval combat substantially; however, a conclusion could rarely be achieved short of ramming, or boarding for the traditional hand-to-hand climax of earlier naval engagements.

Unlike the galley, the galleon had the seaworthiness to make long-range ocean voyages. The principal shortcoming of the galleon—as compared with the galley—was that it was largely at the mercy of the wind. This was only partly offset by the fact that newer vessels were more maneuverable than the old round ships and, thanks to improved sails and rigging, were able to "beat" against the wind.

The English, soon recognizing the tactical change made possible by the introduction of broadside guns, tended to put more and more emphasis on designing their ships for long-range gunnery rather than boarding. As a result the fore and aft castles became lower and lower, and the beaks soon disappeared from English galleons. The proportion of big guns to small guns steadily increased. The Spanish, however, kept the galleon beak, and maintained a balance between man-killing and ship-smashing guns. They followed the English example of lowering the forecastle but retained a towering aftercastle on which was mounted a formidable array of small guns.

The Spanish still considered their ships primarily floating fortresses, carrying garrisons of land soldiers. The English on the other hand, rather than wasting space and manpower by carrying a garrison of landlubber soldiers, trained the individual sailor to leave his gun, or to scramble down the rigging, to pick up pike or cutlass when the time came to board an enemy ship or to repel boarders.

These were the differences in naval tactical theory that led to the decisive Battle of the English Channel in which the English repelled the Spanish Armada, introduced the new era of the broadside sailing warship in naval warfare, and staked out a British claim to mastery of the seas.

The Emergence of Sea Power

Prior to this century naval strategy was largely an adjunct of land strategy. The concept of using sea power as an instrument to project national political and economic interests across wide expanses of ocean was first clearly manifested early in the century by the Portuguese Afonso de Albuquerque when he established a network of bases around the Indian Ocean to give Portugal virtual control of its sea routes and coastlines. The Spanish probably never understood sea power quite so clearly as the Portuguese, but they employed it successfully throughout most of the sixteenth century in consolidating their control of much of the Western Hemisphere and in dominating the sea routes of the Atlantic and the eastern Pacific oceans.

The significance of Spanish bases, and their control of major sea routes, was certainly evident to English seamen like Francis Drake. Confident that the new tactics of broadside sailing ships gave him and his compatriots a clear-cut naval advantage over the Spanish, Drake was probably more responsible than any other Englishman for deliberately initiating the chain of events that were to lead to the supremacy of English sea power.

XV. Ship of the Line: Gunpowder Rules the Sea 1550–1800

The English Challenge to Spanish Supremacy

During most of the century of Spanish domination of European land battles and exploration by sea, the British Isles were ruled by Henry VIII and his daughter Elizabeth I. Between them they established the foundation for the great maritime British Empire, stimulating the growth of English overseas commerce and the beginnings of the Royal Navy. Insular Britain's obvious enemy was the nation then dominating the seas and monopolizing the most lucrative colonial trade: Spain.

However, sporadic warfare with France continued during the century, usually in connection with French involvement in more critical external and internal conflicts. The French attempted landings on the English coast in 1545 and 1546, which led Henry VIII, in the closing years of his reign, to commence an intensive naval construction program, the true beginning of the modern Royal Navy.

When Elizabeth came to power (1558–1603) she adopted a general policy of avoiding involvement in major Continental wars, although she intrigued constantly and sent several small expeditions to the Continent. During her reign the growing hostility between England and Spain came to a climax. British contingents frequently supported the Dutch rebels in their drawn-out and eventually successful rebellion against Spain. Sir Frances Drake, in his circumnavigation of the globe (1577–1580), sacked Spanish Santo Domingo, Cartagena, and St. Augustine, and generally terrorized the West Indies. This decade of undeclared war — on the high seas, in the Americas, and in the Netherlands — led to the outbreak of formal hostilities and the famed Spanish expedition of the Great Armada.

The Great Armada

In 1585 Alvaro de Bazán, Marquis de Santa Cruz, Spain's gifted admiral, recommended a combined naval expedition and land invasion of England. Philip II approved, and in March 1586 he directed the Duke of Parma, Spanish commander in the Netherlands and one of the great soldiers of the era, to prepare to take his army to England under convoy by Santa Cruz's fleet the following year. Drake became aware of Spanish naval preparations for the expedition, and in the spring of 1587 sailed into Cadiz with a fleet of 23 ships. He destroyed 33 Spanish vessels of various sizes, and on his return harassed Spanish shipping off Cape St. Vincent, sacked the installations of Lisbon harbor, then captured a Spanish treasure galleon in the Azores.

Although the damage was repaired diligently, the setback delayed the Spanish plans by a year, and Santa Cruz died before the expedition was ready. His death was probably the most important factor in saving England from Spanish invasion. He was replaced by Alonzo Peres de Guzmán, Duke of Medina Sidonia, a man of courage and ability, but with little experience in high military command and none in naval affairs. Admiral Diego de Valdez was second in command; the Duke of Parma was to assume overall command when the expedition reached the Netherlands.

The English, of course, recognized the danger. On December 21, 1587, Elizabeth selected Lord Howard of Effingham as the commander in chief of her fleet. Drake, England's leading sailor and a commoner, was appointed vice admiral. Howard had little naval experience, and he relied upon Drake and other good seamen serving under him.

The Armada started from Lisbon in May 1588, but stopped at Corunna to take refuge from a storm and to repair a number of unseaworthy vessels. The fleet left Corunna on July 12 and was sighted off Lizard Head by English scout vessels on the nineteenth.* It comprised 130 vessels: 20 great galleons, 44 armed merchant ships, 23 transports, 35 smaller vessels, 4 galleasses, and 4 galleys. The fleet was manned by 8,500 seamen and galley slaves, and 19,000 soldiers. The warships mounted 2,431 guns, of which 1,100 were heavy guns, including about 600 culverins; the remaining cannon, however, were light antipersonnel weapons de-

---

*The dates given here are in Old Style and thus differ by 10 days from those in the best-known account, Garrett Mattingly's *The Armada* (Boston: Houghton Mifflin, 1959).

signed in accordance with the age-old naval tactics of reaching a decision by grappling and hand-to-hand fighting.

The Battle of the English Channel

Naval forces available for the defense of England, under Howard's overall command, consisted of his own squadron of 34 vessels based at Plymouth, Drake's squadron also with 34 and also based at Plymouth, a London squadron of 30 ships, and another squadron of 23 vessels under Lord Henry Seymour that was stationed off the Downs in the eastern English Channel. There were some 50 additional vessels of varying types carrying a few guns, mostly transports and supply ships that took little part in the subsequent action. The principal warships of the English fleet carried a total of approximately 1,800 heavy cannon, mostly long-range culverins.

The first engagement came on July 21 off Plymouth. The English outsailed and outshot the Spanish, who lost one ship sunk and suffered heavy losses and damage from long-range English fire. On the twenty-third there was an all-day engagement off the Devon coast in which much ammunition was consumed by both sides, with no vital damage done to either. By the twenty-fifth the English had replenished their ammunition; the Spanish, having had no such opportunity, abandoned their initial plan of landing on the Isle of Wight, and headed for Calais, hoping to be able to replenish their empty ammunition magazines from Parma's supply depots.

The Spanish fleet, now 124 vessels, anchored off Calais. Howard's four squadrons totalled 136 ships of all types. He anchored most of his fleet out of range of the Spanish guns and contented himself with long-range fire from the few English guns that could reach. He knew he could do no serious damage to the Spanish ships without coming so close as to be in danger of boarding by the Spanish soldiers, a risk he was unwilling to incur. Parma was unable to come to the assistance of the Armada because he was closely blockaded in Bruges by a Dutch fleet.

Before dawn on the twenty-eighth the English sent several fire ships into the Spanish fleet. As they drifted toward his ships, Medina Sidonia ordered anchor cables cut. He planned to return to the anchorage after the danger was past, but his subordinates panicked in predawn darkness. With unfavorable winds, the Spanish vessels, unable to form together, drifted northward in a straggling formation. The English pursued and closed in to begin an all-day running fight at very close range against the most exposed Spanish ships. The English kept to windward, with several ships concentrating against individual Spanish vessels, firing alternate broadsides. The Spaniards fought heroically, but they were unable to reply effectively since they had no heavy ammunition. Their small guns and arquebuses could not effectively reply to the English culverins and other heavy cannon. Despite severe damage and heavy loss of life on the Spanish ships, none were sunk. Toward the end of the day the English began to close in to cut off and capture the hardest hit Spanish vessels. They succeeded in capturing 16, but the remainder were saved by a sudden squall.

Unfavorable winds prevented the Spanish fleet from approaching Dunkirk or Bruges, where Medina Sidonia had planned to refit, to obtain new ammunition, and to join Parma. Unwilling to try to beat back against the wind to the Dutch coast — an operation that would have exposed his now virtually unarmed ships to the deadly English broadsides — Medina Sidonia decided to return to Spain via the North Sea, completely circling the British Isles. By August 2 the Spanish fleet was fairly well concentrated. The English fleet, which had been following, ran short of provisions and returned to home ports.

During August and September terrible hardships and losses were suffered by the Spanish, partly due to storms, but even more to starvation and thirst. Thousands of men died. Out of the 130 ships that started, only 63 are known to have returned, straggling into Spanish ports in September. The English sank or captured about 18; 19 were wrecked on the Scottish or Irish coasts. The fate of the remaining 30 vessels is unknown.

The Development of English Naval Tactics

Because of their revolutionary concepts of naval firepower, so strikingly demonstrated in the war against Spain, English sailors at the beginning of the seventeenth century were tactically far ahead of all possible rivals. Surprisingly, none of these rivals not even the Spanish victims or the aggressive and imaginative Dutch, seem to have fully grasped the secret of English success: broadside firepower. Perhaps the key was superior seamanship, but the English had no monopoly on nautical skills.

The one important development in the early part of the century was a way to harness a gun's recoil with ropes that would bring it to rest far enough inboard from the gunport to permit easy reloading. Previously guns had been tightly bound to bulkheads, their barrels pointed out, to inhibit recoil. This had made loading very difficult — almost impossible in the heat of action. English naval tactics had been based upon groups of about five ships following one another in a circle, only one at a time firing its broadsides at the enemy, while the others were busy reloading. Harnessing the recoil, therefore, increased the rate of fire of each ship and, for all practical purposes, it potentially multiplied firepower by a factor of about five.

From this experience England's great Robert Blake seems to have formalized the concept of the line-ahead formation — all ships in single column, at regular intervals. This achieved maximum firepower by broadside fire and, at the same time, permitted maximum control in an orderly formation responsive to the admiral's will.

The difficulty of controlling a great number of ships stretched across several miles of sea created formidable problems of combining naval tactics and seamanship. Rudimentary flag signals were devised, but even when these reached the peak of sophistication more than a century later, they were frequently inadequate for a commander to communicate precise orders to his subordinates. Even if the flags could have transmitted exactly what he wanted, and transmitted it quickly (neither of which was possible), distance, fog, gunsmoke, and confusion of battle all made this an uncertain means of communication. So the English Navy developed its system of Fighting Instructions, which tried to establish a common, understood doctrinal procedure for dealing with every possible foreseeable contingency. These instructions were augmented by further detailed orders given by an admiral to his subordinates before they put to sea, and again before a battle was expected. But since no two battles could ever be exactly alike, and no two enemies would react in exactly the same way, contingencies constantly arose that the Fighting Instructions did not cover.

This led to the emergence in England of two naval-tactics schools of thought. Both agreed on entering battle with the line-ahead formation, endeavoring to be to the windward of the enemy so as to have the choice of closing or pulling away, as the circumstances of the battle might dictate. But once the battle was joined, the schools differed on how it should be fought. Somewhat oversimplified, the differences were as follows.

The "formal" school believed in adhering to the line-ahead formation at practically any cost, until or unless complete victory was achieved. Each ship would engage with its guns the enemy closest to it, but would at the same time follow the course of the preceding vessel. Thus the admiral would always know where his ships were, and could pull them all out together if necessary.

Those of the "melee" school, however, believed that if an opportunity arose the admiral should be able to release individual squadron and ship commanders to move out of the line in mass attacks against obviously vulnerable elements of the enemy force. The "melee" adherents counted on the judgment and experience of subordinate commanders, and the traditional fighting spirit of the Royal Navy, to make the most of such opportunities, since it was patently impossible to give adequate orders on the spur of the moment.

By the end of the seventeenth century both systems had been tested, each with mixed success and failure. For a variety of reasons, the formalists were in the ascendancy at this time, and they remained ascendant for more than a century.

Continental Challenges

The fighting Dutch were always close behind the British in tactics. Although they adopted the British line-ahead system, they always preferred to board and fight hand to hand. In sheer seamanship the leading Dutch admirals (the two Tromps and de Ruyter) were equal to the very best of the English. Their challenge to English sea power was vigorous and nearly successful. But the English refused to be outfought, and their margin of victory was the clear gunnery superiority they maintained.

By the 1680s, as the English were emerging triumphant from the desperate Dutch wars, the French were also at sea in strength. Louis XIV had approved the advice of War Minister François Louvois to build up French naval strength, against the advice of Economics Minister Jean Baptiste Colbert, who recognized the danger of efforts to be preeminent on both land and sea. The development of scientific ship design and shipbuilding in French shipyards was encouraged and was quite successful. The French adopted the best of what the English had done, and then improved on it. Ship for ship, the vessels of the new French Navy were faster and better than those of the Royal Navy. When the War of the Grand Alliance began (1688), the French Navy was the best in the world, numerically equal to the combined fleets of England and Holland. By all logic, French sea power should have swept the British fleet from the Channel. That this did not occur was due primarily to the failure of Louis XIV to recognize the opportunity, and his refusal to let the senior French admiral, Anne-Hilarion de Tourville, fight the war as he wished. France did not have another comparable opportunity in that war, as Britain grimly built up its navy. But history came close to repeating itself a century later.

Eighteenth Century Developments

Until 1750 naval tactics were simple and crude, with opposing fleets sailing in single columns (line ahead) on parallel courses, attempting to close with one another and engage ship against ship. Individual vessels fought broadside, sometimes actually side by side, pounding away until one or the other gave in. England dominated the seas, not through new concepts of conflict, but through the momentum gained by its great admirals of an earlier era, by determined efforts to excel in gunnery, and by numerical superiority in fighting ships.

The French Navy was second. Ship for ship, French war vessels were still better built than those of the English, but they were usually fewer in number. In general English seamanship was superior. The basic difference between English and French battle tactics was that the French, usually outnumbered, were more conscious of the need to save their vessels, while the English were willing to take greater risks. In consequence French admirals preferred to enter action on the leeward side of their adversaries, which would enable them to break off conflict quickly if necessary. Their guns at the outset of the battle were directed at the spars and rigging of the enemy, to slow him down. The English, too, would use their "Long Tom" bow guns against the masts and rigging of a fleeing enemy to prevent his escape. But once battle was gained, their fire was consistently directed at the enemy's hull, seeking to sink or pulverize it. For this reason they usually sought the position to windward of the adversary, which facilitated closing in.

Broadside and Line Ahead

Broadside firepower dominated the action; seamanship and shiphandling were part and parcel of the art of naval gunnery, for firepower was merely a statistic unless the ship herself was so maneuvered as to bring her almost-rigid guns to bear on the target. There was no room for individualism in the Royal Navy, since the Fighting Instructions had become frozen into law, and the single file of line ahead was gospel. Attempts to experiment or innovate were discouraged; frequently they led to court-martial, disgrace, and sometimes — although rarely — execution. Since no other navy had a system any better, or even as good, the English were generally successful, but only an exceptional naval commander was able to achieve any decisive success against a force approximately the same strength as his own.

Until a new school of British naval officers dared to try it and succeeded, it was unthinkable that vessels should leave the line of battle. During the American Revolution, however — and particularly at the Battle of the Saints — some commanders did sail in, bow-on, toward enemy ships, break through the opposing line, and, falling upon separated parts of the hostile formation, destroy them in succession by concentration of superior firepower. By 1800 this method had been added to naval warfare, but its employment was still exceptional.

This was the golden age of the ship of the line, with her multitiered broadside batteries. As the name signified, this vessel was designed by size and armament to slug it out in the line of battle. The largest of these vessels was a little more than 200 feet in length. The biggest, with a displacement of about 2,500 tons, carried a crew of about 1,000 men.

By the middle of the eighteenth century, warships had become more or less standardized into six "rates." The first three of these classes were ships of the line: a first-rate carried 100 or more guns on three decks; a second-rate had about 90 guns on three decks; the third-rate — the workhorse of the battle fleet — carried from 64 to 74 guns on two decks. The fourth-rater was a compromise, a 50-gun vessel (two gun decks) called a frigate, sometimes used in the line of battle. Like all compromises in naval construction, she was not powerful enough to play a significant part in the line, and she was usually too clumsy to act as a cruiser. The real cruisers were the smaller frigates — fifth- and sixth-raters — carrying from 40 to 24 guns, usually all on one deck. These vessels, lighter and faster than ships of the line, were built for commerce destruction, scouting, and screening. All of the rated vessels — ships of the line and frigates — were in the true nautical term, ships: square-rigged three-masters.

Below these rates came the sloops of war (the term "sloop" had nothing to do with the rig), usually brigs (two masts, square-rigged) or brigantines (two masts, square-rigged on the fore, schooner-rigged on the main), carrying from 16 to 24 guns. Finally came cutters and other small craft, usually known by the name of their rigs (sloop, schooner, or ketch).

Two important innovations in ship construction appeared during this period. By 1700, the tiller — the great beam projecting inboard from the rudder by which the ship was steered — had been rigged by cables to a steering wheel mounted on the quarterdeck, greatly facilitating the conning of the vessel. And underwater sheathing of copper was being introduced, protecting the oaken bottoms to a great extent from the ravages of barnacles and the dreaded teredo (a marine worm that attacks wood).

Naval Gunnery

The main batteries of ships of the line and frigates had become fairly standardized by this time: 16-, 18-, and 24-pounder cannon. The multitiered vessels usually carried 16s on their upper decks, 24s on the lower. Lighter craft mounted 4-, 6-, and 9-pounders, and the big ships frequently carried some lighter guns in addition to their main armament.

Naval gunnery of the period was still of two schools. The British so aimed their guns as to "hull" the enemy, smash in her oaken sides and sink or disable her, while at the same time inflicting maximum damage on the crew. The French aimed for the enemy's top hamper, to immobilize her by shooting away masts and rigging.

The second great French challenge to British supremacy at sea came during the American Revolution, and contributed greatly to American independence. But British technical ingenuity—applied too late to retain the colonies—contributed to retention of mastery of the seas as a result of several innovations in naval gunnery, which assured continuing superiority in firepower. These included a flintlock device that flashed a spark into the touchhole, instead of the loose-powder priming and the linstock—the slow match—previously used. There were also improvements in powder bags, and the wads between powder and ball were wetted to prevent premature firings. Metal springs were added to the rope breechings that held the gun in recoil, and inclined planes of wood were placed under the carriage wheels to ease recoil further. Block-and-tackle purchases enabled the traversing of individual guns to right or left—a tremendous advance in naval gunnery since one no longer had to steer the entire vessel at a right angle to the target when firing. Another innovation was the firing of red-hot cannon shot at wooden ships, a procedure first introduced by the British at Gibraltar in 1782. This incendiary weapon, fired with relative accuracy, was a vast improvement over the previous employment of drifting fire ships and fire rafts, necessarily chancy and haphazard in results.

Perhaps the most important enhancement of British firepower was the introduction of the carronade, a short, squatty piece hurling a ball of 32 pounds or larger; its smashing power at close range was far superior to that of the long 12-, 16-, and 24-pounder guns hitherto comprising the normal armament of ships of the line and frigates. The carronade was cheaper to manufacture than the long gun and, being lighter, easier to handle aboard ship. It had much to do with crucial British victories against the French in the late eighteenth century. But it had one major drawback that would not become critical until the War of 1812. The carronade-armed ship had to be much faster and handier than an opponent armed with long guns, or she would be demolished before her carronades came into range.

The crowning British development was in tactical control: an improved flag signal code whereby for the first time in naval history a commander could maintain control and issue orders right up until battle was joined. These improvements appeared gradually during the period; by the end of the eighteenth century they had proved their efficacy.

Living conditions on board ship in all navies of the period were abominable. It is hard for a twentieth century American to visualize, for instance, how 1,000 men could exist in a 2,500-ton vessel, with perhaps 20 square feet of deck space per man, and sharing that space with ammunition and enough food and water for extended cruises of a year or more without entering port or re-provisioning. Words cannot adequately describe the nature of the food, or its condition after months at sea. The principal item of diet was weevil-infested, brick-hard biscuits, washed down with a few sips of brackish water. The addition of some rum to the water — to make "grog" — helped. The physical effects of the diet were severe. Sailors who survived battle usually aged quickly and died young. The Royal Navy did, however, discover that lime juice inhibited scurvy, and from extensive use of limes by English sailors comes the slang expression of "Limey" for an Englishman.

To these cruel living conditions was added even more cruel discipline. Punishments were atrocious. The gulf between officers and men was at least as great as that in the ground forces, and commanders exercised almost unquestioned life-and-death authority over their men. This was probably the only way of assuring obedience from brutal and brutalized men, many of whom had been impressed into service against their wills.

The century closed with a massive mutiny in England of the enlisted personnel of the Royal Navy (1797). This, as it turned out, was a blessing in disguise, for public attention was drawn to the injustices and horrors suffered by the sailors, which caused substantial remedial action.

XVI. The Age of Gustavus Adolphus: The Marriage of Infantry and Artillery 1600–1700

Transition

The military transition from the Middle Ages to the modern era was completed during the seventeenth century. The musket replaced the pike, the heavy armored horsemen of the gentry and of the reiters were modified and finally outmoded, the basic phalangeal battle formation became linear, and the immobile artillery of siege warfare was transformed into massed mobile artillery that was used as a major combat arm in coordination with infantry and cavalry. Maurice of Nassau and particularly Gustavus Adolphus of Sweden were responsible for most of these developments.

During this period there were several changes in small arms. The transformation of the matchlock musket was significant. Gustavus Adolphus found it a clumsy weapon weighing from 15 to 25 pounds and fired from a forked rest. He trimmed the weight to about 11 pounds, so that it no longer required a rest. He also adopted the paper cartridge — a fixed charge, with powder carefully measured (providing ballistic uniformity) and with the ball attached. The standard musket ball weighed a little more than one ounce — about 12 or 14 to the pound. By the middle of the century the length of the musket had been reduced to a standard four feet, or one and one quarter meters, and during the English Civil Wars it was further reduced to a length of about three feet, or one meter. The result of these changes was a lighter, handier gun, easier to load, with rate of fire more than doubled to one round per minute. This was a very powerful weapon.

The snaphance lock, deriving a spark by striking flint against steel, had been introduced during the sixteenth century. The true fusil or flintlock musket, invented by French gunsmith Le Bourgeoys in 1615, was perfected as a sporting weapon about 1630. However, adoption as a military weapon came slowly, partly because of the increased cost of manufacture, and partly because of the traditional conservatism of military leaders satisfied with the matchlock. The English New Model Army, under Cromwell (1645), included two companies of infantry armed with flintlock muskets; France armed one regiment entirely with the flintlock musket in

1670. Although the flintlock was less accurate and had a slower rate of fire than the improved matchlock, it had offsetting advantages; it was not only less vulnerable to the vagaries of weather, it removed the inherent danger of the lighted match. This meant that infantry soldiers could be placed closer together, thus increasing the number of men and the volume of fire in a given space. By 1699 the flintlock was standard in European armies.

The much more accurate rifled musket was available and in limited use in some armies. The rifled carbine was also coming into fashion for use in a few cavalry units, in conjunction with the sword. The cost of manufacture of rifled weapons, however, ruled out their adoption on a wide scale.

A plug bayonet, inserted into the muzzle of the musket, was widely in use by the middle of the seventeenth century, as partial replacement of the pike. This invention probably resulted when some musketeer picked up the end of a broken pike and rammed it into the end of his musket for hand-to-hand combat. Since this employment rendered the weapon inoperable as a firearm, the pikeman was still a necessary adjunct to the infantry formation to ensure continued firepower. But about 1680, someone — possibly Vauban — invented the ring bayonet, which left the bore clear for firing. This was soon improved by a socket in the bayonet handle that firmly locked it to a stud on the musket barrel. By the end of the century this had been adopted by all European armies. The musketeer thus became his own pikeman; the pikeman himself soon faded from the scene.

In the sixteenth century both the French and the Spanish had revised and reduced the number of calibers of their field artillery guns. In the seventeenth century Maurice of Nassau made further improvements, using only four calibers: 48-, 24-, 12-, and 8-pounders. All of these were mounted on their own wheels, with the trail attached to another two-wheeled cart or limber for movement; the heaviest of these guns were pulled by 30 horses.

Maurice of Nassau

The Spanish square had been devised as a means of making the matchlock handgun an effective infantry weapon. The inevitable next development was to seek a tactical system that would be more flexible and less costly in manpower. The first important steps in this direction were taken by a soldier whose model of perfection in military organization was the Roman legion. Maurice of Nassau, Prince of Orange, moved on to the stage of Europe at the age of seventeen after the assassination of his father, William the

Silent, in 1584. In 1590, he became stadholder of Utrecht and Overyssell and was soon recognized as admiral general and captain general of the United Provinces in their continuing rebellion against Spain. With a background in the study of the military classics and extensive active campaigning experience in the field, Maurice initiated a series of reforms that inaugurated a revolution in military organization and tactics in the seventeenth century.

The main contribution of Maurice to the art of warfare lay in the tactical employment of manpower. With the Roman model in mind he sought to reduce the depth of the infantry formation and to make it more flexible and more effective through discipline and drill. The number of ranks of pikemen in the tercio formation was reduced first from 40 to 10 and then to 5 — the number who could effectively employ their arms at one time. This new formation, 5 deep, with a front of about 50 pikemen at intervals of about three feet, became in Maurice's hands the genesis of modern linear formations. The musketeers were placed on the flanks in three platoons, each of 40 men, facing the enemy in four columns 10 deep, to permit the Spanish countermarch for reloading. Musketeers and pikemen were still linked in a single unit, but they were no longer mixed in such a way that a large portion was ineffective.

With the formation depth decreased, Maurice reduced the size of units by cutting company strength from 150 to 80 men, equally divided between pike and musket. The regiment, or battalion as it was then called, numbered about 500 men — about the size of the Roman cohort. With a maximum front of about 250 meters, with pikemen in the center and muskets on the flanks, the formation avoided the waste of manpower inherent in the tercio and gained in elasticity. The man-for-man effectiveness was virtually doubled. Brigaded in groups of six, the battalions were arranged in three distinct lines of battle in checkerboard fashion like the Roman model.

In frontal engagements against infantry this arrangement worked well, with pikemen effectively engaged and musketeers firing steadily. But against a frontal charge of cavalry, the musketeers had to take shelter under the pikes, a difficult and confusing maneuver. In the case of a flank attack, the battalion had to shift front to flank — another difficult feat.

Maurice encouraged the development of new weapons of an unusual character (including gas and explosive shells); he patronized military mapmakers, and used field glasses for observation, all of which set him apart from his contemporaries. He employed field fortifications widely, and he took many innovative steps in siege warfare, thereby reducing the length of the siege (see Chapter XIII).

The success of Maurice's system rested on morale and on discipline achieved through training and intensive drill. When not on campaign, the men were drilled constantly, to the limit of their endurance, so that they could form quickly and change formation over all kinds of terrain. The system of drill and training was one of Maurice's most lasting contributions. Not only did it alter the duties of the officer corps and make possible the proper handling of the unit, but it also gave the military a task in peacetime and between campaigning seasons. Certain standardized practices, such as marching in step, also date from this period.

Despite his efforts, Maurice's new linear formation could not overcome the rigidity inherent in the combination of pike and musket. Although the individual infantry unit had become more flexible by a reduction in size, it was too small to operate independently. Moreover, it proved to be no less defensive than the system it replaced. The pike retained the same role it had had earlier, and the musketeer was still tied to the pike formation.

Most of Maurice's reforms were completed by 1609. They represent a transition between the earliest forms of warfare in the gunpowder era and the establishment of a system by Gustavus Adolphus that was to last, with modifications, down to the wars of the French Revolution, and — in its fundamental concept of linear mobility — through the twentieth century.

Appearance of Gustavus Adolphus

At the time Gustavus Adolphus assumed the Swedish throne in 1611, the Swedish Army was in deplorable condition: poorly organized, understrength, short on pikes, musketeers equipped with the obsolete arquebus, and badly led. Administration was virtually nonexistent, recruitment at a low ebb, morale poor, and war with Denmark threatened. It was Sweden's great fortune at this juncture to come under a ruler of extraordinary capacity, not only as a tactician, but as a strategist, an administrator, and a leader of men.

Like all princes of his day, Gustavus was educated in the military arts at an early age. Like Maurice he read the classic military works, and was familiar with the Spanish system and aware of Maurice's reforms. By the time he fought in Germany he was an accomplished tactician, not only in the use of his infantry units, but in all aspects of warfare — gunnery, horsemanship, siegecraft, employment of fortifications, drill, and logistics. He had an eye for terrain, and great natural talent for command.

But, more important than his mastery of the techniques of

warfare, Gustavus was an innovator, equally adept at restructuring of weapons, tactics, and organizations.

Gustavus's first task when he inherited the throne was to rebuild his army. He had the choice of a mercenary or a national army. He decided to base his reorganization essentially on a national conscription system, establishing recruiting regions that were responsible for raising and maintaining units. In practice, however, Sweden was unable to meet all of the monarch's manpower needs, and the national army was always supplemented by mercenary units.

Swedish Infantry

The basic tactical infantry unit in the Swedish Army was the squadron consisting of 408 men — 216 pikemen and 192 musketeers. The pikes were formed in a central block, 6 deep, and the musketeers in two wings of 96 men, also 6 deep, on each side of the pikemen. Usually attached to each squadron, however, was an additional element of 96 musketeers, providing a frontage of 184 men, about 700 meters. Since the attached musketeer company was frequently employed for outpost, reconnaissance, and other detached tasks, it was often not available for the squadron.

The squadron clearly resembled Maurice's battalion but — without the attached musketeers — was slightly smaller in size. Like the Dutch battalion, the Swedish squadron was basically defensive in its tactics, but was capable of offensive action if properly employed in coordination with other infantry units and with the cooperation of cavalry and artillery.

The first step in assuring offensive capability was to group three or four squadrons into a brigade. But to provide combined arms versatility, much improvement was needed in Swedish cavalry and artillery.

Swedish Cavalry and Artillery

The cavalry was recruited by voluntary enlistment, and most was light cavalry. Although Swedish horses were small, they proved equal to the tasks Gustavus assigned to his cavalry units. As with the infantry, morale in the cavalry was maintained by regular and high pay, frequently including bonuses in the form of land or income from rents. By 1630 Gustavus had 8,000 native Swedes in his cavalry.

Gustavus recognized that the firepower of his day alone could not win battles; he needed shock power for close-in fighting. This was a job for the cavalry, and Gustavus worked hard to get the most out of the small Swedish horse. He discarded the caracole and deep formations. Instead he formed his horse units in six ranks, later in three. The pistol was a gesture; the real effect came from the saber charge. The first rank fired when it was close to the enemy; the other two held fire, retaining the pistol for emergency use. Detached musketeers stationed between cavalry squadrons provided firepower support to shake the enemy line. While the cavalry charged, the musketeers would reload, to be ready to fire another volley for a second charge or to cover a retreat. To this, at Lützen, was added the fire from the regimental guns of the reorganized Swedish artillery.

Prior to Gustavus, artillery was considered to be a technological specialty, usually operated by mercenary civilians, gunners who scorned the requirements of standard military discipline. Gustavus believed that a more substantial and regularized military organization was needed. In 1623 he formed an artillery company, and in 1629 this was expanded to an artillery regiment of six companies, led by twenty-seven-year-old Lennart Torstensson, the best artilleryman of his time. Of the six companies of the regiment, four consisted of guns and gunners, one of sappers, and one of men trained to handle special explosive devices. Thus, for the first time, the artillery was organized as a distinct and regular branch of the army, manned almost entirely by Swedish troops, which was unusual in an era of mercenaries. But it was new and improved weapons — and the techniques for their use — that, above al¹ distinguished Swedish artillery from its contemporaries.

Swedish Weapons and Equipment

In addition to organizational reforms, Gustavus made important changes in weapons and equipment. Although armor had disappeared in the infantry of most other countries, Gustavus had his pikemen wear breastplates and greaves. To prevent enemy cavalry from severing pikes with their swords, he sheathed the upper length with iron; then to keep the weight manageable, he shortened the pike from 16 to 11 feet. He replaced the arquebus with the matchlock musket, which he made lighter in weight than those in other countries. He standardized the caliber and the powder charge and introduced the paper cartridge. The net effect of all these changes was to increase both the firepower and the defensive strength of the Swedish infantry.

But it was in artillery weapons that Gustavus made his most important technical changes. His objective was to increase the effectiveness of his artillery in combination with infantry and cavalry. This meant not so much increasing the rate of fire — although he strove successfully to do this — as having the guns in the right place at the right time. This required mobility, which in turn meant decreasing the weight of the gun. To achieve this, he reduced the calibers in his army to three — the 24-pounder, the 12-pounder, and the 3-pounder. Thus he eliminated the cumbersome 48-pounder, and replaced the 8-pounder with the very mobile, fast-firing 3-pounder. By improving the quality of the powder he was able to standardize pressures in the tube, thus permitting reduction in the thickness of the barrel. Then he shortened the barrel and also reduced weight by making wider use of copper — a metal of which Sweden had an ample supply — in gun and timber fittings.

Particularly significant was the sturdy 3-pounder, or "regimental gun." This piece, adopted after some experimentation, was four feet long and with its carriage weighed 625 pounds. A packaged cartridge simplified loading and assured a high rate of fire. This weapon completely changed the role of artillery; every regiment in Gustavus's army had one (later two) and thus had an enormous advantage in battle, since it was for several years the only army with such a weapon capable of accompanying the infantry.

Gustavus's development of the regimental gun was an interesting manifestation of a constantly recurring phenomenon in modern war: the search for means of applying increases in firepower and lethality to the requirements of the front-line soldiers. The need for an "accompanying gun" for infantry combat has continually influenced subsequent tactics doctrine, organization, and weapons development.

Drill and Tactics

The new organization and improved weapons would have been of little value without training and discipline. Gustavus was fully the equal of Maurice as a drillmaster. He provided for continuous training of new recruits from the moment of entry into the army. Conscripts were given about two weeks' basic training, marching to drum beat and learning to load the musket or to use the pike. Maneuvers were held frequently by both the small and large units, and the army was never idle. Discipline was strict, and every regimental commander was required to read the Articles of War to his troops once a month. Punishment for infractions of these articles was severe, and Gustavus's soldiers had a reputation for good behavior unusual for troops of the day.

The effect of all these reforms was to fashion an instrument that won consistently on the battlefield. Gustavus's reforms were designed to improve the quality of infantry, cavalry, and artillery; to gain greater firepower in all three arms; and then to make effective use of all of them in combination.

There was one apparent disadvantage to this system of combined arms operations. By tying the cavalry to the infantry and artillery, Gustavus sacrificed the speed and momentum of the horse — except for a final charge of about 100 yards. But the Swedish cavalry could be — and consistently was — used in the traditional cavalry roles of reconnaissance and screening. The system was better than anything yet devised, and it was successful. As a result, it was imitated widely.

In combining firepower with the pike, and missile with shock, Gustavus retained the linear formation of Maurice with six infantry ranks. He combined the use of the two infantry weapons, but with enhanced firepower, having two ranks of musketeers fire before countermarching. Further, the countermarch was so executed that the whole formation moved forward, and the fire was, in effect, a small-arms rolling barrage. During this movement, the musketeers were protected by the pikes while they reloaded. Later, Gustavus introduced the salve, or salvo, further increasing the firepower of his line. In the salvo, three ranks fired simultaneously. This made continuous fire impossible, but it proved effective just before a climactic charge by producing a volume of fire in a few minutes at close quarters that in the countermarch would have taken a half-hour or more. To this small-arms firepower was added the fire from the regimental 3-pounders.

Since the salvo rendered the musketeers impotent while they reloaded, the role of the pike was enhanced in the Gustavian system. The best protection for the musket was offensive action by the pike. Thus this weapon had a broader mission than merely to protect the musketeer. It was to deliver the decisive blow, the salvo being but the prelude to the assault by the pike, as it was for the cavalry charge. Gustavus revitalized the pike as an offensive weapon, combined with missile power, this at a time when it was rapidly becoming obsolete in other armies.

Gustavus also transformed artillery into an offensive instrument, combined with cavalry and infantry. His object in the use of artillery was to secure maximum fire at the decisive point, in collaboration with the other arms. He achieved this goal by mobility. Before his time, artillery usually took its place before the battle was joined and remained there throughout, unable to move as the battle progressed. At Lützen Gustavus moved his fieldpieces to support the infantry and cavalry at critical moments. The light regimental gun could be moved at will, and was therefore employed for a variety of purposes.

The System of Gustavus Adolphus

It is easy and tempting to exaggerate the achievements of Gustavus Adolphus. Most of his innovations were adopted from others, and he was not the only one who improved the military system of the time. But no one else so surely bridged the gap between conception and achievement; none fitted their innovations into a completely integrated system with its own set of unifying principles. His accomplishments were many: he gave to infantry and cavalry a capacity for the offense perhaps unmatched since the army of Alexander the Great; he increased firepower and made it the preliminary for shock; he made artillery mobile; he made linear formations flexible, responsive to the commander's will and essentially viable; he solved the problem of combined arms; and he made the small-unit commander the key to action. He brought to culmination the military revolution that had begun in the middle of the sixteenth century — although there would be refinements before the end of the long reign of Louis XIV. Not all the reforms of Gustavus stood the test of time, but his influence on European warfare was profound.

The Successors of Gustavus Adolphus

After the death of Gustavus his system continued to be improved under the leadership of a number of military men in various countries. Weapons development, especially the introduction of the bayonet, continued to influence tactics and organization. During this period also there were a number of important changes in the size and composition of the armies of Europe that reflected, and in turn affected, political, social, and economic developments of the seventeenth century.

This was the age of absolute monarchs (except in England), and a military system based on strict discipline, exhausting drill, centralized administration, and an army of long-term, highly trained troops was particularly congenial to such a form of government. The monarch was *ipso facto* the commander in chief of his nation's military forces, and most rulers of the time placed great stress on this military role, to the point that their normal dress was a military uniform. The increasing cost of war demanded centralization of the civilian economy and led to the establishment of civilian administrative machinery modeled on military organization. Moreover, it was war — and the maintenance of armed forces to be prepared for war — that placed the greatest demand on the financial resources of the crown, and led to higher taxes and to the creation of tax collection machinery, which in turn augmented the power of the monarch.

The effect of military developments on society — or at least on certain segments of society — was equally profound. War ceased to be the concern only of upper classes. The cavalry, once the exclusive domain of the nobility, was opened to all who could ride a horse. Both mercenary and national regiments began to draw on the middle classes for their officers. The lower classes, however, still found little to attract them to military life, save as members of militia establishments in some countries.

More and more, science and technology were being put to the service of war. Maurice and Gustavus used portable telescopes; cartography was developed for military purposes. Soldiering, at least for the officer, was becoming a profession; systemized instruction increased in importance.

The decline of armor, the appearance of the uniform, and regular pay, all operated to bring into the service many who would formerly not have considered the military life. Also, the emphasis on flexibility and smaller units opened up the ranks of junior officers to commoners — though only those of the gentry. The artillery, which was becoming increasingly important, was more open than any other arm, and drew into the service of the military men who had some technical or scientific training, regardless of birth or background.

In the latter part of the seventeenth century experiments were conducted to demonstrate and to test basic theories of interior ballistics. Mortar trajectories were studied on the basis of the principles of Galileo. In France, Colbert founded the Royal Academy of Science for the express purpose of applying science to war. As war became more technical, knowledge and research and schooling became more important. The first military academy of modern times was established in 1617 by John of Nassau. The nobility, which had traditionally had a monopoly on military leadership, was also forced to study in order to master the tasks of war. Thus to some extent military technology was having a levelling, democratizing effect upon society, blurring the former clear distinction between the nobility and the gentry. Military rank was regularized, and a professional officer corps was born. For reasons more political than they were military or social, this officer corps was as much European as it was national, as officers without strong national ties — like Irish and Scottish adherents of the displaced Stuarts — offered their services first to one monarch, then to another.

The seventeenth century saw a marked increase in the size of armies and the scope of warfare. This was to some extent the result of the changes in warfare and military affairs wrought by Maurice, Gustavus, and their followers, but was due even more to political and economic developments. Before the time of Louis XIV, armies rarely numbered more than 50,000 men. Gustavus had about 30,000 men in 1631; his opponents were only slightly more numerous. But Louis XIV maintained a military establishment of 400,000, with field armies sometimes approaching 100,000 men. In the seventeenth century it was assumed that a country could support an army of about one percent of its population, which was approximately the ratio in France. This trend toward larger armies levelled off in the eighteenth century; then, during the wars of the French Revolution, there was to be another surge forward.

With the increase in sizes of military establishments and field armies went changes in organization, and the relationship of armies to the state. Men and money were needed in larger quantities than ever for waging war, and in the mercantilist view a large population was as essential as natural resources for war. In the Thirty Years' War most of the armies were mercenary; by the end of the century they were largely royal standing armies raised within the state, although mercenary units still abounded. The reason can be found partly in financial and political conditions, and partly in military factors. Although operations were rarely undertaken between October and May, drill and training was a year-round activity in peace and war, and it was necessary to train and retrain troops constantly to be sure of an effective force.

Once armies became permanent institutions, their organizations began to assume the form of modern military establishments. Uniforms became standard; rank was regularized, with the colonel becoming a regimental commander instead of a contractor; regulations and disciplinary standards were developed; supply and support branches were organized to take this function out of the hands of civilians (soon soldiers were to be housed in barracks provided by the crown); weapons were standardized, and so were the men who wielded them. In short, armies became state armies, or armies of the crown, although they did not become truly national armies until a later date.

The French System

Tactics did not alter greatly in the period immediately following the death of Gustavus in 1632. Many French officers had earlier served with the Dutch in joint operations against Spain, and had introduced features of the innovations of Maurice into their own army. Later, because of the French alliance with Sweden, the French also became familiar with Gustavus's system. The Swedish Army in Germany virtually disappeared, and in 1639, after the death of Bernard of Saxe-Weimar, France took over the remains of Gustavus's army, 8,000 men. This force became an elite body in the French Army of Richelieu's day and was retained by Louis XIV. Henri de Turenne, the best French soldier of the era, was a worthy successor of Gustavus.

Under Richelieu and Louis XIV the French Army adopted the basic Swedish infantry formation — a battalion (or regiment) of about 600 men. This unit was usually organized in one line, 6 deep, about 100 yards long, with some 250 pikemen in the center and about 150 musketeers on each flank. An additional contingent of about 150 musketeers was assigned to the battalion, but usually was detached in combat to support the cavalry. The standard infantry battle formation consisted of two lines, with the battalions arranged in checkerboard fashion. The interval between battalions was supposed to be equal to their front, so that the second line, usually 300 to 400 paces behind the first, could pass through. The reserve was usually arranged as a rudimentary third line, about half the strength of one of the two main lines, and at the outset of the battle was generally posted about 600 paces behind the second line.

On his accession to the throne of France, Louis XIV inherited an army of 139 regiments, 20 of which were foreign mercenaries. About 30 of the regiments were cavalry. But France had been through a stormy period of internal disorder and civil war. As a result the army was not well disciplined, and administration was poor. The task of reorganizing and training the army was assumed by Louvois. He hampered field commanders with deadening restrictions, but his organizing talents paid off in improved administration and in the construction of fortifications along the French frontiers.

Louis's cavalry consisted of heavy units, light units, carabineers, and dragoons. The eight regiments of carabineers, totalling at the turn of the century about 3,000 men, were armed with rifled carbines and swords. From one regiment in 1650, the number of dragoons increased until, by 1690, there were 43 such regiments in the French Army, with a total strength of over 16,000 men. They were equipped with muskets with the newly developed bayonet, and an entrenching tool was strapped on their saddles. Both of these categories — particularly the dragoons — combined the advantages of infantry and cavalry, and, being very mobile, proved very useful.

The English under Cromwell

In the sixteenth and early seventeenth centuries the English were not particularly distinguished for their achievements in land warfare and usually lagged far behind the Continent. However, in the last half of the seventeenth century they made rapid strides under the leadership of Oliver Cromwell. At the outbreak of the English Civil War (1642) the militia was a home defense force, a paper organization without training or discipline, and in 1644 Cromwell was authorized by Parliament to organize the New Model Army.

The New Model Army consisted in 1645 of about 22,000 men, organized into 12 regiments of infantry, 11 of cavalry, and 1 of dragoons. About half the men were impressed into service at first, but later the ranks were filled by volunteers.

The infantry regiment had 1,200 men. Its organization and equipment were generally similar to those of Continental armies, the proportion between pike and musket being usually one to two but later increasing to one to three, reflecting the growing importance of firearms.

Infantry tactics and organization were modeled on the Swedish system. Six deep, with pikemen in the center, the formation contained the firepower needed for offense and the pikes for defense, especially against cavalry. But the smaller proportion of pikes made training and maneuver particularly important if the defensive capability of the formation were not to be reduced. There were various ways of using the musket tactically: by fire of successive ranks and countermarch; by fire of successive ranks but advancing, so that the first rank remained stationary and the second rank advanced in front of it to fire; fire by salvo, either by two ranks at a time, or by three ranks (as Gustavus Adolphus did) or all six ranks by doubling (i.e., compressing the formation from six ranks to a crammed three ranks). It was essentially the Gustavian method that the New Model Army used.

For defense against cavalry, the pikemen formed a square in close order, with the musketeers forming two solid ranks in front of each face of the square, the first rank kneeling, the second rank firing over their heads. When the cavalry came within 20 yards or so, the musketeers fired low, either together or in succession, at the horses' legs. If this did not stop the charge, the pikemen were ready, their 16-foot weapons projecting beyond and protecting the musketeers. If the square was broken, each man used what he had, including the butt end of the musket.

Although infantry had assumed the primary role in the seventeenth century, the proportion of horse to foot was still high, between about one to two for the Royal Army and about one to three for the Parliamentarians. In the early years of the English Civil War the cavalry of the New Model Army was of two types: harquebusiers and dragoons. The former was the English designation for a mounted man armed with the carbine, a shoulder weapon about two and a half feet long, firing a bullet about an ounce in weight or sometimes 20 to the pound. The firing mechanism was the wheellock or flintlock. The harquebusier also carried a pistol, a sword, and sometimes a small pole-ax. He usually had light armor or a buff coat of leather, and on his head he wore a "pot" helmet. As the war progressed the cavalry on both sides generally gave up the carbine, relying on the pistol and sword. The dragoons were simply mounted infantry, a cheap form of cavalry that rode any sort of horse. They carried a musket or other firelock, and a sword. Dragoons were used for reconnaissance, to secure bridges or roads in advance or retreat, and to line hedges and control enclosures in enclosed terrain. Often they would dismount and serve as musketeers in support of the cavalry.

Cavalry tactics of the New Model Army, after some debate, were patterned on the Swedish rather than the Dutch model, although the latter had strong advocates. Horsemen were formed three deep and held their fire when they charged, to go in at a rapid trot with swords bared. Cromwell invariably took the initiative, attempting to charge before the enemy did.

Artillery played an important role in the English Civil Wars, the lessons of Gustavus being fresh in the minds of those Englishmen who had served in the Low Countries and Germany. The fieldpieces were culverins, demiculverins, sakers, minion, and drakes (or falcons).* No improvements or modifications of existing practices were made by the English.

The army of the Commonwealth was an efficient and effective instrument. Only two things were needed to convert it to the army

---

*See Table 2, p. 103.

of Marlborough and Wellington: substitution of the flintlock for the matchlock, and the replacement of the pike by the bayonet. Before the end of the seventeenth century both developments were well under way.

XVII. Frederick and the Perfection of Gunpowder Tactics 1700–1780

Eighteenth Century Warfare

The eighteenth century saw the culmination of developments begun in the sixteenth and seventeenth centuries. The trend toward larger field armies continued, albeit slowly. And with this went other trends: the centralization of administration, the growth of higher organizations and multifunctioned staff systems necessary to maintain the larger armies, the increased complexity and growing financial cost of war, and the perfection of precise and mathematical maneuvers for military formations. This maturing of earlier developments was essentially complete by the middle of the century.

Weapons and tactics also underwent gradual but significant change. The flintlock fusil completely replaced the matchlock musket, and the pike disappeared as the bayonet became the weapon of decision. The science of fortifications reached its highest stage with Vauban at the turn of the century. Fortified lines were used by all armies. Operationally and logistically armies became increasingly tied to fortifications, becoming less maneuverable, and war became more deliberate, formal, stylized, and even dilletantish.

Warfare in the eighteenth century was conducted under well-defined and detailed rules. Maneuver, not combat, was the objective, as the opponents sought advantageous positions related to their respective systems of fortified depots or magazines. Since wars were contests among dynastic rulers with limited objectives — seeking a province, an adjustment of boundary, political advantage, or the rights of some members of the family — the conflicts were limited. It was not to the advantage of either side to destroy the other; and war was conducted accordingly. The weapons and tactics of the time to some extent dictated the avoidance of pitched battles with their high cost in men and materials. The flintlock was a more complex and expensive weapon than the matchlock, and each had to be carefully constructed to a standard size to take the new ring bayonet. With the increased emphasis on firepower, more expensive artillery was required, as well as more powder and ball. Everywhere in Europe the manufacture of saltpeter was critical. More men, more materials, more workers, meant higher costs.

Social and economic reasons were even more important in dictating the limited and formal nature of warfare in the eighteenth century. The cost of war had become enormously high. The ever-larger armies had to be equipped, clothed, armed, fed, and housed. No monarch wished — or dared — to face the economic and social consequences of devastation like that of the Thirty Years' War, and so the civilian economy was spared the rigors of war to the maximum extent possible. Generals and their armies were discouraged from living off the country, even on enemy soil. Supplies and equipment were stored in fortified depots; troops were housed in barracks, and on campaign were kept in their encampments and not allowed to go foraging.

All armies contained large foreign elements whose loyalty was doubtful. They fought for pay, not for a cause, and they had no wish to lay down their lives. The national troops usually came from the dregs of society, and were often pressed into service by recruitment measures that bred no love for the army. Given the slightest opportunity, troops would desert. It took rigidly enforced order, discipline, precision, and long training to make a fighting force from this material. Men responded to command; individual will and initiative were undesirable and would have been impossible in the close formations of the time.

The nature of such an army, and the general unreliability of its soldiers, reinforced monarchical reasons for keeping the soldiers under constant control and supervision, with little opportunity to mix with the general populace in the theater of operations, whether this was in nominally friendly or hostile territory. These circumstances tended also to disassociate the general population from the wars of their monarchs, and — save for the effects of taxation — civilians paid little attention to the dynastic conflicts except when the fighting was in their immediate vicinity.

Most armies of the eighteenth century were built on the same model. At the beginning of the century, the French Army was the best in Europe; by the middle of the century it had been surpassed by the Prussians; by the end of the century the French Army had regained its preeminence.

Changes in eighteenth century tactics and organization were in large part the result of the use of the flintlock and the bayonet, and these in turn contributed to the requirements for parade-ground drill and rigid discipline. It took time to load the flintlock, and the depth of the line was related to the reloading factor. Since the weapon was inaccurate, fire had to be by volley, with lines of soldiers delivering volleys on command. One purpose of the drill was to train men to march in step, fire in unison, and reload quickly. The long lines dictated the kind of terrain and weather in which battles would be fought. Hills, ridges, swamps, and villages broke the even formations. Rainy weather could dampen cartridges, which then became useless until they dried.

Interestingly, while the flintlock fusil was commonly referred to as a musket, its users were always called fusiliers. By 1700 the fusilier had virtually replaced the older musketeer. Although he still carried a sword he was less clumsily accoutred, and his fusil — or flintlock musket — was somewhat lighter and easier to use than the matchlock musket. Caliber had been reduced, and the weight of the ball was 1/18 pound, or 18 to 20 to the pound, rather than 12 to the pound as before.

The disappearance of the pikeman did not signify the end of different kinds of infantry, for by this time the grenadier had made his appearance. The hand grenades — a spherical bomb with a short, quick-burning wick fuze, ignited just before being hurled — had been widely used during the Thirty Years' War. In 1670 the French Army had established a separate grenadier company in the Regiment du Roi, and the example soon spread elsewhere. These grenadiers were picked men, tall and strong so as to be able to hurl a grenade weighing three or more pounds. In addition to grenades, they were equipped with standard flintlocks and bayonets. The use of the rather ineffective grenade was later discontinued, but the grenadiers remained, a picked corps for especially arduous tasks. Thus, to all intents and purposes, the grenadier became a fusilier, but he was usually a better and more reliable soldier.

The Rise of Light Infantry

A significant tactical development during the first half of the eighteenth century was the reintroduction of light infantry into European warfare. In various forms light infantry had accompanied armies in earlier eras. Generally, however, these had been irregular troops: archers, slingers, javelin men, and various others, who usually opened battles and then moved aside during the main action. Similar groups were used when firearms were first introduced.

The rigid linear tactics of the early eighteenth century

prescribed a fixed and inflexible role for the regular infantry. During the considerable time it took infantry battalions to take up their battle stations they were vulnerable and needed to be screened from possible hostile action. In addition, the supply depots and convoys that were needed to support the armies were highly vulnerable to enemy raids and needed protection. To perform these screening and protecting tasks, light troops — mainly infantry, although there were some light-cavalry "legions" — were reintroduced into European armies after 1740. In addition, they carried out operations against the enemy's line of communications, raided, and took prisoners. Their principal functions in battle soon became the provision of harassing and screening fire in advance or on the flanks of the main line. In other words, the functions of light troops since the time of Alexander.

The first large-scale appearance of light troops occurred during the War of the Austrian Succession (1740–1748). In 1740, Austria was attacked by the superior forces of Frederick of Prussia and his French and Bavarian allies. Maria Theresa had to muster all the forces at her disposal and did not hesitate to call upon the Borderers — the "wild Croats and Pandours" who had been part of the Austrian frontier defenses against the Turks — to help defend her realm from the northern and western threats. Early in 1741 over 30,000 of these men made their appearance on the battlefields of central Europe. Their effectiveness led the other powers to introduce or build up similar forces. Frederick hastily increased his light cavalry, and raised some irregular "free" battalions to offset the Croats. In France several light regiments, as well as a number of combined infantry-cavalry units (called "legions"), were raised after 1744.

The English Army had no light troops until the line battalions serving in America during the 1750s raised some light companies on an ad hoc basis. In Braddock's defeat at the Battle of the Monongahela in 1753 the rigid linear formation of European warfare succumbed to the elusive individualism of wilderness combat. As a result, experiments were made in the British Army leading to the establishment in each foot regiment of a "light" company, usually detached from its battalion for covering the advance, or for some other special mission. By the time of the American Pevolution it was British practice to separate the light companies from their regiments for action, organizing them into provisional units. In addition, the grenadier companies — also one to each regiment and not to be confused with the Grenadier Guards Regiment — were usually separated and gathered into special units in combat.

One criticism of this British system was that it tended to establish an elite category by inducing a feeling of inferiority among the "line" companies of the regiments. It is doubtful if the question of the values and shortcomings of the establishment of military elite units can ever be satisfactorily resolved, since other issues are invariably involved when such units are formed. (And there will undoubtedly be elites in armed forces in the future.) But in this instance it can be argued that these special units of British infantry were in fact experimental troops, and thus important in the development of the infantry doctrine that was unquestionably the best in Europe in the early nineteenth century. By that time the use of regular troops for skirmishing had led to the establishment of both "light" and "rifle" regiments in the British service, but in practice there was little difference to warrant the distinction.

Light infantry did not, in fact, become a dominant element in European armies. After their first impact, the Austrian Borderers had shown that their ability to influence battle outcomes was limited. In Prussia, Frederick II continued to rely on the massed volleys of the line and devoted much time and effort to measures that would speed up the rate of fire. He formed a number of light-infantry units—called fusiliers in Prussia—but these were trained and generally equipped as line infantry. The Austrians backed into the same solution; the regiments of Borderers were drilled in linear tactics.

Firepower was supreme in infantry combat by this time, after more than two centuries of trial and experiment. Shock action was secondary. The abandonment of the pike was of course offset by the introduction of the bayonet, but something had been lost when the heavy mass of pikes went. The line of flintlocks lacked the offensive shock weight and defensive power of the older phalangeal formations. Fortifications and entrenchments provided the protection needed in the eighteenth century, not only from cavalry, but from fire as well. But the price paid was heavy. Eighteenth century warfare was static, positional and limited, rule-ridden, custom-bound, and generally indecisive.

Frederick the Great and the Prussian Army

The principal exception to these generalities was to be found in the tactical developments of Frederick the Great, which were beginning to make themselves felt by midcentury. No one else accomplished what he was able to do with linear tactics; he achieved the utmost possible within the limits set by technology and by the political and social conditions of Prussia in the eighteenth century.

Under his rule, Prussia gained an eminence in European affairs out of all proportion to its size and wealth.

When Frederick inherited the throne in 1740, his father had left him a first-rate army, already one of the best in Europe. It numbered nearly 80,000 men, an extraordinary force for a country with a population of two and a half million and an annual revenue of about one million pounds sterling. By 1786, the standing army was 200,000 strong, and the population double that of 1740. Four fifths of Prussia's revenue went into the army.

Frederick's personality, accomplishments, and genius defy simple analysis. He was a sensitive, cultured intellectual, and at the same time a ruthless, cold-hearted disciplinarian. A man of great personal honor, as a monarch he was a sly, treacherous, and untrustworthy foe or ally. He accepted the military system as he found it but recognized its weaknesses: slowness, ponderousness, lack of imagination, slow rates of fire. He became a conservative innovator and injected mobility, speed, and rapidity of fire. He used cavalry vigorously, particularly in the approach to combat and in the early stages of a battle. He always attacked first. He created horse artillery to give increased firepower to his fast-moving cavalry. He emphasized the howitzer because its relative lightness made it more mobile, and its higher trajectory enabled it to get at enemy reserves concealed behind hills. He learned that by speed and agility he could concentrate superior power at a critical point before his more ponderous foes could react effectively. He achieved his mobility and speed by reemphasizing the drill and disciplinary methods inherited from his father.

The quality of the Prussian Army depended on the officer corps, drawn almost entirely from the rural nobility. The superiority of the Prussian officer came less from his professional standards or education than from his strict sense of duty and the iron system of discipline. He began his military service at an early age in cadet school and then spent years on active service. Life consisted of constant drilling and review. In compensation for these sacrifices the officer was a member of the first estate of the realm and a companion to the king. Prussian officers took precedence over all other officials and had complete disposition of their men. Failure in combat was often followed by suicide.

More than in any other army of the time, the drill was necessary not only for linear tactics but also for obedience and control. Frederick placed no faith in the loyalty or honor of the enlisted men, who — as in other armies — were recruited from the lowest elements of society. They could not be trusted and must never be detached or allowed away from the army. All the control mechanisms of eighteenth century armies were designed to prevent desertion, and even tactics were shaped by this objective. Because of fear of desertion it was often impossible to speed up the march, to attempt skirmishing, or to pursue a defeated enemy. Despite all precautions, there was more desertion from the Prussian Army than any other, and after an unsuccessful action the number of missing was usually triple that lost in action.

Frederick was able to break away from slavish dependence on depots without resorting to foraging — with its inherent opportunities for desertion. Three days' rations were carried in the Prussian soldier's knapsack, eight days' bread supply in the regimental trains, and a month's supply in the army trains. A well-organized transport system linked Frederick's armies to the few depots that he did organize.

Frederick's father had reduced the infantry line to three ranks and brought these closer together. Iron ramrods, long in use for pistols, had been adopted for the musket, and to this innovation many contemporary soldiers — and subsequent historians — have attributed the then-phenomenal rate of fire of Prussian infantry. Each Prussian soldier could fire as many as five rounds a minute, as compared to two in most other armies. But it is clear that this superiority was attributable more to Prussian drill and discipline than to the mythical superiority of the iron ramrod.

In battle the Prussian infantry line advanced steadily and continuously in step in slow time. Starting at 100 paces the Prussian soldiers fired volleys at intervals on command. The men of the first rank, and later of all three, fired with bayonets fixed. Reduction of the number of ranks and the distance between them made it possible to form a column of march with a front that could be accommodated on an ordinary road. Movement before battle was made in column of division — or smaller units — the marching columns deploying into line by facing, flanking, wheeling, or front-into-line movements like those of modern infantry drill.

Rather than making substantial changes in this army, Frederick got the utmost from it by perfecting its movements through discipline and drill. The infantry was formed in two lines (of three ranks each), about 300 paces apart. The cavalry, formed into two or three single-rank lines, was on the flanks. The army was divided into four commands for control: two wings of infantry and two of cavalry. Maneuver by elements was difficult in this rigid system, discouraged both by organization and by the optimum tactical deployment of the infantry. Frederick the Great, therefore, attempted to accomplish his maneuver by unexpected pre-battle dispositions, and by one particularly effective adaptation of drill-ground techniques to battlefield deployments. This was the oblique order, which Frederick conceived, apparently following the example set by the Theban Epaminondas at the battles of Leuctra (371 B.C.) and Mantinea (362 B.C.).

The success of the oblique order in the approach to battle depended largely upon the perfection of drill and discipline of the Prussian infantry. But to apply it effectively the commander required knowledge of the enemy's dispositions, and an opportunity to surprise the enemy before he could adequately reinforce the flank that was threatened by the Prussian oblique thrust. Reconnaissance and intelligence were therefore emphasized; and every opportunity that might afford surprise — such as weather, terrain, and darkness — was exploited. An advance guard held the enemy in place to prevent shifts in his line to meet the main attack. The attack itself was characteristically vigorous, fire from infantry and artillery almost continuous.

The Prussian cavalry consisted of cuirassiers, dragoons, and hussars. The first two were organized into five-squadron regiments, the last into ten-squadron regiments, about 120 men to the squadron. As noted earlier, Frederick increased the number of hussars, or light cavalry, in response to the appearance of the light-infantry Borderers in the Austrian Army. Otherwise, however, under Frederick there was a return to the importance of the shock power of cavalry in battle, and reconnaissance off the battlefield. Pistols were taken from the cuirassier, and carbines from the dragoons, who thus became unarmored cavalry. All the horsemen were trained to charge at full speed, ignoring the enemy's fire, with sword in hand. The cavalryman's equipment was made as light as possible to enhance speed and increase the fury of the charge. Close order and alignment were achieved by constant drill, and Prussian cavalry could move with the same precision and perfection as the infantry. Eight to ten thousand mounted men could charge for hundreds of yards in perfect order, then after a melee re-form for movement almost immediately. Such cavalry played an important part in most of Frederick's twenty victories.

The Prussian artillery was organized in battalions, ranging in calibers from light 3-pounders to the heaviest 24-pounders. Prior to Frederick's time the Prussian artillery, like that of other armies, was placed in position well forward before a battle began, and an artillery duel usually opened the battle. But Frederick soon discovered that his propensity for vigorous offensive action penalized his cavalry and infantry as they moved to contact, by taking them within range of the enemy's artillery and into areas where their own artillery could not support them. He discovered that the Austrian artillery was particularly effective and caused many casualties among the attacking Prussians. To offset this enemy advantage Frederick increased the mobility of his artillery so that his guns could move with the attack and provide continuous support to assaulting infantry and cavalry.

The problem was particularly acute for the provision of support to the fast-moving Prussian cavalry. Frederick's solution was to create horse artillery (as opposed to horse-drawn artillery), which could keep up with the cavalry. Instead of going on foot or by wagon, as in standard artillery organization, every cannoneer and ammunition handler was individually mounted. Horse artillery units were equipped with light guns and howitzers that could be moved quickly.

Artillery technique was the same for both horse and horse-drawn artillery; the only difference was the greater mobility of the horse artillery. In the approach to combat the artillery (particularly 3- and 6-pounder units) was pushed out ahead of the supported troops. At about 500 paces from the enemy the gunners dismounted and man-handled their guns into position, firing at the enemy until the infantry line caught up with them. Then, by leapfrogging movements, they were able to keep at least half of the guns in constant firing support of the attacking troops. Frederick also exploited the high trajectory of the howitzer by striking at enemy reserves concealed behind trees and hills, and in the process gave artillerymen a tantalizing glimpse of the potential of indirect fire.

The Battle of Leuthen

The Battle of Leuthen, perhaps the tactical masterpiece of history, illustrates the workings of Frederick's system. By this time — 1757 — Frederick had had sixteen years of combat command, and so the battle represents his matured views and his direction of an army that was the product of his own work. Having just won a victory over much larger French forces at Rossbach, Frederick marched to Breslau, where — with reinforcements — he had an army of 36,000 men. The Austrians under Prince Charles of Lorraine had more than twice this number available for battle near Breslau, nearly 80,000 men.

As Frederick marched east from Breslau, he found the Austrian forces drawn up in a five-mile-long line of battle, in undulating country, partially hidden behind a low range of hills. (It was a tribute to Frederick's skill and reputation that the Austrians, despite their two-to-one advantage, decided to fight a defensive battle.) On the Austrian right was a marsh; the left flank was protected by wooded hills. Cavalry covered both flanks, and the reserves lay behind a partially entrenched left wing, in anticipation of a possible Prussian flanking effort against that side. Instead, Frederick moved his army toward the Austrian right and center in four columns, the inner two made up of infantry, the outer ones of cavalry.

Charles hastily shifted his reserves to meet the obvious Prussian threat. However, when his advance was concealed from the Austrians by a low range of hills, Frederick changed the direction of march of his main body obliquely to his right, leaving only a portion of his left-hand column of cavalry — still in the enemy's field of vision — to begin a demonstration against the Austrian right. Out of sight of the Austrians, the infantry was marching past the enemy front in two columns, the cavalry (save for the demonstration detachment), screening the flank, and covering the front and rear of the infantry columns.

When the Prussian marching columns, still concealed behind the hills, began to overlap the Austrian left, Frederick faced his infantry to the left and advanced in two lines echeloned from the right in his now-famous oblique order. The Prussian artillery charged over the hills, and went promptly into action, massing fire at the apex of the Austrian left flank, ranged in a V, just before the leading infantry battalions hit the surprised Austrians. As successive infantry battalions closed in to the left, the pressure on the Austrians increased, and their line began to waver. The Prussian cavalry — on both flanks of the infantry — now charged the Austrian left wing and drove it back on the center.

Charles attempted to form a new line against this attack, while throwing his right-wing cavalry against the Prussian left flank, but the Austrian horse-cavalry was met and scattered by Prussian cavalry units waiting for this reaction. These horsemen then charged in on the Austrian right flank. The Austrians, thus caught off balance on both flanks, never rallied. Nightfall facilitated the escape of the remainder of the vanquished forces to Breslau, but the army was ruined, and only about half of the original Austrian strength returned to Bohemia and winter quarters.

Frederick's victories had a powerful effect upon military thinking throughout Europe. Many of his contemporaries sought to emulate his system. Foreign officers flocked to Potsdam to witness and admire the complicated maneuvers of the Prussians, then went home to train their own troops in these movements. Frederick had developed the linear system to its utmost, and few could rival, much less surpass, him at this. Without the genius of Frederick himself, however, it was impossible to achieve comparable results. Spain adopted Frederick's system, as did Russia, but neither produced outstanding armies. This should have had a meaning for Frederick's successors in Prussia, after his death. But it did not. There was no real test of the system for another quarter of a century, and "the melody lingered on."*

XVIII. Napoleon and the Revolution in Warfare 1795–1815

The last of the Great Captains is able to take all Europe for his stage, while his great naval opponents conduct coordinated campaigns in the Mediterranean and Baltic Seas, and the Atlantic and Indian Oceans.†

The Significance of Napoleon

The first coherent new concept of warmaking since that of Genghis Khan was demonstrated in the early campaigns of young Napoleon Bonaparte in Italy and Egypt. In his hands this concept continued to dominate warfare directly for the first fifteen years of the nineteenth century, and its influence still persists. Although his enemies copied the Napoleonic system to the best of their abilities, and although they finally defeated him by force of numbers, they never fully understood the concept that underlay Napoleon's tremendous revolution in warmaking.

The French Revolutionary Army

It is only fair to note that the military instrument Napoleon used as the basis for this system had been to a large extent inherited. The army, its discipline, and particularly its artillery system, had been developing during the second half of the eighteenth century. Despite the violent perturbations in the officer corps and in structure during the early years of the Revolution, this development had been continued by the military organizational genius of the Revolution, Lazare N. Carnot. During the first decade of the nineteenth century, Napoleon unquestionably modified and substantially improved the French Army, but these were essentially refinements, rather than revolutionary innovations. What was revolutionary was the manner in which he used this instrument: his

---

*I am indebted to Hugh Cole for this observation.

†Professor Theodore Ropp, in a letter to the author.

operational methods — or "grand tactics" — and his strategic employment of armies.

The only country that had not been strongly influenced by the reintroduction of light infantry into European warfare early in the eighteenth century was France. French thinking had been influenced by the Chevalier Folard and Marshal Maurice de Saxe, who, because they had a basic mistrust of firepower and the thin line, recommended tactical schemes based on Alexander's phalanx and the Roman legion. The result was battle tactics culminating in shock action delivered by "columns." Saxe's victory over the British at Fontenoy (1745) was the classic example of such tactics. During the last half of the century, however, there was debate among French soldiers as to the extent to which fire should precede and support columnar assault, and whether this fire should be delivered by line, line and skirmishers, or skirmisher swarms. During this period French tactics were in flux.

During the early years of the French Revolution the "column" came to be used generally, although it was really an adaptation of the linear system. The so-called column, in fact, was the deployment of a number of linear units (usually battalions) in depth, to provide physical and psychological weight to an attack. The individual units could and did still operate in a linear formation, if desired.

The great tactical value of the French column lay in its flexibility and versatility. It permitted the commander to move large numbers of men over the battlefield more rapidly and with better control than had been possible with more rigid lines. In particular, the column could operate more effectively than the line in hilly terrain. It could easily change into different formations. The shift from marching column to attack column, in particular, took far less time than had the deployment of linear formations from the marching column. Skirmishers could be detached without necessitating major readjustments in the formation. Two- or three-rank firing lines and squares could be formed rapidly. The earlier need to maintain tight flank connections between units in the line fell away; the tactical situation opened up and became more dynamic.

The attack column had two main functions. First, it could be used to bring men in close order rapidly to the enemy. The success of such an action was largely dependent on adequate preparation by artillery and skirmishers, and it was their firepower that inflicted most of the casualties, rather than the column itself, which possessed little firepower once it started to move. Bayonet charges actually driven home against a steady enemy were rare.

The far more common employment of the attack column was as

a sustaining force. The column sent out skirmishers to start the firefight and served as a replacement pool for the skirmishers and as their immediate tactical reserve. If it encountered firm resistance the column might deploy into lines to carry on the fight with volleys. Once the enemy wavered, these lines could resume the advance, or they might again reduce their front and move forward in column.

It should also be noted that an important part of Napoleon's impact on world history was due to his ability to harness (and to show others how to harness, as well) the tremendous new economic and social forces of which the French Revolution was only an early manifestation. The "mass army," first put into the field by Carnot and other early leaders of the Revolution, was an essential ingredient in Napoleon's whirlwind campaigns — and those that eventually overthrew him. The mass army was possible, of course, only because the first fruits of the Industrial Revolution were releasing manpower from farms, and because this manpower could be influenced to fight in support of attractive social goals. Napoleon's successes were greatly aided by the motto of the Revolution, "Liberty, Equality, Fraternity." It is interesting to speculate on the possibility that Napoleon might have been able to make better use of this revolutionary philosophy. On the other hand, it must be recognized that there were inherent contradictions between this philosophy and the dictatorial and totalitarian requirements of military and political success. Furthermore, he had too many enemies.

The introduction of the attack column as a standard combat formation in the wars of the French Revolution did not by itself lead to a revolution of infantry tactics. The utility of the column was dependent on other innovations on the battlefield. Circumstances and combat leaders together ultimately fashioned that combination of close-order columns and loose-order skirmishers which constituted the new tactics of the revolutionary and Napoleonic infantry. Skirmishers would so occupy the enemy that the assault columns could move up without being unduly exposed to the fire of the enemy line.

In the War of the First Coalition (1792–1795) the practice of skirmishing spread throughout the French infantry, and by 1793 all battalions were acting as light infantry, dissolving into skirmisher swarms as soon as action was joined. These fighting methods, sometimes called "horde tactics," were in turn superseded after 1795 by a tendency to return to properly controlled assault columns, preceded by skirmishers whose functions were reconnaissance and disruption of the enemy by individual aimed fire. The important point about this French skirmishing system was that it was not performed by special light troops but by integral parts of the regular bodies. Infantry became more flexible, suggesting that specialized light troops would soon be eliminated by one all-purpose infantry.

The most effective answer to the French system, however, was provided by the British light infantry. Although the tactical specifics were different, the British, too, were becoming all-purpose infantry. Their system was largely based on the effects of controlled, aimed musketry, delivered by troops combining as far as possible the mobility of skirmishers with the steadiness of the line. Under Sir John Moore and Sir Arthur Wellesley (later to become the Duke of Wellington), the British tended toward defensive tactics to maximize available firepower. Typically the British would take advantage of cover, usually behind the crest of a ridge, in a line only two ranks deep. When the attacking French columns approached, the British line arose from its cover to deliver devastating fire.

The character and functions of light infantry were greatly changed by the introduction of the rifle, which came slowly into military use toward the end of the eighteenth century. Originally a sporting weapon, this heavy, cumbersome handarm, whose grooved barrel imparted a spin to its bullet, achieved amazing accuracy and range as compared to the smoothbore musket. It crept overseas to North America from its original habitat, the Rhineland, where huntsmen had used it for nearly two hundred years. German craftsmen in Pennsylvania began turning out a somewhat lighter and longer-barreled rifle for colonial woodsmen.

The rifle had a slower rate of fire than the musket, since the loading process required that each bullet (wrapped in a greased patch of cloth) had to be hammered down into the grooved barrel with a mallet. The rifle was not equipped with a bayonet, since this adaptation could be made only at the risk of impairing the weapon's accuracy, and also made precise marksmanship more difficult. It was an individual arm, used by skilled individualists along the western fringes of the thirteen colonies. As a result of experience in the American Revolution, the rifle and the rifleman had become elements in European warfare as the century closed. Rifles were expensive, however, and because of this and their slow rate of fire only select units and select individuals in line companies were equipped with them until well into the nineteenth century.

The first important adaptation of the rifle to the demands of formal warfare was to be found in the English light infantry of the early nineteenth century. The small proportion of men armed with the rifle could take their place in a close-order line of muskets, and maintain a high rate of fire by using a subcaliber bullet, which did not engage the rifle grooves. When individual aimed fire was required, the rifleman would use regular-sized bullets in greased patches. Obviously the rifleman so equipped had to be a cool, well-trained, highly disciplined soldier. By his ability to operate individually or in close order, he represented in essence the all-purpose infantryman of the future.

The political implications of the new light-infantry tactics of the French and British were revolutionary. The light infantryman often fought as an individual skirmisher in open order, much less under the direct supervision of his officers than was possible in the close-order column or line. Both the French revolutionary armies and the British system abandoned the brutal and degrading discipline of the eighteenth century armies. Instead, performance was encouraged by combining a firm but just discipline with intense training and appeals to regimental pride, revolutionary élan, and the spirit of nationalism.

Artillery played a decisive role in Napoleon's battles and was the major factor in the lethality of his warfare, inflicting more than 50 percent of the battle casualties suffered by his opponents. The French Revolutionary Army inherited from the monarchy an excellent field artillery system, developed by an artillery officer, Jean-Baptiste Vaquette Gribeauval (1715–1789), and introduced into the French Army in 1776. Influenced greatly by Frederick the Great, Gribeauval made mobility the main feature of French artillery, obtained by reducing the length and weight of the gun barrel and the weight of the gun carriage. This reduction of weight was facilitated by providing the carriages with iron axletrees and rugged wheels of large diameter to facilitate movement in difficult terrain. Range and precision were preserved by more precise manufacture of cannonballs of true sphericity and correct diameter; this also made possible a reduction in powder charge, which in time permitted lighter gun barrels. Prefabricated cartridges replaced the old loose powder and shot and increased the rate of fire. Draft horses were disposed in double files instead of single. Six horses now sufficed to draw the 12-pounder, while four were used for smaller guns, which included 8- and 4-pounders, and a new 6-inch howitzer.

Napoleon's System of War

Napoleon took full advantage of the maneuverability of the French artillery and made out of it the most important tool of his operations. One of his favorite techniques, particularly employed in later years of the Empire as the demands of war caused a decline in troop quality, was employment of the *grande batterie*. This technique, notably employed at Wagram in 1809, physically massed a preponderance of artillery weapons in support of his main effort on the battlefield, literally blasting a section of the enemy line to shreds to permit his infantry to advance.

During this period cavalry remained the shock arm, with lance and saber the principal hand weapons. However, because of Napoleon's exploitation of all of the traditional roles of cavalry, the distinction between "heavy" and "light" cavalry was as marked in the imperial armies as it had been in the forces of Alexander the Great and Genghis Khan. Heavy cavalrymen were partly armored cuirassiers on big horses, while light-cavalry units were made up of more agile troopers on smaller mounts, who could harass as well as shock.

Napoleon's cavalry, provided with horse artillery and used in great but articulate masses and in surprise operations against hostile cavalry and infantry, was very effective. It was usually thrown against enemy infantry already shaken or shattered by massive artillery fire or by infantry attack. The French horsemen were particularly effective against retreating infantry. Cavalry was less successful, however, against fresh infantry that had time to form squares. By its vigorous action in pursuit, French cavalry exploited victory with minimum losses to its own army. Napoleon also used his cavalry very effectively for reconnaissance and for screening.

During the early Napoleonic Wars, under outstanding dynamic leaders, and by its impetuous charges, French cavalry was generally superior to the best cavalry in other European nations. Later, as casualties and the passage of years took their toll, Napoleon found it difficult to maintain the same high standards of performance in his mounted units. At the same time, his enemies steadily improved their cavalry by copying the French organization, tactics, and methods, devoting more attention to its organization and training. In the Iberian Peninsula, for instance, cavalry played a minor role in Wellington's campaigns. At Waterloo, however, the English cavalry played a major role in slowing and stopping French infantry attacks, including the final assault of Napoleon's Old Guard.

The decline of French cavalry during the latter years of the Empire provides an excellent example of a process that had been affecting all of the French Army to some extent. All military institutions operate from a socio-economic base. A cohesive society and a strong economy do not automatically guarantee excellence in the military institutions, but they are essential if the institutions are to survive and flourish. French livestock — and particularly the equine resources — was used up in two decades of almost uninterrupted war.

The infantry division as a large permanent tactical and administrative organization appeared in France in the eighteenth century. In 1759 the Duc de Broglie introduced into the French Army a divisional formation: permanent mixed bodies of infantry and artillery.

In 1794 Carnot, the Revolutionary minister of war, developed the idea of a division embracing all three arms, infantry, cavalry, and artillery, which was capable of carrying out independent operations. By 1796 the divisional system had become universal in the French Army. It was Napoleon Bonaparte, however, who developed all the potentialities of the divisional system and used it as a maneuver tool in mobile warfare. The men were trained and toughened by fast marching in maneuvers, and the supply system was modified to support more rapid movement of large and small forces. The mobility of the division was also enhanced by the improved artillery, which could follow infantry and maneuver on the battlefield.

When the size of the French field armies increased to more than 100,000 men it became necessary to group divisions into army corps to simplify the problems of command and of control. The first such organization was made in 1800, when Moreau concentrated his span of control by grouping the eleven divisions of the Army of the Rhine into four corps. In 1804, as Napoleon was readying his Grande Armee of 200,000 men for an invasion of Britain, he introduced permanent army corps in the French Army, employing them as he had previously used divisions. However, the division remained the major tactical unit, now usually composed of two arms — infantry and artillery — and entrusted with a definite mission. The corps included cavalry as well — also usually in divisions — which conducted reconnaissance for the whole corps. In addition, Napoleon formed corps of cavalry alone.

Napoleon's infantry division consisted of two or three infantry brigades, each comprising two regiments, and of one artillery brigade, consisting of two batteries, each with four field guns and two howitzers. He deliberately varied the size of his divisions — by varying the number of component brigades and artillery batteries — to confuse and frustrate the intelligence services of his enemies.

In combat operations Napoleon always sought a general battle as a means of destroying the enemy's armed force, after having gained a strategic advantage by maneuver—if possible, by seizing or threatening the hostile line of communications, or by interposing his army behind scattered enemy units. Tactically he endeavored to use mass and maneuver in combination, seizing the initiative as soon as possible to force the enemy to conform to his plans. There was no precise tactical pattern, but he always used maneuver to operate against the hostile flanks. Often he directed his main blow against the enemy's flank while simultaneously attacking his front; alternatively he would launch his main thrust against the center of the enemy's battle front with the aim of breaking through, while at the same time carrying on an enveloping maneuver against one of the opposing flanks. Divisions assigned missions of attacking important objectives were often supported by massed fire from Napoleon's artillery reserves. Divisions with exposed flanks were protected by corps cavalry or even by the army's cavalry reserve. After the victory that usually ensued, Napoleon would launch an energetic pursuit with his cavalry, followed by the whole army. Only after destruction of the main force of the enemy did he occupy the principal strategic and political centers of the enemy's country.

To deceive and confuse his enemies, whose combined military strength almost always exceeded his, as well as to permit rapidity of movement and efficient foraging, Napoleon kept his forces spread out until the last possible moment. Then, concentrating rapidly, he would bring superior forces to bear at some critical point. (One of his favorite expressions was, "We must separate to eat, and concentrate to fight.") In a favorite variant, he would endeavor to place his concentrated army between two hostile armies, defeating them in turn. His first and last campaigns, Montenotte and Waterloo, are both brilliant examples of this. His failure in the latter was due to the failure of performance (his and his subordinates') to match his superb strategic concept.

Napoleon's Principles of War

The essence of Napoleon's system of war can best be described in terms of the Principles of War—and it was essentially by the study of Napoleonic campaigns that subsequent students of warfare came to recognize the existence of such principles, which began to be codified about a century later.

Objective. Napoleon's principal objective was always the main body of the enemy; his aim was to try to place the main body of his opponents in an unfavorable situation as quickly as possible, and then to destroy its effectiveness in a major battle. Geographical objectives — commanding terrain, important communications centers, supply depots — were always secondary and intermediate to the basic objective of destroying the combat capability of the enemy's army.

Simplicity. There were a number of reasons for Napoleon's preference for simple strategic and tactical plans. It was important to him that the efforts of all of his subordinates be coordinated to achieve maximum effectiveness. Because of his awareness of "friction in war" (a phenomenon later identified by Clausewitz, probably the greatest and most perceptive of the students of Napoleonic warfare), he recognized that complicated plans could be misunderstood and misinterpreted, and that they usually were dependent upon close timing that was rarely obtainable in military operations — particularly when those operations were being opposed.

Unity of command (or *cooperation*, or — as seen by Napoleon — *control*). In some respects *unity of command* was a result of *simplicity*. In any event, Napoleon's simple operational combinations demanded — and usually obtained — the coordination of the efforts of all elements of his army to achieve his intermediate and ultimate objectives.

Offensive. Napoleon invariably seized the initiative in his campaigns and, even when superior enemy numbers forced him to a defensive posture, he always attempted to force his enemy to respond to his actions, rather than the other way around. He was far from reckless; his calculations were always cool and calm; and (though usually outnumbered by his enemies) he always endeavored to have superior numbers present on the battlefield. Thus he viewed offensive action in climactic battles as the culmination of prior arrangements to place the enemy at a relative disadvantage.

Maneuver. This was one of the two principal means Napoleon used to offset hostile numerical superiority, while placing his enemy in a disadvantageous position. Maneuver — both strategic and tactical — was Napoleon's hallmark. His first great victories at Montenotte and Dego in 1796 — like his tactical masterpiece at Austerlitz in 1805 — were won by maneuver that permitted him, even when his army was greatly outnumbered, to bring superior numbers to the critical battlefield. His brilliant strategic maneuvers in the Marengo, Ulm, and Jena campaigns, put his army in a position astride his enemies' lines of communications in such a way that the campaign was virtually won before the climactic battle was fought.

Mass (or concentration). Napoleon was fond of quoting Voltaire's aphorism that "God is on the side of the heavier battalions." He knew that — all other things being equal — superior numbers on the battlefield were the principal determinants of battle outcomes. He always attempted to have superior numbers, greater combat power, at the critical point on the battlefield. However, he knew that military skill could be used to multiply numbers (he has been only slightly misquoted as saying that "the moral is to the physical as three is to one"). And his two major tools to achieve effective combat power superiority over a numerically superior foe were the principles of *maneuver* and *surprise*.

Economy of forces. This is the opposite side of the coin from *mass*. To achieve concentration or mass at the critical point — particularly if his forces were outnumbered by the enemy — Napoleon had to reduce strength drastically at less vital positions. He recognized (as Clausewitz later wrote about his battles) that "defense is the stronger form of combat." So he counted on small numbers of troops in defensive posture to stop or delay larger numbers of enemies, while he concentrated maximum combat power against the most critical or most vulnerable portion of the enemy's forces. Thus *economy of forces* was usually an essential contribution to *mass*.

Surprise. Napoleon recognized that of all of the moral forces in war surprise is perhaps the most effective, and the greatest multiplier. He endeavored to achieve surprise in many ways: by moving rapidly to places where the enemy did not expect him, by attacking in places where the enemy thought he was weak, by crossing terrain that the enemy thought was impassable, by attacking when the enemy thought he and his army were resting, by being present at battlefields where his enemies thought he was absent. (The significance of this latter point is clear when we consider that his two most able foes — Wellington and Blücher — are both quoted as saying that the presence of Napoleon on the battlefield was worth 40,000 men.)

Security. Napoleon knew that surprise was a two-edged sword. Although he knew that none of his enemies could match his own fertile brain and imagination, he also knew 'that he must try to guess every possible action that his enemies might take. Thus he always was careful to dispose his forces to minimize the possibility of surprise — by use of spies, by aggressive reconnaissance with his cavalry, by always retaining a reserve to meet unexpected contingencies — and to be able to react calmly and effectively in the event that he actually was surprised. Even at Waterloo his security measures were adequate — but his subordinates (particularly Grouchy) failed to accomplish the security missions he had assigned them.

Napoleon was not only a tactical and strategic genius, he was a master of planned and improvised supply, and completely changed the depot-oriented system of eighteenth century warfare. Divisions had often been billeted in towns and villages, where the local population was required to provide food. Each soldier carried four days' provisions; another four days' supply was on the wagon trains following the troops. These eight days of provisions were to be consumed only in emergency; insofar as possible daily food requirements were to be obtained by local requisitions or foraging. In addition, provisions were stored at the army's main base and in intermediate depots, the latter moving forward behind the advance of the troops.

This system of logistics proved very satisfactory until the Russian campaign of 1812, when it completely broke down because of bad roads in Russia, the poverty of the country, the activities of the Russian partisans and the "scorched earth" policy adopted by Emperor Alexander and General Kutusov.

Napoleon never committed his concepts to paper in systematic form. But his methods of warfare and the concepts underlying those methods are deducible not only from his random writings but also from the record of his accomplishments. He avoided stereotypes and attempted to develop his plans for every campaign and every battle in such a way that his enemies could never know what to expect from him. Insofar as possible, Napoleon tried to win a campaign strategically before the first battle was fought. Whenever there was an opportunity, he would combine rapid marching and skillful deception to pass around the enemy's flanks to reach the hostile line of communications, and then turn to make the enemy fight at a disadvantage.

After the first defeats inflicted on them by Napoleon, other European military leaders tried to imitate him. They gradually introduced divisions and army corps into their armies, modified linear tactics by introducing deep combat formations, applied concentration of forces on the battlefield in general and in its decisive areas in particular, and formed reserves. But though Napoleon's enemies learned much from him, and greatly improved their military instruments and performance, they could never match the great master and never really grasped the secrets of his genius. They finally overwhelmed him through numerical superiority and the effects of the attrition of war on France, both traceable to Napoleon's diplomatic failures. As noted above, even the generals who defeated him recognized Napoleon's superior genius.

Wellington's Army and Tactics

Linear tactics remained in use for a good part of the nineteenth century, since it was held by many that Wellington's victories in the Peninsula and at Waterloo demonstrated the superiority of the line. Time would show that this conclusion was at best dubious, especially when improvements in military technology vastly increased firepower, mobility, and communications. But the tactics of Wellington are well worth study, especially since they were so often successful against a system that ultimately replaced them.

The British did not adopt the division until 1807, and Wellington's army in the Peninsula in 1809 was still composed of independent brigades. Despite the early successes of the French system, the British retained the two-deep line, in which every man could employ his weapons to produce a greater volume of fire than could the column. Wellington's success was due undoubtedly in part to this; but it was due also to his tactics. (It should be remembered that Wellington met Napoleon only once — at Waterloo — and the victory there was due more to the arrival of the Prussians than to Wellington's skill.)

Wellington decided he could overcome French tactics in the Peninsula with three techniques: not exposing his line until the action opened, protecting his line against French skirmishers, and securing his flanks. The first he usually achieved by placing his infantry whenever possible on reverse slopes, the second by building up his light troops. The third was accomplished by the use of natural obstacles and skillful use of cavalry.

The British Army was a volunteer force and necessarily smaller than the French. But it had the advantage of more training and drill. The infantry was superior to any other in Europe in the excellence of its musketry, an advantage enhanced by its two-rank line. The British Army was the only European force in the Napoleonic Wars that consistently inflicted more than half of the casualties on the enemy with small-arms fire.

During the Peninsular War (1809–1814), Wellington's army at first was organized into eight brigades of two or three battalions each. Reorganized as its size increased, it consisted finally of seven divisions, a light division, and a separate cavalry division. Although the elements of the divisions varied, they were usually about 6,000 strong, composed ordinarily of two British brigades and one Portuguese brigade, usually with three battalions each. The cavalry division consisted of three brigades of two regiments each. The light division served as a protective screen for the entire army, operating far to the front.

One of the more interesting and important aspects of Wellington's organization grew out of his efforts to secure a strong screen of skirmishers to meet the French *tirailleurs*. Wellington added to every brigade in his army an extra company of light riflemen to reinforce the three light companies that were by now standard in the British brigade. Furthermore, each of the brigades of the light division had a number of rifle companies.

British light infantry therefore was armed with two different kinds of weapons, the rifle and the musket. The light-infantry musket was a special type, lighter, shorter, with better sights, and somewhat more accurate than the basic infantry weapon, the famous "Tower musket" or "Brown Bess." The line battalions used the Brown Bess, a stout reliable weapon the British (probably wrongly) considered superior to those used on the Continent. Weighing about nine pounds, with an effective range of 300 yards (but accurate enough to hit a man only at about 100 yards), it was a heavy flintlock with all the virtues and faults of the type. It fired a round lead ball and used a heavy paper cartridge.

Cavalry played a minor role in Wellington's Peninsular Campaigns, in part because of the difficulty of shipping horses from Britain. But Wellington did pay considerable attention to defense against French cavalry. The steady line and accurate fire of the British infantrymen were usually able to repulse a French cavalry charge. On one occasion, an infantry line advanced against cavalry and drove it from the field. In a square formation, the British infantry could rarely be broken, and there is recorded the instance of the light division, formed into five squares, retreating for two miles with only 35 casualties, under attack by four French cavalry brigades.

Wellington's sparing use of cavalry in the Peninsular Campaigns should not be taken to indicate that he was unable when the occasion offered to use it with good effect. In one of the culminating actions of the Battle of Waterloo, a brigade of dragoons (1,000 sabers) passed through the British infantry to fall unexpectedly upon the advancing French infantry, which had no time to form squares. Although French horsemen soon drove the British cavalry back, the French momentum had been killed. Some Englishmen (forgetting the decisive role of the Prussians) go so far as to claim that the British cavalry charge was the main cause of the French defeat.

Wellington employed his artillery selectively: in small numbers and individual batteries, at carefully chosen sites, at critical moments. They were placed all along the front as support for the infantry and played a minor but important role in his defensive-offensive tactics.

The British Army did not do well initially against the revolutionary armies of France, but under the leadership of Wellington it began to win victories and to earn the reputation it held toward the end of the Napoleonic period. Military glory came with the successful campaigns in the Peninsula and the victory at Waterloo, both led by Wellington.

Congruence of Weapons, Theory, and Practice

Under the direction, or stimulus, of Napoleon Bonaparte, the weapons of the age of gunpowder were finally assimilated into consistent patterns of military theory and practice. For the first time since gunpowder had appeared on the battlefield, there was a substantial congruence among weapons, tactics, and doctrine. The bayoneted flintlock musket and the smoothbore cannon had each been perfected to a point closely approaching its maximum potential. After centuries of experimentation, the tactical means of employing these weapons in combination with each other and with cavalry had been refined to the point where a skillful commander could exploit the full potential of his weapons and his arms to achieve decisive results with minimum cost. The last time that commanders had been able to exercise comparable discriminating control over the means available to them had been in the thirteenth century, in the Mongol and English tactical systems.

Yet just as those two tactical systems had approached perfection in the employment of men and weapons at a time when the systems were doomed to early obsolescence because of the emergence of gunpowder weapons, so the principal tactical systems of the early nineteenth century (French and British on land, and English at sea) would be equally short-lived under the impact of the Industrial Revolution.

The congruence of weapons, tactics, and doctrine was bound to come during this half-century as a logical result of earlier developments. But the achievement was probably hastened, and certainly made more significant, through the genius of Napoleon Bonaparte. No man has more indelibly stamped his personality on an era than did Napoleon. In his own time and for more than a century to come, military theory and practice were measured against his standards and related to his concepts of warmaking, while masters of naval warfare were trying to retrieve that "Nelson touch" that had done so much in the end to assure Napoleon's defeat.

Part Three: The Age of Technological Change

XIX. Technology and the Industrial Revolution 1800–1900

Technology and Warfare, Early Nineteenth Century

The transformation of warfare that occurred in the century following the defeat of Napoleon in 1815 was a prolonged revolution created and sustained by many forces — political, economic, and social — of which technological advance was only one, though in many ways the most dramatic, as well as most profound. In the realm of technology, the developments with which we are here concerned — metallurgy, chemistry, ballistics, and electronics — were prominent but far from all-embracing factors in the military revolution. The weaponry of this revolution, along with the immense volume and variety of mass-produced tools and consumable articles of the new industrial civilization, were also products of machines, themselves the creation of a revolution in mechanics and engineering without which the new knowledge of metals and new sources of power would have remained as sterile as the scientific theories and gadgets of the Greeks two thousand years earlier.

Throughout the nineteenth century the application of new scientific and technical knowledge to military technology characteristically lagged behind other applications. As late as 1860 the naval guns in actual service did not differ in essential respects from guns in use three centuries earlier. The Royal Navy's smoothbore 68-pounder, for example, which had been adopted in 1840 and was the heaviest gun then in service — so heavy and violent in recoil that it was used as a pivot gun only on the largest warships — was fundamentally the same as the heavier naval guns of Queen Elizabeth's day. This is not to ignore the numerous improvements and refinements that had occurred over the intervening centuries (particularly the last) in the quality of casting, the mixing of powder, and the precision of boring. But the basic principles of gun operation and construction remained the same.

Yet great changes were already in the making. Many, in fact, were already proved and known, even though they had not yet made their way into the standardized equipment of armies and navies. By 1863 virtually all the basic principles embodied in the modern naval gun had been introduced into the ordnance of the period.* In other types of materiel, and in the weaponry of land combat, changes of almost equal moment had also made their appearance. Thereupon, for another quarter-century or more, a developmental lull ensued while armies and navies endeavored to assimilate the new technology.

Weapons and Tactics, Early Nineteenth Century

By the close of the Napoleonic Wars, the dominant weapons of the battlefield were the combination of flintlock and bayonet, supported by smoothbore, muzzle-loading cannon. Cannon had marked superiority in range over the flintlock, and probably inflicted nearly half the casualties in combat. In battle, armies formed in line to defend, or to attack by fire, and usually formed in greater depth (the so-called column) to charge. This tactical system by 1820 was about two hundred years old. Until the Napoleonic era, the proportion of casualties (killed and wounded) to total effective forces under the linear system had declined steadily from 15 percent for victors and 30 percent for losers in battle in the Thirty Years' War to about 9 percent and 16 percent respectively during the French Revolution. Napoleon's later insistence on — or tolerance of — columnar attacks without thorough preparation drove the casualty rates up sharply to 15 and 20 percent. In the several minor wars fought under the system after Napoleon, casualty rates fell even below those of the French Revolution. This would suggest that a balance had been struck between lethality of weapons used and the combat effectiveness of linear tactics by men so armed.

The Mexican War was the last fought by the U.S. Army with smoothbore muskets and linear tactics against a similar doctrine. Casualty experience there began a significant century.†

In 1858, the United States adopted the conoidal bullet, fired from a muzzle-loading rifle-musket. This was the standard weapon used by North and South in the Civil War, and it was lethal at longer ranges than canister or spherical case shot fired from contemporary cannon. Solid shot and shell from smoothbore cannon could reach as far as the conoidal bullet from the rifle-musket. But contemporary shells, if they burst, broke into only two to five fragments, while direct hits with solid-shot cannon were extremely

---

*Bernard Brodie, *Sea Power in the Machine Age* (Princeton, 1941), p. 198.

†Gilbert W. Beebe and Michael E. De Bakey, *Battle Casualties* (Springfield, Illinois: Charles C Thomas, 1952). Table 4. Note, these are *annual* figures, and not single battle figures as discussed above. Note also, these do not include wounded, usually about 3.5 times as numerous as those killed in action.

TABLE 3

Name of War	Killed in Action per 1,000 per year
Mexican War	9.9
Civil War	
North	21.3
South	(loss data incomplete)*
Spanish – American War	1.9
Philippine Insurrection	2.2
World War I	12.0
World War II	9.0

*But generally greater than Union losses; see Thomas L. Livermore, *Numbers and Losses in the Civil War* (Bloomington: University of Indiana, 1957), reprint.

rare. In short, the relation of lethal capability between infantry weapons and artillery had been reversed. As a result, of a sample group of 144,000 Civil War casualties the causes were:

TABLE 4

Conoidal rifle bullet	108,000
Smoothbore musket, round ball	16,000
Shell fragments	12,500
Canister, grape, and cannonball	359
Explosive bullets	139
Edged weapons (mostly sabers)	7,002
	144,000

In summary, small arms (mostly rifles) caused 86 percent of the casualties, cannon caused 9 percent, and edged weapons caused 5 percent.

Both sides used linear tactics during the Civil War. On many occasions, most notably when fighting over broken ground, troops would spontaneously break into little groups and fight from one cover to another. But to attack or defend, men would be formed in lines of two or three ranks; to weight an attack, one regimental line would follow another to make a great column, as in Napoleon's day. The resulting imbalance between infantry weapons of greater potential lethality, on the one hand, and tactics better suited to the weapons of a previous generation, on the other, sent casualties on both sides soaring to levels comparable to Napoleon's bloodiest battles. By the end of the war, however, there was a clear, although slow, trend toward dispersal.

From 1866 on in western Europe breech-loading rifles were standard issue. The increased rate of fire seems to have compensated for the increase in the capabilities of field artillery that resulted from the slightly later introduction of breech-loading and rifling in cannon. Thus, in the Franco-Prussian War as in the Civil War, casualties from rifle bullets were about ten times those from artillery. It does not appear that the implications of this fact were appreciated initially in the Prussian or French services any more than they had been by either North or South in the American Civil War. Adaptation to the new situation came somewhat more rapidly in the Prussian Army, perhaps, but even at the end of the Franco-Prussian War the linear tactics of Gustavus Adolphus were still in vogue.

Appreciation of the impact of the significant increase in lethality of infantry weapons resulting from rifling and breech-loading was first shown when the Prussians dropped the close-order bayonet charge from their tactics. And Prussian combat formations spread out into "open order," so that all infantrymen acted as skirmishers, much as had been the unofficial practice in America a few years earlier, at the end of the Civil War. The difference, however, lay in the fact that the Germans studied the lessons of their nineteenth century wars — reinforced by observation of the Russo-Japanese War — more intently, and with better results, than their contemporaries.

Scientific and Technological Background

In order to relate the new developments of the early nineteenth century military revolution to the relevant technologies, it is necessary to go back somewhat to pick up the threads of antecedent knowledge in the fields of metallurgy, chemistry, ballistics, and electronics.

We have seen in early pages how the discovery of iron and the development of new techniques in reducing the ore to molten metal influenced weapons manufacture from 1400 B.C. onward. With the development in the mid-sixteenth century of techniques for casting heavy ordnance, the technological basis was laid for the manufacture of artillery during the next two and a half centuries.

By the latter part of the eighteenth century, the rising cost of wrought iron (or charcoal iron), resulting from the depletion of European timber resources, posed a serious problem. The eventual response to this need was the use of the so-called puddling process, in which the molten metal was agitated by a long steel bar in a reverberatory furnace fueled by coke; this had the effect of exposing all the metal, not merely that on the surface, to the air, thereby achieving a more complete decarburization, which transformed it into malleable iron.

Wrought iron produced by puddling was inferior to charcoal iron, but it was far cheaper. A further improvement came in 1829 with the introduction of preheated blast air, using the spent gases from the blast furnace itself. This innovation made it possible to produce three times as much puddled iron with the same amount of fuel. Still another development was the "wet" puddling method, by which the floor of the furnace was coated with small pieces of slag containing iron oxide, which combined with the carbon in the metal to produce carbon monoxide under the surface, resulting in an effervescent agitation that accelerated the decarburization. The total production of iron in England in 1720 was only 20,000 tons. It had risen by 1806 to 250,000 tons, and by 1850 England was producing 2.5 million tons of iron annually, reflecting the expanded output of both cast and wrought iron.

Since ancient times there had been no fundamental change in the methods of making steel. It remained a product of small-scale individual craftsmanship. The basic material used in England was Swedish bar iron of high quality and commensurate cost. As a result, steel cost five times as much to make as wrought iron.

The first significant improvement in the ancient processes was developed about the middle of the eighteenth century. Benjamin Huntsman placed small crucibles of special clay inside a melting chamber fired by coke, and through intense heat and a special flux succeeded in producing a cast steel completely free from silica or slag at a slightly lower cost than that yielded by other existing methods. However, the product unfortunately could not be welded, and its very hardness was disadvantageous for certain uses. This technique, nevertheless, became the basis of the Sheffield steel industry and was widely copied in Europe. No other notable improvement occurred until the middle of the nineteenth century, and the high cost of steel, together with the imperfections of the material itself, continued to deter its use in the manufacture of heavy ordnance.

The Krupps of Rhineland Prussia built their reputation during the first half of the nineteenth century on the manufacture of fine cast steel, and by midcentury they were producing steel artillery pieces in very limited numbers. One model of advanced design, shown at the Great Exhibition of 1851 in England, attracted much attention and proved a harbinger of future developments. Krupp steel had four times the tensile strength of cast iron and twice that of wrought iron. Yet artillerists generally regarded steel as too brittle (several Krupp steel guns had burst since the first was built in 1847) and lacking in uniformity to supersede the more dependable wrought iron, cast iron, and bronze weapons, particularly since this very period was witnessing the beginning of a revolution in large gun design and manufacture, using these traditional metals.

The manufacture of steel of fairly good quality in quantities and at cost comparable to the manufacture of cast and wrought iron was first made possible through the Bessemer process. At about the same time, the Siemens brothers in England were developing a process of heat regeneration using hot waste gases or gases produced from low-grade coal to preheat incoming fuel and air. The Siemens-Martin "open hearth" process, developed a few years later, used a regenerative furnace to melt pig iron mixed with scrap iron or steel; the Siemens process used pig iron with iron ore. The basic product of all these processes was "mild" steel, harder than wrought iron but less so than the "blister" steel produced by older processes. It provided the material for a wide variety of uses — rails, boiler plate, structural steel (for ships, houses, and reinforced concrete), and sheet metal. Between 1856 and 1870 the price of steel dropped by 50 percent, and its production increased sixfold. In 1863 the first steel ship and the first steel locomotive were manufactured. Some idea of the rise in total production is given by the increase in British output of steel from 220,000 tons in 1870 (practically all by the converter process) to 4.9 million tons in 1900 (of which 3.1 million were by the open hearth process). American steel output in 1900 was 10 million tons, that of Germany about 8 million.

The most significant avenue of subsequent development in the metallurgy of steel was in alloy steels for special applications. Faraday had made chromium and nickel steel as early as 1819, but it was not until 1868 that Mushet began to manufacture high-carbon tungsten-manganese steel, from which highly durable tools could be fashioned without the quenching technique. Chromium steel for armor-plate and shells was produced commercially in France in 1877. Sir Robert Hadfield of Sheffield discovered how to make manganese steel by quenching, in 1882, and Le Creusot started making nickel steel in 1888. All these advances derived from the new science of metallography, the study of the structure of metals From the discovery of X rays in 1895 by Wilhelm Röntgen came, among other things, the science of crystallography, which led to further refinements in the uses of metals.

Matching the development of these mass-production techniques in smelting, there were also improvements in the finishing processes in the latter part of the nineteenth century. Hammer forging gave way largely to rolling processes. A basic refinement was the reversing mill, which passed the metal ingots and sheets to and fro with major savings in time. The three-high mill used a third roller to pass the metal back without reversing the machinery; the continuous mill had roller-stands in a series of diminishing size and power. All these methods appeared in the 1860s and underwent subsequent refinement.

Aluminum, which has become the basic material of the modern aircraft industry, was first produced from ore experimentally in the early nineteenth century, but the process was too expensive for widespread application. In 1886 Charles Martin Hall developed a process of electrolytic production of aluminum from molten alumina (oxide of aluminum) dissolved in molten cryolite (mined in Greenland but later produced synthetically). This inaugurated the age of light metals and their alloys, based on mass production with cheap electricity. Aluminum and magnesium alloys, with other light metals, have challenged steel and copper in many fields of manufacture that the latter formerly dominated, including air transport, electric power transmission, cooking utensils, and building construction. Since World War II aluminum and its alloys can be cast, forged, extruded, rolled, spun, beaten, and sprayed to meet many applications.

The eighteenth and nineteenth centuries saw extremely significant additions to man's knowledge of chemistry and physics, as interest in research expanded, and new discoveries spurred industrial development. But there was no concentrated effort to apply new knowledge to the improvement of weapons. When the revolutionary government of France attempted in the 1790s to mobilize science in defense of the nation, the focus was on improving methods and rates of production rather than on the creation of better or more lethal weapons. The cannon, muskets, powder, and shot were the same, or nearly the same, as those that had been in use for some time. It was not until the middle of the nineteenth century, when great strides had been made in scientific knowledge, that that knowledge began to be applied seriously to solution of battlefield problems.

Three developments were of particular importance. The first of these was the canning and preservation of food. As early as 1795 the French Revolutionary Government saw the possibility that food preservation might make it easier to supply and feed its greatly enlarged mass armies. A prize of 12,000 francs was offered to anyone who could produce a practical method of food preservation. It was not until 1809 that the prize was won, by Nicolas Appert, who was able to preserve foods that had been sterilized in special glass containers. (Why this was so, however, was not known until Louis Pasteur's work, about 1860.) It was obvious to both military men and scientists that metal containers were more practical than bottles. But the problem was to devise a welding or soldering method that would provide a perfect seal and prevent the contents of the can from being contaminated while in storage. By the middle of the nineteenth century the problem had been substantially solved, but it was not until the end of the century that truly efficient mass production of canned goods was possible.

A related area was the manufacture of cartridge cases for small arms. The first completely metallic cartridge cases appeared about 1850, the result of considerable parallel but independent research and experiment in France, Britain, and the United States. There was little problem with the concept of an all-metal cartridge with a protected detonating compound that would be activated by the firing pin of the weapon. But the practical problems were substantial. How to get the right consistency of metal that would be both strong enough to withstand the pressures of the powder charge and soft enough to be indented by the firing pin? And once that combination was found, how to design a machine that would extrude the cartridges on a mass-production basis. Until this was accomplished — in the late 1860s — the concept of the machine gun could never become practical reality.

Third was the introduction of antisepsis and asepsis to field surgery. Pasteur in the 1860s demonstrated that infections and diseases were caused by bacteria, and by 1867 Joseph Lord Lister translated this discovery into practical means of antisepsis. Applying antiseptic procedures in field surgery in wartime, however, was another matter. The problems of carrying out other antiseptic procedures soon led logically to the concept of asepsis: the packaging of sterile materials so that they would not be contaminated before use. Asepsis was able to profit, of course, from the achievements of canning, in which food was also kept sterile until just before it was eaten

The New Weaponry

One of the most important nineteenth century contributions to weaponry was the percussion cap, which brought about marked changes in the infantry musket. In 1798 L. G. Brougnatelli discovered silver fulminate, and in the year following, E. C. Howard produced fulminate of mercury. These were the first developed of several explosives that could be ignited through concussion. In 1807 the Reverend Alexander Forsyth, a Scottish clergyman —. presumably a man of peace — succeeded, after years of experimentation, in developing a mercuric fulminate that would readily explode under a hammer blow and communicate the flash through the touchhole of the gun to the powder charge in the barrel. A percussion cap employing this powder was invented in 1814, using successively iron, pewter, and finally copper caps. After being adopted slowly, the percussion cap became the basic method of igniting the propelling charge in both small arms and artillery. Used at first in the form of a separate cap, which the user had to affix to a nipple beneath the weapon's hammer, it was subsequently incorporated into the combined cartridge and projectile.

No real improvement in gunpowder itself was achieved until about 1860, when the principle of progressive combustion was discovered. It was found that the rate of combustion and therefore the pressure of the expanding gases in the bore could be slowed by compressing the grained powder into pellets of greater density. Since the compressed pellets exposed a smaller surface initially to be ignited, less gas was evolved during the early instants of combustion, and the evolution of gas continued as the projectile moved down the bore. The result was higher muzzle velocities and lower maximum pressures. This discovery resulted in successive improvements in the ordinary black powder that continued to be the basic propellant for small arms throughout the remainder of the century. It had an important consequence in the development of rifled artillery, in that it made it possible for a gun of any given caliber to eject a heavier projectile than before. By lengthening the bore, greater muzzle velocities could be attained. By the end of the century, as a result, muzzle velocities had mounted to almost 3,000 feet per second, and ranges increased in proportion.

The development of slow-burning powders was associated with smokeless powders, which began to come into use late in the century. Apart from the advantage of not betraying a gun's position, the new powders were also relatively slow-burning, giving the thrusting type of propulsion described above. Their most effective use was in rifled pieces (which now could be made larger since the pressures to be sustained were smaller) whose elongated projectiles were both more accurate — particularly at the longer ranges — than spherical shot and could sustain higher velocities against air resistance.

Late in the century, largely through Alfred Nobel's work, the nature and the technique of detonation of the new explosives TNT, tetryl, picric acid, PETN, and cyclonite became known. Picric acid was first used in battle in the Russo-Japanese War (1904–1905); TNT was not a standard military explosive until World War I.

Other applications of chemistry to military technology, which can only be mentioned here, were the whole field of toxic chemical agents, the internal combustion engine, rocket and jet propulsion, and the improved and high explosives of the twentieth century. In this connection, too, should be mentioned the solution of the ancient problem of gunpowder shortages resulting from the scarcity of saltpeter — first, through the discovery of abundant sources of saltpeter in the nitrate deposits of India and Chile, and later through development of processes for extracting nitrogen from the air and from by-products of the manufacture of coke.

One of the presumed founders of ballistics, the sixteenth century mathematician and engineer Niccolo Tartaglia, wrote two treatises on artillery and one on fortification and tried to compute the ranges of cannon by tables derived from a theory of dynamics — but he was devoid of military experience and had no technical knowledge of artillery. His most useful contribution to posterity was a gunner's quadrant, a tool for measuring true angle of elevation. Tartaglia's numerous academic successors wrote voluminously and spun many refinements of his basic theories, but failed to correct his errors (which were fundamental) and added nothing useful.

In the following century, Galileo revolutionized the whole approach to ballistics as one aspect of his study of the laws of physics and dynamics. Fascinated by the theory of projectiles, he studied the artillery pieces of his day as the best means of testing his mathematical theories. From his studies came the parabolic theory (1638), which, although itself erroneous, did correct the most basic errors of Tartaglia's theories. Tartaglian theory retained its hold on popular belief, however, until a popularization of Galileo's views appeared in 1674, after which Galilean theory was accepted as gospel well into the eighteenth century.

The art and practice of gunnery and of gun design, meanwhile, remained unaffected. Whether scientifically accurate or not, the ballistical theories of the textbooks were scarcely relevant to the warfare of the time. The utter lack of uniformity in firearms, and the erratic, wholly unpredictable path of a projectile's flight, made analysis almost meaningless. When Benjamin Robins, a British mathematician, did attempt to experiment in the eighteenth century, he found that at a range of 800 yards the cannonball diverged as much as 100 yards to the right or left of the line of fire, and varied as much as 200 yards in the first contact with the ground. Only in the growing use of mortar fire in late seventeenth century warfare did there appear to be some connection between theory and practice, and even here the imperfections of the materiel made the theories of the scientists useless from the gunner's point of view.

Benjamin Robins, however, did achieve a first measure of success in providing a scientific basis for gunnery. He studied not only exterior ballistics, the subject of all previous theorizing, but also interior ballistics (the motion of projectiles inside the gun), and terminal ballistics (their behavior at the end of flight). Robins perceived the many errors in the theories of Galileo and Newton — such as ignoring the effect of air currents — and perfected the ballistic pendulum, invented by Cassini in 1707, into an effective instrument for measuring the velocity of a projectile.

The triumph of scientific ballistics came in the nineteenth century. Only then had metallurgy and mechanics reached a stage of development that made possible the design and manufacture of weapons sufficiently precise in their dimensions and predictable in their behavior to provide a basis for scientific analysis. The effects of scientific ballistics on military technology can best be viewed along with those of the new scientific metallurgy in the general context of the military revolution of the nineteenth century (see Chapter XX).

Appearance of Electricity in Communications

It is doubtful that anyone has yet (1980) been killed by the military use of a purely electronic weapon, although the potential clearly exists. The military function of electronic devices has been, throughout their history, to enhance the lethality of other types of weapons. The earliest were devices to send orders, information, and firing data from point to point without the inherent physical limitations of voice, visual signals, or messenger.

The telegraph, the first of these devices, appears to have been brought into commercial use almost simultaneously in Europe and America about 1830. It consisted of a single wire strung between the places in communication, a battery at one or both of them, a manually operated switch, called a key, by which connection of the battery to the wire could be made or broken, and a coil of wire wound on an iron rod. When current flowed through this coil the iron became magnetic and attracted to itself a movable piece of iron; the click produced when the two came together was noted and interpreted by the operator at the receiving end. The intervals between clicks at the receiving end were the same as operations of the key at the sending end, and a code translated sequences of clicks into the letters of the alphabet. It became possible to transmit as many as fifty letters per minute. Two stations could communicate through intermediate points by means of a "relay," which permitted passing messages over indefinitely long lines. Telegraphs were first used militarily in the Crimean War. Submarine cables came into use about 1851, the first between Dover and Calais, and led to long-range telegraphic communication between London and Paris on the one hand and the Allied Crimean War base at Varno on the other. Telegraphs were used extensively in the American Civil War by both sides. Trans-Atlantic cables were functioning by 1866.

The telegraph originated in an industrial environment that could furnish almost nothing to support it; the wires (bare and insulated), the pole insulators, and the batteries were all completely new inventions. There were never enough telegraphic instruments manufactured to stimulate new industrial forms or products. It was the appearance of the electric light, not the telegraph, that made such equipment available for industrial exploitation in new industries.

When the telephone and radio appeared, they were more effective and eclipsed the telegraph in military importance. Recently, however, the telegraph has come back into its own, in the form of the teletype and more sophisticated devices. It can process information far more rapidly than is possible verbally, and it is the natural means of communication between the robots that loom ever larger on civil and military horizons.

Like the telegraph, the telephone appeared almost simultaneously at several places in America and Europe. Its first usable version — in 1876 — is usually attributed to Alexander Graham Bell. There was an electrical industry ready to support the telephone when it appeared. This derived mostly from the electric light trade and the electricity generating system that supported it. There were also the beginnings of a mathematical theory of the flow of electricity through long lines, which had come from efforts to improve the telegraph.

Radio can be used to transmit telegraphic, telephonic, or more complicated types of signal. Its essential feature is the transmission of electrical signals without wires, allowing communication where wire-laying is difficult. This communication can be between mobile stations as well as between fixed stations. Radio phenomena were first demonstrated in Germany by Heinrich Hertz in 1885 but were first adapted to communications by Guglielmo Marconi about 1908. In contrast to the telegraph and telephone, radio was developed largely on the initiative of military authorities. It is noteworthy that although the requirements that developed radio were largely military, the work was done almost entirely in private industrial laboratories.

The multiplicity of technological developments in the late nineteenth and early twentieth centuries forced sometimes reluctant military professionals to broaden their horizons and to create new standards while coping with the unprecedented changes in warfare made possible by the Industrial Revolution. In addition to the direct effect of new and improved instruments of warfare, industrialization had other significant consequences in the conduct of war. Perhaps the most significant change from an essentially agricultural economy to industrialization was the release of a greater percentage of national manpower to both the armed forces and the developing war industries. Larger armies could be raised and supported than in the past, and the development of steam transportation and the electric telegraph facilitated the movement and control of these larger forces.

But it was in the refinement and proliferation of weapons that the new technology had its greatest effect.

XX. The Great Transition: Sail to Steam, Wood to Iron, Broadside to Turret 1800–1865

The Naval Revolution

During the last half of the eighteenth century the political and economic consequences of Britain's naval supremacy made the importance of sea power evident to the leaders of all European nations. Horatio Nelson, shattering the old order of naval tactics, had an influence upon naval thinking comparable to that of Napoleon in land warfare. However, just as the practice of the naval art under Nelson's genius attained its highest possible limits with the technology available, the Industrial Revolution arrived to release navies from dependence on the wind, on primitive, almost rigid, guns, and (eventually) from the tyranny of flag signals.

During the fifty-six years between the Battle of Trafalgar and the Battle of Hampton Roads there occurred a revolution in naval warfare that brought more sweeping changes than that which had occurred in the three previous centuries, and that was at least as remarkable as that which occurred in the century that followed. The warships with which Nelson defeated French Admiral Pierre Villeneuve at Trafalgar on October 21, 1805, were not remarkably different from those with which Howard and Drake defeated Medina Sidonia in the English Channel more than two centuries earlier. Either of the vessels that fought at Hampton Roads on March 9, 1862, could have singlehandedly destroyed the combined fleets of Nelson and Villeneuve.

Nelson and Trafalgar

But in 1805 those two fleets, the most powerful naval forces their respective nations had ever put to sea, were to meet in the climactic battle that was to decide, once and for all, their century-long struggle for mastery of the seas and worldwide colonial domination. On October 21, 1805, Nelson's fleet of 27 ships of the line intercepted Villeneuve's 33 ships 20 miles off Spain's Cape Trafalgar.

Villeneuve, who had been in Cadiz, was sailing for the Straits of Gibraltar and the Mediterranean in response to orders from Napoleon. The emperor, about to initiate his victorious Ulm-Austerlitz campaign against Austria, wanted the French fleet to support that campaign by attacking Austria's ally Naples. Villeneuve knew that the English fleet was not far away, but he hoped to reach Gibraltar and reinforcements in the Mediterranean before Nelson realized his intentions. But Nelson's strategic sense immediately grasped the French admiral's intentions, and, when the two fleets sighted each other, Nelson had the weather gauge; the French could not avoid the battle.

Nelson, aware that decisive outcomes were rare in sea battles between fleets of wooden, broadside-firing ships of the line, had been thinking tactically about this battle while waiting for the French fleet. He had written a memorandum for his captains in which he gave them his general tactical plan for "bringing the enemy to battle in such a manner as to make the business decisive. . . ." Leaving them freedom and flexibility to engage hostile ships as seemed best, he told his captains that the British fleet would be in two columns — one under his direction, the other under his second in command, Admiral Lord Collingwood. He would strike the center of the anticipated French line-ahead formation and overwhelm its rear half "before the van of the enemy could succor their rear." He concluded his memorandum with the following paragraph, summarizing his tactical philosophy:

> *The second in command will in all possible things direct the movements of his line by keeping them as compact as the nature of the circumstances will admit. Captains are to look to their particular line as their rallying point. But in case signals can neither be seen nor perfectly understood no captain can do very wrong if he places his ship alongside that of an enemy.*

Two American naval historians have written that "this Memorandum is noteworthy especially for its spirit of aggressiveness, its trust of juniors, its simplicity, and its confidence of victory."* It was also noteworthy as the final word in the long argument between British naval tacticians about the melee versus the line. Nelson had the best of both: he retained the controlled approach to battle provided by the line—but with two lines he was planning to break up the enemy formation in the fashion advocated by the melee school, and to bring maximum firepower to bear against a fraction of the enemy fleet.

As the fleets approached each other, Nelson's HMS *Victory* led the northern British column toward the van of the French line, making the French believe this would be a traditional line-ahead battle. At that time he had a signal hoisted to the yardarm: "England expects that every man will do his duty." Then, with the fleets nearly in gunshot of each other, he ordered his column to change course for the center of the French line, and had another signal displayed: "Engage the enemy more closely."

That signal remained at the *Victory*'s yardarm until it was finally shot away during the bitter battle. Nelson's tactics worked as well as was possible in the days of sailing warships, when—as he had written in his memorandum—"nothing is sure in a sea fight beyond all others." It was perhaps the most decisive fleet action of broadside sailing vessels: 18 French and Spanish ships were captured without loss of a single English vessel.

There was a grievous English loss, however. Nelson was mortally wounded, and died shortly after the conclusion of the two-hour battle. But England's loss was also England's gain: the glorious death in victory of a hero whose reputation could never be tarnished. Because, in fact, England had no more need of Nelson

---

*E.B. Potter and Chester W. Nimitz, eds., *Sea Power; A Naval History* (Englewood Cliffs: Prentice-Hall, 1960), p. 163.

living. He had destroyed French naval power and established Britain as mistress of the seas in the most decisive major naval victory — tactically and strategically — of history.

Furthermore, the Industrial Revolution had already initiated the chain of events that would soon eliminate fleets like Nelson's — but not Britain's mastery of the seas. The first successful steamship had been launched on the Saône River in France in 1783. And Robert Fulton had initiated the work that would lead to the voyage of the steamship *Clermont* up the Hudson River from New York to Albany and back, less than two years after Trafalgar.

The New Naval Ordnance

But the first great impact of the Industrial Revolution on naval warfare was not in the area of ship construction but rather in heavy naval ordnance. And the most revolutionary innovation was the hooped or built-up gun, which, in conjunction with rifling at a later stage of development, would initiate the transition toward the powerful ordnance of the twentieth century.

At least as early as 1829 a French naval officer, A. Thiery, succeeded in shrinking an iron envelope over a cast iron gun barrel. By 1843 Professor Daniel Treadwell of Harvard University was constructing a few built-up guns by this method for the U.S. Government. The built-up technique produced a strong compressive tension on the barrel, so that the expansive force and heat of the exploding powder charge encountered the resistance of his compression from the first instant of the explosion. Not only would this type of construction not have been possible with the techniques of casting and forging available fifty or a hundred years earlier, but its very purpose would not have been understood had not the knowledge of the properties of metals and of interior ballistics been developed. It appears, in fact, that the method was a direct product of that growth of knowledge and technique, and was not responsive to the pressure of any specific need; necessity was not the mother of this invention.

However, the built-up gun was not adopted readily by naval services, which preferred improved cast iron guns. In 1851 Commander John A. Dahlgren, U.S. Navy, developed a cast iron gun that was adopted by the Navy five years later. The Dahlgren guns were muzzle-loading smoothbores, and their distinctive feature was their shape, which resembled a beer bottle. The shape was due to a design that placed the greatest thickness of metal at points of greatest stress. In 1860 Major Thomas J. Rodman, U.S. Army, invented the hollow-casting process, by which a gun was cast around a core chilled by a coil of running water. This method — a logical progression from early experiments with built-up guns — caused the interior of the bore to harden first. The outer layers of metal, shrinking inward as they cooled, exerted continuous pressure on the hardened interior. Thus the explosive force of the charge was absorbed by the entire thickness of metal surrounding the bore, rather than by successive layers expanding outward. The hollow-casting technique was applied in the construction of Dahlgrens and most other heavy cast iron guns of the U.S. Navy during the Civil War and for twenty years after. The great Dahlgren and Rodman smoothbores, cast in calibers up to 15 inches, proved their effectiveness in smashing through the armor of Confederate ironclads, causing these guns to be rated as the best in service in their day.

In 1859 the British Admiralty Board, in response to the impending completion of the French ironclad *Gloire*, ordered a large number of 40-pounder and 70-pounder rifled guns of built-up construction from the prominent gunmaker William Armstrong. Armstrong's guns combined three advanced features: breech-loading, built-up construction, and rifling. The projectiles were ringed with soft metal bands — rotating bands — to be gripped by the grooves of the rifling. Because it assured accuracy and greater terminal velocity, rifling was widely regarded as the best answer to armor.

Built-up construction had not yet attracted much attention. There was, however, a close relationship between rifling and built-up construction. Rifling, which was mainly designed to improve accuracy, placed extra strain on the tensile strength of large gun barrels because of the tight fit of the projectile and the resulting greatly increased pressure from the exploding powder on the walls of the barrel. In addition, elongated projectiles, a natural corollary of rifling, since they permitted both greater range and greater accuracy, placed a heavier inert mass in front of the powder charge than did spherical shot of the same diameter. As a result, early rifled cannon were prone to burst. The barrels had to be made stronger. Although it was not immediately apparent, the built-up technique was the answer.

About this time the Krupps of Essen, who had for some time led in developing steel for use in artillery, perfected the Bessemer process. By providing cheap case steel of good quality, they contributed further to the development of new guns.

The Emergence of Steam Propulsion

Meanwhile, in the late 1830s and 1840s the navies of the world had begun to experiment with steam propulsion. Aside from the inherent conservatism of naval men there had been two major practical deterrents to the adoption of steam for naval vessels. First was the fact that until the early 1840s propulsion of ships powered by steam was provided by large paddlewheels on each side of the vessel. Not only did the paddlewheel reduce the space for placing guns by as much as one third, they, and the exposed engines that drove them, also were very vulnerable to enemy cannonballs. Second, a steamship could cruise only a few hundred miles before it required refueling, while a sailing vessel could go thousands of miles and many months without having to put into port.

Actually, during the War of 1812 Robert Fulton had designed a steam warship that attempted to solve the first of these problems. The USS *Demologus*, intended to break the British blockade of America's Atlantic seacoast, had a single paddlewheel between two hulls, with outer walls five feet thick. She was not finished before the war ended, and never operated at sea. Not for more than twenty years did any navy attempt another steam warship. And the first models that did appear, in the mid-1830s, used steam only as an auxiliary to sail.

Then, in 1837, John Ericsson, a Swedish-born engineer, introduced the screw propeller, which would in time eliminate the paddlewheel problem and permit the emplacement of machinery below a vessel's waterline. One of the first to realize this was U.S. Navy captain Robert F. Stockton. When the British Admiralty refused to try the screw propeller, Stockton persuaded Ericsson to come to the United States to help him design and build a new steam warship.

Ericsson, Stockton and the USS *Princeton*

This was the USS *Princeton*, the first screw-propelled warship in the world, and also the first to have all of its machinery below the waterline. Stockton planned two 12-inch guns for the *Princeton*, making her at least theoretically the most powerful warship of her time. Brilliant, erratic, and one of the most controversial figures in American military history, Stockton turned down an offer to become President Tyler's Secretary of the Navy in order to complete the *Princeton* and her powerful armament.

Ericsson was even more brilliant, perhaps the greatest naval designer of history. Not only did he begin a revolution in warship construction by inventing the screw propeller, he produced the first large wrought iron, built-up gun, the 12-inch "Oregon," which was mounted on the afterdeck of the *Princeton*. He would later complete the warship construction revolution he started by inventing both the big-gun turret and the first all-iron warship to go into battle — the USS *Monitor*.

Sparks soon flew between these two exceptional men. The principal cause of the dispute that later estranged them was the design and construction of the other 12-inch gun for the *Princeton*, a weapon which Stockton called the "Peacemaker." Ericsson protested that the Stockton method of working the wrought iron barrel of the Peacemaker could result in undiscoverable flaws that might dangerously weaken the gun. Stockton imperiously dismissed Ericsson, completed his gun, and invited the principal officials in Washington to observe the test-firing of the Peacemaker as the newly commissioned *Princeton* steamed down the Potomac River below the capital.

When the gun was fired it blew up, killing the Secretary of State, the Secretary of the Navy, and several congressmen. Stockton, standing beside the gun when it exploded, miraculously escaped. So did President Tyler, who was below decks chatting with other distinguished guests and their wives at a sumptuous buffet that Stockton had provided. Stockton was exonerated of blame (as he should have been) by a board of inquiry, became a commodore and the senior officer of the Navy, and went on to a dramatic confrontation with General Stephen W. Kearny during the conquest and pacification of California in the Mexican War.

Despite the fact that Ericsson's Oregon had already been successfully test-fired, the U.S. Navy barred further use of wrought iron and built-up guns, and the arts of metallurgy and gun design suffered a severe setback.

Sinope

However, by the mid-1850s the greatly improved cast iron guns, combined with improvements in shell projectiles, had greatly increased the power of naval ordnance. This was dramatically demonstrated on November 20, 1853, when a Russian squadron armed with the new shell-firing guns destroyed a Turkish fleet at Sinope. Not only did this precipitate the Crimean War, it demonstrated the devastating potential of improved naval ordnance, and revealed the total vulnerability of wooden ships to these weapons. Both sides in that war hastily created armored floating batteries, which took part in subsequent naval operations of the Crimean War. A logical evolution led to the creation of the French wooden-hulled armor-plated *Gloire*, which caused the panic in Britain when she was commissioned in 1859. The reluctant admiralty was forced to rush construction of its own first armored warship, HMS *Warrior;* the iron-hulled, armored vessel was launched in 1860, and commissioned the following year.

The *Virginia* and the *Monitor*

But it was an armor-plated Confederate vessel that, on March 8, 1862, conclusively tolled the bell for wooden warships.

When Virginia seceded from the Union in April 1861, Confederate troops seized the Norfolk Navy Yard. In the port was the 50-gun steam frigate USS *Merrimack*, one of the most modern ships of the Navy. Not having steam up, the vessel was unable to escape, and was scuttled by her crew. However, the Confederates raised her and—following the example being set by France's *Gloire* and Britain's *Warrior*—they constructed an armored casemate on top of the hull of the *Merrimack*. The vessel was renamed CSS *Virginia.*

Spurred by the outbreak of the Civil War, the United States Navy had also been studying the French and British innovations. When Secretary of the Navy Gideon Welles and his advisors learned about what the Confederates were doing at Norfolk with the *Merrimack-Virginia*, they quickly recognized that this new ironclad Confederate warship might break the Union blockade of the Confederacy, and even steam up the Potomac to threaten Washington, possibly winning the war. Faced with this challenge, the Navy Department hastily approved a completely new warship design submitted by John Ericsson.

The Ericsson design was for a relatively small, low-lying, iron-hulled, armor-plated and armor-decked warship carrying only two guns in a single revolving turret. But these were 11-inch, smoothbore Dahlgrens, considerably more powerful than any of the *Virginia*'s three 9-inch Dahlgrens, and two 6-inch and two 7-inch rifles. In mid-September 1861 Gideon Welles signed a contract with Ericsson, and in the incredible time of 101 working days the new vessel, named USS *Monitor*, was completed. She was commissioned on February 25, and on March 6 set out from New York on her shakedown cruise. This was also her cruise to battle, to Chesapeake Bay. It was known that the *Virginia* was almost ready, and so the *Monitor* was to join the Union fleet blockading Norfolk and the James River.

On March 8, as anticipated, the *Virginia*, under Flag Officer Franklin Buchanan — former commander, USN — steamed out of Norfolk into Hampton Roads. In about three hours of one-sided battle, the *Virginia* destroyed the 44-gun sailing frigate *Congress* and the 21-gun sloop-of-war *Cumberland* and severely damaged her former sister ship, the 50-gun screw frigate *Minnesota*, which ran aground. The 50-gun screw frigate *Roanoke*, the 44-gun sailing frigate *St. Lawrence*, and various other smaller vessels of the blockading squadron escaped a similar fate only by withdrawing to shoal waters near the protective batteries of Fort Monroe. The *Virginia* — off which iron cannonballs had been bouncing all afternoon — probably could have endured the fire of the shore batteries, but the weight of armor had so increased her draft that the Confederate commander was reluctant to go too close to shore. Furthermore, when she had rammed the *Congress*, that vessel sank so rapidly that the *Virginia*'s ram had broken off, causing a slight leak. Also the protruding muzzles of two guns had been hit, and the guns put out of action. The *Virginia* returned to Norfolk to repair this slight damage and to refuel, and prepared to come out on the ninth to complete the destruction of the blockading Union squadron.

That night, the *Monitor* arrived from New York. It had been a difficult trip for the new warship, since she proved not to be very seaworthy. At 9:00 A.M. she joined the battered Union ships in Hampton Roads. Thus dramatically was the stage set for the battle that forever changed naval warfare. Lieutenant John L. Worden, captain of the *Monitor*, took station as directed to protect the grounded *Minnesota*, and anchored his ship.

The following morning the *Virginia* came out, expecting to break the blockade, to find her way barred by the *Monitor*. During the next four hours the two vessels maneuvered near the *Minnesota*, pounding each other with their great guns at point-blank range, neither inflicting serious damage on the other. The *Monitor* was able to outmaneuver the clumsy *Virginia*, and had somewhat the better of the exchange. The *Virginia* finally went aground, and had not Lieutenant Worden been injured at the same time by a lucky hit on the narrow eye-slit of his low pilothouse, the Confederate vessel probably would have been destroyed or captured. As it was, she was able to pull herself free, and, taking advantage of the temporary confusion in the Union pilothouse, the badly leaking *Virginia* withdrew from the action, and limped back to Norfolk.

Tactically the battle was a draw, but strategically the *Monitor* had won a decisive victory. The Union blockade was reestablished, never again to be seriously damaged, and the Confederacy was doomed.

Two other new naval developments first found significant use in the Civil War. The first was the submarine, on which Confederate naval engineers made important developments. The problem of underwater propulsion would remain a hindrance until development of the gasoline engine and the electric storage battery after the turn of the century.

The second development was submarine mines (originally called torpedoes), which came into common use during the Civil War, and were used effectively by the Confederates to protect their ports and coastal defenses from Union warships. The South and North both used such mines offensively by attaching them to the ends of spars or booms attached to submarines or other small craft. By the end of the century, these spar torpedoes had been transformed by compressed air self-propulsion into a much more lethal threat as prototypes of the modern torpedo. With this development there came into being in the world's navies the fast but fragile torpedo boat, and close on its heels the larger, faster torpedo-boat destroyer.

But the most important naval consequence of the Civil War was that the *Monitor* and her turret had ushered in a new era in naval warfare. The unseaworthy *Monitor* foundered in a gale off Cape Hatteras later that year. But other ironclads had already joined the Union Navy. And Ericsson and other naval architects soon solved the problem of wedding his revolving battery — introduced on the *Monitor* — to a seaworthy armored hull.

The experience of the American Civil War broke down the skeptical resistance of professional naval men to the substitution of iron for wood in ship construction and virtually completed the transition from sail to steam that had been well underway before the war began. This first of modern wars started trends in naval construction and warfare at sea that would come to fruition in the world wars of the next centuries.

XXI. Rifle, Conoidal Bullet, and Dispersion
1800 – 1875

The Appearance of the Rifle Musket

The earliest significant technological change affecting land warfare in the nineteenth century was the invention and introduction of the percussion cap, already described. It eliminated most of the uncertainty from what had for centuries been one of the least reliable of the many actions involved in using a hand firearm on the battlefield, namely the act of firing itself. Flintlocks had misfired about every seventh shot; percussion caps reduced misfires to fewer than one in two hundred rounds.

Even more revolutionary, however, was the cylindro-conoidal bullet, which finally made practicable the replacement of the inaccurate, short-ranged smoothbore musket by the highly accurate, much longer-ranged rifle that became the basic infantry weapon. Until the development of the new bullet, the rate of fire of rifles had been slower than that of smoothbores, because they were much more difficult to load. The expansible feature, provided by the action of the powder gas on a cavity in the base of the lead bullet, made possible a bullet small enough to load easily, yet large enough upon firing to fit tightly into the spiral lands and grooves of the barrel and to acquire maximum spin for consistent accuracy. Range and accuracy were further facilitated by a shape that gave less resistance to the air after firing.

To equal the performance of a rifle musket the smoothbore required twice the quantity of ammunition expenditure at 200 paces, five times the quantity at 300 paces, and at least ten times the quantity at 400 paces. Beyond 400 paces the smoothbore was completely useless, while the rifle could hit larger targets, like troop formations, at 800 yards, and at 1,000 yards the bullet retained sufficient terminal energy to penetrate four inches of soft pine.

The introduction of the rifle musket and its conoidal bullet in the decade between 1850 and 1860 was to have the greatest immediate and measurable revolutionary impact on war of any new weapon or technological development of war before or since. When and if tactical nuclear weapons appear on the battlefield, presumably they will have an even greater effect. But certainly not even the high-explosive shells, airplanes, or tanks of the twentieth century were to have effects of contemporary scale and significance comparable to the rifled musket in its early days.

The principal reason for this dramatic rise in the lethality of small arms in comparison to artillery and cold steel was that with the rifled musket every infantryman had a weapon with the same effective range as the largest and most powerful cannon—in other words to the limit of effective vision, or the crest of the next hill or ridge. At the same time, artillery gunners became much more vulnerable to infantry fire, and, save when in defensive fortified emplacements, artillery was unable to sustain the firepower that had made it dominant on Napoleonic battlefields.

Breech-loading was another feature of early firearms, long in disuse, which the science and technology of the nineteenth century liberated from its ancient disabilities. Traditionally the difficulty with breech-loading weapons in the days of imprecisely fitting metal parts had been the leakage of gas and flame from the exploding charge through the seams of the breech. Associated with the development of nineteenth century breech-loading weapons was the metallic cartridge, which combined projectile, powder charge, and percussion cap in a single capsule. Made from a special alloy of copper or other soft metal, it expanded under the heat of the explosion and effectively sealed off the rearward escape of released gases. Breech-loading allowed a rifleman to reload more quickly and without standing and exposing himself to enemy fire.

The principal and only really basic subsequent development in small arms was the principle of repeating and, later, automatic fire, which found an immense variety of applications in the late nineteenth and twentieth centuries. Automatic weapons did not stem from new metallurgical developments but from mechanical invention, made potent by the earlier metallurgical and ballistic advances.

The New Artillery

It was in the development of artillery, especially large weapons, that the new metallurgy, chemistry, and ballistics of the nineteenth century eventually had their most spectacular effects, although these were not consummated until the twentieth century. Cavelli in Italy made the first successful rifled cannon in 1846 — breechloaders bored with two spiral grooves and using cylindrical shot. A little later, Joseph Whitworth, a leading English gunmaker, produced a "rifled" gun, also a breechloader, in which a twisting hexagonal bore was substituted for spiral grooves.

In the Italian War of 1859, Napoleon III's rifled artillery proved decisively superior to the smoothbores of the Austrians in both range and accuracy. Yet most armies clung to smoothbores until well into the third quarter of the century, mainly because they were cheaper and more reliable than the new experimental cannon. In fact, because their effective range on the battlefield was limited to the limits of vision of the gunners, the new artillery ordnance could not be truly cost effective until that range of vision could be substantially increased. In the American Civil War, both rifled and smoothbore artillery were used on both sides, but the favorite piece, for Federals and Confederates alike, was the muzzle-loading, smoothbore, bronze "Napoleon." This serviceable gun, actually a

12-pounder gun-howitzer, was already obsolete in Europe, and its days were numbered in America. The comparative softness of bronze had always been a serious shortcoming, and the new metallurgical techniques, together with the scientific study of interior ballistics, now made it possible to exploit the superior hardness and durability of iron.

The rifled musket itself was not a product of either the new metallurgy or the new ballistics, since the principle of increasing accuracy and range by rifling had long been well known. The development of rifled weapons in the nineteenth century profited greatly, however, from the increase in knowledge in both these fields. With the improved techniques and machinery of metal working that became available, it was possible to bore and rifle barrels with far greater precision than ever before. For centuries the manufacture of handguns had been the task of the skilled gunsmith, who produced each weapon as an individual product, often a work of art. The basic metal had been wrought iron, the usual process one of wrapping and welding a strip of metal around a core. The first rifled barrel drilled in a bar of cast steel was made in the nineteenth century in the Remington gun factory in New York. The Remington shop was also one of the first to develop assembly-line techniques of production, based on the principle of interchangeable parts introduced early in the century by Eli Whitney and others. In the new rifled weapons of this period, the science of ballistics found a medium for systematic experimentation and rapid accumulation and refinement of knowledge of all aspects of the behavior of projectiles.

The Effects of New Weapons on Tactics and Organization

With the weapons of war undergoing this impressive technological revolution and becoming progressively longer ranged, more accurate, and capable of much greater rates of sustained fire, clearly there was need for matching improvements in organization, tactics and logistical support. The development of the division and corps during the Napoleonic era was followed by a long period of stagnation, if not retrogression, in organization and tactics. For example, the one notable conflict between 1815 and 1845, the Russo–Turkish War (1828–1829), was remarkable for the obsolescent infantry tactics employed, and the Russian departure from the Napoleonic operational and strategic principle of concentration of forces. In like respect, the French and British armies reverted to parade-type drill at the expense of combat training.

In organization and tactics armies responded slowly to the weapons changes, largely because the new weapons demanded battlefield dispersion, which professional soldiers feared — quite understandably — would lead to loss of control. The problem, of course, was that if soldiers were dispersed to make it more difficult for the enemy to find them it would be equally difficult for their own commanders to see them. Problems of coordination between adjacent units, difficult at best, would also be greatly acerbated if intermediate commanders could not adapt their tactical maneuvers to clear and easily identifiable lines of friendly troops. It would take another phase of the Industrial Revolution — the electrical-electronic phase — before tactics could catch up with weapons development.

The new weapons developments were discussed thoroughly, and sometimes heatedly, in the professional military literature of the period and in the upper echelons of military commands of many nations. But mainly because of their concern about battlefield control, most professionals in midcentury agreed that no basic changes in organization or tactics were required, and that the role of cavalry was not affected by them. In retrospect it is obvious that such preconceptions caused military specialists to disregard clear evidence. There were to be disastrous consequences in the years ahead.

In most of the armies that were at war during this time, in Europe and in the United States, either the brigade or the regiment was the tactical element. However, the division was the standard organization for convenience in administration and maneuver. The term "division" was rather loosely used, generally designating either some portion of the battle line, as in medieval practice, or a force of infantry and artillery larger than a brigade, but otherwise indeterminate in size. (In fact, the term is still used loosely and without standardization.)

Great Britain and the United States provided by law and regulation for maintenance of divisions, but in peacetime neither maintained active organizations larger than regiments. In war these regiments were more or less haphazardly organized into brigades and divisions that were disbanded at the end of hostilities. There were no peacetime staffs for the larger formations, and so wartime staff officers had had no opportunity to practice their grave responsibilities.

In those armies that did maintain peacetime divisions and corps, both structure and staffs were rudimentary by modern standards. Even in Prussia, where long strides had been made toward a functioning general staff, it was concentrated primarily at army level. But staffs in other armies were predominantly concerned with administration and supply, rather than with planning and directing operations, which were still considered to be the prerogative of the commander — or of the council of war, when the commander wanted advice from subordinate commanders (not from his staff). And Prussian commanders, as new General Staff Chief Helmuth von Moltke discovered in 1864, were no exception.

Theoretically, in all armies where it existed actually or prospectively, the division was a combined-arms force, consisting basically of infantry, with artillery, cavalry, and sometimes engineer support organic or attached. In general, it comprised two infantry brigades with two regiments each; its combat support varied from country to country and often from division to division. In France and most other European countries a war-strength division usually was no larger than 5,000 men, and often as small as 2,500. In Russia and Prussia, however, the division consisted of 12,000 or more effectives. Strength figures were unreliable since, even in those countries that managed to provide manpower to paper or establishment strength, units were soon reduced far below their authorized complements as a result of sickness, desertion and straggling, and ultimately battle casualties. Study of the campaigns of this period is hampered by the fact that it is usually difficult, and often impossible, to determine whether strengths given in the accounts are those of effectives actually present, or only the paper strengths of the units involved.

The most important conflicts of this period were the United States-Mexican War (1846 – 1848), the Crimean War (1854 – 1856), the American Civil War (1861 – 1865), the Austro-Prussian War (1866), and the Franco-Prussian War (1870 – 1871).

The Mexican War was virtually ignored in Europe. Its principal military significance was the demonstration of an exceptionally high order of professionalism in the officers of the small United States Army, permitting it to defeat a much larger Mexican Army decisively.

Most of the lessons of the Crimean War were negative; it presented no radical, or even evolutionary, departures in weapons, organization, and tactics. In fact, standards of tactics were generally abominable on both sides. Nevertheless, it provided an almost unnoticed indication of the efficacy of field fortifications against the weapons of the time. This was demonstrated at the siege of Sebastopol. There the British and French fired 2,381,042 rounds of artillery ammunition from 2,587 guns over a twelve-month period. This rate of consumption and relative paucity of results were contrary to all current military expectations, yet they aroused only passing professional interest. Also significant was the introduction of electronic communications, in the form of the telegraph.

The American Civil War

Many historians have termed the American Civil War the last of the old and the first of the modern wars. This does not overstate the case; in this war occurred the revolution in weaponry and tactics which, although not perceived by European soldiers, was to come to bloody fruition in 1914.

At the outset of the war both armies were equipped principally with muzzle-loading percussion-cap smoothbore muskets of various makes and calibers. The universal infantry weapon of the Union armies ultimately became the Springfield .58-caliber rifle, firing the minié conoidal "ball," but still a percussion-cap muzzle-loader. Produced by Southern arsenals, it also became the standard Confederate infantry arm, supplemented by small numbers of rifled muskets purchased abroad. Captured Union equipment also contributed to the Confederate inventory.

Some special Union units, such as Colonel Hiram Berdan's two regiments of sharpshooters, were armed with the Sharps breech-loading rifle of .58 caliber. And in the last two years the Union cavalry was increasingly armed with the Sharps breech-loading carbine and the Spencer and Henry magazine carbines. Some Spencer rifles were also issued to Union infantry units. When captured by the Confederates, these arms could not be adapted to their own use, since they took metallic rim-fire cartridges unobtainable in the South.

The new fixed ammunition affected the use of all weapons. In artillery the wrought iron rifled gun of three-inch bore, still muzzle-loaded, had come generally into use as a Union fieldpiece. Percussion and time-fuzed shells, of low fragmentation, were commonly employed by both sides, and shrapnel was in general use. Counterbattery fires were employed extensively, with large-caliber guns dedicated to this purpose. Mining was common on both sides, especially toward the end of the war when the increasing lethality of their weapons had forced both sides to resort to dispersal and field fortifications.

Infantry tactics in the Civil War were linear at the outset and continued so to the end, but with some marked alterations with the passage of time. In the early battles both sides stood in close ranks and fired, by volley or at will, until one or the other launched a charge to bring the issue to bayonet point. As the use of rifled muskets increased, these charges became so costly that dispersal was the general procedure on the defensive, and rudimentary systems of infiltration were being tried on the offensive as the war ended. Entrenchments became the rule and provided firepower bases for both offensive and defensive maneuver.

This was a logical development from the tendency of both sides, without sanction of regulations or manuals, to seek cover from the increasingly lethal rifle fire, at first behind walls and fences, then in hasty field works, and finally in elaborate fortifications, as at Vicksburg, Petersburg, Richmond, and Knoxville. The marked increase in lethality in the hand weapons used in the Civil War was offset to some extent by this increasing tendency of both sides to defend themselves by taking cover. Nevertheless no officially sanctioned innovation in infantry tactics took place during the war.

By the end of the first year the Union forces had been reorganized into divisions and corps, each corps consisting of two or three divisions, and each division of two or three brigades of four (occasionally three) regiments each. Artillery, generally four batteries, was assigned to each division, and one regiment of cavalry was assigned to each corps, with a troop or squadron sometimes at division level. This organization, with two major exceptions, persisted to the end of the war. The first exception was that cavalry eventually was concentrated in its own divisions and corps, where its value was tremendously increased. (This was a reversion, of course, to the Napoleonic concept of mass employment; the comparison with modern practices of employment of armor is obvious.) The other exception, also a reversion to Napoleonic logic, was that artillery reserves were created at corps and army, significantly enhancing the usefulness of that arm.

Confederate armies were organized into divisions during the winter of 1861–1862. There was lack of uniformity in divisions as well as in brigades, divisions consisting of two to six brigades and brigades of three to six regiments. Occasionally a battery of artillery was assigned to a brigade, but, in general, this arm was concentrated under corps or "wing" command. In the Confederate armies of the West, corps were organized in temporary "wings" under one of the division commanders until late 1862, when a permanent corps organization was adopted.

In both armies throughout the war the tactical infantry element was the brigade disposed in line. The Confederate armies from the first tended to concentrate cavalry and artillery, a practice adopted by the Union armies after the utility of these arms had been repeatedly demonstrated by Confederate successes. In no way did this conflict revolutionize the division structure, nor did the division organization itself directly affect the conduct of the war.

The Impact of Moltke and the Prussian General Staff

In the seven weeks during which the Austro-Prussian War lasted, the breech-loading rifle was given its first full-scale test in battle. Despite a serious shortcoming in design, the Prussian breech-loading "needle gun" (so called because of its long firing pin) met this test so well in the crucial Battle of Königgratz, or Sadowa, that objections to breech-loading guns were thenceforth silenced in all armies.

However, Moltke realized that Prussian cavalry had not performed as well as it could have and should have. His failure — and that of lower commanders — to push the Prussian horsemen aggressively in advance of the army for screening and reconnaissance purposes could have had disastrous consequences in the week before Königgratz, as the Prussian armies were blindly pushing their way through the Bohemian mountain passes. As a result some advanced Prussian elements literally blundered their way into unforeseen meeting engagements with Austrians around the periphery of northern Bohemia. Thereafter Moltke saw to it that Prussian commanders at all levels were reminded of the crucial importance of cavalry; for reconnaissance, to establish contact with the enemy, and then to maintain constant surveillance over all hostile activities. Equal stress was laid upon the use of cavalry to screen the movements of the main elements of the army, to prevent enemy cavalry from gaining comparable information, and to provide outpost cover to delay and harass an approaching foe.

Hardly less important were the deficiencies Moltke discovered in Prussian artillery weapons and doctrine. As for the weapons, the answer was clearly to hasten and complete as soon as possible the partial conversion of Prussian artillery to steel, rifled, breech-loading cannon. But more fundamental was the employment of these cannon. It had been the Prussian practice to have the artillery toward the rear of the marching columns, on the understandable premise that the artillery generally would be deployed behind all of the infantry except the reserves and rear guard. But what this meant was that the columns debouching from the mountain passes were unsupported by artillery when they met the Austrians in the Bohemian foothills. The same problem of delay in providing artillery support to the engagement elements occurred, although less seriously, on the main battlefield of Königgratz. From that time, however, all available Prussian artillery would be engaged in battle at the earliest possible opportunity. The Prussians pioneered the modern concept that the artillery's reserve is its ammunition.

With characteristic thoroughness the Prussians applied to their army the lessons of 1866 and entered the Franco-Prussian War (1870–71) better prepared in organization, equipment, command, and tactical doctrine than any army up to that time. The result was a surprisingly quick and overwhelming victory over France's Second Empire.

The French, as well as the Prussians, had taken cognizance of the lessons of 1859, 1861–1865, and of 1866, but had grossly misread them. From the devastating effects of rifle-fire use in defense in the Civil War and Austro-Prussian War they had reasoned that the proper tactic was to defend in place, allowing the enemy to waste himself against their rifle fire. The Prussians had also noted the power of the defense but had reasoned further, looking to a well-conducted tactical defense not merely as the proper base for attack against a weakened enemy, but as the logical result of a strategic offensive.

Even before the Austro-Prussian War Moltke had noted the effectiveness of the new infantry rifle-musket, with its long-range, accurate conoidal bullet. This observation had led him to urge that the Prussian Army adopt the Dreyse breech-loading needle gun, to get maximum firepower volume combined with improved accuracy and range. Then in the 1864 war against Denmark he had observed the effectiveness of Danish defensive fire against attacking Prussians. It is possible, also, that reports of the American Civil War convinced him that a true revolution was taking place in weapons effects.* As a result, in mid-1865 he wrote:

> *The attack of a position is becoming notably more difficult than its defense. The defensive during the first phase of battle offers a decisive superiority. The task of a skillful offensive will consist of forcing our foe to attack a position cho-*

---

*Moltke's writings reflect little interest in the American Civil War, but there does not seem to be any solid authority for the reputed contempt attributed to him in the apparently apocryphal remark that the Union and Confederate armies were "armed mobs." His own experience in the 1864, 1866, and 1871 wars confirmed much of the Civil War experience, in which infantry rifles inflicted 85 to 90 percent of the casualties, while artillery accounted for only 9 to 10 percent. This was in marked contrast to early nineteenth century experience, evidenced as recently as the U.S.-Mexican and the Crimean wars, in which artillery accounted for nearly 50 percent and infantry firearms for barely 40 percent of casualties. The increasing effectiveness of infantry small arms also raised the total casualty rates significantly above those of the early nineteenth century, even above the rates of Napoleon's bloodiest battles.

sen by us, and only when casualties, demoralization, and exhaustion have drained his strength will we ourselves take up the tactical offensive. . . . Our strategy must be offensive, our tactics defensive. [*Emphasis added.*]

There was not time before the outbreak of war with Austria for this concept — almost as revolutionary as the weapons effects that prompted it — to be translated by the conservative Prussian Army into effective tactical doctrine, although Moltke may have had this in the back of his mind when he formulated his encirclement plan at Königgratz. But the effects of firepower on that and the other battlefields of the war provided further evidence that the concept was sound, and he soon translated concept to doctrine.

In the Franco-Prussian War both the French and Prussian armies were armed with breech-loading rifles, the Prussians with their needle guns and the French with the new .51-caliber Chassepot, a bolt-action piece with a rubber ring that sealed the breech against the escape of gas. Like the Prussian weapon, it employed paper cartridges with the cylindro-conoidal bullet. Save for rate of fire, it was a much better weapon in all respects than the needle gun, particularly in accuracy and range.

Although the Prussian field artillery had been completely equipped with Krupp steel breech-loading rifles, the French still depended on muzzle-loading rifled guns. In addition, they had adopted the *mitrailleuse,* a crank-operated machine gun they had cloaked in secrecy so impenetrable that no tactics for its employment had been developed. It was used as artillery rather than as an infantry weapon. Its adoption was in essence a calamity, for it aroused in the French high command an unwarranted sense of superiority. Substituted for artillery pieces, however, it was a dismal failure. Unfortunately, this failure would be so misread by many observers (except the Germans) as to delay the later adoption of the machine gun in the French and British armies — a cruel handicap at the opening of World War I.

Actually some British soldiers had recommended the adoption of the machine gun in the closing years of the nineteenth century. However, considerations of cost lêd Parliament to refuse to appropriate funds for machine guns. As a consequence, the British Army resorted to "rapid fire" drill with the standard infantry rifle, a procedure which in 1914 did in fact lead some of their German opponents to believe that the British Regular Army infantrymen at Mons were equipped with machine guns. It should also be noted that at about the same time the British were considering the machine gun, a similar debate was going on in Germany. One reason the Germans adopted machine guns was to rectify unavoidable deficiencies in the musketry capabilities of their reserve formations. But the Germans also equipped their regulars with these weapons.

Cavalry continued to be the elite arm of most armies, its traditional role in shock action unaltered by its failure in 1866. Even though in 1870–71 it was properly and aggressively used by the Prussians in screening, cavalry again failed against the new infantry weapons. Despite this, horsemen in most armies were still certain that the failure was due to improper use of cavalry, rather than to an inherent vulnerability to lethal weapons.

The organization of the Prussian Army was essentially the same with which it had fought in 1866, although Moltke had reorganized and improved the General Staff. French organization was centered on the army corps as the administrative and maneuver element. Each corps contained two divisions, the divisions being composed of two brigades of two regiments each, with attached artillery, usually four batteries. A serious weakness was the lack of a central coordinating staff, either in the capital or with the field armies.

Tactics on both sides were a combination of linear and columnar, drill being designed to convert from one to the other as required at or just before contact. The French continued to use clouds of skirmishers, who greatly reduced their effectiveness by opening fire at excessive ranges and by failure to press their attacks in advantageous circumstances.

The most significant tactical development of the war was Moltke's masterful demonstration of the validity of his concept of "strategic offensive, tactical defensive." This was the deciding factor in the two major battles of the war: Gravelotte-St. Privat and Sedan. In both of these battles Moltke, assisted by the superb screening and reconnaissance performance of his cavalry, was able to swing his major forces behind the opposing French army in a wide envelopment that placed the Prussians on the French line of communications. The French had no choice but to attack immediately to try to escape from the Prussian trap, while the Prussians won the battles primarily through the superiority of their defensive firepower.

Moltke's concept of strategic or operational offensive maneuvers to place infantry where they could employ tactical defensive firepower against hostile flank or rear was in fact not new. It had been pioneered by Lee and Jackson at Second Manassas and Chancellorsville in 1862 and 1863, improved by Grant in the bitter fighting around Richmond in 1864 and early 1865, and employed brilliantly by the Union general in his final pursuit of Lee to Appomattox.

Nothing in the organization or employment of the combined-arms division during this period had any appreciable effect on the conduct of war, strategically or tactically. It is true that from 1845, when the smoothbore musket was still largely in use, to 1878, when the breech-loading rifle had become commonplace, a major revolution had occurred. But it was technological, not organizational or tactical. The rifled, percussion-cap musket had indeed driven artillery out of the infantry line, forcing artillery also to adopt rifling and breech-loading, and these ultimately were to enhance vastly artillery's utility on the battlefield. The rifled musket, and later the breech-loading rifle, had rendered linear tactics in battle unacceptably costly, a lesson most clearly demonstrated by the American Civil War. Yet close-order linear tactics persisted, at great and unnecessary expense in casualties.

The Railroad and War

Near the middle of the century the railroad had emerged as a valuable logistical ally for the new weaponry. Armies were quick to take advantage of its capacity for transporting men and equipment rapidly. In the Italian War of 1859 the French Army, in a period of three months, transported 604,000 men and 129,000 horses by rail.

In the Civil War railroads demonstrated that they could play an essential role in keeping armies effective in the field for long periods. Spurred by Moltke, who made a thorough study of the potential role of this new mode of transport, the Prussian Army made extensive use of it in 1866 and again in 1870–1871. By the end of the century it was so important that the huge armies employed in the wars before and after the turn of the century could not have been mobilized, maneuvered, or supplied without it.

XXII. Battleship to Dreadnought to Carrier
1865 – 1945

The Rise of the Battleship

The eighty years following the American Civil War saw a revolution in naval warfare almost as dramatic as that of the first five and a half decades of the nineteenth century. The critical point on the continuum of change in naval warfare had been the introduction in 1862 of John Ericsson's *Monitor*, with its revolving, armored, big-gun battery. By the end of the century the battleship was queen of the seas, the new ship of the line, soon to be brought to its ultimate potential by Sir John Fisher's *Dreadnought* and its successors.

During these decades steam power had become a critical consideration in broad national strategic planning. Location of a coaling station not only became a limiting factor but also in many cases directly determined the direction and extent of colonial expansion. Two classic examples were provided in the Spanish-American War. Lacking coaling stations, Admiral George Dewey could move his squadron from Hong Kong to Manila only by the outright purchase of British colliers and their cargoes. And the long cruise of the USS *Oregon* from San Francisco around Cape Horn to join the fleet in Cuban waters (nearly 13,000 nautical miles) sparked the later American acquisition of the Panama Canal Zone and the construction of the canal itself.

Hand in hand with revolutionary developments in ship design and steam propulsion was the continuing, dramatic improvement of armaments.

By the early 1860s large, rifled cannon had fallen into temporary disfavor, since they appeared to be less effective in smashing armor than giant smoothbores firing spherical projectiles. It was obvious to a naval generation not far removed from the carronade that spherical shot could be used with heavier charges than the heavier elongated projectiles of the same caliber, and therefore could deliver a more powerful blow at short range. This was demonstrated over and over again during the Civil War by the success of the great Dahlgrens and Rodmans against Confederate ironclads. The full potential of heavy, rifled ordnance was not realized, in fact, until the development of slow-burning powders in the 1860s. By giving the projectile a prolonged rather than an instantaneous propulsion, charges of slow-burning powder could hurl heavier projectiles and attain higher muzzle velocities and ranges than could the quick-burning powders.

At about the same time that the Armstrong built-up guns were coming into vogue, British captain A. T. Blakely developed and systematized the principles of reinforcing gun tubes by hoops shrunk on at points of greatest stress, and also the technique of concentric tubes of different degrees of elasticity. As we have seen, steel guns also became more common with the advent of cheap Bessemer steel; and combinations of steel, wrought iron, and cast iron were produced, using the techniques of hooped and built-up construction. After about 1881, the use of steel became general, following the perfecting of the Siemens-Martin open-hearth process of steel making, which made possible more complete control over quality. Thereafter, the most powerful naval guns had cast steel tubes with forged steel or wire-bound reinforcing tubes. Even as the refinement of steel metallurgy was vastly increasing the strength that could be built into a gun, the slow-burning powders, with their greater propelling force combined with reduced pressures in the powder chamber, were reducing the need for strength — which made it possible to construct longer, slimmer, and immensely more powerful guns than ever before.

The smokeless powders of the 1880s allowed clear vision for repeated firing, and quick firing was made possible by an engineering development — the short-recoil carriage. New explosives were then applied to shell development, and the high-explosive shell became the final essential element of World War I naval artillery.

In combat the line ahead (ships in a single file) was still the normal tactical formation in the mid-nineteenth century, and broadside fire was optimum. However, at Lissa, on July 20, 1866, in the first major fleet action involving ironclads on both sides, victory was gained by the smaller and theoretically weaker Austrian fleet by a concentrated thrust in wedge formation through a gap in the traditional line-ahead formation of the Italian fleet. Austrian admiral Wilhelm von Tegetthoff again demonstrated that the principle of mass was as applicable on sea as on land, as had Nelson in his similar thrusting attack at Trafalgar sixty-one years earlier.

Nevertheless, these examples of bold deviation from conventional naval tactics, by making and taking advantage of unexpected opportunities, did not alter the fact that a tight, well-controlled line ahead provided opportunities for firepower concentration impossible in other formations. And, as naval guns gained in range, this concentration capability in line ahead became more significant.

In the next important fleet action — the Battle of the Yalu River, September 19, 1894 — the disparity in strength between the stronger Japanese fleet of Admiral Sukenori Ito and the Chinese fleet of Admiral Ting Ju-ch'ang was roughly comparable to that between Italians and Austrians at Lissa. In a very general way the situation at the outset of the battle was similar, as the Japanese approached in line ahead, and the Chinese formed in a somewhat ragged wedge. This was partly because Admiral Ting's two largest vessels could fire the heaviest weight of shell ahead; however, he seems also to have been influenced by the example of Tegetthoff at Lissa, or was unconsciously following his example for one of the tactical reasons that had influenced Tegetthoff: the hope of an opportunity to use his vessels' rams against the broadsides of the Japanese ships. But Ito combined the firepower of a tightly controlled line with the maneuver of his two squadrons, to destroy most of the smaller Chinese vessels at long range, and to force Admiral Ting's surviving heavily armored battleships to withdraw to the coast of China.

Meanwhile the United States, which had ended the Civil War with by far the most powerful ironclad fleet in the world, had allowed that fleet to decay until, twenty years after the war, "naval officers were ashamed to meet even the officers of those small South American republics whose navies were more modern than their own."* And more numerous!

However, between the mid-1880s and the late 1890s there was a remarkable change in American naval affairs, influenced in large part by the writings of Captain Alfred Thayer Mahan. And so, when American fleets were involved in the next two significant naval actions, in 1898, in the Spanish-American War, their vessels were modern, their crews competent, and their commanders skilled. And, since they were opposed by an enemy that was gallant but technologically outclassed, the one-sided outcome in both instances was essentially the result of the overwhelming numerical and firepower superiority of the American Navy over the Spanish Navy. The first of these battles, Admiral George Dewey's victory in the Battle of Manila Bay, May 1, 1898, confirmed the United States as a Pacific Ocean power. And at Santiago Bay, July 3, 1898, Admiral William T. Sampson's fleet demonstrated American naval supremacy in the Western Hemisphere.

In spite of the addition of torpedoes, torpedo boats, and torpedo-boat destroyers to late nineteenth century fleets, the line ahead continued to be the preferred basic formation for battle fleets. New emphasis was placed on attempting to "cross the enemy's T," that is, to maneuver one's line of vessels across the leading end of the enemy's line. This maneuver, approximately the same as what was known as "raking" in the days of sail, permitted the ships of the crossing line to concentrate fire on the leading ships of the enemy who could bring only the forward guns of his ships to bear on those ships of the crossing force that were within range. At the same time, or independently, the speedy torpedo boats and destroyers would harass the enemy line by attacking individual ships.

At Tsushima on May 27, 1905, both of these new tactical

---

*Potter and Nimitz, *Sea Power; A Naval History*, p. 340.

developments were effectively employed by Admiral Heihachiro To-go's superior Japanese fleet to destroy the Russian Baltic Fleet under Admiral Zinovy P. Rozhdestvenski. Aided to some extent by the disruption created in the Russian line by Japanese torpedo boats and destroyers, Togo's faster, more powerful Japanese ships defeated the more numerous Russians as they crossed Rozhdestvenski's T. Once the Russian line was smashed, the surviving Russian warships fled in confusion, most to be hunted down during the night by Japanese armored cruisers, destroyers, and torpedo boats.

The overwhelming Japanese victory—in combination with only slightly less dramatic successes on land—abruptly halted Russian colonial expansion, and brought to an end an era of three centuries of almost unbroken European successes against Asian military opponents on land and sea.

World War I: Dreadnought and Submarine

Britain's *Dreadnought*, launched February 10, 1906, combined heavy armor, immense weight of metal hurled by a homogeneous group of ten large-caliber (twelve-inch) guns, and all-round fire capabilities. All previously constructed battleships were rendered obsolete. In consequence, the great powers were forced into a naval armament race. Naval designers, searching to combine firepower and mobility, soon brought out the battle cruiser, gunned to near equality with the *Dreadnought*, but lacking its protective armor belt—a sacrifice to achieve greater speed. The battle cruiser, like most naval hybrids, proved its inefficiency in the battle of Jutland in 1916 and soon began disappearing from the world's navies.

Jutland marked the end of an epoch in naval warfare. It was the last great fleet action in which the opponents slugged it out within eyesight of one another. A much more numerous British fleet won a clear-cut—but far from decisive—victory over hard-fighting, skillful Germans. Had British admiral Jellicoe been less cautious, however, the Germans would probably have been destroyed. As in land warfare, when naval opponents in direct contact are closely matched in fighting quality, numbers determine battle outcomes, but leadership shapes the scope of the result.*

The most significant development in naval warfare in the early twentieth century was the introduction of the improved submarine as a weapon of blockade and counterblockade. Although British

---

*See *Encyclopedia of Military History*, pp. 964–967.

supremacy on the surface of the waves was challenged only once (at Jutland), and was never seriously jeopardized, the German U-boat offensive against merchant shipping came close to bringing Britain to its knees in 1917, when sinkings by submarines threatened to starve England into surrender. The introduction of the convoy system — combined with the availability of American destroyers — permitted the British to ride out the crisis.

Less spectacular than the German submarine blockade of Britain, the Allied surface blockade of Germany was more decisive. The slow strangulation of the German economy became significant in the final months of the war, and caused the war-weary German people to demand peace and — when the Allies refused to negotiate with the kaiser's government — to overthrow the monarchy in order to achieve an armistice. The continuation of the blockade then forced a reluctant government and a starving people to accept the terms of the Versailles Treaty.

When the United States entered World War I the Navy, whose personnel increased to 800,000, was primarily concerned in antisubmarine and convoy activities, though a division of five battleships joined the British Grand Fleet, and three other battleships operated in Irish waters against surface raiders. In all, 79 American destroyers took part in convoy work, and 135 sub-chasers also operated near the European coast. An important part of U.S. Navy participation was the laying of 56,000 of the 70,000 mines comprising the North Sea mine belt, which stretched from Scotland to Norway, a partially successful effort to bottle up German submarines. Naval air squadrons played a role by taking part in bombings of German submarine bases along the Belgian coast.

Electronic Communications

Radio was an important factor in defeating the German sea raiders in World War I, although the spark equipment and elementary receivers in use at that time were not very reliable. To transmit and receive at long distance, ships trailed long antennas behind them — some a mile or more in length. Between the world wars the tremendous burgeoning of electronics, particularly the invention of radar and improved radio communications, was to play an even greater part in naval operations.

Shortly after World War I the three-electrode tube was developed for generating and controlling transmitter power, and the amplifier based on smaller versions of this tube came into use in radio receivers. Long antennas were no longer needed, and where formerly it had required kilowatts to reach a few hundred miles, a few watts of electrical power now sufficed to girdle the earth. The three-electrode tube and its more complicated descendants also made possible the transmission of voice over the radio, which had been impossible with spark sets.

In contrast to telegraph and telephone, radio was developed largely for military use. The U.S. Navy took the lead in this effort. There appears to have been no opposition to radio innovations in the fleet; new developments were accepted as fast as they became available, partly because radio solved a need for open-sea communications that had long been felt by naval strategists and tacticians, a need that had intensified as the advent of steam power forced them to cope increasingly with the problem of security of movement. And its advantages had been demonstrated in combat in the Sea of Japan, the Falkland Islands, and in the most publicized maritime disaster in history — the loss of the *Titanic* — little more than a decade after its introduction.

Radar — following radio by nearly two generations — was also entirely a military requirement and development. It had no civilian applications until after World War II. Radar was a by-product of radio. It transmitted high-frequency signals that were bounced off distant objects. Then, using strongly directional antennas to pick up the signals as they returned, angle and distance of the object were measured by comparing echo times with the speed of light (or the speed of radio transmissions).

The first practical demonstration was made at the U.S. Naval Research Laboratory about 1938. A decisive advance in radar technology was made in England, however, about a year later. This was the invention by Sir Robert Watson-Watt of the magnetron, a vacuum tube quite different in concept from the three-electrode tube. It permitted the generation of brief bursts of high-power signals at very high frequencies. British radar was perhaps the most significant element in the several factors that brought victory to the Royal Air Force in the crucial Battle of Britain in the summer and fall of 1940. Although it achieved decisive results at sea and in the air, radar had no demonstrable influence on the tactics of land warfare.

Improvements and refinements in weaponry, transport, and communications brought tremendous changes in tactics and techniques of warfare in the first half of the twentieth century. Logistics developed into a science in itself, on land and sea. The U.S. Navy's Logistic Support Groups, developed in World War II, solved one of the most annoying problems of naval warfare: the necessity that vessels return to some land base for fuel, supply, and repair. The necessary withdrawal from action of naval fighting units became a matter of merely a few days or even hours, instead of weeks and months, when sea trains of fast cargo ships and floating repair shops became components of each task force.

Air Power at Sea

One of the most important, perhaps *the* most important, influence on the character of naval warfare and the composition of modern battle fleets was the development of the airplane. After its first use in World War I, in support of the battle in northern Europe, the airplane soon became a source of controversy involving its capabilities, and in particular its ability to render large surface vessels obsolete. Most vocal in his insistence that with the advent of the airplane the battleship and other large naval vessels could not survive was Major General William Mitchell of the U.S. Army Air Service. A staged demonstration of the ability of aircraft to sink ships at anchor in 1921 and 1923 convinced many influential people of the validity of his view. Nevertheless large naval vessels continued to be built. And naval strategists promptly capitalized on the ability of aircraft to sink ships by developing ways of taking them to sea. This included at first the carrying of small planes on large ships from which they were catapulted into the air, and the conversion of old hulls into launching platforms. Ultimately it led to the large aircraft carriers of World War II, which sent aircraft roaming far ahead of the vessels of the fleet to attack enemy ships, and rendered ship-for-ship engagements of large ship formations obsolete.

Naval Operations in World War II

The effectiveness of land-based (and carrier-based) bomber and torpedo aircraft against surface warships was in fact so pronounced at the outset of World War II that it soon became evident that air superiority also automatically included surface superiority, almost regardless of the relative strength in surface warships of opposing forces. This was demonstrated beyond all doubt in the dramatic naval battle at Midway, where the destruction of the Japanese fleet carrier force assured victory to a considerably smaller American fleet.

It became apparent early in the war that carrier-based aircraft were not mere supporters of surface naval forces, but were in fact the primary naval striking element. The carrier, providing the weapon to destroy enemy surface forces — a dramatic extension of firepower — thus quickly displaced the battleship as the capital ship of the fleet. This was at the very moment that the all-big-gun superdreadnought reached its apogee of firepower and of invulnerability to gunfire in such formidable warships as the German *Bismarck* and the Japanese superbattleships *Yamato* and *Musashi*. The *Yamato*, largest battleship ever built, was completed in December 1941. She carried nine 18.1-inch guns with a 42,000-yard range, the most powerful in the world. Her sister ship, *Musashi*, was completed in July 1942.

The change from battleship dominance to that of carrier and carrier-based aircraft started with the Japanese carrier blow at Pearl Harbor. Two days later the loss of HMS *Renown* and *Prince of Wales* off the coast of Malaya demonstrated the inability of surface vessels to resist vigorous and well-delivered air strikes, either land- or carrier-based. Before the war ended, great fleet actions were contested and won in the air by bombs and torpedoes delivered by airplanes launched from surface vessels that never sighted each other. The first such carrier battle took place in the Coral Sea, May 7-8, 1942. During the engagement no surface ship on either side sighted the enemy.

Nevertheless, there were still a number of World War II naval actions in which surface vessels slugged it out with gunfire. Notable were the battles of the River Plate and the Komandorski Islands, while the Battle of Surigao Strait, in itself a contest of surface maneuver and gunfire, was a component of the large-scale Battle of Leyte Gulf in which carrier-based air power played the major role. However, the epitome of modern naval surface warfare came in the Solomon Islands, August of 1942 to February of 1943, as the Japanese Navy fiercely but vainly attempted to isolate U.S. Marine Corps and Army units on Guadalcanal. Not since the Anglo-Dutch naval wars of the seventeenth century had two powerful navies engaged in such prolonged, intensive, and destructive warfare at sea.

As in World War I, the submarine loomed large as a component of sea power, its primary mission being commerce destruction. Germany's Atlantic U-boat campaigns almost, but not quite, weighted the scales in favor of Nazi victory. In the Pacific, despite possession of the "Long Lance" torpedo, technically the best weapon of its category, Japan never quite understood the strategic employment of the submarine, was not very effective in its tactical employment — particularly at the Battle of Midway — and was unable to develop an effective antisubmarine doctrine. In consequence, the U.S. submarine campaign was able to strangle the Nipponese merchant marine. What emerged from the conflict was the sound premise that submarine warfare, in both offense and defense, was a highly specialized affair and, like all military operations of the period, demanded professional competence and vision of high order.

On the other hand, the use of submarines to evade surface blockade, first attempted by the U.S. Navy during the opening Luzon campaign, became highly developed by the Japanese in the Southwest Pacific. Underwater vessels carried troops and materiel, supplementing the use of fast destroyer-transports for the same purpose.

A striking development in surface operations was the use of naval firepower in support of landing operations. In operations around the periphery of Europe, and across the reaches of the western Pacific, refinements in fire control and direction enabled U.S. and British naval craft to put down most effective gunfire support for ground troops before and during the initial sensitive period prior to debarkation of the assaulters' artillery.

Technological inventions, radar and sonar in particular, together with other electronic communications innovations, constituted a vast and delicate refinement in command control. The interception of radio transmissions became routine, and the decoding of such transmissions influenced the movements of both submarine and antisubmarine forces significantly in the Battle of the Atlantic.

An important result of developments in electronics was the emergence of the command ship. In fleet actions, no longer were the admiral and his staff an irritating excrescence on some unfortunate capital ship. In amphibious operations the floating command post enabled close personal cooperation between the naval commander, responsible for putting the ground forces ashore, and the ground commander, who assumed control once the troops gained a toehold on the beach.

The strategy of island-hopping from the Central and South Pacific required the rapid development of effective tactics and techniques of amphibious warfare. This special type of combat had been a subject of study by naval theorists since the fiasco at Gallipoli in World War I. Japanese forces were put ashore with little opposition in a number of places in the first months of World War II. But landing large forces in a combined Navy–Marine Corps or Navy–Army operation on a hostile beachhead under fire became the primary pattern of the war against Japan and reached its ultimate in size and complexity in the landing of Allied troops in Normandy in June 1944.

As nuclear power was developing into a practical source of propulsion in the period after World War II, the navies of the world were faced with a new power source with a potential far greater than the two changes that had previously revolutionized war at sea: the change from galley slaves to sail, and the change from sail to steam.

Thus, in less than a century, navies made a transition from propulsion by wind and sail, through propulsion by steam produced by coal, and steam produced by oil, to steam produced by nuclear fission. The change in naval weaponry and equipment was more dramatic than the change in the armies of the world, as the advances in metallurgy and heavy machinery made possible the change from wooden ships to heavily armored vessels that could carry guns of a size and power that could not be easily handled on land.

Changes in naval tactics were less dramatic in the nineteenth century, however, and in tactics the changes in land warfare were much more extensive than those at sea. This may be attributed in large part to the lack of opportunity for fleet action in the period between the appearance of the ironclad in the Civil War and the end of the century. While naval tacticians prepared for combat, and fleets simulated battle action, such things as amphibious operations, scouting, blockade, and combined action of various types of vessels in a fleet engagement were studied little and practiced less before World War I. There were, after all, only two major fleet actions between 1860 and 1914.

The lessons of World War I and the developments in technology that followed the war were very carefully studied, however, and 1939 found the navies of the world better prepared for world war than they had been twenty-five years earlier.

XXIII. Trenches, Barbed Wire, Machine Guns, and High Explosives 1870–1918

Tactics and Doctrine Fall Behind

The half-century that followed the American Civil War spawned a series of technical innovations that greatly increased the potential lethality of weapons while undermining the *raison d'être* of contemporary tactical doctrines of land warfare. Writing in 1902, the American translators of French colonel Charles J.J.J. Ardant du Picq's masterly assessment of human behavior in war, *Battle Studies*, quoted from a letter Ardant du Picq had written in 1870, shortly before the Franco-Prussian War, and commented that it was still as true as when the words were written:

> *In the last century, after the improvements of the rifle and field artillery . . . improvements to which the recent Prussian successes in war in part are due — we find all thinking men in the army asking themselves the question: "How shall we fight tomorrow?" We have no combat doctrine. And the various contradictory methods [that are suggested] confuse the intelligence of military men.*

The words could just as well have been written in 1950 or 1980.

Among additional improvements that followed the Franco-Prussian War — in which Ardant du Picq was killed — one of the most important was the perfection of smokeless powder in 1885. This eliminated the smoke clouds that had previously betrayed one's own position while obscuring the vision of the enemy. No further comment on the military preparedness of the United States Army in the closing years of the nineteenth century need be made other than to note that in the Spanish-American War the Americans used black-powder ammunition, while the "decadent" Spanish had smokeless powder.

But the most important developments in land warfare in this half-century were the gradual return of artillery to the position of battlefield preeminence it had held before 1850, and the introduction of the rifled musket. This return swing of the pendulum resulted from a number of innovations in military technology — or acceptance and adoption of older innovations. Smokeless powder, rifling, breech-loading, and the development of recoil-absorbing devices and the non-recoil carriage, combined to make possible highly accurate, long-range, quick-firing artillery pieces. The high explosive artillery shell, first introduced in 1886, proved to be fantastically more lethal, as well as more effective against hard targets, than the old black-powder shell. A three-inch high-explosive shell of the kind standard in World War I burst into about 1,000 high-velocity fragments, while a black-powder shell of the Civil War period had burst into 2 to 5 fragments, and that of the Franco-Prussian War into 20 to 30.

The principal reason that the quick-firing artillery piece had become the dominant weapon on the battlefield was improvements in communications techniques. Using immediate reports from observers stationed at the best visual vantage points, artillery units could take advantage of the parabolic trajectory and increased range of newer guns, move back from the front lines, and provide support to the infantry by indirect fire over the heads of the infantrymen from positions screened and covered by hills and trees.

The need to get exposed, vulnerable, and relatively defenseless gunners out of the infantry lines had been apparent as soon as the rifled musket had demonstrated its dominance early in the Civil War. The obvious solution was to take advantage of the cannon's longer range and trajectory — if a way could be found to aim the gun so that it could hit the enemy from positions in which the gunners could not see the target. Balloons had been tried as early as 1794 and had been used seriously during the Civil War, without much success. Experiments were made with the new telegraph, and with the heliograph, and with signal flags using adaptations of the new Morse code. But such communications were slow, and the heliograph was limited by weather conditions. Signal flags of course were almost as old as warfare, but new semaphore techniques with dual-flag messages permitted more precise transmission at great speeds. By the beginning of the twentieth century this technique was widely employed; an observer on top of a hill from which he could observe the enemy would give commands via a "wig-wag" signalman to the guns — concealed and protected in defilade behind the hill. The observer would then adjust the fire on the targets by additional commands sent through his signalman.

But about this time the introduction of the field telephone brought the revolution in artillery technique to logical fruition. No longer did the observer have to be within sight of both targets and guns. No longer was the transmission of fire commands delayed while words were converted to the signal-flag letter code, and back again at the far end. Furthermore, the fire of several guns and batteries could be concentrated on one target. It was this new flexibility in controlling and directing fire, as much as the improvements in guns and ammunition, that made artillery even more predominant on the battlefields of World War I than it had been in Napoleon's time.

Between 1886 and 1900, most armies had abandoned single-shot infantry weapons using black-powder cartridges with soft lead bullets and had adopted repeating rifles generally patterned after the prototype Mauser rifle adopted by Germany. These Mauser-type weapons were bolt-action, clip-fed magazine rifles that fired projectiles from smokeless-powder cartridges. The bullets were covered with hard metal and were between 8 and 10 millimeters in diameter, or about three tenths of an inch, or .30 caliber. The new ammunition more than doubled the speed of flight of the projectile, from approximately 1,300 foot-seconds to a supersonic muzzle velocity as high as 2,800 foot-seconds. At the higher velocity — in conformance with the simple energy formula of MV^2 — the projectile struck the target with much greater force and caused far greater damage to the body or other object it might hit. The bolt-action feature — by which the spent cartridge was ejected and a new one shifted from magazine to firing chamber by one movement of the rifleman — greatly speeded reloading and rate of fire.

The same period — 1885–1900 — witnessed the introduction of the modern machine gun into military inventories. Attempts to produce multiple-firing weapons had been made as far back as the fifteenth century. But development of the automatic machine gun had to await perfection of the metallic cartridge. The first effective machine gun was the multibarrelled Gatling gun, adopted by the Union Army in the Civil War. Manually operated by a hand crank, but with automatic loading and ejection of cartridges, the Gatling could have been called "semiautomatic" had that term been in use then. But the fully automatic modern machine gun used the energy of the gun's recoil (Maxim, about 1885) or the energy of the gas from the powder combustion (Hotchkiss, 1897) to reload as well as fire the gun. The automatic machine gun when perfected had a theoretical rate of fire many times that of the bolt-action magazine rifle's maximum rate of about 30 shots per minute.

As had been the case forty years earlier, the new technological advances in weapon lethality generally failed to elicit corresponding innovations in tactics. Both the South African War (1899–1902) and the Russo-Japanese War (1904–1905) provided unequivocal evidence regarding the battlefield efficacy of bolt-action and clip-fed rifles, entrenchments, and quick-firing artillery. But these examples did not stir military thought to an adequate reappraisal of the presumed psychological and practical effectiveness of seizing the initiative and conducting mass attacks that would carry all before them.

Nearly a century earlier Clausewitz had written that the defensive was "the stronger form of combat," though he warned that offensive operations were necessary to bring war to a successful conclusion. And in the 1860s Moltke had developed his concept of strategic offensive and tactical defensive. But even Moltke had been aware of the importance of seizing the initiative, and of the tremendous psychological effect on both attacker and defender of a vigorously pressed charge of a mass of disciplined soldiers with inspired leaders.

The Germans, partly because of Moltke's perceptive observations, and partly because their general-staff system caused them to evaluate the new weapons more objectively than did most other armies, had some awareness of the effectiveness of the new weapons. Their tactics at the beginning of the twentieth century were more flexible; they had more machine guns per man,* and more artillery pieces (particularly in heavy calibers) per man than did other armies. But they remembered the success of the Prussian charge at Duppel, which had won the Danish War in 1864; they remembered the near success of French charges at St. Privat in 1870, and they were impressed by the writings of French theoretician Ardant du Picq regarding the importance of moral factors in war. They were also very much aware of the theories of offensive action advocated by French colonels Foch and Grandmaison at the beginning of the century. However, even German tactics did not adequately take into account the greatly increased firepower of the new weapons in relation to the psychological factors of war.

In the four decades preceding 1914, the European states engaged in a race for numerical and qualitative supremacy in arms and in mobilizable soldiers, with all but Britain adopting short-term national conscription. All powers also adopted some version of the Prussian general-staff system. The universal assumption of the various general staffs, reflected in the lack of long-range economic planning, was that because of the power of new weapons, war, if it should occur, would probably be brief, its course decisively determined by an heroic offensive thrust.

> [The] theorists' picture of the next war was surprisingly like that of the wars of 1866 and 1870, which had been decided by a series of initial shocks from which the defeated armies had never recovered. Then, arguing from these historical examples, these theorists had built mass armies which seemed capable, to their builders, only of fighting the kind of war which had been posited by these historical examples.†

---

*Like the British and French armies, the Germans had only two machine guns in the standard infantry battalion, but they had additional Jäger battalions with six machine guns per battalion in their corps troops and in cavalry divisions in the standard infantry corps.

†Theodore Ropp, *War in the Modern World*, (Durham, N.C.: Duke University Press, 1959), p. 204.

World War I

When World War I broke out in midsummer of 1914, five of the six major European powers (France, Britain, Russia, Germany, and Austria-Hungary) put into effect their long-prepared war and mobilization plans as members of the Triple Entente and Triple Alliance. (Italy remained neutral; taking advantage of a loophole in the terms of the Triple Alliance, refusing to join Germany and Austria-Hungary since this necessitated war with Great Britain.) None of these war plans envisaged a protracted war of attrition.

Significantly, however, the German war plan — a watered-down modification of a strategic concept developed by German chief of staff Alfred von Schlieffen in 1905 — had been initially designed in recognition that such a war was possible. Schlieffen, fearful of a stalemate, believed Germany could prevent this by using small forces to hold off the slowly mobilizing Russians in the East while the bulk of the German Army swept through the Low Countries and northern France to encircle and crush the French armies. Mostly because of the younger Moltke's inept modifications of the original Schlieffen strategic concept, but partly because the tactics to carry out the concept were not compatible with the new weapons, the German plan failed, and World War I became the long, bloody stalemate Schlieffen had tried to avoid.

The war opened with the Germans pushing through Belgium into France in accordance with the modified Schlieffen plan. The small (100,000 men) but highly trained British field army of long-service regulars, equipped with the Lee-Enfield rifle, fired with such deadly accuracy at the Battle of Mons, near the French-Belgian frontier, that successive German assaults were mowed down by what some Germans mistook for machine-gun fire. The British high command was also misled by this experience into underestimating the necessity of immediately procuring large numbers of machine guns. They had not been needed by the men at Mons, but those men were soon gone. British losses in the first three months of the war were 85,000 killed, wounded, and captured. French losses were 854,000 for this same period, and German losses 677,000. The combat lethality of the machine gun, the French and German quick-firing artillery pieces, and the modern rifle were amply demonstrated. Stalemate ensued for three years.

In the period 1915–1917, it was usually the Allies who attempted to break the stalemate on the Western Front, always with appalling casualties and only a few yards gained. The opposing lines of trenches stretched from the North Sea to the frontier of neutral Switzerland; there were no flanks. Thus the offensives were direct frontal attacks on strong field fortifications, which included machine guns (by this time 32 per battalion in the British Army, for instance), protected and made more lethal by barbed-wire entanglements.

Because of the way these attacks were conducted, surprise was impossible. Concentration of men and ma†erial and preliminary bombardments lasting as long as two weeks indicated clearly where the attack was to be directed, and to some extent when. The obvious response to these indications was to concentrate reserves within one or two days' march of the threatened point and use them for defense in depth and counterattack. The heavy British casualties of the Somme offensive of July–November 1916 (about 410,000 — nearly 60,000 the first day) brought protests in Britain's Parliament and from the British public. French general Nivelle's costly Aisne offensive of 1917 brought a wave of mutinies involving 54 French divisions. In assault, casualties were frequently twice as great as those of the defender, despite the preliminary artillery bombardments.

One reason why the pulverizing power of artillery failed to achieve the firepower advantage that commanders sensed was essential to successful offensive action was that artillery was proving itself even more effective in the defensive role. In combination with barbed wire and machine guns, which slowed down the attackers and increased their exposure to artillery fire, the high-explosive shells of the artillery inflicted prohibitive losses that stopped even the best-trained, best-disciplined, and most enthusiastic troops. Counterbattery fire by attacking heavy and medium artillery attempted to destroy, or at least temporarily silence, the defending artillery, but could never be completely successful. Defensive artillery fire could always (at least until March 1918) slow down the attackers enough so that reserves could arrive in time to bolster threatened positions and stop all hope of a breakthrough.

Particularly effective against both advancing troops (outside the shelter of their trenches) and soldiers in trenches, was the use of shrapnel. There is perhaps no military term more consistently misused, even by professionals who should know better, than the word "shrapnel," and it is thus useful to explain what the word really means, as well as how it has become so misused.

Early in the nineteenth century an English artilleryman, Henry Shrapnel, developed a novel improvement of grapeshot, which during the late eighteenth and early nineteenth centuries was the principal artillery antipersonnel ammunition. Grapeshot was a packet of small iron balls held together by cloth, or netting, or a wooden case, fired from a cannon. The effect of grapeshot against infantry advancing in the open could be devastating. Its major shortcomings were a very short range and ineffectiveness against an enemy taking advantage of undulations of the ground.

Shrapnel's adaptation of the concept was to encase the small balls (usually smaller than in grapeshot, and often made of lead rather than iron) in a cannonball shell. A fuze was set in the shell and timed to go off while the cannonball was still in the air, over the enemy infantry. It completely overcame the two disadvantages of grapeshot: the cannonball could be fired to a considerable distance before it was exploded by the fuze; and troops in the open could not hide from the pellets raining from the sky with the force of the explosion combined with the force of gravity. However, this new kind of ammunition — named shrapnel after its inventor — had a serious disadvantage of its own. It was very difficult to get the fuze to go off at precisely the right instant, and it required a very skillful gunner to combine range, direction, and height of burst over an enemy formation, even when the fuze worked perfectly. So despite some spectacular successes, shrapnel was not much used in the nineteenth century.

The fragments from a thicker-walled iron shell were found to be about as effective as the lead pellets of shrapnel, but even that was not used much because of the fuze and skill problems. Furthermore, there were not too many opportunities for a gunner to see enemy infantry far enough away to use either early shrapnel or early shell. And when the enemy was close, grapeshot was easier and more effective. And so in 1847, at Buena Vista, five years after the death of Sir Henry Shrapnel, Zachary Taylor supposedly uttered the words that helped him become President of the United States: "A little more grape, Captain Bragg!" (In fact, he is more reliably quoted as saying: "Double-shot your guns, Bragg, and give 'em hell!")

But the concept of shrapnel became more viable with the advent of indirect fire in the early years of the twentieth century. And it was particularly effective in the trench stalemate of World War I. The far more powerful point-detonated high-explosive shell was not very effective against entrenched troops, but shrapnel pellets rained down with deadly effect on trenches and troops in the open. There was still a problem with height of burst, even though fuzes were much more reliable. If the burst was too high, the pellets scattered and were not very effective; if it was too low it was even less lethal. Successful use of shrapnel required a high order of gunnery skill by the observer who adjusted the fire on the target. But in the stalemate of 1914–1917 there was lots of time, and almost unlimited ammunition and opportunity for gunners of all armies to perfect such skill.

Later in the war it was found that high-explosive shell, detonated in the air by a similar timed fuze, was even more effective than shrapnel, the jagged shell fragments striking with greater force and far greater damage effect than the shrapnel pellets. Infantry soldiers, unaware of the technical distinction between shrapnel pellets and shell fragments, and having learned earlier that air bursts were "shrapnel" bursts, began to refer to the wounds caused by shell air-burst fragments as "shrapnel" wounds. So, too, did the doctors who treated those wounds. And since there was no difference between the effects of a shell fragment from a point-detonated high-explosive burst and an air high-explosive burst, all shell-fragment wounds were soon called "shrapnel wounds." The incorrect terminology was perpetuated in World War II, and there is probably nothing an old artilleryman can do to set the record straight.

One of the most dramatic artillery weapons developed in World War I was the long-range German gun commonly known as the "Paris gun," or sometimes erroneously called "Big Bertha." (Big Bertha was the designation of a powerful 18-inch German siege mortar-howitzer, relatively short ranged, employed successfully early in the war at Liège, Namur, and Antwerp, and somewhat affectionately called Big Bertha by its users in honor of the ample lady who had recently inherited leadership of the house of Krupp.)

The Paris gun, which was first used in combat on March 23, 1918, was about 9 inches in caliber, and had a barrel 117 feet long—the longest artillery tube ever used in battle. By virtue of that barrel, and a powder charge about 10 feet long, the gun could fire a projectile up to a maximum range of 80 miles. Actually there were seven such guns in all, active between March and August 1918. At first the arrival of shells in Paris, with no aircraft overhead, and the front line almost 70 miles away, nearly caused panic, since the longest-ranged guns known could not fire more than 30 miles. But French ordnance experts quickly and accurately analyzed the shell fragments and, using increasingly sophisticated counterbattery detection techniques, soon found the gun position, and employed their own big guns quite effectively in counterbattery from positions near the front.

New Weapons of World War I

In addition to these improvements in weapons, there were three significant new weapons introduced in the war. These were aircraft, poison gas, and the tank. However, neither poison gas nor the tank proved decisive (battle-winning) because of technical imperfections, inadequate quantities, failure to adopt appropriate tactics for their use, and the lack of adequate reserves to exploit transitory advantages achieved when the weapons were first introduced.

Aircraft, on the other hand, had a more significant effect on the conduct of military operations. By late 1915, aircraft had become the principal means for reconnaissance — previously limited by the lines of entrenchments stretching from the North Sea to Switzerland, which prevented effective ground reconnaissance. They had also become useful for artillery observation and for long-range harassing bombardment. And by 1918, aircraft became important participants in the land battle by providing close support to troops on the ground.

The Introduction of Armor

Tanks were developed in England and France, more or less concurrently, for a single specific purpose. They were designed to beat a path for infantry in frontal attacks against entrenched and wired-in rifles and machine guns. Thus the tank was developed and employed solely as an instrument of rupture. Due in large part to the enthusiastic support of First Lord of the Admiralty Winston Churchill, the British first introduced the new weapons into battle on September 15, 1916, in the hope of revitalizing the offensive that had bogged down on the Somme.

By this time the British had two companies, with 60 tanks, in France. But few of the officers and men of these companies had ever before seen a battlefield. The tanks were distributed without regard to organization among nine divisions attacking on a three-mile front. Of the 60 tanks available, only 49 were able to leave their parks, and 36 of these reached the line of departure. These 36 tanks attacked ahead of or with the infantry with excellent local results, but only 9 returned under their own power. The rest were disabled by mechanical breakdown, ditched, or put out of commission by German artillery fire.

Seven months before the first commitment of British tanks, Colonel Ernest Swinton, one of the early protagonists of the tank, had proposed a doctrine for employment of armor. In it he made these points:

1. Some means of communication from commanders to tanks — other than through the telephone lines of accom-

panying infantry — should be worked out. (Swinton clearly envisaged radio, which was not yet sufficiently sophisticated to be installed in tanks.)

2. Artillery and mines were most to be feared. The former should be attacked by supporting aircraft and also taken under counterbattery fire.

3. These machines "*should not be used in driblets*" (emphasis Swinton's), in order to keep their existence secret until sufficient were ready and their crews trained for "one great combined operation." (He vigorously protested the September 15 attack as premature, but was overruled.)

4. The sector of attack should be carefully chosen to minimize the tank's limitations and enhance its capabilities.

5. Approach to the line of departure should be at night from assembly areas not more than two miles back. The attack should start just before dawn.

6. The tanks should precede the infantry by a distance sufficient to allow the enemy's rifle and machine-gun fire to be concentrated on the tanks when the infantry reached its attack objectives.

7. Once the infantry arrived, the tanks should move on to the next trench line, bringing it under enfilade fire and attacking enemy reserves and bombing parties moving up.

8. The tank attack should be in such force that it could continue, without halting, through the enemy's artillery positions (about 12 kilometers).

9. The momentum necessary to achieve deep penetration in a single attack would require carefully planned logistical support to assure a continuing, adequate supply of fuel, ammunition, and other necessities.

10. Smoke should be used to conceal the tank attack to the maximum extent possible.

To an armor officer today these concepts would seem elementary. But in 1916, and for a long time thereafter, they seemed radical, based on undemonstrated theory, and inconsistent with the realities of contemporary warfare. As a matter of fact, Swinton somewhat overestimated the capabilities of the contemporary tank.

At Cambrai on November 20, 1917, the British tankmen were given a better opportunity to put their theories to the test in a limited-objective attack on a six-mile front. Of more than 450 tanks available, about 300 reached the line of departure. More than half of those committed, however, were disabled or broke down in the first twelve hours, and most of those remaining were either mechanically incapable of going on at the end of twenty-four hours, or their crews were exhausted. Nevertheless a few tanks were collected for another day's fighting. By the end of a second twenty-four hours of attack a salient 12 miles wide at its base had been driven 6 miles into German territory. This was the most spectacular penetration on the Western Front since 1914, and it was achieved in what was then an incredibly short time.

The British high command has been severely criticized for its failure to appreciate the revolutionary tactical value of the tank and to convert the Cambrai battle into a decisive penetration. (One of the principal critics was Major General J.F.C. Fuller who, as a staff officer, planned the attack, and who was at that time disappointed by the failure of the high command to seize the opportunity.) Some of this criticism is frivolous and emotional. The World War I tank was not mechanically capable of sustained operations; it lacked the speed and range necessary for very deep penetration, and its lack of other than visual communication made unplanned mass maneuver on the battlefield impossible. Some critics have judged the employment of the tank of 1917 as though it had had 1940 performance capability. This, however, was not true of the criticisms of J.F.C. Fuller — who disagreed as much with those who exaggerated his criticisms as with those against whom it was directed.

Perhaps the most valid lesson of Cambrai, but one that did not impress itself on the world's soldiers for many years, was that the prime virtue of the tank was its ability to control ground without necessarily occupying it. Recognition of this factor was to be the basis for later audacious exploitation of tank successes in apparent violation of the classic principles of security and mass.

A lesson that did impress itself, although at first too narrowly, was the overwhelming morale effect of tank attack. Fuller, for instance, observed of the tank at Cambrai that its "predominant value [was] its morale effect. It showed clearly that terror and not destruction was the true aim of armed forces." Of all the nations to go to war in 1939 only the Germans and Soviets had written this lesson into their armor doctrine — and the Soviets had gotten the idea from the Germans during their seven years of close collaboration from 1925 to 1933.

Although the tank had far to go before reaching its tremendous potential, in World War I automatic weapons and quick-firing artillery had achieved essentially all that could be expected from these weapons. This was so because industry and technology had also provided the means for new and improved logistics systems that not only supplied them with ammunition, but also distributed to the millions of men who were their users (and their targets) food, fuel, clothing, and a wide range of other goods and services. The railroad was primarily responsible for making it possible to keep large armies in contact for long periods of time. It could bring up more food from greater distances than had ever been possible for the largest wagon trains, and it brought up the millions of pounds of ammunition that mass production poured out of the factories.

The internal combustion engine also contributed to the exploitation of the lethality of the weapons. Without trucks the forward railheads would have been constricting bottlenecks, because horse transport, with its great demands for forage, would have limited what could be brought forward. As it was, trucks could bring supplies to distribution points in operational zones, from which horse-drawn transport could finally take over distribution. In all, during World War I, fuel for truck, train, and horse was about half of the supply tonnage shipped to the British Army in France.

By the end of 1917 Germany had succeeded in eliminating Russia and Rumania from the war, which released large forces from the Eastern Front. The availability of this trained manpower, combined with the exhaustion of the French and British armies, and the success of the submarine campaign against Great Britain, appeared to the German high command to provide an opportunity to end the war by a clear-cut military victory or at least by forcing a favorable negotiated peace. Increasing the pressure for an early decision were the declining quality and morale of German troops, the entry of the United States into the war, the worsening economic conditions in Germany as a result of the Allied naval blockade, and the success of Allied countermeasures against the submarine.

General Erich Ludendorff, Quartermaster General (in effect, Chief of Staff), recognized that positive military results were possible only through offensive action; a strategy of attrition would not suffice. A decision could be achieved only by a deep tactical penetration at some point where the strategic results would be disastrous to the British or the French. Up to this time, despite repeated efforts, neither side had been able to carry out such a penetration, regardless of the force applied, the weaponry employed, or the frontage attacked. Even the British tank attacks had achieved only a limited success at Cambrai, and aggressive German counterattacks had recovered most of the lost ground. Nor could the Germans think of a tank offensive in the near future.

Although they had started producing tanks in haste after the British introduced them, they had very few of these new weapons, even including those captured from the Allies.

The New German Tactical Concept

Ludendorff and his general staff believed, however, that a tactical solution was possible. A new tactical system was developed as a result of intensive study in 1917. The factors deemed requisite for success were identified as, first and foremost, surprise; finding and penetrating weak points in the enemy defenses and avoiding prolonged attack against formidable defenses; rapid, violent, and deep exploitation of penetrations; maximum fire support at all times; and maintaining the momentum of attack.

The following tactical measures were adopted by the Germans to achieve these factors on the battlefield.

1. Surprise
    a. Measures were to be taken to minimize indications of the time of attack, including elimination of the long premonitory bombardment; preassault artillery preparations were limited to not more than four hours.
    b. The buildup of artillery in the attack sector would be concealed by limiting registration fire of newly arrived batteries.
    c. Attacking troops would be moved forward only at night and held in concealed assembly areas behind the portion of the front where they would attack.
    d. Deception would be maintained by false preparations in other areas along the front.
2. Penetration at weak points
    a. The troops would be indoctrinated in the "soft spot" tactical doctrine of infiltration, which dictated that attacks would be pushed to the limit and closely followed up only where resistance was weak or ineffective. This doctrine was to apply to all echelons from the squad to the field army.
    b. Points or areas of strong resistance were to be bypassed by the assault elements and dealt with later — "mopped up" — by successive echelons.
3. Exploitation
    a. When penetrations were achieved, the penetrating units, of whatever size, were to press the attack vigorously straight ahead.

b. Units following the assault elements were to widen the gap by exerting pressure against the flanks of the penetration, and by enveloping those flanks.

c. Regiments and divisions widening the gaps were to use the same infiltration and weak-point tactics by which the initial penetration was created.

4. Maximum fire support

a. The infantry squad (a half-platoon of 14 to 18 men in the German Army) was to be reinforced with an automatic rifle (or light machine gun) and a light mortar. (The automatic rifle generally was the 20-pound Madsen, though no doubt some Bergmann 26-pound and Parabellum 22-pound rifles were used.) The automatic rifle and the mortar were to serve as firepower bases for maneuver of the riflemen in the squad.

b. Rifle grenade launchers (recently adapted from the French *Vivien Bessieres* grenade cup) were to be distributed to each rifle squad, and the allotment of hand grenades was to be increased for each man.

c. In addition to standard artillery support techniques, light artillery pieces were to be attached to infantry rifle battalions to provide immediate close-fire support.

d. Battalion machine-gun companies were to be assembled close behind the assault infantry, and individual guns were to be detailed to move ahead, find cover, and provide supporting fire overhead and through the intervals between infantry formations.

e. Supporting light, medium, and heavy guns were not to be emplaced rigidly in line as had been customary, but irregularly in covered positions; batteries and battalions were to be prepared to displace forward by bounds (leap frog) to provide uninterrupted fire support.

f. Direct support was also to be provided by fighter and light bomber aircraft, which would attack targets of opportunity, such as enemy pockets of resistance, or enemy reserves moving up, or reconnaissance aircraft adjusting artillery fires.

5. Maintaining momentum of attack

a. Engineers equipped with light bridging materials would be attached to the assault elements to facilitate the advance of accompanying artillery and supply vehicles.

b. Leading assault elements would be given no objective points, but rather would be instructed to push straight ahead regardless of delays to units on their flanks.

c. Reinforcements and replacements, especially of automatic rifles and mortars, were to be fed directly from rear to front, and replacement of exhausted or depleted assault units was to be accomplished in the same way.

d. Local successes were to be promptly and strongly developed and expanded by closely following reserves of infantry, machine guns, and artillery.

If the foregoing appears to be a summary of modern battlefield tactics, that impression is correct. Ludendorff's innovations of 1918 — especially in the organization, equipment, and tactical employment of the squad and larger battle groups — were the basis for current organization and battlefield tactics. The modern combat team concept is an extension of Ludendorff's squad organization, and combat team tactics are, on a larger scale, those of Ludendorff's squads.

These innovations were not adopted by the German Army without protest from a number of German officers. First, the emphasis on independent action by small semiautonomous units required a decentralization that seemed contrary to the tight control on which German doctrine long had insisted. Second, it affronted the pride of many German officers to give great tactical responsibility to junior officers, noncommissioned officers, and individual soldiers. Nevertheless, the German army already had shown its receptiveness to the lessons of combat when — in part because of manpower shortages — it triangularized the infantry division in 1916, years ahead of any other.

The new system was used with great success by General Oscar von Hutier in his offensive against Riga in September 1917, and achieved a spectacular victory over the Italians at Caporetto in October and November. Because it was first employed by General von Hutier, the new system was soon called the "Hutier tactics."

The German Offensives of 1918

Confident that he held the tactical key to victory, Ludendorff and the general staff undertook a study of how these tactics could bring strategic decision in 1918. They decided that the most vulnerable portion of the Allied front was at the junction of the British and French armies in the upper Saverne Valley. The British Fifth Army was undermanned and stretched thin. A breakthrough there would threaten both Paris and the Channel ports, upon which the British Expeditionary Force was dependent. The natural result would be for the French to withdraw to protect Paris, and the

British to withdraw to protect their lines of communication. Because of these diverging withdrawals, the breakthrough would become permanent.

During the winter the Germans worked energetically to prepare themselves both tactically and strategically. All men over thirty-five were transferred from active infantry organizations to those on occupation duty, from which men under thirty-five were transferred to join active units. All divisions, including those on the Eastern Front, were put through a program of intensive training in the new tactics during the winter of 1917–1918. It was stressed in this training that the task of unit infiltration was not one for specialists but a function of all infantry. In addition, artillery was trained not only in firing from defilade, but in map registration, in the use of forward observers with improvised signalling, and in maintenance of a creeping barrage moving at about 40 meters a minute.

The Hutier tactics were used against the British Fifth, Third, and First armies on March 21, 1918, between Noyon and Arras. The attack was preceded by a short but heavy artillery preparation, using about 50 percent gas, against artillery positions, command posts, road junctions, vehicle parks, and other sensitive areas behind the front. After about two hours the bulk of these fires were shifted to the British front and support lines, and after another two hours the German infantry began moving forward behind a creeping barrage. A feature of this barrage was that it was delivered by specially designated batteries within battalions, so that there was no abrupt cessation of fires, with consequent warning that the infantry assault was starting.

The infantry squads performed as expected, assisted in surprise by a heavy fog, which, however, delayed the planned German air support and, to some extent, hindered machine-gun and close artillery support. The ultimate result of the new tactics was a maximum German penetration of some 40 miles in 15 days, which took the German Second Army within nine miles of Amiens, a crucial rail center. No such penetration had been achieved by any of the belligerents on the Western Front since September 1914.

It seems probable that the German strategic objectives would have been attained had their transportation movement and logistical capabilities measured up to those they had developed in tactics. By April 5, when the advance finally was halted, the attacking troops were exhausted, without food and ammunition, and had far outrun their artillery support. This logistical and transportation failure has been generally attributed to the German election to conduct the offensive over terrain they themselves had utterly devastated in their withdrawal to the Hindenburg Line in 1917. In this region they found nothing whatever to sustain themselves or to help themselves advance, having to depend entirely on what they could move forward by their own efforts over a wide extent of shell-ravaged, muddy, roadless ground cut laterally by deep trench systems and heavily laced with wire.

Ludendorff tried four more offensives in subsequent months. All of these also failed, not only because of the continuing inability of German artillery and supply to keep up with the infantry advance, but also because losses were exhausting and discouraging the German infantry. Another reason was that in this crisis the Allies finally appointed an Allied supreme commander — General Ferdinand Foch — who perceived what the Germans were doing, and quickly took adequate countermeasures.

Despite strategic failure, the German offensives of 1918 impressed their tactical lessons deeply on the Allied commanders. In July, using adaptations of the same tactics in conjunction with tanks and tactical airpower, the Allies launched their own counteroffensive, which was to continue without cessation until the armistice of November 11. Postwar reorganizations of all armies were based in varying degrees on the German 1918 tactics.

Perhaps the salient feature of this tactical innovation was its revolutionary use of the squad. Prior to 1918 the squad universally had been an internal element organized primarily for low-echelon administration and for convenience in maneuvering from column into line and back into column. Since 1918 the infantry squad has been a tactical element, built around a firepower base of one or more automatic weapons, organized for fire and movement within the platoon and company. The concept of squad organization and the tactics devised by Ludendorff and his staff have been extended to the battalion, regiment, and division, so that each is now a tactical element capable of maneuver with the support of its own base of fire. In 1937 American field experiments under direction of Brigadier General Leslie J. McNair led to adoption by the U.S. Army — twenty-one years after the Germans — of the triangular division, itself a combat team capable of fragmentation into various smaller combat teams with specific capabilities.

The Ludendorff innovations of 1918 may thus justly be regarded as revolutionary, with an impact on the conduct of land battle comparable to those of the Macedonian phalanx, the Roman legion, compact bodies of Swiss pikemen in the attack, similarly compact bodies of English archers in defense, the Spanish square, and the line of Gustavus Adolphus.

XXIV. Buildup to Blitzkrieg
1919–1945

The Lessons of World War I

The twenty-year period following World War I provided an opportunity for armies to assimilate the advances in weaponry that had been introduced during the war, notably the tank and military aircraft. The means of assimilation was the concept, based on the German tactical innovations of 1918, that we have called the twentieth century combat team. This is the combination of a base of fire and a maneuvering element, each given a composition related to the other and to the overall plan. The armored division of 1939, the air assault team, the Anglo-American landing team, are examples of application of the base of fire and the maneuvering element in a way that fully exploited the capabilities of such diverse military entities as air transport, combat aviation, armored vehicles, landing craft, and naval gunfire. The joint-service task force is an attempt to concentrate the lethality and support capabilities of land, sea, and air services for the execution of a single mission.

Assessment and Action by the Allies

The years between the world wars saw a peculiar ambivalence in military thinking about armor among the western nations. The enthusiasts — notably Major General J. F. C. Fuller and his disciples Basil Liddell Hart in England and Major General J. B. Estienne in France — were remarkably prophetic, although their theories were still beyond the capabilities of the contemporary tank. (Fuller, of course, recognized this, but did not communicate this realization to many critical readers.) Perhaps this fact, coupled with the sometimes impetuous and polemic advocacy of their cause by these three thoughtful but prickly soldiers, contributed to underestimation of the latent capabilities of armor by their superiors. More important, however, there was an understandable reluctance by military leaders to supplant proven weapons and doctrine with some that still were experimental. Furthermore, in all of the armies of the recent western alliance there existed an undeniable degree of apathy toward innovation. In France, for instance, when Defense Minister Paul Reynaud sought to introduce armored formations in 1935, the effort was successfully opposed by military as well as political leaders, who were convinced that defense, not offense, was the key to success in modern war.

This general survey — like all generalizations — oversimplifies the problem. There were many factors operating against the armored-force concept, some of them basic and some stemming from national temperament and politics. Among these were French reliance on the proven effectiveness of lethal firepower in defensive fortifications, and Britain's faith that it could avoid future Continental involvements by relying upon its air force and navy to ensure its insular security. And throughout the West revulsion against the horrible losses of World War I contributed to a wave of militant pacifism that — especially in Britain and the United States — simply denied the relevance of war to international intercourse. In the United States this pacifism was related to a sentiment of isolationism based upon the security provided by the broad oceans that separated the nation from all other major powers. Let them fight their own wars; our nation with its abundant resources should not become involved again.

None of the major western armies was considering the abandonment of the tank, but it continued to be considered solely as an instrument of rupture, tied closely in an auxiliary role to the infantry. This concept was supported not only by the experience of World War I but by the fact that there was a residue of thousands of tanks from the war. The slow speed (4 – 8 mph), limited range (12 – 25 miles), mechanical unreliability and inadequate armor and armament of these tanks held the armored units to the pace and doctrine of infantry until the old tanks were worn out.

Improvements in tank design and performance abounded, and in the 1930s new tanks were being built embodying them. The most important changes were in suspension, armor, power plants and transmissions, and communication means of the vehicles themselves. Among innovations were hydropneumatic mechanisms permitting use of more powerful guns without longer recoil, gyro-stabilizers that theoretically would enable tanks to fire effectively when moving, and radio communications systems such as Swinton had foreseen. Although by 1939 none of these innovations had come close to their theoretical potentials, and the tanks of the 1930s were still far from achieving the capabilities visualized by Fuller, they were as much an improvement over the clumsy armored vehicles of 1918 as was the 1906 *Dreadnought* in comparison with the 1862 *Monitor*. The result was a series of tanks of increasingly greater speed, range, trafficability, mechanical toughness, and maneuverability — individually and in mass.

Nevertheless, the doctrinal fixation on the tank as an infantry support weapon continued to restrict its armament to antipersonnel automatic weapons and small-bore cannon. Very few tanks in any army at the outbreak of World War II possessed an antitank capability, although the doctrine espoused by the exponents of armor must inevitably have resulted in tank-versus-tank battles. This possibility was vaguely foreseen and provided for in a general sense, by heavy armor in France and high mobility in England. The eventuality does not seem to have impressed itself on planners in the United States, where, as a result of an intraservice squabble between infantry and cavalry, the tank was restricted by law to employment as an infantry weapon.

England maintained its Royal Tank Corps at greatly reduced strength and developed armor along two distinct lines: the "cruiser" tank to operate in all-tank units and the "cooperation" tank to work directly with and under control of the infantry. The United States experimented with mechanized combined-arms forces in maneuvers in 1928 and 1930, and in 1932 established the 7th Cavalry Brigade (mechanized) at Fort Knox, Kentucky. In order to accomplish this the Army found it necessary to adopt the absurd expedient of designating cavalry tanks as "combat cars" to circumvent the statutory restriction on tanks as infantry weapons. France maintained tank battalions for the sole purpose of infantry support, and even when, just before World War II, it began to organize armored divisions, could not resist the temptation to fragment these for distribution among its infantry formations.

Assessment and Actions by the Germans

In Germany the story was quite different, although at first as much for reasons of necessity as for superior foresight and imagination. The Versailles Treaty limited Germany to an army of 100,000 men and specifically prohibited any German armor or combat aircraft. Although Germany had made little use of the tank in World War I, in large part because of industrial constraints, much stress was placed on armor and armor doctrine in its surreptitious postwar training under General Hans von Seeckt. German attention was initially directed toward mechanization primarily by the need for some substitute for the manpower denied it at Versailles. Intensive general-staff study of the lessons of World War I, in combination with experience in experimental use of armored vehicles in field training, led ultimately to a means of meeting the manpower substitution requirement that was to produce earthshaking military results.

The covert German experimentation program had to be carried out under the surveillance of an Allied Control Commission, charged with enforcing the Versailles Treaty restrictions. The Germans were able to enter into secret cooperation with the Russian Army as one means of deceiving the Control Commission. In its training areas in Russia the German Army evolved the armored division with organic motorized infantry and engineers. Development of self-propelled artillery, except as a short-range infantry arm (assault gun), was slow. Training initially with mocked-up tanks on truck bodies, in lieu of the tanks denied them by the treaty, the Germans developed a doctrine of surprise and speed in armored operations far ahead of anything envisaged by the former Allied countries.

This development did not come about with the universal approbation and support of the German military hierarchy. Armor enthusiasts in postwar Germany met with much the same obstacles of inertia, parochialism, and downright antagonism within the professional officer corps that were frustrating similar enthusiasts in the other western armies. But in Germany certain powerful factors were working for them that were denied to their western counterparts.

The German Army had inherited no specific tank doctrine from World War I. Nor were there surplus tanks such as the Allied armies were saddled with. With a general-staff tradition of study and analysis of military problems it was easier to accept new and improved tanks and doctrine for their use. When the Germans were able to buy or build tanks they were tanks of advanced design, capable of performing according to new and advanced theories. They came, moreover, at a time when voice radio had developed to a point where it was available for command, control, and communications for armored forces.

Farsighted as the German doctrine and organization were, relative to those of the Allies, armor remained with them an instrument of rupture. But while the Allies tended to employ the instrument as an adjunct of infantry, the Germans believed the concept was best achieved by masses of armor, organized in divisions and corps, operating with motorized infantry divisions that were designed to exploit the successes of the rapidly moving tanks. In the absence of organic self-propelled artillery, the clandestine Luftwaffe began to consider the possibility that dive-bombers could provide the equivalent of mobile artillery support for fast-moving tanks.

The Luftwaffe came out of hiding in 1935, and began testing the prototype of the Ju-87 dive-bomber. The success of these tests overcame the opposition of many German officers to the dive-bombing concept, and the first operational Ju-87s appeared in 1937. They were put into formations to substitute for mobile artillery under the relevant group commander. Ultimately these dive-bombers were equipped with screaming devices to maximize the moral effect stressed by Fuller.

This employment of aircraft did not originate with the Germans. Swinton had pointed out its utility in his 1916 draft armor doctrine. And in the British offensive at Amiens in August 1918 a squadron of two-seater Armstrong-Whitworth aircraft had been allotted to the tank corps for close support, and a squadron of Sopwith Camels experimented with antitank guns. Fuller wrote in his *Lectures on FSR III* (1932) that "the tank and the aeroplane are complementary machines and for a long time to come the one is unlikely to be able to operate safely without the other. . . . In future warfare, cooperation between tanks and aeroplane is likely to prove far more important than cooperation between tanks and infantry." Yet it was the Germans, under the dual pressures of necessity and field experiment, who really developed the tank-air team.

By the early 1930s the German Army had secretly placed orders for construction of 37mm-gun light tanks and 75mm-gun medium tanks, to be built of mild steel rather than armor plate. Under the impetus provided by Lt. Col. Heinz Guderian — a general-staff officer — an armored force began to take shape in 1931, and in 1932 training tanks were constructed on a number of Carden-Lloyd tracked antiaircraft mounts purchased in England. This vehicle actually went into battle in 1939–1940 as the Mark I tank.

When Hitler became chancellor not only did he approve and support the aims of the young armored force, but in 1934 he authorized overt construction of tanks fully armored and designed to conform to the new doctrinal requirements. So energetically was this work pressed that on October 15, 1935, Germany's first three panzer divisions were organized. These divisions were constituted as follows:

> One panzer brigade consisting of two panzer regiments, each of two four-company tank battalions, with 15 tanks per company, a total of 240 tanks to the division.
>
> One motorized rifle brigade of one rifle regiment and one motorcycle battalion, a total of about 3,000 infantrymen.
>
> One antitank battalion of three companies, armed at first with 37mm guns.
>
> One armored reconnaissance battalion of two armored-car companies, one motorcycle company, and one mixed company, a total of about 50 armored cars.
>
> An artillery regiment of two battalions (six batteries each)

of truck-drawn light howitzers, a total of 72 pieces per division.

A motorized signal battalion.

A motorized light engineer company.

Tests of armored forces and doctrine in the Spanish Civil War (1936–1939) were generally disappointing or inconclusive. However, the Germans rightly attributed failures and disappointments to the lack of experience or other inadequacies of tank crews, higher commanders, and other units. They were more satisfied with the results of air reconnaissance and the use of dive-bombers versus artillery. On balance they believed that their organization and doctrine had been confirmed by the Spanish experience.

The Opponents at Outbreak of World War II

At the outbreak of World War II in 1939, in addition to nearly 100 infantry divisions, Germany mustered six armored and four motorized infantry divisions designed for exploitation. Three "light divisions" had also been organized at cavalry insistence for the traditional cavalry roles of reconnaissance and exploitation. In the Polish campaign the panzer divisions were used as instruments of rupture, and the nature of this campaign was such that the true exploitation potential of armor formations was not fully realized.

After the 1939 Polish campaign, the panzer division was strengthened by addition of an antiaircraft battalion, an air reconnaissance squadron, and a supply battalion, and the engineer company was increased to a battalion. The light division had been found neither to be strong enough, nor to have sufficient additional mobility to justify its existence. So all three were converted after the campaign into panzer divisions. A new panzer division was also formed during the following winter so that for the 1940 invasion of France ten panzer divisions were available.

This force of ten divisions was equipped with 2,574 tanks, all but 135 of which (used for command) were combat vehicles. The 2,439 combat tanks represented four German and two Czech models, of which the German Mark II, armed with 20mm guns, was by far the most numerous (40 percent).

During the fall and winter of 1939–1940 Guderian, by this time a general commanding the XIX Corps, vigorously urged employment of armored forces for exploitation as well as for rupture. Although he found himself in complete agreement with Major General Erich von Manstein, chief of the planning division of the general staff, the recommendations of these two officers were at first met with skepticism in the army high command. However, in two important map maneuvers — on February 7 and 14, 1940 — Guderian employed his corps in an exploitation role with unmistakable effect. He and Manstein won over General Franz Halder, chief of the general staff, and formerly one of the skeptics. Manstein's plans for surprise breakthrough in the Ardennes, and Guderian's concept of the breakthrough, were adopted. When the assault came in May 1940, Guderian was able to maintain the momentum that took him to the English Channel in fifteen days.

While Germany was preparing for an armored blow with materiel and doctrine in congruence to a degree unseen since the heyday of Napoleon, belated efforts to organize armored forces were begun in France and England in the late 1930s. The French concept of armor solely as an infantry support weapon held so firmly, however, that the first French armored division was not formed until September 1938. This division consisted of four battalions of heavy tanks formed into two demibrigades and two battalions of motorized infantry, with rudimentary support elements. In January 1940 a second such division was organized, and by May 1940 a third was in existence and a fourth was being organized. By this time each demibrigade had been reorganized to consist of one battalion of 34 heavy tanks and one of 45 light tanks, a total of 158 tanks in the division. The motorized rifle contingent had been reduced to one battalion, and the artillery to two *groupes* of 12 truck-drawn guns each. These divisions were underequipped and only partly trained when committed to battle in May and June 1940. Furthermore, for the most part they were committed piecemeal and with little effect.

Great Britain, although the home of some of the most advanced and articulate advocates of armored warfare, lagged even behind France in development of the armored division. Despite considerable experimentation with mechanized formations of various sorts, the British did not organize an armored division prototype until 1938, as a mechanized cavalry division. The first armored division along modern lines was started in April 1939. It consisted of two tank brigades, one light and one heavy, of three battalions each, with a total complement of 321 tanks, one motorized rifle battalion, and a "support group." This last included a 16-gun motorized artillery regiment and a company of engineers. The division was not fully equipped at the outbreak of war, did not reach France until after the first German victories, and was not engaged.

The Introduction of Blitzkrieg

The German concept of armor organization and tactics, and their aggressive and imaginative employment of armor and close-support aircraft in close collaboration with each other, has been known since 1939 as *blitzkrieg* — lightning war. Its epitome was the campaign in the West in 1940, one of the most overwhelming victories in the annals of warfare. Armored spearheads of von Rundstedt's Army Group A, making the main effort through the Ardennes, reached the Channel in fifteen days. Then they turned north into Belgium, joined with elements of von Bock's Army Group B, and penned the Allied forces between them and the Channel. With the all-out support of the Royal Air Force and Royal Navy, most of the British Expeditionary Force was evacuated in the "Miracle of Dunkirk" — but the British troops left all their heavy equipment behind. On June 5 — one day after the British completed their evacuation of Dunkirk — the regrouped German armies struck southward across the Somme, and within three weeks France capitulated. The pattern for the war had been set.

The New Weapons of World War II

Amazing inventions and refinements in technique emerged from the crucible of World War II. Among these were such things as the proximity fuze, "shaped" charges, the bazooka (prototype anti-tank missile), recoilless rifles, rockets (returning from a century of oblivion), and concomitant refinements in artillery fire direction and control. Vastly improved mobile ordnance, fast tanks and tank destroyers, and other cross-country vehicles combined to produce a mobile warfare capability at speeds previously impossible.

The United States Army demonstrated the most significant development in the enhancement of artillery firepower since the time of Gustavus Adolphus. Between the wars the U.S. Field Artillery School at Fort Sill, Oklahoma, developed the technique of massed fires, whereby a single fire direction center could rapidly and accurately shift the fire of many batteries, and sometimes many battalions, across a wide front, multiplying artillery effectiveness many times. This capability, and particularly the "time-on-target" technique of massing the fires of large numbers of guns on one target in a demoralizing crescendo of destructiveness, gave the Americans a firepower superiority on the battlefield that was not matched by any other nation in the war. It should be noted, however, that the Soviets were equally impressed with the importance of firepower, substituting numbers of guns for technique.

Almost accidentally the Germans discovered that their high-velocity 88mm antiaircraft gun was very effective as an antitank gun. It was, in fact, the best in the world, and was also useful in the normal artillery support role in level or rolling areas where its flat trajectory was not a handicap. Probably the most effective use made of the 88mm gun was by General Erwin Rommel in the desert fighting in North Africa, where he aggressively sent batteries of 88s forward with his armor, to form deadly firepower bases around which his tanks maneuvered rapidly, to the dismay of his British opponents.

In 1941 the United States and Britain agreed to divide between them the efforts of producing new weapons then in development, or on the drawing boards in the two nations. The United States was given responsibility for developing a proximity fuze, first conceived by the British. British scientists had been working toward a device to detect changes in the atmospheric electric field, but U.S. scientists decided that the electrostatic device held less promise than radar, and this was the form used in the ultimate development. The fuze was a tiny radar set fitted into the point of an ordinary artillery shell. When it sensed any electricity-conducting body near it, the shell was detonated. Proximity to any solid object — trees or ground or aircraft — activated the fuze; the effect was an air burst 20 to 50 feet from the solid object resulting in a lethal spray of hundreds of shell fragments.

The proximity fuze was first used in ground combat in the Battle of the Bulge. Soon thereafter it was being used effectively against V-1s in England and in antiaircraft shells in the Pacific. No longer was there need to adjust for height of air burst — a difficult procedure that had been developed in World War I — or to trace aircraft with pinpoint accuracy. When the fuze was first used the devastating effect of fragments from shell air bursts was plainly evident to the hard-pressed American infantry. But, according to Dr. Hugh M. Cole, author of The Battle of the Bulge, the effect was "grossly exaggerated."

Before the war the British, Americans, and Japanese — quite independently — devised weapons, equipment, and techniques to improve assault landings. All three developed shallow-draft, ramp-unloading landing craft that would get troops to the edge of the beach and enable them to unload rapidly. During the war the British and Americans produced ocean-going vessels such as the landing ship tank (LST) and landing ship infantry (LSI) that could carry assault troops across an ocean and land them in combat-ready formation on hostile beaches.

Rockets were used in both land and naval warfare during the

nineteenth century, but their effect was more spectacular than lethal. It was not until World War II that rocket-type missiles became
truly effective as military weapons, and significant improvements
in this class of weapon have taken place at a rapid pace since 1945
(see Chapter XXVII).

Soon after World War I, American Dr. Robert H. Goddard conducted laboratory experiments and made computations that indicated that more thrust and terminal velocity could be obtained
from the burning of a mixture of liquid chemicals than from the
solid propellants previously used. The rocket invented by Dr. Goddard was a free-flight vehicle with a simple pressurized type of
propulsion system. In addition to presenting technical papers in
the United States describing his experiments and the results, he
discussed them extensively in correspondence with scientists in
other nations.

The significance of this development was recognized in
Europe, especially in Germany, before much attention was paid to
it in the United States. The German Rocket Society was founded in
1927. Experiments with liquid-propellant rockets were also carried
out in Austria, England, and Russia. Hitler was so impressed with
the potential of rocket-type missiles that he created a special group
of engineers and scientists to develop them. He poured almost unlimited funds into the development of these "secret weapons" and
believed that their use against England would break the British will
to fight because of the destruction and casualties they would
produce.

The subsonic pulse-jet German V-1 was first used just after the
Normandy invasion in 1944, but it was quite inaccurate, easily de-
tected, and fairly easily shot down by aircraft or antiaircraft
weapons. The larger supersonic V-2 was the first ballistic missile
used in warfare. Its trajectory was computed on the same basis as
that for the "Paris gun" of World War I. The tremendous energy produced by the burning alcohol and liquid oxygen pumped in the
rocket engine enabled the V-2 to carry a half-ton high-explosive
warhead to a range of up to 200 miles. Although Hitler had several
thousand V-2 ballistic missiles available in early 1944, he did not
authorize their use until September. Between that time and early
in 1945 they were used in great numbers against England and the
Channel ports to inflict extensive losses in lives and property. Hitler
thought of them as vengeance weapons, to be used against non-
military targets in retaliation for the Allied strategic bombardment
of Germany.

The German V-2 burned about two tons of liquid oxygen and
alcohol to produce 20,000 pounds of thrust for 62 seconds — or a

little over one minute. The weight at takeoff was about eight tons, but the rocket energy raised the missile to an altitude of about 80 miles during the time of burning. At "burn-out" the velocity of the rocket was over 3,000 miles per hour or more than four times the speed of sound.

The rockets used tactically in ground and naval warfare in World War II and since are of course much smaller than the V-1 and V-2, and almost all of them are driven by solid propellants. The first "bazooka" rockets, and the British antiaircraft rockets for the defense of London, used cordite as the propellant. A fast-burning modified nitrocellulose propellant gives the necessary "boost" to the projectiles launched from recoilless rifles.

World War II was a war of maneuver, personnel, and logistics. While the value of fortifications — both fixed and temporary — as springboards for maneuver was again attested throughout the period, sieges *per se* had no appreciable effect other than psychological. Air power emerged as a combat force equal in importance to land power and sea power.

XXV. Air Power
1935 – present

The Origins of Air Combat

Mythology and folk legend provide ample evidence that attack through the air has been a wistful dream of man since he invented organized warfare. There are numerous tales of warriors on flying horses and troops carried by trained eagles, to say nothing of Munchausen's story of riding a cannonball over the enemy lines.

Since the first flight of a hot air balloon in 1782 the dream of delivering troops or projectiles over the enemy's head to his sensitive rear changed to an achievable goal in the imagination of many practitioners and dilettantes of warfare. The first military use of a balloon in battle was in the French Revolutionary War at Maubeuge in 1794. Balloons were used extensively — without much success — in the American Civil War. And during the four-month siege of Paris in 1870 – 1871 a total of 65 balloons, filled at the Paris gas works, carried on a one-way air transport operation, lifting 23,485 pounds of dispatches, 164 passengers, and 381 carrier pigeons out of the city.

This operation demonstrated why no balloon-borne attack has been attempted in war and why it would almost certainly have failed had it been attempted. Many of the Paris balloons landed in the German lines, some drifted out to sea, and at least one was carried to Norway before it returned to earth. Man's dream of flying to the enemy's rear clearly had to await some more tractable forms of lift and propulsion.

In 1903 the Wright brothers' invention led the way to those better forms. In a span of only eleven years, from the time of this first powered flight to the outbreak of World War I, the airplane was developed into a weapon of combat. The first aircraft were intended to supplement carrier pigeons for communication and to augment cavalry reconnaissance. In 1907 the U.S. Army estalished an aviation section of the Signal Corps for these purposes.

Air Combat in World War I

From the outset American soldiers and military aviators were considering ways of using aircraft for direct combat purposes as well. This possibility became a requirement in all of the opposing armies in World War I. The evolution from the reconnaissance plane, used solely for observation, to the fighter plane was not long in coming with the attachment of a machine gun that could be fired by pilot or observer. Thus, although observation still remained an important function of military aircraft, active fighting now lay within the plane's capability. Increasingly, the task of gaining control of the skies over the battlefield became the role of these flying guns.

The idea of placing machine guns in airplanes was conceived early in the war on both sides, but the technical shortcomings of both the weapons and the aircraft of the day made it difficult to place guns that would load and fire efficiently on the wings, outside the radius of rotation of the propeller blades. A logical solution was to put the machine gun in the cockpit, beside the pilot, so that he could aim plane and weapon simultaneously at a foe, in the air or on the ground. The trouble with this, however, was that machine-gun bullets struck the propeller, soon sawing it off.

The French improvised a crude solution by fixing steel plates to the propeller blades, thus deflecting bullets that would otherwise go through them. The Germans, having observed the crude French device in a captured plane, soon took the lead in this area of development when they mounted an efficient fixed machine gun in their Fokker monoplane. The German gun was synchronized with the propeller, so that the bullets went out between the whirling blades. The French, in turn, improved upon the German development with their Nieuport in 1916. The practice of mounting machine guns in the wings, however, continued to a limited extent.

By the end of the war there were three separate types of military aircraft: the observation plane, the fighter, and the more heavily constructed bomber, usually a multiengined aircraft. Most aircraft were biplanes, but there were also triplanes and a few monoplanes.

The combined fighter-bomber developed in 1917 by the chief of the British Royal Flying Corps, General Hugh Trenchard, was one of the most important steps forward. This was a fighter plane slightly modified to carry up to four light (25-pound) bombs for ground support purposes. The plane's characteristics remained unchanged; thus, after a fighter had achieved the main objective of superiority in the air, it could then be employed in ground support, either by using its machine gun alone, or by dropping its light bombs as well. In 1918, the use of the fighter-bomber contributed somewhat to the initial success of the great German offensives; British fighter-bombers played a more important role in stopping those German drives. The British Somme counteroffensive (August 1918) and the American St. Mihiel offensive (September 1918) marked the first major utilizations of bombers and fighter-bombers in mass preparation for offensive battle.

The concept of creating a separate arm for air combat, comparable to the army for fighting on land, and navy for conflict at sea, was strongly urged by many leading airmen, particularly General Trenchard. His efforts were rewarded early in 1918 when the Royal Flying Corps became the independent Royal Air Force (RAF). While the issue is debatable, this seems in general to have contributed to a more flexible and more aggressive use of air power by Britain and other nations that followed that policy.

The Apostles of Air Power

In the 1920s and 1930s the issue of the role of air power in future combat was hotly debated by military theorists. A few countries — Italy and Germany among them — followed the British example of establishing an independent air force, coequal with their armies and navies. But most nations retained their military air contingents as elements of the army or — in many cases, as in the United States — army and navy.

Although Great Britain led the world in the creation of an independent air force, the Royal Navy insisted that it must retain control over aircraft at sea, and particularly over aircraft that were based upon naval vessels, and so the Naval Air Arm was a contingent of the Royal Navy, not of the Royal Air Force. American sailors were just as adamant that they must control air power at sea, but the issue was less hotly debated in the United States since non-naval military aviation also remained under Army control.

The most noted of the early apostles of air power was Italian aviator Giulio Douhet, whose book, *Command of the Air*, published in 1921, led some people to call him "the Mahan of the air," a comparison with the great American apostle of sea power. It was Douhet's thesis — shared by many airmen around the world, particularly in the United States and Great Britain — that future wars would be won by air forces, striking far behind national boundaries and fighting fronts on the ground, that would destroy the warmaking capabilities of industrialized nations, and so terrorize their populations that the will to continue the war would be destroyed long before a decision could be reached by embattled ground armies. Thus he visualized the air force as first among equals in a nation's armed forces, with armies and navies dwindling to little more than supporting elements for air power. Not surprisingly these ideas were rejected by most generals and admirals, although the Douhet thesis was endorsed by many (if not most) airmen and a number of civilian writers on military and strategic affairs.

It is interesting that when World War II came the Douhet thesis was adopted as enthusiastically by American military airmen — even though they were still under Army control — as by those of the RAF. Equally interesting is the fact that Germany, which did have an independent air force, used its air power almost exclusively as an adjunct of land and (to a limited extent) naval power, and never really tested the Douhet thesis — which was considered the Trenchard thesis by many Britons, and the Mitchell thesis by many Americans.

In fact, as we shall see, air power had much greater influence on both the conduct and outcome of World War II than most generals and admirals had predicted before the war, but never came close to having the influence foreseen by Douhet, Trenchard, and Mitchell. In fact, it became evident during the war that the strategic air power thesis could be successful only if weapon lethality could be increased by orders of magnitude. High-explosive bombs could wreak terrible damage, but they could not by themselves destroy nations and their warmaking capabilities as Douhet had foreseen. It was to take the atomic bomb (which Douhet had never foreseen) to give real significance to his theories.

Technology and Aircraft Development

Technological advances between the First and Second World Wars, particularly in propulsion and aircraft frames, gave marked improvement in speed, range, and load-carrying capacity. The period saw the emergence of prototypes of modern high-speed fighter planes and both short- and long-range bombers.

Between the world wars the British demonstrated that aircraft could be highly effective punitive weapons in colonial border and tribal wars. Not only did this use of aircraft permit quick response to local disorders, it frequently obviated the necessity for costly punitive expeditions on the ground.

The low-wing, single-engine, monoplane fighter was typified in Britain by the Hurricane and Spitfire in particular, and in Germany by the Messerschmitt Me-109. These planes were armed with as many as six or eight wing-mounted machine guns and could be adapted to carry light bombs in the fighter-bomber role. They could fly at speeds between 350 and 400 miles per hour.

The two-engine, low-wing bombers (Dorniers, Heinkels, Blenheims), that also appeared during this period, were the pre-World War II prototypes of the modern light and medium bombers. Their increased range, greater speed, and large cargo capacity permitted delivering a significantly more lethal load at ranges up to 500 miles, and they could be mass-produced.

In 1935, the U.S. produced the prototype of the strategic bomber, intended by its designers to wage war as foreseen by Douhet, Trenchard, and Mitchell. The B-17, or "Flying Fortress," was the first modern four-engine long-range bomber. With the essentially similar B-24 "Liberator," and the more advanced B-29 "Super Fortress," which appeared toward the end of the war, the B-17 was to play a major role in the defeat of Germany and Japan.

In 1939, the British perfected fighter direction based on the new and revolutionary development of radar. With improved radio communications and control centers, radar made possible highly efficient use of the fighter-interceptor. These new systems increased effectiveness of the RAF fighters, individually and collectively, and contributed significantly to victory in the Battle of Britain. In addition, there was a slight qualitative superiority of the Spitfire over the Me-109. Actually the full potential of the Spitfire was not exploited in the Battle of Britain. Most of them were equipped with Very High Frequency (VHF) radios, but since some Spitfire squadrons and most Hurricane squadrons were not so equipped, radio control had to be performed by standard HF communication.

The Luftwaffe and Blitzkrieg

The increased capabilities of the new fighters and light and medium bombers furnished the means for creation of the first modern tactical air force: the German Luftwaffe. As with ground weapons and concepts, the Spanish Civil War provided a testing ground for aircraft and air operations, and gave the Germans and Italians — who supported the Spanish "rebels" under General Franco — and the Soviets (who assisted the "Loyalist" forces of the leftist Spanish Republic) considerable combat experience in the tactical employment of these aircraft. Later the Luftwaffe, in conjunction with German armored and infantry divisions, made possible the rapid overrunning of Poland, France, the Balkans, and western Russia. German blitzkrieg tactics very nearly resulted in an early German victory in World War II.

Blitzkrieg, of course, owed much of its overwhelming effectiveness to the Germans' revolutionary handling of tactical air support. They welded the fighter plane, dive-bomber, and medium bomber into a weapons system of tactical warfare within the blitzkrieg concept. Although both the Germans and British had experimented with the idea, using fighter-bombers during the last part of World War I, the invasion of Poland was the first example of highly effective tactical air support. The Germans accomplished the coordination of aircraft with armored vehicles that had been visualized by farsighted Englishmen like Swinton and Fuller some twenty years earlier.

The enveloping movements of armored columns were supported by aircraft (dive-bombers and fighter-bombers) performing what would soon be recognized as the three basic functions of tactical air power: (1) gaining air superiority by defeating the enemy in the air and by destroying or neutralizing enemy air bases; (2) interdicting enemy lines of communication to inhibit movement of reinforcements and supplies; and (3) providing close firepower support of ground forces as flying artillery, attacking battlefield targets. The Germans initially placed the most importance on the second aspect of air support, since their first opponents could give but weak resistance in the air and their tactical air weapons were most effective against exposed, stationary targets. After eight months of "phony" war stalemate in the West, the pattern was continued in Holland, Belgium, and France. There too, ground movement was strongly supported by Stukas and Messerchmitts, which were particularly deadly against communications centers and vehicle concentrations, but which also performed the mission of flank protection.

British and American Air Support Doctrine

Ironically, it was the British and the Americans who went on to exploit the full potential of tactical air support. The most important developments after the beginning of the war took place in the Middle East theater, where the RAF played a major role in stopping Rommel's drive into Egypt in 1943. Procedures for flexible cooperation between air forces and ground troops were worked out between the local British commanders, who, for the first time, spelled out the three classical missions of tactical air support that had been demonstrated by the Germans. The principal difference between the British and the German methods was in the relationship of air and ground command. In the German system the air commanders were subordinate and were forced to deploy their units in accord with the desires of the ground commanders. This caused no problems as long as there was no substantial air opposition. But the British discovered that they could achieve air superiority over a dangerous foe or prevent him from gaining air superiority only if their first objective, regardless of the course of the ground battle, was to seek air superiority. And to do this, of course, the air commander must deploy and use his units as seemed best for the air battle, with little or no concern about ground targets.

When the Americans entered the war, at first they followed the German system. After suffering serious losses in the air and on the ground in early actions in Tunisia, however, they adopted the British system, which became accepted U.S. air doctrine. There has been much postwar controversy over its validity in the light of dramatic changes that have taken place in aircraft. But with the aircraft and weapons on hand in 1942–1945, there is little doubt that the doctrine then adopted was the one that best exploited existing capabilities.

In the war against Japan the problem of priority of fighter task allocation was never so serious as it was in North Africa and Europe. This was partly because, after the early months of the war, the Japanese were not capable of offering the same kind of opposition in the air as the Germans did in the West. Accordingly, in the Pacific and on the Asian continent, the roles of Army, Navy, and Marine Corps aircraft in tactical support were very similar to that of the Luftwaffe in its early European campaigns. The most significant use of aircraft in the Pacific ground campaigns was in softening up beachhead defenses, and in supporting amphibious landings. In the central Pacific these functions and subsequent close air support of the ground operations were performed mainly by carrier aircraft.

In the southwest Pacific the air support mission was usually the responsibility of Fifth Air Force fighters, operating from fields within 500 miles of the beachhead. Only in the Hollandia and Leyte landings were the assault troops initially dependent upon carrier plane support. This was highly effective in both instances, although the results of the naval battle for Leyte Gulf very briefly permitted Japanese land-based aircraft to gain air superiority over the beachhead from depleted U.S. carrier units. The hasty construction of an airfield ashore, and the expeditious arrival of land-based fighters, plus the arrival of carrier reinforcements, soon rectified this situation. No further serious air opposition was encountered by American ground forces in the Pacific war.

In operations in Burma and China the Japanese had air superiority in late 1941 and early 1942. By 1943, however, the situation had changed, mainly because the Japanese were forced to allocate most of their available air effort against the Americans in the Pacific. Thus the Allies completely dominated the skies in Burma and were rarely challenged in southern and central China.

During World War II there were two major varieties of weapons relating to the tactical air support of ground forces (aside from the weapons of air-to-air combat) that permitted or restricted air superiority. The first of these were antiaircraft weapons that ground forces used to fight back against the attacking aircraft. The second category included the weapons that the aircraft used against ground targets.

Defense against Air Attack

The first antiaircraft weapons were the ground soldiers' rifles and machine guns, used in World War I against strafing fighters. These were generally ineffective and merely helped to sustain the morale of troops subjected to the somewhat terrifying experience. Later, specially mounted .30-caliber and .50-caliber machine guns were employed, with rudimentary sighting devices to permit them to "lead" the attacking planes. And some light cannon with similar crude sights were employed to use high-explosive shells with both percussion and time fuzes. Again, none of these was very effective.

Antiaircraft artillery was greatly improved in all countries between the wars, and the requirement to develop an effective antiair capability gave great impetus to the adaptation of electronic developments to military uses. By the outbreak of World War II rather sophisticated computing devices were available that (in combination with modern optical equipment) permitted accurate tracking of aircraft, predicting flight paths, and calculating range, altitude, and time of flight for a high-explosive shell to reach a predicted point of interception. This machinery could then electrically traverse and elevate the pieces, and set a proper time setting on time fuzes, or make it easy for soldiers to do this manually by matching pointers. The results would have been deadly against World War I planes. But at the outset of World War II aircraft performance was such that even these marvelous weapons were relatively inaccurate and did not account for a very high percentage of planes lost in the war.

The development of the VT, or proximity, fuze (see Chapter XXIV), greatly increased the lethality of antiaircraft artillery. This capability was still further enhanced for low-flying aircraft, by the development of radar tracking devices and by improvements in electronic equipment. Once again, however, countermeasures were taken to reduce the effectiveness of each new technique. "Window," or myriad strips of metalized paper, were released by Allied bombing planes to jam and confuse German electronic defenses during the bomber offensives of 1943. And the increasing capabilities of high-speed, high-altitude aircraft with "pathfinder" systems, which located targets by radar and marked them, largely offset the new antiaircraft techniques.

More recent developments in antiaircraft weapons involve large rockets firing target-seeking or electronically guided missiles.

Air Weapons and Ground Targets

For air-to-ground attacks, at least until the 1950s, primary reliance was on the two weapons first employed in World War I: machine-gun fire and small, antipersonnel, high-explosive bombs. Two important additions to these, the napalm fire bomb and the rocket, came into use in World War II. Both of these have added to the actual effectiveness of air support, as well as contributed to the moral effect of air attack.

The effectiveness of air attack on ground targets, in terms of destructiveness and lethality, is considerably less than might be expected from the formidable quantity of firepower that can be assembled on a relatively small aircraft. This is due in large part to the inaccuracy inherent in finding and attacking a distant target while passing over it at great speed, and in the relative instability of the aircraft as a weapons platform, in comparison with ground-based weapons. Nonetheless, aircraft frequently have demonstrated that they can have an important role in supporting troops when artillery support is limited, or cannot reach targets effectively. In particular, however, ground-support aircraft have a tremendous moral influence on ground troops — a very negative effect upon troops being attacked, and a positive effect on those being supported.

Air Power and Logistics

The logistical potential of aircraft was incompletely perceived at the outset of World War II. The employment of transport aircraft for airborne assault had been foreseen by most nations before the war, and this combat concept was developed further by the Germans and Russians. But the concepts of large-scale logistical support of ground forces by transport aircraft, of strategic air deployment of substantial ground units, and of regular and massive air evacuation of wounded were all pioneered by Americans, with substantial cooperation from the British.

It was in the China-Burma-India theater of World War II that the most extensive use was made of air transport. The operations of General Stilwell's force in north Burma (eventually reaching a combat strength of more than six divisions) were almost completely supported by air supply for nearly two years. The long-range penetrations of Wingate's Chindits were made possible only by air power, including air assault, combat air support, and air logistics. Finally, the climactic, successful offensive of General Slim's Fourteenth Army in central Burma was also mainly supported by air supply, at the same time that the Chinese-Americans were still operating on air supply farther north, in a truly amazing display of the capabilities of air logistics.

Airborne Operations

The air assault team, like the armored division, is a type of twentieth century combat team. Its troops, training, weapons, and tactics are tailored to a specific mission. The doctrine under which it is employed must be consonant with these characteristics and with the mission. Coordination is necessary not only within the team but with all other operating elements involved in the common military effort. In the case of airborne attacks, for example, one cardinal point of doctrine that has emerged is the necessity of a prompt linkup with conventional troops armed with heavy weapons.

In World War I mechanical unreliability, limited payload capacity, and uncertain airworthiness of aircraft precluded their use for the tactical delivery of troops in combat. Furthermore, not until near the end of World War I was a compact portable parachute with quick release and a pilot chute perfected. By the end of the war, however, the essential requisites for troop transport had begun to coincide in manageable form, and the chief of the American Service in France — Brigadier General William Mitchell — was planning for large-scale airborne operations in 1919 had the war continued.

It is perhaps pertinent that the most serious and persistent experiments in airborne operations between the wars were undertaken in the two countries whose political philosophies were overtly aggressive. The Soviet Union began tests in 1930, and Nazi Germany followed suit after Adolph Hitler came to power in 1933. In both of these countries airborne development was carried to the point that both had parachute and air-transported units of division size ready at the onset of war in 1939.

Progress in the western nations was more pedestrian. In the United States a small delivery of men and equipment by parachute was made in training operations in 1928 by the Army, and occasionally thereafter. But it was not until 1938 that airborne operations were incorporated into U.S. Army doctrine, and it was 1940 before organization and training of airborne units was begun. England organized no airborne units until 1940, although experiments there had been undertaken as early as 1927. France and Italy had no airborne formations prior to World War II.

The Russian development of airborne forces exceeded that of any other European nation, although in combat operations they were of relatively little worth. Unsatisfactory experience in the Spanish Civil War (1936–1939), followed by the failure of airborne troops to meet expectations in Finland in 1940, led to deemphasis on airborne operations until after the German successes in Holland in 1940 and Crete in 1941. These brought about a revival of Soviet interest, but by the time of the German invasion of Russia (June 1941) only one parachute brigade in each of three projected corps had been fully equipped. Subsequent repeated failure in major operations, together with shortages of aircraft and the immediacy of combat requirements, led to employment of the troops principally as conventional land forces.

German development of airborne forces and doctrine was little publicized before 1940, but it was highly productive. Behind the early German success lay not only a realistic appreciation of the limitations of airborne forces but an equal regard for mission and objective in assessing their capabilities. Thus, with one or two exceptions, airborne units were not assigned tasks for which their necessarily light armament was not adapted, and prompt linkup with more heavily armed conventional forces was written into their doctrine. Finally, the principle of surprise was exploited to the utmost.

In the spring of 1940 Germany had available 4,500 trained parachute troops, concentrated in the 7th Parachute Division — under command of the Luftwaffe rather than the army. The parachute elements were organized in three rifle regiments, supported by a signal battalion, an artillery regiment, an engineer battalion, and antitank and antiaircraft battalions. The auxiliary troops and one of the rifle regiments were transported in gliders.

In extension of the capabilities of this one Luftwaffe parachute division, the army's 22d Infantry Division (12,000 strong) was trained in air-landed operations. The transport aircraft employed for all airborne operations, parachute delivery, glider towing, and troop lift, was generally the Junker Ju-52, a three-engine monoplane with a capacity of 22 equipped troops. The 1940 glider was the DSF 230, with a troop capacity of nine.

These two divisions, only one of which was an airborne division in the current sense, plus one rifle battalion that could be airlanded, constituted the entire German airborne capability on May 10, 1940, when the western assault was launched. That its accomplishments were out of all proportion to its size was the result of the imaginative doctrine already discussed, as well as certain other tactical devices. One of these was the use of dummy parachutists to divert attention from actual drop zones and to increase the impression of strength in those zones. Another was intensive preliminary bombardment of the drop zone by aircraft and, where possible, by artillery.

The main airborne effort of May 10 was directed against Holland, with only 500 troops reserved for use in Belgium. The principal targets in Holland were the bridges at Rotterdam, Dordrecht, and Moerdijk, with The Hague a secondary target. Four parachute battalions and one airborne regiment were used against the three principal targets with complete success and negligible losses. The attack on The Hague, carried out by one parachute battalion and two airborne regiments, failed with severe casualties.

In Belgium, success was precariously achieved but was spectacular beyond expectation. The objectives of this operation were the two bridges over the Albert Canal west of the Dutch "Maastricht Appendix" and Fort Eban Emael, which guarded the flank of this zone. The canal bridges and the fort were seized without difficulty in a brilliant operation, but the Dutch succeeded in blowing up the Meuse bridges in Maastricht, delaying the linkup forces from the east. This delay did not affect the outcome.

German airborne operations were undertaken only four more times during the war. Only one of these was large-scale — the invasion of Crete. It constituted the only major operation in history carried out solely by airborne forces, but it so crippled Germany's airborne capability, in both troops and aircraft, that — despite success — no subsequent major effort was attempted.

The assault on Crete was made by the 7th Parachute Division supported by the 5th Mountain Division from Greece. It was planned that immediate support would be provided by seaborne forces, but seaborne support was prevented by the British Navy. Although the landing of the 7th Division was thoroughly protected by the Luftwaffe against extremely meager British fighter defenses, the airborne forces, once landed, were unable to make progress and suffered prohibitive casualties. It was then decided to land the 5th Mountain Division. Even this reinforcement might have failed had not a landing also been made under British artillery fire on Maleme airfield, which became the base of the ultimately successful attack.

Although limited, German airborne operations yielded useful lessons to all participants, some of which were substantiated by subsequent Allied experience. Surprise is a highly important factor that should be augmented by rapid and vigorous exploitation, presenting the enemy with no opportunity to recover and react. Division of command between army and air force can lead to difficulties. Since parachute and glider-landed troops cannot be adequately armed, especially in artillery, armor, and antitank weapons, to match a determined ground defense, linkup with conventional forces within a brief interval after landing is essential to success in major operations. Finally, airlift is adaptable to movement of all ground troops.

As the war progressed airborne operations were used frequently during U.S. and British offensives. The troops were transported in planes and parachuted to the ground, or carried in towed gliders for "crash" landings.

At sea the aircraft mission of support of surface forces was similar in concept to that on land though it differed in some important details. As the war drew to a close professional opinion about the capabilities and limitations of air power was widely divided, but there was a consensus that it had become an indispensable member of the combat team.

XXVI. Landing Team to Joint Task Force
1940 – present

The Origins of Amphibious Warfare

Since man first began to go "down to the sea in ships," whatever might be his "business in great waters," his voyages frequently involved going ashore on some foreign land. And frequently people on the land attempted to prevent those on the ships from going ashore. In such instances, of course, a classic confrontation situation was created, with those on the ships fighting to get on shore, and those on the shore fighting to prevent the landing. There was nothing unusual about such fighting, as far as those who were defending the shoreline were concerned. But to those attempting to land, the fighting was far from routine. For sailors involved there was an awkward transition from nautical activities to unfamiliar land combat. More often than not, however, the sailors stayed on their vessels, while soldiers who had been passengers on the craft carried out the task of getting established on shore. The transition from passenger to fighter was also an awkward one.

It was this awkward period of transition that made landing operations — only recently referred to as "amphibious operations" — both tricky and dangerous. To reduce the danger, and to minimize the awkwardness, it was the responsibility of the sailors operating the ships to put the soldiers (or sometime other sailors) ashore where they could reach solid ground quickly and easily, and yet also where enemy opposition was not likely to be serious. Obviously considerable planning and cooperation were necessary between those who were controlling the ships and those taking part in the fighting if the operation was to succeed.

Over the course of history there have been numerous landing operations; many of these were successful, but a large number failed. And with a few exceptions, during the process of planning and preparation there were usually disagreements between the sailors — responsible for their ships and for getting soldiers to the shore — and the soldiers, whose duty it was to fight once they had reached land. The differences between naval operations and land operations, and the differences in perspective that soldiers and sailors brought to the tricky landing operation, were such that friction was almost inevitable.

The sailors wanted to make sure that their ships did not go aground, and they did not wish to be caught unready for naval battle by the possible untimely arrival of a hostile fleet. The soldiers not surprisingly wanted to be put ashore without getting wet, and without meeting an enemy until after all troops were ashore and organized for battle. It was rare that these conflicting desires could be completely reconciled. Not unnaturally, therefore, both soldiers and sailors avoided amphibious or landing operations whenever possible. There were only a few significant historical exceptions to this generalization before the twentieth century: the ancient Greeks, for geographical reasons, were almost as much at home on the waters of the Aegean as on their rocky promontories; and the Vikings gloried in their ability to fight at sea, on land, and on the beaches in between.

Of course, until the end of the seventeenth century the distinction between soldier and sailor — particularly among officers — was often transitory, and sometimes nonexistent. When fleets went to sea in ancient and medieval times, the fighting men and their commanders were usually soldiers. Thus most admirals of those eras were usually even more at home as generals. But the perfection of gunpowder weapons, and the simultaneous emergence of the seagoing fighting sailing ship, brought increasing specialization to, and greater differences between, land and naval warfare. The era of commanders equally at home on quarterdeck or on horseback ended with England's famous "generals at sea," Blake and Monck, in the latter years of the seventeenth century.

For the next two hundred and fifty years the naval and military professions continued to diverge and specialize, and the problems of coordination for landing operations, when these were required, became more difficult. There were exceptions: General Wolfe and Admiral Saunders cooperating at Quebec in 1759; and Admiral Keith and General Abercrombie at Aboukir in 1801. Despite some friction, considerable misunderstanding, and provident extemporization, the British land and naval commanders in these two instances at least tried to cooperate; they planned jointly, and the operations were truly joint endeavors.

As these examples might suggest, the maritime and colonial interests of Great Britain forced the Royal Navy and British Army to work together in amphibious operations rather more than they cared to. In the nineteenth century the British had a mixture of successes and failures — including the landing that culminated in the capture of Washington, D.C., in 1814, and that which preceded defeat at New Orleans in early 1815.

The Americans also had some experience in that century. One of the most capable of early American practitioners of amphibious warfare was Winfield Scott, with successes to his credit at Fort

George on Lake Ontario in 1813, and at Vera Cruz on the Gulf of Mexico in 1847. (By interesting coincidence, the first of these had been planned and carried out in collaboration with Commodore Oliver Hazard Perry, the second with his younger brother, Commodore Matthew Galbraith Perry.) In the Civil War, Fort Fisher, at the mouth of North Carolina's Cape Fear River, was the scene of two of the several amphibious operations undertaken by Union troops. That which was attempted in December 1864 under the command of inept General Benjamin Butler was a failure; the one a month later, planned and directed by General Alfred H. Terry in cooperation with Admiral David D. Porter, was successful.

Landing Operations in World War I; Failure at Gallipoli

However, it took two British failures in World War I to demonstrate to Americans and Britons that maritime powers needed to develop, and maintain, landing doctrines that were fully abreast of current weapons technology. At Tanga, in November 1914, German general Paul von Lettow-Vorbeck initiated his four-year string of successes in East Africa by repulsing a British landing force. But it was the British failures at Gallipoli, in April and August of 1915, that most clearly revealed the gap between the military and naval professions.

The British experience in fact led many authorities to believe that successful amphibious operations had become impossible against modern sophisticated armies. The advantages defenders reaped by virtue of the shelter of field fortifications from which they could fire modern high-lethality weapons at troops wading ashore on open beaches seemed overpowering. But other military analysts interpreted the results of Gallipoli differently. The nature of their debate, and its results, warrant a survey of what happened.

Forewarned by the Allies' abortive naval attack on the Dardanelles in February 1915, the Turks, under the command of German general Otto Liman von Sanders, had concentrated troops in the area, and constructed defenses in places where landings seemed most likely. By late March 1915 a vast Allied armada was assembled in the Greek islands near the mouth of the strait. The defenders braced themselves.

Then unexpectedly the Turks were given more time to prepare themselves. The British commander — General Sir Ian Hamilton — as he readied his troops for the landing, discovered that they had been loaded on troop ships, and their equipment and guns had been loaded on cargo ships, efficient for peacetime troop movements, no doubt, but quite inefficient for an amphibious landing. The ships had to be sent back to Alexandria to be combat-loaded by units, with men, their guns, ammunition, and equipment all on the same ship.

Meanwhile Liman von Sanders had made good use of the extra month. He organized his command of about 60,000 men in an elastic defense, as ready as he could be to react to a British landing that might be made, of course, anywhere along a coast of several hundred miles.

When the landing came, on April 23, naval gunfire supported the troops as they went ashore in heterogeneous flotillas of ill-matched small craft of all kinds. Despite very heavy losses, the British achieved two major footholds, and came very close to seizing the two heights that dominated the peninsula and the strait. But due to incredibly slow and inefficient leadership, the opportunity was missed, and the hastily assembling Turks seized the heights, and ringed the narrow beachheads with entrenchments.

Analysts who studied this operation after the war recognized that it had not been Turkish firepower that had prevented the British success — even though it made the British failure terribly costly. The analysts noted that the firepower advantage had been on the side of the British, who had been able to concentrate sudden, heavy, and powerful naval gunfire on the selected landing points, whereas the Turks, not knowing where the assaults would come, had to keep most of their men and guns in reserve until the British committed themselves. And so, when the British troops came ashore, despite losses inflicted by the well-entrenched Turkish forces covering the several beaches, the British had a tremendous numerical superiority at the outset. And they could bring reinforcements ashore more quickly than the Turkish reserves could arrive overland. It was lack of doctrine, lack of planning, lack of coordination, and lack of aggressive leadership that had brought the British failure.

By midsummer of 1915, with the troops ashore confined to several shallow and tormented beachheads near the peninsula's tip, the British — reinforced by a fresh infantry corps of 25,000 men — were prepared to try again.

With the object of regaining freedom of movement for the whole enterprise and lifting the pressure from the embattled perimeters, the new corps was put ashore at Suvla Bay on the night of August 6. The landing was scheduled for 2230, just in time to beat the rise of a waning moon. The operation was commanded by Lieutenant General Sir Frederick Stopford, not known for brilliance or aggressiveness, but chosen for this crucial task because of his seniority.

He and his troops were without battle experience, and their junior leaders, wholly ignorant of the very special tactical problems of the venture, had received no special training. And the Navy had sent many of its vessels, including its most powerful battleships, home, and was unable to provide adequate gunfire support.

The landing in darkness placed insupportable burdens on command and organization, and on inexperienced officers and men. Units became intermingled, officers could not command, and troops hesitated to obey, since no one knew to whom he was speaking. When enemy fire was added to this chaos, uncontrolled panic naturally resulted.

There was very little enemy fire against the landing melee, but that little bit proved decisive enough. So great was the inertia that settled on these troops through their night of shock that when morning came it was impossible to stir up enough men and to boot them along from the beach and adjoining salt flat to the distant high ground. A few brave parties struck out to the east; the mass stayed inert not far from blue water. Stopford, aboard a British warship, seemed incapable of regaining control. Without guidance or direction, his division commanders did not do much better. The Turks closed in to secure the ridges overlooking the bay — ridges that the British could have seized early on the seventh, even without naval gunfire. The Gallipoli hope turned to ashes, and the inevitable sequel was the liquidation of the one great amphibious effort in World War I.

Amphibious Doctrine Between the World Wars

Between Gallipoli and World War II, amphibious operations changed dramatically. History makes it perfectly clear that there is no other way to account for Allied victory in World War II than to follow the curve of development in amphibious operations during that period. At the most critical period of the conflict, the European Axis Powers dominated the whole coastline of the European continent, and the Japanese were emplaced along a perimeter covering the whole western half of the Pacific, leaving open only the sea lanes between the Americas and Australia-New Zealand. There was no other way to victory but — in one theater — to invade continental Europe from the sea and — in the other — to wrest back, chain by chain, the island groups and atolls the Japanese had fortified to keep hostile forces distant from their homeland.

That these things were done, and that no Allied amphibious attack was defeated in the course of the recovery, seems almost incredible. The inherent vulnerability of the men in the assault forces was unchanged; the advantages of the defenders were still powerful. The phenomenon can be explained only by the development of a sound body of amphibious doctrine during the interwar period and by improvements in fire support — including that of air power — and the creation of new, specially designed vehicles and vessels during World War II.

The basic amphibious doctrine of World War II was developed largely between 1922 and 1935 by the U.S. Marine Corps. Although numerous adjustments had to be made when the tremendously larger forces actually required engaged in amphibious assault, the doctrine proved fundamentally sound. The doctrine was, in fact, an adaptation of the precepts set forth a century earlier by the European military thinker Jomini: "to deceive the enemy as to the point of debarkation, to select a beach with hydrographic and terrain conditions favorable to the attacker, to employ naval guns in preparing the way for the troops, to land artillery at the earliest practicable moment, and strenuously to push the invasion by seizing the high ground commanding the landing area."[*]

The U.S. Marine Corps *Tentative Manual for Landing Operations* (1934) stressed the role of naval gunfire in replacing the artillery fire support an infantry attack would ordinarily expect to have. Emphasis was placed on combat-loading of men and supplies — both arranged so that the first landed and unloaded would be the first used ashore. Troop units were to be kept together, so that unity and control were maintained. Shallow-draft landing craft — most with quick-release bow ramps to permit rapid debarkation of men and equipment — were designed. Beach regulation parties were to be landed first to mark beaches, then to maintain communication with the ships and to direct units off the beach, and thus reduce congestion and confusion on the beach. Air superiority of three-to-one was considered necessary for a successful assault, and air-to-ship and air-to-ground communication techniques were worked out.

Amphibious Operations in World War II

The doctrine was refined and improved throughout World War II and used by Army units as well as Marines. Among the more important of the new developments were: (1) a new accent on preliminary air bombardment of all hostile defenses in the landing area, of troop assemblies, roads, railroads, and particularly in the

---

[*]Jeter A. Isely and Philip A. Crowl, *The U.S. Marines and Amphibious War* (Princeton: Princeton University Press, 1951), p. 4.

area behind the beaches; (2) great improvement in support fire control and a new order of magnitude in the volume of ship fires; (3) creation of a whole new family of small and medium-sized landing craft with lower silhouettes, more speed, better protection, and overall dependability assuring uniformity of delivery, the more advanced types having true amphibious characteristics in that they were mobile both afloat and ashore; (4) development of another new family of oceangoing transports; the most representative, LST, with a bow ramp that closed, could discharge cargo (men, heavy weapons, supplies) directly upon the beach, thereby affording a quick buildup ashore and energizing the attack. Ship-to-shore logistics became greatly simplified, support fires were enormously expanded, and movement of the assault element was more accurately synchronized with the air and naval bombardment, all of which compounded the shock to the defenders. The development of voice radio communication was essential to these advances.

Both British and Americans had experimented with flat-bottomed landing craft in the 1930s, and independently had developed similar craft with bullet-proof front loading ramps to provide protection while approaching the beach, and a means of quick debarkation once the bow of the craft grounded near the water's edge and the ramp was dropped. The Japanese also had been experimenting and practicing in their war with China. They were producing much larger craft and barges than the Anglo-Americans. First used in the invasions of Malaya and Java, these initiated a chain reaction of imitation by Britain and the United States. With only a little exaggeration, President Roosevelt spoke on August 13, 1944, of "the landing craft, a wholly new type of ship, one we didn't dream of two years and a half ago." It was not the British defeats in Flanders and Dunkirk that spurred the massive British production effort of World War II, but rather the disasters that followed Pearl Harbor.

But another production effort was also found to be necessary. The ammunition demands of preassault bombardment proved to be far greater than anticipated. Indeed, following Operation "Galvanic" (the invasion of the Gilberts in 1943) Admiral Richmond Kelly Turner had to cable the Navy Department that in this one brief operation his fleet had exhausted 60 percent of the ammunition that had been expected to last it through the war.

An amphibious assault force or landing team, in its initial movement ashore, has certain similarities to an airborne assault force. In both cases, and in contrast to infantry during other attacks, the assaulting force is almost helpless in its final approach to the battlefield; it is already vulnerable to the defenders' firepower, and its own weapons are almost completely ineffective. In this respect, the individual airborne trooper is even more alone, and more exposed to hostile fire than is the amphibious soldier, who has at least some protection from hostile fire while he is in his landing craft, and has the companionship of his fellows in the craft. But this airborne disadvantage is to some extent offset by the fact that the soldier's unexpected appearance from the sky is likely to be more demoralizing to the defender than is the well-advertised approach of landing craft to the beach. However, the landing force is protected not only by the fixed weapons (usually machine guns) on the craft transporting it to the beach, but also by supporting ship fire, including heavy guns offshore and closer-in rocket batteries, and has been able to observe the devastating preassault air bombardment of the defending positions.

But as the first assault wave reaches the beach, this is infantry in its hour of greatest moral and physical weakness. Indeed, the physical drain of stress and fear on the resources of men in the boat waves is invariably greater than on emplaced forces ashore, even though surprise may have been achieved and the over-water approach relatively unscathed. Despite the effects of the preliminary bombardment, World War II experience demonstrated that defending forces protected by conventional earthworks can survive "saturation" fire by air bombardment and naval artillery and remain effectively operational.

The men in the embarked assault force, meanwhile, are likely to be wretchedly ill from crowding on the transports, from seasickness, and from the long strain of fearful anticipation during the haul shoreward, when they are doing nothing and unable to respond should they be fired on. Literally hundreds of assault landings were made by American joint task forces on the coasts of Europe, North Africa, and islands in the Pacific and Mediterranean. Many of these were able to avoid heavily defended beaches; many others, however, encountered deadly defensive fire at the waterline. In at least three of the more important of these — Tarawa (or Betio) in the Central Pacific, Salerno in Italy, and Omaha Beach during the invasion of Normandy — the outcome was in grave doubt from the beginning, with the issue remaining in the balance for many hours. In all three cases a repulse would have been a shocking, perhaps disastrous, defeat for the United States. But the margin of victory in each case was provided, in somewhat varying proportions, by four resources available to the attacker: effective air support in an environment of Allied air superiority; effective and accurate naval gunfire support; the ability of the attackers to bring up reinforcements across the beaches more abundantly or more rapidly than could the defenders; and the resource of a sound amphibious doctrine in which the troops had been effectively trained and their leaders made aggressively confident.

A critical element of that doctrine was the well-understood objective not just of crossing the waterline, but of crossing the beach, getting to the shingle, and on from there to the high ground, just as rapidly as possible, and in cohesive units with all possible weapons and essential supply. As proven at Gallipoli, a landing force trapped on the beach is doomed. Once the force has debouched from the beach exits, it proceeds as it would in other field operations, using fire and movement to fragment and dislodge enemy forces. The only significant differences from other operations from then on is that described in the old manual of landing operations published by the Joint Board in 1933, which defined an amphibious landing as "in effect the assault of an organized defense position modified by substituting naval gunfire support for divisional, corps and army artillery, and generally navy aircraft support for army aircraft support."

During World War II the demands for amphibious operations in North Africa, the Atlantic and Mediterranean coasts of Europe, the coasts of Southeast Asia, and the islands of the Pacific were such that the supply of small amphibious craft never came abreast of requirements. In consequence, despite commonality of doctrine, there was no real standardization of such specifics as: lift for the ship-to-shore movement; what type of craft should be used in the boat wave, and in what numbers; and how much supporting, nonorganic firepower and armor should cover the basic battalion landing team — the BLT — as it closed on the shore.

The rule followed in such matters was to do the best possible with the available materiel. In Europe, until the last invasion, the BLTs were largely carried in Higgins boats — landing craft infantry (LCIs), landing craft vehicular personnel (LCVP), and landing craft tank (LCT) — and amphibious trucks, all highly conspicuous and soft-skinned craft, because nothing else was in sufficient supply. In Pacific operations, however, in addition to these basic craft the real amphibians of World War II appeared in ever-increasing numbers. These were the Alligator (tracked, unarmored), the Buffalo (tracked, armored, carrying a 37mm gun and two machine guns in its turret), and the ubiquitous DUKW — or "duck" — the amphibious truck. The extent to which the boat waves could be mounted in these craft, which offered less target area and (save for the DUKW) gave better protection, varied from operation to operation, not according to the lessons of experience, but according to the flow of materiel from the factories in the United States across the seas to the theater of operations.

Problems of Naval Gunfire and Air Support

The pattern and volume of naval gunfire support, and of tactical air bombardment, also varied greatly. Support fire depended on how much emphasis was placed upon surprise, how many warships could be present, the distance between home base and the target, and command estimates of the point of diminishing return in softening-up fires.

There was no such thing as the typical preparation. There are only illuminating examples. Two examples of fire support in amphibious operations demonstrate that, although fire support is essential, even the most abundant fire support does not, by itself, ensure combat superiority over defenders.

In preparation for Operation "Galvanic," November 1943, the 7th Air Force repeatedly bombed the two targets of Tarawa and Makin in the Gilbert Islands for one week prior to the direct assault, as the seaborne convoy approached its target. There was only superficial damage to enemy works and (it was learned later) little loss of military personnel. Navy carrier-based bombers struck at Makin directly ahead of the boat wave on November 20, 1943, dropping one-ton and half-ton bombs for one-half hour against coast artillery positions, heavy antiaircraft guns, pillboxes, stores, and personnel. The works remained relatively undamaged when this phase was completed and only four craters were found either in or immediately adjacent to them.

Meanwhile there were two naval gunfire bombardments in support of two separately staged landings on Betio — the principal island of Tarawa atoll — one soon after dawn and the other in the late morning. The firing plan called for the expenditure of 1,990 rounds of 14-inch, 1,645 rounds of 8-inch, and 7,490 rounds of 5-inch shells from four battleships, four cruisers, and six destroyers; nearly 3,000 tons of naval projectiles being thrown against the enemy during the four hours before the first assault troops hit the beaches. (Actually the preassault firing lasted slightly less than three hours.)

Eyewitnesses to these massive bombardments, especially those aboard the capital ships and troop transport APAs, who had a better chance for objective observation than troops embarked in the circling small boats, truly believed that they would shatter all resistance. Rear Admiral Howard F. Kingman, who commanded the fire support group in the attack on the main island said: "It seemed almost impossible for any human being to be alive on Betio." But these impressions were illusory. The main effect wrought on the defense was disorganization from the blasting of communications, the obliteration of roads, the shattering of radar installations, and the destruction of wire. While Japanese resistance was no longer unified, its elements remained deadly, saved for the most part by ground cover. Although most surface structures had been destroyed or knocked about, entrenched works and log-covered strong points remained almost intact. In fact there had been too many targets to be destroyed for the time allowed, and too much of the fire had been wasted on open space.

The taking of Tarawa yielded an estimated 4,690 Japanese killed; Marine Corps casualties in the attack were 3,178. At the end of the fighting on Makin, 550 of the enemy were either dead or taken prisoner (all but one POW were Korean labor troops) and total American battle casualties were 218. Thus, overall, for every three Japanese soldiers killed, two Americans were either killed or wounded. The figures demonstrate that the lethality of the preparatory bombardment did not significantly affect the ability of the defenders to resist. There remained on both islands garrisons in numbers and state of morale still capable of engaging and standing off a force of equal size. The attack prevailed because of the superior resources and reserves of the attackers, whereas the defense could not reinforce.

The next major target of Admiral Nimitz's central Pacific forces was Kwajalein atoll in the Marshall Islands. On Kwajalein there was literally no place to hide from air bombing and no natural feature that afforded any protection against fire from the sea. The island is almost perfectly flat, except for a few coral outcroppings. The earth crust is extremely shallow. The average elevation above sea level is roughly the height of a man. The vegetation, after the Japanese cleared ground for their base and road network, was not lush. Except for the works protecting the coastal battery at one end of the island, there was no conspicuous concrete construction. The island is approximately two and a half miles long and averages 800 yards in width over most of its length. It is thus an area of about one and a half square miles, with no natural features to limit the effects of high-explosive blast.

Preceding Operation "Flintlock," there was plenty of time for the Americans to carry out systematic land-based bombing of the targets from the new airstrips in the Gilberts, and by carrier-based naval aircraft. The first 7th Air Force strike against Kwajalein proper was on December 21, 1943, when four B-24s dropped six tons of bombs. There were nine subsequent missions, running through January, with about 200 tons of bombs dropped on the atoll.

The island was hit by Navy bomber planes of Task Force 58 for two days beginning on January 29, 1944. There were four separate groups of carriers, battleships, cruisers, and destroyers in this attack, with 700 carrier-based planes.

Early on D-Day, January 31, the offshore bombardment resumed, the battleships having moved up to within 1,500 yards of the main island. The official U.S. Army history describes the resulting fire as "unprecedented in volume and effectiveness." Two shells per second were exploding into Kwajalein. On that day almost 7,000 Navy rounds (14-, 8-, and 5-inch) raked it from end to end. From nearby Carlson Island five battalions of field artillery added another 29,000 rounds to the hammering of Kwajalein, in what may have been the most intense one-day shoot of World War II. Six Liberator bombers, flying well above the artillery trajectories, dropped fifteen 1,000-pound and 2,000-pound bombs on the same target, striking at the island's heavy-gun installations. They were followed by 18 dive-bombers and 15 torpedo bombers, which struck one end of the island while an equal number of fighter planes strafed the far end with machine guns and rockets. All told, 96 sorties were flown off the six carriers in this round.

At day's end the island was a rubble heap. Even to the eye of a sophisticated witness who had viewed other battlefields, it looked as if all life on Kwajalein had been extinguished. Here was devastation unimaginable, the most chaotic scene ever wrought by American guns and bombs until that hour. That night many fires blazed amid the wreckage.

On February 1, two regiments of the U.S. 7th Infantry Division landed from small boats on the southern end of Kwajalein and crossed the beach with little opposition, only to run into effective defensive fire almost immediately. Thereafter they fought their way to the extreme end yard by yard, at which point — on February 7 — the battle ended. The direct and general support fires from the five artillery battalions on nearby Carlson Island kept moving in front of this line and rarely slackened.

On the third day of the battle, enemy bodies strewn over an area of approximately six acres were examined to determine, if possible, the cause of death. Based upon such considerations as the nature of the wounds, the near presence of craters, and allowing some margin for error, it was calculated, on the basis of the sampling, that in excess of 70 percent of the enemy who died above ground had been killed by Army-delivered shellfire, either field artillery or mortars. All of the surface dead examined had apparently been killed after the American troops had landed.

From this and other evidence it was calculated that only 4 percent of the total Japanese losses were due to the massive preparatory bombardment from air and sea. Yet this relatively small loss, combined with the accompanying shock to survivors, had been sufficient to so disrupt the defenders that they offered no group resistance to the attackers until they were well ashore, and their subsequent opposition was far less effective than that at Tarawa. There can be no question that the three-day preassault bombardment of Kwajalein was — as planned — massive and intense enough to reduce the Japanese resistance capability to a much greater degree than was done at Tarawa after only a three-hour preassault bombardment.

The field artillery shoot against Kwajalein Island was the most intense, and the most methodical, of any delivered in a World War II landing, and the target was ideal for providing a moving curtain of fires to shield the infantry advance the length of the battlefield. The relatively small target measured approximately 4,500,000 square yards. Since about 65,000 105mm and 155mm rounds were laid on it, that means there was one shell burst for every 69 square yards. During the preassault bombardment there had been a shell burst or bomb burst for about every 100 square yards. Yet the results showed that even this was not truly "saturation" fire. Men will survive, little hurt or shocked, just a few yards beyond the lip of the crater, if they are in protected trenches, dugouts, or concrete emplacements.

In summary, the killing impact of all power loosed with the object of enabling the BLT to get ashore and help establish a beachhead during World War II, under the most optimum circumstances, was never more than 3 to 5 percent of the defenders. This means that in excess of 95 percent of defending personnel survived the preassault preparation. Yet the effect of the fire, in suppression and disruption, was enough in each case to ensure the success of the landing. One important effect of the preparatory fires was the disarrangement of the defenders' communications. But the irreparable damage was the effect of shock, disruption, and dislocation upon the individual defending soldier, caused by the massive firepower hammering, which degraded the defenders' effectiveness by a dividing factor that can be estimated at between 1.5 and 3.0.

World War II, with operations spread over vast areas and a large proportion of these involved in amphibious landings, demonstrated the prime importance of joint task forces. Although interservice rivalries made it difficult to develop a doctrine for unified command at the strategic level, certainly combined-arms tactical doctrine proved itself. The former rigid compartmentalization of land and sea operations disappeared, and a new, coordinated "triphibious" warfare evolved, with ground, naval and air elements making essential contributions.

XXVII. Nuclear Weapons, Guided Missiles, and Deterrence
1945

Hiroshima and Nagasaki

On August 6, 1945, President Truman announced that "an American airplane dropped one bomb on Hiroshima, an important Japanese Army base." He added: "That bomb had more power than 20,000 tons of TNT. It was an atomic bomb."

The now-famous experimental pile under the stands of the University of Chicago's Stagg Field became a self-sustaining system at a power level of one-half watt on December 2, 1942. This tiny output proved the potential for all later power-generating reactors. From it was produced about half a gram of plutonium that was successfully separated from the uranium and the fission products by chemical procedures deemed adaptable to mass operations. The problems of making a bomb — most notably the assembly of components within a portable size and weight — were, together with immense procurement and processing projects, successfully handled in a massive, secret scientific engineering and administrative effort in the amazingly short period of thirty months.

Among the earliest newspaper comments on the new development may be found the theme that has concerned mankind ever since: "The atomic bomb means the end of war or the end of the human race."* Prospects and problems of war with these new weapons have emerged in the nuclear age as the central concern of governments and peoples influencing and often dominating important political, military, and economic policies of major nations.

A discussion of nuclear weapons logically starts with the performance and capabilities of those that fell on Japan on August 6 and August 9, 1945. The actual yield of the Hiroshima bomb was apparently somewhat less than the 20-kiloton estimate initially reported by President Truman; it was probably closer to 15 kilotons.

---

*Robert Boothby, M.P., in *News of the World*, London, August 1945

The yield of the Nagasaki bomb was apparently somewhat greater. Statistically, the results of these bombings are impressive. At Hiroshima there were 144,000 casualties (68,000 deaths) among a population of about 300,000 with a density of 8,400 per square mile. The toll at Nagasaki was 59,000 casualties (38,000 deaths) in a population of 200,000, about 5,700 per square mile. About 67 percent of the buildings in Hiroshima and 40 percent of those in Nagasaki were destroyed or damaged. Extensive fires started in both cities. In Hiroshima a fire storm gutted the center of the city. The postexplosion fires at Nagasaki were smaller.

A significant casualty factor, the high incidence of fatal burns, resulted because of the hot, cloudless weather and the scanty, thin garments worn by the victims, plus lack of medical attention for most of the injured during a period of at least forty-eight hours. A tally of survivors' injuries shows 70 percent from blast (almost wholly secondary, or mechanical, effects), 65 percent from burns, and 30 percent from radiation (not counting long-term radiation effects). Since many suffered from multiple injuries, the total exceeds 100 percent. Of casualties among people in the open, 50 percent occurred within an average distance of 1.3 miles from the center of the explosion. Among people within buildings, 50 percent of the casualties occurred within an average distance of 0.8 miles.

Emergence of Tactical Nuclear Weapons

Not surprisingly it was several years after 1945 before serious thought was given to a role for nuclear weapons on the battlefield. Several factors combined to suppress development of concepts for tactical use of such weapons: the circumstances under which the first bombs were used; the emphasis upon strategic bombing in World War II; the early bomb's weight and girth, requiring a very large bomber aircraft to deliver it; and a general assumption that only a few bombs would be made and they would be reserved for targets of critical importance. Tests in the South Pacific with obsolete Navy ships as targets began at Bikini Atoll in 1946. But no significant new vistas seemed to be opened.

By 1950, progress in slimming the new weapon while increasing its yield severalfold coincided with the appearance of jet aircraft in United States Air Force inventories. Obviously smaller weapons could be delivered by smaller — and faster — planes. Serious thinking about tactical nuclear weapons had begun.

In order to give the Atomic Energy Commission a little more "room," as it worked on designs for nuclear devices for tactical weapons — and also as a result of Army efforts to share nuclear weapons development funds with the Navy and Air Force — it was decided to change the design of a new 260mm cannon (being developed in 1949) to a bore diameter of 280mm. The gun and carriage were designed as conventional artillery but with the additional specification that a projectile with an atomic warhead could be fired from the gun. As the result of tests of the prototype projectile in 1951 and 1952, the design was accepted. The Army Chief of Staff, General J. Lawton Collins, relying upon this surprisingly mobile behemoth, insisted that the Army must develop atomic-capable artillery. Though doomed to early obsolescence, the "280" became the forebear of modern nuclear or dual-capability artillery in the United States.

As lighter and smaller nuclear devices entered the U.S. inventory, parallel developments hastened improvements in the design of tactical nuclear weapons. And in 1951, two nuclear explosions in the Soviet Union confirmed previous evidence of the first Russian test in 1949. The Russians now also had "the bomb."

Already, work had begun on development of an even more lethal device, based on the fusion of atoms rather than fission. Authorized by President Truman, the first hydrogen bomb was tested at Eniwetok in November 1952. Its potency was attested by the fact that in one test a small island near Eniwetok disappeared, leaving a hole in the ocean floor a mile in diameter and 175 feet deep. In the summer of 1953 the Soviets exploded a fusion device. So both superpowers had weapons with yields equivalent to millions of tons of TNT — megaton weapons.

Emotions were mixed with political and economic considerations as ground forces tried to meet the organizational and tactical demands of the nuclear age. There was considerable, and inconclusive, professional discussion of the possibility of using atomic weapons in Korea. (Actually the issue had been settled in the first year of the conflict by an American commitment to British prime minister Clement Attlee, who had expressed deep alarm during a frantic trip to Washington following a hint by President Truman that he was considering the bare possibility.)

Search for Doctrine for Nuclear Wars

Recognizing the possibility that nuclear weapons might be employed on future battlefields, armies began to search for dual capability — conventional and nuclear — in tactics and doctrine. In the U.S. Army it was determined that this called for "greater dispersion, more mobility, logistic austerity, small-unit dependence," and several divisional reorganizations were made toward achieving these objectives.

At the same time, however, serious questions arose as to whether — in practical operational terms — war could be fought in a nuclear environment and, more serious, whether employment of tactical "nukes" by one side in a war would precipitate a swift escalation into Armageddon.

The term "general war" came into use, interchangeably with "strategic nuclear war," meaning the employment of nuclear weapons against an enemy's homeland, by means of bombs carried by long-range bombers or intercontinental ballistic missiles (ICBMs) with nuclear warheads. The results of nuclear exchange would be unimaginably horrible, yet both the United States and the Soviet Union rapidly developed the capability to carry out such an exchange. The development of nuclear capabilities by Great Britain, France, and later China, complicated but did not fundamentally alter the bipolar nuclear standoff between the United States and the Soviet Union.

In the face of Soviet expansion into central Europe in the immediate postwar years, the United States had joined with many of the nations of western Europe to form the North Atlantic Treaty Organization (NATO), for the purpose of discouraging further westward moves of the Soviet Union. In response the Soviets and the satellite nations of eastern Europe established the Warsaw Pact, which officially announced the availability to the Soviet Union of the territory and the forces of these nations.

The presence of the United States in NATO extended a "nuclear umbrella" over its allies there. In the mid-1950s NATO promulgated a doctrine that any Warsaw Pact aggression would be countered with a tactical nuclear response. How this would be done was not immediately worked out, but it was assumed that statement of the doctrine would deter Soviet aggression, since NATO had more tactical nuclear weapons than the Warsaw Pact, the United States had more strategic nuclear weapons than the Soviet Union, and escalation to their use would be almost inevitable.

By the late 1970s the tactical use of nuclear weapons was a topic to which considerable attention was being paid by planners and analysts, but whether they would in fact ever be used, and how, remained unclear.

Related Technological Developments

Nuclear weapons were not the only new developments that came in the period after World War II. Advances in technological capability came rapidly, partially under the impetus of the space programs of the United States and the Soviet Union. Old weapons were extensively modified, and new weapons and equipment have strongly influenced the nature of warfare. With rapid changes, some weapons have become outmoded almost as soon as they were operational. It is impossible to discuss all the new weapons, both because of the numbers and because many are guarded in secrecy. In general, similar concepts have resulted in similar weapons in the United States and the Soviet Union in particular, and in smaller numbers in other countries as well. U.S. weapons tend to be better publicized, and some of those will serve to represent more or less universal types.

In the forefront of new weapons are rockets of many types. Rocket projectiles, capable of carrying either nuclear or high-explosive warheads, range from the giant ICBM, with practically worldwide range, to the one-man bazooka antitank weapon of the foot soldier. The development of guidance systems and homing devices has significantly raised the probability of hitting targets with weapons that can be described as "smart bombs." The continuing search for higher energy and more stable propellants has been of prime importance in extending range, thus making more targets theoretically available.

Rocket missiles fall into four general operational categories: surface-to-surface (including subsurface-to-surface), surface-to-air, air-to-surface, and air-to-air. The first postwar American prototype model of a free-flight rocket with a solid-propellant booster and a liquid propellant-sustaining motor was the U.S. Army's WAC Corporal, first launched successfully at White Sands Proving Grounds (New Mexico) on a very high parabolic trajectory in late September 1945. A larger version of this antiaircraft weapon, with terminal guidance added, was developed between 1946 and 1950. It had ballistic trajectory during most of its flight, and became the Army's long-range tactical weapon. The Sergeant, a solid propellant ballistic guided missile, with many improvements in mobility, reliability and accuracy, replaced the Corporal. Other weapons — Redstone, Honest John, Lance, all with dual-capability — have followed.

Meanwhile, an Aberdeen Proving Ground report dated February 28, 1947, gave conclusive evidence that antiaircraft artillery projectiles, despite a maximum time of flight of about 40 seconds, were ineffective against jet aircraft at ranges that required 30 seconds flight time. Thus it was evident that effective engagement of a jet aircraft required an antiaircraft rocket-type missile. As a result the Nike Ajax guided missile was developed from the WAC Corporal. Nike Ajax units became operational in 1953. But already the more advanced all-solid propellant Nike Hercules guided missile had been perfected. This was many times more effective than its predecessor and soon replaced the Ajax in most air defense installations around the nation.

Many types of solid propellant antiaircraft and antitank rockets and launchers have been developed since 1945. Soviet-made surface-to-air missiles (SAMs) were effectively used against U.S. aircraft in Vietnam and against the Israeli Air Force in 1970 and 1973. Assessment of both Israeli and Egyptian comments about the American-made Hawk missiles, which the Israelis installed around their key airfields, suggests that these SAMs had a hit-and-kill capacity at least as high as any of the Arabs' Soviet-made SAMs, and they were probably even more accurate.*

The U.S. Army TOW was designed as a surface-to-surface anti-tank missile. It is a "second generation" weapon, an improvement on a design pioneered in France. A self-propelled missile weighing about 54 pounds, it can be fired from a jeep or a tripod. It carries a large charge accurately over a range up to two miles. When it is fired, two thin wires unreel behind it to carry the impulse by which its flight is guided. As the gunner holds his target on the cross-hairs of his gunsight, a small computer converts the information into commands that activate flaps on the missile to correct its course. During the Vietnam war helicopters also were used with great success as TOW platforms. However, since the helicopter had to remain stationary during firing, it was highly vulnerable to ground fire. During the 1973 October war the Egyptians used the similar wire-guided Soviet-built Sagger antitank missile, as well as an improved bazooka-type weapon, the RPG-7.

Two air-to-surface homing bomb systems (HOBOS) were used by the United States in Vietnam. One of these "smart bombs" used an electro-optical system and a miniature computer to fix the bomb on target and automatically release it when the plane comes in range. While the bomb falls by the force of gravity, its memory operates fins that keep it on target. The other guidance system uses a laser beam that is projected from the plane to the target. The bomb locks onto the beam and follows it to the ground. Both systems

---

*See Table 5, which shows characteristics of missiles and rockets used in the October War (from *Elusive Victory*, pp. 610–611).

TABLE 5
Characteristics: Missiles and Rockets, October War 1973

Name	Desig-nation	Length (cm)	Diameter (cm)	Wingspan (cm)	Max Speed (mach)	Launch Wt. (kg)	Warhead Wt. (kg)	Warhead Type
Air-to-Air Missiles – AAM								
Israel								
Shafrir		260.0	16.0	60.0	2.0	93.0	11.0	HE
Sidewinder	AIM-9	284.0	12.7	60.9	2.0	75.0	11.4	HE
Arab								
Atoll	K-13A	280.0	12.0	53.0	2.0	69.8		HE
Air-to-Surface Missiles – ASM								
Israel								
Walleye	GW-Mk-1	344.0	38.1	114.0		499.0	385.0	HE
Maverick	AGM-65	246.0	30.0	71.0		209.0	59.0	HE-shaped
Bullpup	AGM-12	320.0	30.5	95.3	2.0+	258.0		HE
Shrike	AGM-45	304.8	20.0	91.4	2.0	177.0		HE
Standard ARM	AGM-78	457.0	30.5	139.7	2.0+	826.0		HE frag
Arab								
Kelt	AS-5	940.0		460.0				HE
Surface-to-Surface Missiles – SSM								
Israel								
Jericho	MOD-660							
Arab								
Frog		900.0	55.0	105.0		2,000.0		HE
Scud		1,100.0	85.0		5.0	6,300.0		HE
Surface-to-Air Missiles – SAM**								
Israel								
Hawk	MIM-23A	512.0	35.0	122.0	2.5	580.0	130.0	HE
Arab								
Guideline*	SA-2	1,070.0	70/50	122.0		2,300.0		HE
GOA*	SA-3	670.0	60/45					HE
Gainful*	SA-6	620.0	33.5			550.0	40.0	HE
Grail* (Strela)	SA-7	125.0	7.0					HE
Antitank Rockets & Guided Missiles – ATR & ATGM***					(m/sec.)			
Israel								
TOW	BGM-71A	117.0	15.2		278.0		18.0	HE-shaped
LAW	M-72	65.3	6.6		145		1.25	
Super Bazooka	M-20A1	153.0	8.9		148.9		3.31	HE-shaped
Arab								
Snapper*	AT-1	113.0	15.0		89.0		22.25	HE-shaped
Sagger*	AT-3	88.0	12.0		120.0		11.3	HE-shaped
RPG-7			4/10				2.5	HE-shaped

*NATO codename.

**AA guns: Israel: 2 × 20mm, 4 × 40mm, 2 × 40mm, mounted on AML (Panhard) or M-42 chassis. Arab: ZSU-23-4 (4 × 23mm). mounted on PT76 chassis; Su-57, twin 57mm on armored track chassis.

***AT guns: Israel: 106mm RR.

Arab: Su-100/100mm, SP, armored; D-48 (85mm); 57mm. M-1943: B-10 (82mm recoilless rifle); B-11 (107mm recoilless rifle).

TABLE 5 (Continued)
Characteristics: Missiles and Rockets, October War 1973

Propulsion	Guidance	Homing	Range (km)	Launch Platform	Altitude
Solid fuel rocket	Infrared	Infrared		Mirage. F-4	
Solid fuel rocket	Infrared	Infrared	3.24	Mirage. F-4	
Solid fuel rocket	Infrared	Infrared	2.74	MiG-21	
Gravity	TV	Lock-on		A-4. F-4	
2-stage solid rocket	TV	TV	17.00	F-4	
Liquid rocket	Radio comd.	Radio comd.	16.00	A-4. F-4	
Solid rocket	Passive radar	Passive radar	25+	A-4. F-4	
Dual-thrust solid rocket	Passive radar			F-4	
Solid rocket	Spin stabilizer	None	320.00	Tu-16	
Liquid	Inertial		450.00	Not used. little info	
2-stage solid rocket	Radar	Radar	60.00	Tracked (PT-76)	
			280.00	Wheeled transporter	
2-stage liquid solid	Radar	Radar	35.00	SP	11.600/30
2-stage solid	Radar	Radar	50.00		18.600/-
			30.00	SP	
Integral rocket ram-jet	Optical	Heat seeking	60/30	Shoulder. BRDM	18.000/4.000
2-stage solid rocket	Wire guided	Optical track	3.75/.065	M-113 APC	
Solid rocket	Aimed		.25	Shoulder	
Solid rocket	Aimed		.15	Shoulder	
Solid rocket	Wire guided	Visually guided	2.3/.5	(Hand-carried box)	
Solid rocket	Wire guided	Visually guided	3/.5	(BRDM. BMP)	
Solid rocket	Aimed		.3	Shoulder	

allow high-flying planes to pinpoint small targets with fewer and, therefore, larger bombs than is possible in less precise scatter bombing.

By the late 1970s the Strategic Air Command's aging B-52s were carrying 20 air-launched cruise missiles. These in effect are pilotless jet planes programmed to fly specified routes to their targets. The guidance system is a terrain contour matching (Tercom) computerized radar system that upon release enables the missile to fly about 100 feet above the ground as the radar compares the terrain below with a three-dimensional map that has been preset in the missile's computer.

The Navy Sidewinder, a supersonic guided missile, was the first air-to-air missile to destroy an enemy aircraft under actual combat conditions. Equipped with an infrared homing device, it seeks and destroys high-performance enemy aircraft at elevations from sea level to more than 50,000 feet. The Chinese Nationalists on Taiwan successfully used the Sidewinder, armed with a conventional warhead and propelled at Mach 2.5 by a solid-fuel rocket motor, against Chinese Communist MiGs during the Quemoy crisis of 1958.

Many naval guns have been made obsolete by guided missiles with massive explosives guided by sensors or other devices. The U.S. has the Tartar surface-to-surface missile (SSM), the Terrier and Talos surface-to-air missile (SAM), and the ASROC and SUBROC antisubmarine missiles (ASWM). There are similar Soviet weapons.

Weapons and Issues of Strategic Nuclear War

During the 1950s and 1960s both Russia and the United States developed intercontinental (ICBM) and intermediate range (IRBM) ballistic missiles, which attain extreme accuracy at great distances. In the United States, the Atlas and the Titan series were early liquid-propellant intercontinental missiles, and the Jupiter and Thor were intermediate-range varieties. The more modern Minuteman ICBM, using solid propellants for its power, replaced the Atlas and Titan.

The United States also pioneered with multiple-warhead missiles, and by the late 1970s both the United States and the Soviet Union had them in their inventories. These are of two principal varieties. The first provides for separation of the warheads during the missile's final approach to the target area. The spread pattern of several warheads gives a greater blast pressure than is possible with one large warhead of the same or greater yield. Decoys have been developed to be used with these missiles to prevent defending radars from distinguishing between the real warheads and dummies. The second type of multiple warhead, the multiple, independently targetable reentry vehicle (MIRV), is designed to have its trajectory corrected after separation from the booster rocket. After each correction one reentry vehicle can be released in order to attain the desired dispersion of the warheads.

Submarine-launched ballistic missiles (SLBM) — the United States has Polaris and Poseidons — have become a principal deterrent force of the U.S. They are carried on nuclear-powered submarines (SSBNs), which can be dispersed all over the world for long periods of time. The submarines can remain submerged for months, and are designed so that missiles are carried in upright position, ready for firing from below the surface.

The awesome development of missiles with almost unlimited range and with the ability to deliver nuclear warheads with deadly accuracy soon compelled both the United States and the Soviet Union to try to develop an antiballistic (ABM) defense. The task seems almost hopeless since the chances of intercepting incoming missiles would inevitably be small, and only one warhead need get through to devastate an area. Advances in phased-array radar and computer techniques have increased chances of detecting objects at long distances, discriminating among objects — rocket boosters, warheads, decoys, and all trash floating in space — and in tracking and guidance of interceptors to destroy the warheads. But the expense of trying to defend against all incoming missiles is formidable.

There were extensive studies carried on in the U.S. Government in the 1950s and 1960s as to what should be defended by an ABM system: cities, the population in general, the seat of government, or the retaliatory force. It was finally concluded that only the retaliation force could be defended with a significant degree of success, and that the ability to defend that force would be the best deterrence against a hostile decision to start a war. In 1972 — as part of the first strategic arms limitation treaty (SALT I) — the United States and the Soviet Union agreed to limit ABMs to the Galosh system already deployed for defense of Moscow, and two sites in the United States containing no more than 200 missiles.

Nuclear Warfare at Sea

At sea, nuclear power, combined with advances in rocketry, has brought radical changes in both weaponry and propulsion, necessitating equally radical changes in ship construction. The nuclear-powered vessel, surface and submarine, can remain at sea indefinitely (without need for replenishment of fuel) if given periodic replenishment of victuals and ammunition from floating depots.

The nuclear-powered carrier task force remains the queen of maritime weapon systems, although some observers doubt its survivability in a general nuclear war. The nuclear-powered submarine, armed with SLBMs, has extended sea power inland as never before. To many sailors the submarine is the prototype of the future capital ship.

It is generally believed that conventional landing operations face almost certain destruction by nuclear weapons, should general war break out. However, for smaller amphibious operations with so-called conventional weapons, the helicopter has appeared to be the answer, with vertical assaults largely replacing the surface assaults. But the apparent vulnerability of helicopters has made control of the air an even greater requirement than had been the case in World War II.

Air Power in the Nuclear Age

The principal problem of air power has centered about the crucial question of the respective capabilites of the manned bomber and the missile in delivering nuclear warheads. On the right choice rests, it appears, the efficacy of the free world's doctrine of deterrence. Opinion is still divided.

Meanwhile, important developments have brought more speed and range in all areas of the air power spectrum, both missile and manned aircraft. Range and rate of climb of aircraft have increased. Concurrently, technological advances in optics have gone hand in hand with increased altitude for reconnaissance. The increasing power of weapons has not altered the necessity that air and land power work together as a close-knit tactical team.

But achievement of such teamwork has become increasingly difficult. The tactical use of fixed-wing aircraft in close support has been complicated by the fact that the increased speed of a jet-propelled combat aircraft restricts its firepower efficacy to a minimal fleeting moment over the target, thus greatly reducing the pilot's capability for identification of target and delivery of fire. This same condition also impedes the value of fast-flying aircraft in reconnaissance, while vast refinements in ground-based air defense weapons range, fire control, and direction have greatly complicated the problems of applying air power to ground combat. The complexities have been further increased by the necessity for an instantaneous and almost infallible communications system of command control, if prior air superiority and isolation of the battlefield — an enormous area where nuclear warfare is contemplated — could be attained. Such communications will have to operate in an environment of electronic warfare against hostile countermeasures as sophisticated as the communications system itself.

The Superpower Confrontation and Arms Control

Political and military strategy of all nations has been decisively influenced by the confrontation between the United States and the Soviet Union. The two superpowers have towered in political, economic, and military strength over the other nations of the world, and the most important strategic fact of life for each is the existence and power of the other. The friction, or conflict, that has resulted from this confrontation was in the 1950s and 1960s called the Cold War. Cold War grimness has been only partially ameliorated by determined American and Soviet efforts to achieve a form of "peaceful coexistence," which both sides prefer to call "detente," but their confrontation is still a major factor of world affairs.

During the nineteenth century there were numerous attempts to establish controls and limitations on the employment of armed force among nations. There had been nothing to compare, however, with the worldwide intensity, sincerity, and sophistication of the search for arms control of the post-World War II era. This was in large part the result of growing realization by all mankind of the potentialities of nuclear weapons, and a feeling of desperate need to control the use of such weapons before they are allowed to destroy civilization.

XXVIII. Warfare under the Nuclear Umbrella: Korea, Vietnam, and the Middle East 1950 — 1973

Background

The confused, tangled, and momentous events of the three decades following World War II do not readily yield to systematic historical analysis, partly because they are still too close to be seen in true historical perspective, partly because it was a time of rapid transition. However, it is a period in which the interrelationship of weapons and warmaking is readily discernible, even if the implications are still clouded. During a quarter century of war, and threats of war, military men struggled in a fog of experimentation and frustration, seeking on one hand to harness the new nuclear capability in weaponry, and on the other to maintain and improve postures of the so-called conventional means of warmaking without resort to the use of nuclear fission or fusion.

The abrupt break-up of colonial empires in a very brief span of time following World War II created many new states where — more often than not — no one was adequately prepared for leadership. There were leaders, of course, drawn to their roles by the vacuum, but unrest and instability were the inevitable consequences. In many countries poverty, ethnic rivalries, and political or social inequities encouraged acceptance of the promises of Communism, and the Soviet Union and to some extent the People's Republic of China worked to exploit disorders and unrest, developing a worldwide net of Communist parties.

Both the United States, directly, and the Soviet Union, covertly or indirectly, became involved in wars in this period, as Communist objectives of conquest conflicted with U.S. objectives of establishing and maintaining stable situations in developing nations. Besides supplying money and military equipment to friendly nations, the United States sent troops to fight in Korea and in South Vietnam. The Soviet Union also participated — with arms and supplies, training, and with proxies from other Communist states, but not by overtly sending troops — in three kinds of conflict in various areas: civil wars, wars of "national liberation," and wars in defense of Communist regimes.

The nature of warfare in the middle of the twentieth century was strongly influenced by the existence of nuclear weapons in the arsenals of the United States and the Soviet Union, by their basically opposed political concepts, and by the technological developments that produced such weapons as have been described and new means for using and controlling them. Both superpowers relied, in their national stategic thinking, on the mutual deterrence value of their nuclear weapons to prevent a direct military conflict. Although there was no direct confrontation on the battlefield, in most of the wars of the period the superpowers were in some fashion arrayed on opposite sides.

The possibility that any conventional warfare could escalate into nuclear war caused political leaders to keep very close observation of day-to-day developments on the battlefield, and electronic devices made it possible for the U.S. President during the Vietnam War, for example, to observe the progress of combat and communicate directly with the participants. Unfortunately, this provided the temptation to civilian authority to meddle unnecessarily, and generally counterproductively, in minor administrative and tactical details that were not always fully understood.

Korea

During the first six months of the Korean conflict the pendulum of military success swung widely. It went from an overwhelming initial victory by the North Koreans as a result of their surprise invasion of South Korea to an equally overwhelming victory by U.S. forces — representing the United Nations in opposing the aggression — in a brilliantly conceived and executed counteroffensive, to a serious setback to United Nations forces when Communist China intervened on the side of North Korea.

The most important lesson from this latter defeat was the necessity that U.N. troops — primarily American troops — relearn the rudiments of fire and movement on foot. Roadbound at the outset, they had found themselves too dependent upon supporting tanks, artillery, or aircraft. The lightly equipped Chinese troops, on the other hand, utilized fluidity, surprise, and concealment in the rugged regions of north and central Korea to compensate for their inferiority in firepower. They moved and attacked by night, and lay camouflaged during daylight. Their attacks all followed the same pattern: infiltration, encirclement, and ambush. Frontal assaults were in effect holding attacks in small force, but the penetrations were deep. Each engagement was initially one of small units. It was a platoon commander's war. At no time was the U.N. able to employ its firepower superiority to optimum capability.

At the end of the first year of the war the Communist forces were overextended, supplies expended, and communications under continuous aerial attack, and the U.N. front moved slowly north all across the Korean peninsula. As the advance accelerated, the Soviet representative in the United Nations proposed a ceasefire on June 23, 1951. The U.N. commander was ordered to halt, despite his plea for approval of "hot pursuit" of an enemy on the verge of collapse. With Chinese intervention fresh in mind, the U.S. Government was sensitive to implied Soviet threats, and to the consequent alarm elsewhere in the free world, and it was decided to do nothing that might risk World War III. (In retrospect it is easy to confirm what perceptive stategists saw at the time: there was no risk of Soviet involvement.)

Delegations from both sides met near the fighting front, first at Kaesong and later at Panmunjom. Negotiations dragged on interminably, while minor actions flared continually all along the front.

The Communists took advantage of the time to build up their strength. By the year's end an estimated 800,000 Communist ground troops — three fourths of them Chinese — were in Korea, while heavy shipments of Soviet artillery, including excellent radar-controlled antiaircraft guns, were brought in. However, U.N. command of the air was never seriously threatened, and the Communists were forced to continue their practice of taking shelter during daylight hours in concealed, deep-dug bunkers and other underground installations.

After the breaking off of negotiations several times, with the renewal of attacks by one side or the other, then the resumption of talks, an armistice was finally signed on July 27, 1953. The *de facto* boundary was the existing battle line, generally a little above the thirty-eighth parallel, which had been the prewar dividing line between North and South Korea.

This war was significant on several counts. It was the first major struggle of the nuclear age. While no nuclear weapons were employed, the threat of the atom bomb hung heavy over all concerned but particularly affected the United Nations forces since it throttled exploitation of success.

The conflict reaffirmed the critical importance of air power as an essential ingredient of successful combat in modern war. It also was a reminder that air power alone can neither assure adequate ground reconnaissance nor bring about final decision in land warfare. The initial superiority achieved by the U.N. in the air caused the Communist side to bring in MiG-15s, which were then the latest Soviet jet fighters, quite superior to America's F-84s and in some respects surpassing the F-86s. MiGs, first seen in Korea in late 1950, increased in number during 1951, but the superior training and competence of U.N. pilots, mostly Americans, compensated for any inferiority in materiel. While the U.N. pilots were never permitted to pursue the MiGs across the Yalu, they were able to neutralize all Communist efforts to establish bases south of the river.

Also, the potential of the helicopter was clearly demonstrated as a new means of mobile transportation, reconnaissance, evacuation, and rescue work.

Even more important than the contribution of air power, and in particular the U.S. Air Force, was the contribution of sea power and the U.S. Navy. It included not only the maintenance of supply lines across the Pacific but participation in the form of amphibious operations, naval gunfire attack on targets within range of the sea, naval and Marine Corps air attacks on ground targets, both in close support and in interdiction, and installation of a blockade that prevented the Communists from supplying their forces by sea.

Vietnam

Meanwhile, there was a long-continuing conflict in Vietnam, which started in 1945 as a colonial uprising against French control, and in 1954 became a civil war between Communist and non-Communist Vietnamese factions. It developed into a major international war from 1965 to 1973 as the United States became an active participant. American forces were pitted against the North Vietnamese and Viet Cong, both supplied by Communist China and the Soviet Union (independently and without coordination). The United States had entered into the longest, oddest, and by far the most unpopular war in its history. It was a war without a fixed front; the enemy was here, there, and everywhere. General Vo Nguyen Giap, North Vietnam defense minister and victor in the previous war (1945–1954) against France, had made the operations of guerrilla warfare a science. American forces held only the soil on which they stood in a war of thousands of savage engagements without a single major battle in the conventional modern sense. The war was a phantasmagoria of brutal combat, political and social entanglements, and unceasing frustration. The military effort was heavily influenced by political considerations in Washington.

The U.S. troops operated from fortified bases, carrying out search-and-destroy missions designed to eliminate Communist forces and base areas rather than capture and hold blocks of territory. Combat, except in sieges, consisted of clashes at platoon to battalion strength, even in the occasional large-scale operations. The ubiquitous helicopter—gunship, personnel and cargo carrier, vehicle of rescue and evacuation of wounded—furnished amazing flexibility to the U.S. and allied troops.

In mid-1966 the U.S. forces launched their first prolonged offensive with lengthy and continuous sweeps rather than short, swift raids. But when the Communists were hard pressed, relying on their knowledge of the terrain, they were generally able to break contact and disappear into the jungle, and across the convenient neighboring borders with Laos and Cambodia. When the allied sweeps receded, the Communist forces generally moved back into the territory they had held before.

Early in 1968, well-publicized optimistic reports from U.S. field commanders were followed by the surprise Communist Tet Offensive—a callous breach of an armistice agreed for the Chinese New Year holiday called Tet. The size, scope, and fury of this offensive shocked the American public and resulted in demands by many for a U.S. withdrawal from Vietnam.

Though the Communists were completely repulsed, had suffered heavy casualties, and gained neither new territorial footholds nor increased support among the South Vietnamese, the offensive was a major strategic victory for the North Vietnamese and Viet Cong. It was perhaps the decisive factor leading to eventual U.S. withdrawal from Southeast Asia in 1973.

The Middle East

In 1917 a declaration by Britain's foreign minister, Lord Arthur James Balfour, set in motion forces that led first to thirty years of unrest, followed by thirty years of war, in the ancient land of Palestine. This unrest and war directly or indirectly involved all of the Middle East, and affected the entire world. Neither Lord Balfour nor the British government should be blamed (other than incidentally) for these events; the forces contributing to them were already active or emergent, and would eventually have been set in motion by some other incident had there been no Balfour Declaration.

Antagonisms between Arab and Jew, which flared into fighting even before Israel officially became an independent state, focused in four wars between 1948 and 1973. More than the others, the last of these, the October War of 1973, which followed the patterns of modern conventional wars more closely than had either the Korean or Vietnam war, and which was fought by forces that had been supplied with arms and training by the superpowers, provided an opportunity to test the effectiveness under combat conditions of some of the new weapons and tactics developed since World War II by both the Soviet Union and the United States.

After initial Arab victories on both the Golan Heights and Suez Canal fronts, by the time a U.N.-ordered cease-fire was finally in effect on October 25, the Israelis had recovered the initiative, had gained substantial local successes on both fronts, and had cut off the Egyptian Third Army east of the Suez Canal. Significantly, however, in the closing days of their offensive west of the Canal, the Israelis were repulsed in efforts to take the cities of Ismailia and Suez; and on the Golan front the Syrians, with support of Iraqi and Jordanian reinforcements, were planning to mount a counterattack. Although the Israelis had unquestionably had the better of the fighting, it was in no respects a one-sided conflict, as the previous encounters of 1948, 1956, and 1967 had been.

On both the Suez and the Golan fronts, planes of the Israeli Air Force (IAF) appeared over the battlefield about forty minutes after the Arab H-Hour. They immediately encountered Soviet-made Arab missiles in unexpected quantity and effectiveness. Before dark the Israelis lost more than 30 aircraft. In the following days Egyptian mobile SA-6 missiles and self-propelled four-barrelled ZSU-23-4 machine cannons claimed many Israeli planes. The light, hand-carried Strela (SA-7) was less effective; it made many hits but damaged more planes than it destroyed. Israeli close air support was therefore negligible for several days. Later, employing hastily devised tactics and utilizing chaff and other electronic countermeasures (ECM), Israeli aircraft began to make a greater contribution to the ground battles, particularly on the northern front.

The Soviet-made SAMs, particularly SA-6 and Strela, demonstrated that air superiority was no longer an automatic result of superior effectiveness in the air as had been the case since World War II. Desperate Israeli efforts to deal with the missile threat, particularly in the employment of ECM measures, regained only a slight measure of air superiority for the Israelis over the battlefield. The most significant influence on the air battle, however, was the result of ground action. At first some results were achieved by long-range artillery fire, which suppressed the missiles. Later, and even more important, the Israeli advance west of the Canal forced the displacement of many Egyptian missile sites, permitting the Israeli Air Force to provide more effective support to the ground troops.

At sea the Israeli *Saar*-class missile vessels, armed with the Israeli-made Gabriel missile, completely dominated the coastal waters off Syria and Egypt. Not a single hostile shell or missile was fired from the sea against the Israeli coast. On the other hand, the Egyptian blockade of the Strait of Bab el Mandeb (southern entrance to the Red Sea) cut off all commerce to and from the Israeli port of Eilat, and the declared Egyptian blockade of Israel's Mediterranean coast also severely reduced ship traffic.

Both Egypt and Syria were almost completely dependent upon the Soviet Union for replacement and repair, equipment and parts; and two days after the opening of hostilities Israel began to fly supplies from the United States. At the end of the first week, the United States began to use American planes to supplement the El Al lift of supplies. By the time of the cease-fire the Soviets had airlifted about 15,000 tons, the U.S. more than 20,000.

On October 27, 1973, the U.N. Security Council, with both the U.S. and the U.S.S.R. voting affirmatively, agreed to establish for six months a 7,000-man international peacekeeping force to enforce the cease-fire along the Suez Canal and on the Golan.

Other Wars

There were a number of other conflicts throughout the world during this period. The largest — and perhaps the most momentous — of these was the concluding phase of the Chinese Civil War, in which the Nationalist Government of President Chiang Kai-shek was driven from mainland China in 1949 by the Chinese Communist armies of Mao Tse-tung.

The most important military lesson of the Chinese Civil War was a demonstration of the politico-military theories of Mao, particularly how a successful guerrilla war can be converted to a climactic conventional struggle for national power.

The most important development in the 1970s was the introduction of war by proxy by the Soviet Union and its Cuban satellite. In the former Portuguese colony of Angola, a pro-Soviet faction defeated a pro-United States faction, and in the mid-1970s gained control of the country with the help of a large contingent of Cuban troops equipped with Soviet weapons. Similarly, Soviet-equipped Cuban troops plus a Soviet field command were the decisive elements in 1978 in bringing victory to Soviet-equipped Ethiopian troops against Soviet-equipped Somalis in a struggle for the long-disputed Ogaden Province.

Assessment

It is tempting to seek some common denominator of change and startling new dimensions in the conflicts that have occurred since World War II and the dawning of the nuclear era. But, nuclear weapons were *not* used in any of them, and no such common denominator emerges clearly. Certainly new technology greatly influenced the performance of one or both of the opponents in most of these wars — particularly in the Middle East, Korea, and Vietnam. But this, in itself, is nothing new, and is typical of warfare for at least the past four centuries. The continuing, and increasing, importance of communications could perhaps be cited; but this is nothing new. It is merely a manifestation of a trend well established for more than a century, dating back at least to the Crimean War.

One might note that a backdrop to most of these wars was the looming presence of a superpower rivalry without a direct confrontation of the major rivals on the battlefield, a confrontation avoidance resulting from mutual deterrent policies. This, in fact, is perhaps as close as one can come to a new common denominator, because implicit in that untested rivalry, and in the deterrent strategies, was the potentiality of disastrous employment of the unprecedentedly destructive power of nuclear weapons. Yet there is really nothing new in the phenomenon of relatively minor wars as proxy conflicts, or protagonist-proxy encounters in which the ultimate principal adversaries were deterred from combat through fear of the consequences.

It was a phenomenon that marked much of the rivalry of Rome and Carthage, of Rome and Parthia and Persia, of the Byzantine Empire and Islam, of the Byzantines and the Franks, of Britain and Russia in central Asia in the nineteenth century, of Austria-Hungary and Russia in the Balkans, and of Britain and France in colonial America, colonial Africa, and colonial Southeast Asia. In some of these instances the showdown confrontations eventually occurred; in others they never did. So, even though unused nuclear weapons have to a substantial degree altered the strategic context of these proxy, or partially proxy, wars, historical patterns have predominated in each of them.

The Korean War, for instance, can be likened to Rome's Macedonian wars during the confrontation of the Italian republic with Carthage, or to Britain's Afghan wars during the British Empire's confrontation with Imperial Russia. The parallels are not exact, since, for reasons discussed earlier, history can never precisely repeat itself. But the paraphrase, or the pattern of similarity, is evident.

Patterns abound of great power involvement in local war or insurgency while the principal opponent watches from the sidelines, as in Vietnam. Or — in 1978 and 1979 — in Afghanistan, where the United States was the observer. There was, for instance, turmoil in Israel in the second century B.C., as the Jews successfully fought against Seleucid Syria while first Ptolemaic Egypt and later Parthian Persia observed from the sidelines. The script was similar, but the outcome different, three centuries later in Israel as Rome suppressed Jewish insurgency, again with Parthia watching nearby. A more modern parallel was the long, bitter British struggle against the dervishes of Sudan in the latter years of the nineteenth century, while France took advantage of the situation to gobble up nearby regions of Africa. Common to all of these — and other parallel examples of major power involvement in foreign insurgencies — was the frustration of regular troops in dealing with an elusive foe operating with the tacit and actual (but usually covert) support of the local populace.

Historical examples of proxy wars like those of the Middle East and Africa since 1956 are comparably abundant. In modern times the Balkan Wars of 1912, 1913, and the Spanish Civil War, provide interesting comparisons. But comparisons would be just as apt in ancient Greece, when Athens and Sparta were trying to avoid the conflict that eventually destroyed both of them, or in the Roman-Macedonian confrontation after the fall of Carthage.

The common factor, therefore, appears to be that no matter how weapons and technology may change, that technology and those weapons are employed — or brandished — in consonance with ancient and repeated patterns of human conflict.

A number of historians, philosophers, and perceptive authors have found different ways to suggest why each generation of humanity needs to study history to understand what is going on in its own times. But in describing the relationship of the new to the old — in weapons to warfare, for instance — no one has put it better than Alphonse Karr: *"Plus ça change, plus c'est la même chose"** (The more things change, the more they remain the same).

XXIX. Lethality through the Ages

All weapons have at least one common characteristic: lethality — the ability to injure and if possible to kill people. The history of warfare is a review of the manner in which groups of men have endeavored to impose their will upon other groups of men by using their weapons more effectively than the opponents, or in other words, by realizing, or at least approaching, the ultimate degree of lethality of their weapons.

Lethality is necessarily a comparative thing. Nothing is more lethal than a sword in the hands of someone who can wield it to kill his single opponent. But its comparative lethality is limited by the factors of time, range, and the physical limitations of the man who wields it. By assigning values to these and other factors it is feasible to compare the lethality of the sword with the lethality of the hydrogen bomb, or the tank, or whatever other weapon one pleases. Obviously the weapons that kill more people in shorter periods of time have greater lethality. Table 1 and Figure 2 show the result of calculating the lethality of representative weapons over the course of history, using a standard formula to produce for each one a Theoretical Lethality Index, or TLI (as in Table 1, p. 92) and plotting them semilogarithmically (as in Figure 2, pp 288-89).

The reader will not be surprised to find that through the period we have called the "age of muscle" the curve is quite flat. Since the

---

*Alphonse Karr, *Les Guêpes*, January, 1849.

introduction of gunpowder weapons, however, and particularly since the mid-nineteenth century, the curve rises steadily and sharply.

As man has tried to produce more and more lethal weapons, there have been two major results: First, men have had to alter their methods of fighting in order to exploit the new weapons capabilities to their maximum. Second, men at the same time have adopted active and passive means of limiting the increased effectiveness of these new weapons when used by the enemy.

These two combined — and in large part offsetting — activities: using weapons to their maximum capability against an enemy, while limiting the effects of the enemy's weapons, have required the development of what we call tactics: the employment of troops in battle. Tactics has three components: (1) firepower, or lethality; (2) movement, for the purpose of getting troops and their weapons in positions from which they can inflict the greatest harm on the enemy, or — alternatively — to where the enemy can do the least harm to them, or — practically — some combination of both of these; (3) deployment of troops, for the dual purpose of maximizing the effectiveness of the weapons when we use them and, even more importantly, of minimizing by dispersion the effectiveness of the enemy's weapons.

The Constants of War

From everything that has gone before in this book it is evident that the story of warfare is an account of continual change. The alterations have been in technology, which has changed weapons, which then have changed tactics. Yet despite this unceasing flux and change, there are certain constants in war, and these constants are at least equally as important as the changes.

There are three major constants. First is the objective of war: the employment of lethal implements for the purpose of imposing one's will upon an enemy. Second is the way in which wars are fought, commonly summarized in a handful of principles, usually called Principles of War (p. 161). Third — and the essential constant in war — is the unchanging nature of man.

As is readily seen from Table 1 and Figure 2, there have been few major advances in weapons lethality through the ages, and most of them have occurred since about 1850. A major advance may be defined as a new development that changes the nature of warfare. It is a revolutionary change, which may be followed by a series of evolutionary changes, with which it should not be confused. Thus, the Maxim recoil-operated, belt-fed machine gun was

288

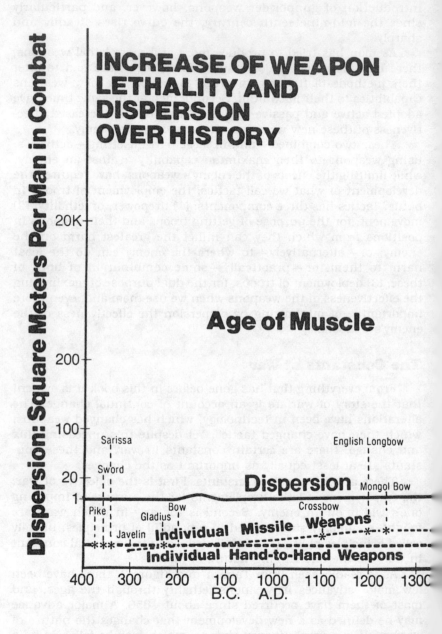

FIGURE 2.

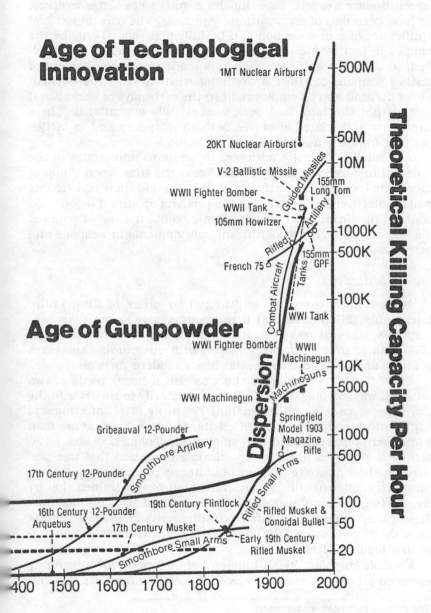

Age of Technological Innovation

1MT Nuclear Airburst — 500M

20KT Nuclear Airburst — 50M

V-2 Ballistic Missile — 10M

WWII Fighter Bomber
WWII Tank
105mm Howitzer

155mm Long Tom

French 75 — 500K

155mm GPF

WWI Tank — 100K

Age of Gunpowder

WWI Fighter Bomber

WWII Machinegun

WWI Machinegun — 10K
— 5000

Gribeauval 12-Pounder

Springfield Model 1903 Magazine Rifle — 1000
— 500

Smoothbore Artillery

17th Century 12-Pounder

16th Century 12-Pounder
Arquebus

19th Century Flintlock

Rifled Small Arms

Rifled Musket & Conoidal Bullet — 100
— 50

17th Century Musket

Smoothbore Small Arms

Early 19th Century Rifled Musket — 20

400   1500   1600   1700   1800   1900   2000

Theoretical Killing Capacity Per Hour

Dispersion

Guided Missiles

Artillery

Rifled

Combat Aircraft

Tanks

Machineguns

a revolutionary weapon. Later machine guns were better weapons but have been part of an evolutionary process. The true impact and significance of a new weapon can be fully appreciated only by the changes in tactics and organization that occur when it is assimilated, or when a significant change is made in the employment of existing weapons to resist it or to act with it. Thus the German panzer division and its employment in the early days of World War II showed that the tank had been successfully assimilated. There were major and related advances both in weaponry and in tactics resulting from the assimilation of the tank.

The number of major advances in weapons and tactics in the course of history is relatively small. From the time when Philip of Macedonia increased the lethality of the pike and then exploited its combat effectiveness by building the phalanx around it (about 355 B.C.)*, to the introduction of the atomic bomb, the earlier pages of this book reveal eighteen significant developments in weapons and their lethality.

Age of Muscle

Macedonian sarissa. Lengthened by order of King Philip shortly after 359 B.C. so that it was appreciably longer than contemporary pikes, it was used in the *phalanx*, an organization of 4,096 trained professionals, employed with outstanding successes by Philip and Alexander somewhat like a modern division.

Short sword. The Roman short sword, a heavy weapon, two feet long, was adopted about 250 B.C., primarily to thrust into the vital organs, causing either instant death or fatal infection; its weight and breadth also permitted its use as a hand ax. Roman swordsmen were organized into small units (*cohorts*) of about 120 men each, deployed in battle in a flexible formation that was prepared on short notice to move or fight at any point of the compass, with each soldier fighting as an individual, but so trained that by his efforts he was an element of a coordinated fighting machine. These cohorts, plus light infantry and cavalry, formed a combat team, the *legion*, some 4,500 men strong, again roughly comparable to a modern division.

English longbow. Welsh hillmen before A.D. 1200† apparently developed a longbow made of yew that could be fired rapidly, and

---

*This process may have been inverted.

†There is evidence that a full-scale prototype of the longbow existed in Egypt nearly 3,000 years before the Christian era. There is also some question of the Welsh origin of the English bow; it may have been developed in England.

reputedly could drive its arrow through four inches of oak. But men had to train from childhood to use the weapon effectively. Although it was a significant increase in lethality over all other European hand-bows, it was in fact not much more inherently lethal than the slower-firing, somewhat clumsy crossbow, which appeared in Europe about a century before the longbow was adopted by the English. The longbow was not significantly effective in combat until the English kings Edward I, and his grandson Edward III, used longbowmen in great numbers to provide a base of fire for defensive-offensive tactics in which bowmen, light and heavy infantry, and small parties of elite armored cavalry operated in close and disciplined cooperation.

Mongol bow. This was a quite different kind of bow, of the reflex variety, and about as long as the English longbow, built up from horn and wood, and fired from horseback by men trained from childhood to ride and shoot. Grouped under the sophisticated command and control system developed by Genghis Khan, guided by exceptional competence, and used in coordination with more heavily armored lancers, Mongol bowmen had weapons significantly more effective than any weapons they met, and the Mongol forces were virtually invincible during most of the thirteenth century.

Age of Gunpowder

Gunpowder by itself is merely a mildly dangerous explosive. It was known in Europe by 1250, and probably earlier in China. It was fifty to seventy-five years before someone discovered how to make it lethal by confining and igniting it in an open-ended tube. The full assimilation of gunpowder took nearly four hundred years more, but by the middle of the fifteenth century gunpowder weapons were clearly demonstrating a potentially significant increase in lethality.

The first cannon. By A.D. 1326 gunpowder was being used to hurl small missiles at castle gates. The device it was fired from, however crude, was a cannon, and made gunpowder lethal. It was, therefore, the fundamental jump to lethality for gunpowder.

Arquebus. About 120 years later, the first reliable handgun was invented. From it the matchlock arquebus was developed by the middle of the fifteenth century. Its slow rate of fire offered real problems to the user, who was both ineffective and defenseless while reloading. Solution of these problems was sought in a combination of (a) protecting the vulnerable arquebusier by formations of pikemen and (b) having arquebusiers form in files ten deep to fire in turn, each man countermarching to the rear to reload. This tactical solution was best exemplified in the Spanish square (early 1500s).

Weapon improvements of Gustavus Adolphus. The improved and more lethal weapons introduced by this king were a major element in his generally reformed military system, whose tactical and organizational changes were the foundation of European military practice for the next three centuries. By issuing cartridges (first large-scale employment of an idea developed much earlier) he sharply increased the rate of fire of musket and cannon. To exploit increased infantry firepower he initiated *linear tactics* by forming his soldiers in a shallow line rather than the relatively deep mass of the Spanish square. To exploit increased artillery firepower he lightened tubes and carriages, and improved artillery organization, providing a significant increase in tactical mobility and efficiency over previous contemporary practice.

Flintlock and bayonet. This combined a simpler, more reliable gun with a hand-to-hand weapon that made the gun lethal even after it had been fired. Introduction of the ring bayonet ended the long transitional period in gunpowder, since pikemen were no longer needed to protect a soldier with an unloaded gun. Becoming general in Europe about 1700, this combination remained standard until well into the next century, *i.e.*, about 125 years. Linear tactics and smoothbore cannon were perfectly matched to the inherent lethality of the flintlock and bayonet.

Age of Technological Change

The weapons of this period as a group constitute a quantum jump in lethality over their predecessors of the age of gunpowder. Since they were introduced in modern times and better records are available, the circumstances of their invention and of related developments are much clearer and lend themselves more readily to analysis.

The conoidal rifle bullet (1849–1860). Known commonly as the minié ball, this conoidal projectile, fired from a muzzle-loading rifle that was discharged by a weatherproof percussion cap, had a high muzzle velocity and an effective range equal to that of contemporary smoothbore cannon, and was considerably more accurate than the old flintlock. The primary infantry weapon of the American Civil War, it caused most of the casualties in that war and initiated a revolutionary readjustment in infantry tactics. The adjustment, however, proceeded comparatively slowly. Because of its casualty effects, it was the most dramatically revolutionary weapon that has ever been introduced to warfare, at least up to the 1980s.

Breech-loading rifles (1848–1864). By permitting the user to lie prone while firing and loading, the breech-loading rifle made the muzzle-loader obsolete. The idea was not new, and workable prototypes had been in use more than a century earlier. Mass adoption for all infantry came first in the Prussian Army in 1848, although the needle gun was not unveiled until the Danish War of 1864.

Breech-loading rifled artillery (1845–1870). Although the first workable prototypes appeared about 1845, they were not widely used for twenty-five years. After steady improvement they revealed themselves in the Franco-Prussian War (in German hands) as clearly superior to the old-style French muzzle-loaders. Sharply increased range and rate of fire made them significantly more lethal.

Maxim machine gun (1883). This belt-fed, recoil-operated weapon is the prototype of modern automatic weapons. In World War I the machine gun proved to be one of the most significant of all advances in lethality since the introduction of gunpowder.

High-explosive shell (1886). Light artillery shells filled with high explosive could produce more than 1,000 lethal fragments 20 feet from the point of burst. The old black-powder shell of the American Civil War produced only from 2 to 5 fragments; Prussian shells in the Franco-Prussian War broke into as many as 30 fragments. Thus, on fragmentation alone, high-explosive shell was theoretically 35 to 200 times as lethal as black-powder shell.

Bolt-operated magazine rifle (ca. 1895). There had been numerous magazine rifles in various armies for nearly half a century, but the vastly improved Mauser became the prototype of the standard infantry rifle of the world's armies on into World War II. The principal factor increasing lethality was greatly increased rate of fire. Outstanding was the American Springfield, M1903. Largely for financial reasons these rifles were slow in being superseded by the semiautomatic rifle (an adaptation of the machine gun concept), nearly half a century later.

Tank (1916). The internal combustion engine driving an endless track made it possible to give cross-country mobility and armor protection to machine guns and light cannon. This made them significantly more lethal than unprotected horse-drawn or man-carried weapons. The tank was a mechanical step toward solving the tactical stalemate created in World War I by the recent previous advances in lethality.

Fighter-bomber (1917). This aircraft introduced new dimensions of flexibility, range, and reaction time to the problem of putting a relatively large projectile (or machine-gun bullet) on a point target. (Also note that medium and heavy bombers could be used on the battlefield on an ad hoc basis. The German Stuka dive-bomber was a briefly successful freak early in World War II, rather than a significant increase in lethality, because the environment could be made too effectively hostile to it.)

Ballistic missile (1944). By its range, all-weather capability, and relative imperviousness to countermeasures, this German invention* (unveiled in 1944) greatly increased the lethality of its warhead. It was the prototype of a whole family to which tactics and organization are still responding and — if only because of its quantum jump in range — constituted a significant increase in lethality.

Atomic bomb (1945). In part because its first use in strategic bombardment was universally publicized, and its lethality generally appreciated, this weapon has been unique in forcing changes in tactics and organization even though it has never been used tactically in battle. The adequacy of responses to nuclear weapons is perhaps the most serious military problem of this or any previous age.

Major Ancillary Technological Developments

It is important to an understanding of the evolution of warfare to recognize that advances in lethality have not been exclusively caused by weapons. It is of course the weapons that do the killing and maiming that make them the implements of the objectives of warfare. But the actual capability of weapons to do their dread work has in many instances been affected or enhanced by ancillary technological developments.

Just as there has been only a small number of truly major or revolutionary advances in the lethality of weapons themselves, so there has been a mere handful of revolutionary technological developments directly affecting the lethality of weapons. From them have come almost numberless evolutionary changes flowing from these major advances.

Listed below are nineteen major technological advances that seem to have been truly revolutionary in their influence on warfare. As with the weapons themselves, most of these major advances have occurred in the era of technological change since the middle of the nineteenth century.

---

*Based largely upon theoretical rocket developments pioneered by an American, Robert H. Goddard (1882–1945).

Age of Muscle

Armor. Prehistoric men protected themselves from the blows of their opponents with crude shields of hide and then of wood. Rudimentary armor was worn by soldiers in Egyptian and Mesopotamian armies, reaching a new sophistication in Greece with the development of the metallic helmet, cuirass, and shield. An important development in body armor was the introduction of mail early in the Christian era. Mail continued to be the main defense of the body and limbs through the twelfth and thirteenth centuries, until the fourteenth century when plate armor began to displace mail. Armor, of course, was intended to inhibit the lethality of a foe's weapons, while its protection provided moral encouragement for more aggressive — and it was hoped more lethal — employment of one's own weapons.

Stirrup. Although possibly used in parts of Asia as early as the first century A.D., the stirrup came into general use in Europe during the sixth or seventh century. This device significantly increased (a) the lethality of the lance by putting the total weight of horse and rider behind its impact and (b) the lethality of the bow and the sword, by giving the horseman a secure mounting from which to use these weapons.

The result of both the above developments was a system of armored cavalry that became the dominant arm in Europe for the next eight hundred years until the successive impacts of the longbow and the Swiss pike were felt.

Age of Gunpowder

Stable gunpowder (corned powder). About 1450, someone found a way of preparing gunpowder so that it retained its explosive qualities and did not separate into its basic ingredients. This made it reliable and so greatly enhanced its effectiveness.

Matchlock mechanism. In the fifteenth century, the Spanish developed an ignition system for the arquebus that made firing a more secure and safe process and permitted the user to aim the weapon, thus considerably increasing both its accuracy and its lethality.

Flintlock mechanism. This was a safer, surer and speedier method of ignition of the musket that superseded the arquebus with matchlock mechanism. It involved basically the use of mechanical devices in which pyrite or flint was struck against steel to produce sparks, igniting the priming powder in the pan. This development increased the effectiveness of the musket by concealing its ignition during night operations, preventing hazards to the individual, permitting operations in rain, and lessening delay in firing when attacked by surprise.

Iron ramrod. In the early part of the eighteenth century, according to some historians, Frederick William I of Prussia introduced an iron ramrod to replace the former fragile wooden ramrod. The new implement, when exploited by training (the weapon itself being unchanged) permitted an increase in the average rate of fire of the Prussian infantry from twice to at least three times a minute.*

Age of Technological Change†

Steam engine (1769). The patenting of the steam engine by Englishman James Watt, and the subsequent development of the railroad and the locomotive, made it possible to move large masses of men and for them to use weapons with faster rates of fire by bringing forward ammunition in the quantities these weapons could use. Steam power also revolutionized naval warfare and permitted mass production of weapons for mass armies and for fleets of unprecedented power.

Percussion cap (ca. 1815). In the early nineteenth century, the percussion cap, introduced by American Benjamin Shaw, superseded the flintlock mechanism. In addition to its application to the military musket, it made possible the invention in 1835 of the Colt revolver.

Electronic communication. In the mid-nineteenth century electricity first made possible long-distance, instantaneous communication, permitting the command and control of large masses of men in combat.

   a. *The telegraph (ca. 1840)* was the first important manifestation of this development. Telegraph was used extensively in the Civil War for strategic and tactical direction of large forces.
   b. More recently, instantaneous voice transmission was achieved first by *field telephone*, first used on a large scale in World War I, primarily for artillery communications, in transmission of firing data and corrections from artillery observers to the guns.

---

*Other historians believe that the increase in rate of fire was due almost entirely to training and discipline.

†Not mentioned here, but also contributing to overall military capabilities, were such advances as mass-production techniques for weapons and supplies, food preservation, advances in medicine, and engineering.

c. *Voice radio* also appeared in primitive form in World War I, but became the primary means of strategic and tactical control in World War II. It supplemented the telephone and replaced it entirely in operations of highly mobile units over great distances.

Barbed Wire. Originally a harmless farming device, barbed wire more fully exploits the lethality of automatic weapons by holding their targets in the line of fire and by keeping them away from the gun and its crew. It was first adapted to these military purposes in 1874, but its full significance was not appreciated until World War I.

Smokeless powder (1885). Because it permitted users of the weapons to continue to see their targets while maintaining a steady rate of fire, its introduction marked a significant increase in the lethality of the weapons, which also became less vulnerable to countermeasures since their concealment was not betrayed by smoke.

The internal combustion engine (1887). Soon after it appeared in workable form, this engine made possible both tanks and aircraft, and permitted dramatic new concepts of warfare. By propelling trucks and tracked vehicles it has given both road and cross-country mobility to infantry, artillery, and supply trains.

Recoil mechanism, quick-firing artillery (1890 – 1910). The full capabilities of breech-loading cannon could not be exploited until means had been found for the carriage to absorb the recoil, so that the cannon did not have to be manhandled back into place and relaid for direction and range after each round. After this was accomplished by sophisticated recoil mechanisms, a whole family of cannon appeared, marked by long range, greater accuracy, and (particularly) greatly increased rates of fire. Other improvements in heavy-ordnance construction methods, such as built-up tubes, also contributed to this advance in artillery lethality. By 1914 this significant increase in lethality, among others, contributed to rendering linear tactics obsolescent.

Observation aircraft. First developed in 1907, but not fully exploited until World War I, these helped reveal targets (mainly for artillery) that would have been hidden in past years.

Photography. In conjunction with the observation aircraft, the camera, another development of the technological age, has become an essential means of target acquisition, primarily, although not solely, through air photographs.

Radar. In essence, this electronic device sends out impulses that are reflected back from objects in their path.

a. *Defensive use (1938).* Radar has given observers a completely new capability for acquiring and identifying targets in the air, on the ground, and on the surface of the sea; this in turn more fully exploits the lethality of weapons for which they are observing. Its capabilities were first understood and employed by the British in their air defense system, and it was a major factor in their decisive victory in the Battle of Britain (1940).

b. *Offensive use (1944).* The *VT-fuze,* or *proximity fuze,* took advantage of the radar principle to accomplish the detonation of a high-explosive shell when it came near a target. Previously, a time-mechanism fuze was used to detonate shells in the air. This process was expensive, and required complex and sometimes relatively unreliable calculations. Consequently time fuzes were only marginally effective in battle. The inclusion of a tiny radar set in a fuze, however, caused the fuze to detonate the shell when it came within a prescribed distance of the earth, or of an object projecting above the earth, or of any clearly defined object in the air, such as an airplane. Thus for the first time, the maximum lethal potential of high-explosive shells could be achieved against any target if the shell were aimed to pass close enough to it.

Inertial and electronic guidance. These are methods of guidance or navigation to provide accuracy in direction and range for long-range ballistic missiles, for aircraft, for naval vessels and for ground vehicles.

Computers/automatic data processing (1940). The first really workable military prototypes of the modern computer were developed by the British in World War II as an element of the process of deciphering German coded messages. The ultimate potentialities of increasingly smaller and more lightweight electronic mechanisms for calculation and for information storage and retrieval are still only dimly perceived in the early 1980s.

Earth satellites in space. This development is included here with considerable diffidence, since there is no historical basis in warfare for its inclusion, and since satellites are — at least to some extent — refinements of ballistic missiles. Yet there is enough difference, and their potential for observation, communications, and even as weapons platforms, is so obviously significant to warfare of the future that some mention seems to be called for.

The Stimuli of Peace and War

Before the nineteenth century, the creation of major advances in lethality and the assimilation of these advances was the work of individuals, whose appearance was in large measure a matter of accident. In the nineteenth century—beginning with steps away from the old flintlock, in the 1830s—industrial, military research, and administrative institutions began to emerge in the several great powers of Europe and in North America which could exploit the "greatest invention of the Nineteenth Century . . . the invention of the method of invention."*

New interest in research, and communication among various institutions engaged in research, made it possible for military thinkers, as never before, to take advantage of the scientific and technological changes that began to come even faster. Thus, in the mid-nineteenth century, major advances in weapons lethality and in tactics and organizations that could best exploit them began to be linked with general changes in science and technology brought about by the Industrial Revolution, although the process was very slow at first, and for much of the century military developments lagged behind.

The dates of the significant advances of the age of technological innovation are curiously bunched. The conoidal rifle bullet, an effective breech-loading rifle, and breech-loading rifled field artillery appeared between 1841 and 1849. The modern machine gun, the high-explosive shell, the Mauser bolt-operated magazine rifle, smokeless powder, and quick-firing modern artillery appeared between 1883 and the mid-1890s. The tank and fighter bomber appeared in a two-year period in World War I (1916–1917). Ballistic missiles and the atomic bomb were introduced within a year of each other in World War II.

The nineteenth century advances were conceived in peacetime, or at least the first workable models appeared in peacetime, about fifteen years after the end of the most recent major hostilities. This time lag may perhaps be explained by budgetary problems and a sort of apathy in the wake of major wartime expenditures of money and energy, and by the availability of time for thought and experimentation.

The twentieth century increases in lethality (tank and fighter-bomber, ballistic missile and atomic bomb) were wartime developments. In each case, the basic concept originated in peacetime,

---

*Alfred North Whitehead, *Science and the Modern World* (New York, Macmillan, 1925), p. 141.

but the impetus to develop the device was lacking until national danger supplied both the overriding need and the resources. The Austro-Hungarian Army of 1911 turned down a workable tank; it is certain that the U.S. Congress of the interwar years would not have voted billions for the Manhattan Project.

Identity of Originators

Who has been responsible for significant increases in lethality in modern times? Individuals and groups, private and government agencies. In general, the men associated with the development of small arms, artillery pieces, and ammunition were civilians, who worked essentially as individuals, although there were a significant number of military men involved as well. Because of the foundries, laboratories, and metal-working machines required, major developments in artillery and its ammunition were sponsored by private manufacturers in Great Britain and government arsenals in France and Germany.

Up to 1900, the principal problems involved in gunpowder weapons were those of weight, smoke, recoil, rate of fire, range, fuzing, fragmentation, and accuracy. (The major problem of obturation — or sealing a breech-loading weapon — had been solved earlier by the introduction of self-contained, metal-cased cartridges.) These problems were centuries old and well known. There seems to have been no case of a government's placing a requirement that any of these weapon deficiencies be solved. When advancing technology offered the possibility of a solution, some individual would eventually see the opportunity, would create something, and then offer it to the government. The role of government arsenals in this process was distinctly minor, limited to a few artillery developments. The classic picture was that of the inventor trying to sell his new discovery to a government agency. That a government agency should ask inventors to produce new and more lethal weapons is decidedly new.

In World War I the process of originating significant increases began to change. As a result, while aircraft, the tank, ballistic missiles, and the atomic bomb, all trace their origins to the basic concepts of civilians, in each case they were made into weapons through major effort of one or more government agencies, with both military and civilian participation. The shift was from small private industry to large governmental agency.

By nation, most of the pre-1914 innovations divide almost evenly among the three industrialized great powers: France, Germany, and Great Britain. Hiram Maxim, the inventor of the modern machine gun, was an American, but it is indicative of the temper of the times in the United States that he moved to Great Britain and did his work there in connection with the great Vickers arms factory. These three powers, very conscious of their need for effective arms, possessed of advanced technologies, and with ample budgets, offered the best prospects to inventors and manufacturers. After 1917, the United States joined this group and has since taken the lead.

Stages in Introducing Major Advances in Lethality

In every case, the idea for a significantly new device or a more lethal version of an existing one came far ahead of the development of a workable model. For instance, Leonardo da Vinci thought of the tank and the airplane some 450 years before they could be built. Experiments were tried with breech-loading cannon and explosive shell in the same period.

With the coming of the Industrial Revolution it became possible to transform drawings into models — although some inventors were unaware of the earlier ideas — and then to improve significantly upon them. The intervals from concept to prototype to item of issue also shrank progressively in keeping with the ever faster rate of technological progress. Thus, from the first breech-loading cannon to a safe, practical model took at least 400 years. From this cannon to the "French 75" took 51 years. From the first flight of a tiny model aircraft in 1795 to the Wright brothers' man-carrying model in 1903 the interval was 108 years, and from then to the fighter bomber in 1917 only another 14.

Assimilation of Weapons

The invention of a weapon that is potentially more lethal is only the first of three steps toward realization of that lethality. It must be adopted by a military establishment, and it must be assimilated into tactics, doctrine, and organization. As we have seen, the invention and adoption of weapons have been increasing and accelerating, but there seems to be no significant acceleration in the process of assimilation of weapons into military systems.

The invention of a workable weapon has not in the past guaranteed either that it would be promptly purchased by any armed force or that, if bought, it would be purchased in sufficient quantity to be standard issue. British major Patrick Ferguson invented a serviceable breech-loading rifle in 1776. (Both the French and Austrian armies had experimented with breech-loading musket carbines as much as fifty years earlier.) And it was another sixty to seventy years before the major powers began, haltingly, to adopt such weapons, some eighty years after Ferguson's death. In the American Civil War, the Union bought enough repeating breechloaders to equip a portion of its forces, but for the most part Union soldiers fought the war with single-shot muzzle-loaders. Not until the Seven Weeks' War in 1866 was the muzzle-loader really superseded in operational military inventories.

The interval between invention and adoption reflects several things. Man, of course, is not everywhere and at all times at war. But industry, commerce, law, medicine, and engineering are continuous. New devices and new ideas in peaceful activities can be tried out at any time. Ever-present competition provides an incentive to use new and improved methods. In sharp contrast, there are often very long intervals between wars. There was one such interval before 1914. Thus, a German officer commissioned in 1872 at twenty-one years of age would have been sixty-three, virtually at the end of his career, before he faced a European enemy in 1914. In no other major profession or institution is it possible — as in the armed forces — to go for more than a generation with no practical test of professional skill, performance, or competence, and no combat experience for testing weapons.

It must also be remembered that major wars leave behind two legacies: first, budgetary problems, and second, large stocks of materiel. The budgetary problems put pressure on the armed forces to use up the inherited wartime stocks. (The Allies of World War I probably did the German Army of the 1930s a real service in forcing it to scrap the materiel of 1918.) These budgetary problems, these masses of obsolescent materiel, suggest why the first of two groups of significant advances in lethality prior to 1914 followed about fifteen to twenty years after the Napoleonic Wars and the second followed a similar period after the American Civil and Franco-Prussian wars.

Another very important reason for this delay is that the military generation of the previous war, which was accustomed to, and made its careers with, this older materiel and the ideas associated with it, had to vacate positions of authority before new ideas could have an impact. In this connection, a great physicist observed: "New scientific truth does not triumph by convincing its opponents

. . . but rather because its opponents eventually die and a new generation grows up which is familiar with it."*

These considerations apply everywhere; there are no clear patterns of national behavior in regard to adopting weapons. Instances can be found where national problems or practices caused a power to lag in adopting a certain weapon, but these are cases, not patterns. The Russians stressed the bayonet and lagged in adopting the machine gun; the Germans stressed the machine gun and lagged in adopting the tank—which the British had invented to counter German machine guns. To draw conclusions about national behavior from these cases is dangerous, if not impossible.

Interval between Adoption and Effective Use

It has always taken a while for a weapon to become a fully contributing member of the current arsenal of weapons, to be used in a way that capitalized to the greatest possible extent on its characteristics and potentialities. This is understandable, since experimentation is ordinarily required to see how any new device will perform best, and no peacetime testing—no matter how realistic it may appear—can replace the terrifying environment of real combat. This time lag is further influenced by current modes of military thinking, which invariably tend to try to fit a new weapon into existing tactics. Changes in tactics come later only as it becomes apparent that the new weapon permits, or demands, such changes.

This pattern was clearly evident in the case of the arquebus, the first handgun that was sufficiently developed to be adopted on a large scale. It was adopted generally in the second half of the sixteenth century, but it was first used in the manner of fighting that was usual at the time, by massed infantry, firing in volley. In this process the men firing the weapon were defenseless, able to contribute nothing to the battle during the long period of time it took to reload the arquebus, and they required protection by massed pikemen. It was some fifty years before the technique of the countermarch was developed, so that the men in the first rank of files fired, then moved to the rear of the line to reload while the nine successive ranks followed the same procedure.

This was the first effective solution of a basic problem in the use of individual gunpowder weapons in combat. From then on, other types of handguns could be used effectively on the battlefield

---

*Max Planck, *Scientific Autobiography and Other Papers*, trans. F. Gayner, (New York, 1949), pp. 33–34.

practically as soon as they were invented. It does not follow, however, that this initial use was their most effective use; in general there was a period of experimentation of twenty to thirty years until the best tactical use was developed. The same was true of the first radical changes in artillery weapons, late in the nineteenth century. The uses of both tanks and combat aircraft were postulated before or with their introduction in combat; the problem with each was that of properly exploiting its inherent lethality. From the time of its introduction, the ballistic missile has been used essentially as long-range artillery, but again assimilation into operational doctrine has been slow. Nuclear weapons have offered fundamental tactical difficulties of a conceptual nature at least roughly comparable to those that affected the introduction of effective gunpowder small arms; at present there seems to be no reason to think that assimilation will be any easier or quicker.

It was apparent at the outset of the nuclear age that there would be a lapse between invention and demonstration of nuclear weapons, and the determination of doctrine for their application in battle. The first two were used in 1945 as weapons of mass destruction and terror. By the time of the Berlin blockade of 1948 tactical nuclear weapons were practicable, but the United States had evolved neither policy, tactics, nor doctrine for their tactical use in ground combat. Indeed the first major attempts to consider changes in army tactics, doctrine, and organization to include nuclear weapons were not made until the next year, 1949.

The Assimilation Process

It is fairly easy to ascertain from observation or from the record that a weapon has not been assimilated, that is, that its capabilities are not fully realized and it is not being used to the best advantage. It is almost as easy to recognize that a weapon has in fact been assimilated and is an effective part of a military establishment. But it is less easy to pinpoint exactly when the process of assimilation was accomplished.

When a radically new weapon appears and is first adopted, it is inherently incongruous with existing weapons and doctrine. This is reflected in a number of ways: uncertainty and hesitation in coordination of the new weapon with earlier ones; inability to use it consistently, effectively, and flexibly in offensive action, which often leads to tactical stalemate; vulnerability of the weapon and of its users to hostile countermeasures; heavy losses incident to the employment of the new weapon, or in attempting to oppose it in combat. From this it is possible to establish the following criteria of assimilation:

a. Confident employment of the weapon in accordance with a doctrine that assures its coordination with other weapons in a manner compatible with the characteristics of each.

b. Consistently effective, flexible use of the weapon in offensive warfare, permitting full employment of the advantages of superior leadership and/or superior resources.

c. Capability of dealing effectively with anticipated and unanticipated countermeasures.

d. Sharp decline in casualties for those employing the weapon, often combined with a capability for inflicting disproportionately heavy losses on the enemy.

There have been three basic preconditions historically for assimilation of new weapons or ideas:

1. An imaginative, knowledgeable leadership focused on military affairs, supported by extensive knowledge of, and competence in, the nature and background of the existing military system.

2. Effective coordination of the nation's economic, technological-scientific, and military resources.

3. Opportunity for battlefield experimentation as a basis for evaluation and analysis.

When these conditions have been present, there has usually been a time lag of approximately twenty years, or one generation, between the initial experimental adoption of a new weapon and its full assimilation. It is notable that this time lag does not seem to have changed much over the course of the past century, despite the fact that science and technology have been producing new weapons, or adaptations of weapons, in accelerating numbers and at an accelerated pace. When the conditions have not been present (which was frequently the case before 1830), the process of assimilation has been slower.

New weapons, or modifications of new weapons, have generally been developed because scientists, technicians, or soldiers have perceived an opportunity to develop a new weapon or improve an existing one. Only rarely have new weapons been designed for the specific purpose of coping with a tactical problem.

There has been a natural reluctance to make a sweeping change in tactics, or organization, by widespread adoption of a new and untried weapon before it has been thoroughly investigated under battle conditions. There is some evidence (not conclusive) that intelligent boldness in this respect can pay handsome dividends (as in the case of Prussian adoption of the needle gun). Despite this reluctance and despite the likelihood that optimum assimilation will be impossible without battlefield testing, the increasing pace of invention is placing pressures on the military today to make such sweeping changes.

The substantial leadership in military affairs (of land warfare) enjoyed by Prussia, and then Germany, over a period of about a century (ca. 1840–1942) did not stem from any inherent intellectual, scientific, or fighting superiority on the part of the Germans. Rather it stemmed from their earlier realization of the significance of the impact of the Industrial Revolution on warfare in terms of increased complexity in weapons and of the methods of employing them. Much earlier than other nations, the Prussians so organized themselves as to acquire systematically, and without dependence upon chance, the kinds of competence indicated in the first and second preconditions for assimilation of weapons, and this systematic organization also permitted them to exploit fully and promptly their own battlefield experimentation and that of others.

The German experience and those of the other great powers who have followed the German pioneering work in general-staff concepts and in relating military affairs to national society as a whole suggest additional preconditions for assimilation in the mid-twentieth century:

a. There must exist industrial or developmental research institutions, basic research institutions, military staffs and their supporting institutions, together with administrative arrangements for linking these with one another and with top decision-making echelons of government.

b. These bodies must conduct their research, developmental, and testing activities according to mutually familiar methods so that their personnel can communicate, can be mutually supporting, and can evaluate each other's results.

c. The efforts of these institutions — in related matters — must be directed toward a common goal.

It is evident that the process of systematic development of new and more lethal methods of warfare has become a very expensive one; the annual military budget of the United States makes this very clear. To assure cost effectiveness, there is a need for maximum efficiency in the coordination of the efforts of the institutions concerned and in the procedures followed within the institutions. What is *not* yet clear is whether our new methods of peacetime experimentation — through sophisticated war games, computerized evaluations, and carefully designed field tests — are in fact sufficiently realistic to provide adequate substitutes for battlefield experimentation (the third precondition). There is good reason to believe that, at present, they are *not*.*

XXX. Lethality, Casualties, and Tactics

Since weapons have steadily increased in lethality over the ages, and the trend has become particularly pronounced in the past century and a half, it would seem logical to assume that wartime casualty trends have also been going up, and that war has become steadily more horrible and deadly.

Whether nor not war has become more horrible, it is clear that as weapons have become *more* deadly, the results of exposure to standard weapons concentrations for standard periods of time have become *less* deadly, since the rate at which weapons inflict casualties on the battlefield has been declining. (By casualty *rate* is meant the percentage loss per day of forces exposed to weapons effects.)

This paradox is occasionally noted by military theorists, military historians, and operations research analysts, but for all practical purposes it is ignored in historical works, in theory, in planning, and in analysis. The result has been a gross misinterpretation of recent wars, and — in all probability — an equally gross misperception of wars of the future.

It is not possible, of course, to make any truly satisfactory comparison of lethality and casualties, or of the changing relationships among them, without being able to measure lethality. And to anyone who says that lethality is a quality that cannot be measured, it can be answered that we have already intuitively quantified lethality — no matter how much we may protest to the contrary — by the mere fact that reasonable men agree that lethality has grown; and growth is a concept that automatically presupposes a comparative standard and some form or degree of scale.

Thus we *must* turn to quantification. And to those who insist that Clausewitz and Napoleon eschewed quantification, what I suggest is that they read or reread *On War*, and the *Maxims* and

---

*See T. N. Dupuy, *Numbers, Predictions and War*, (New York: Bobbs-Merrill, 1979).

correspondence of Napoleon. Few men were as intuitively mathematical-minded as Napoleon. And Clausewitz was fond of making comparisons based upon relative measurements. This in no way invalidates or contradicts the frequently expressed realization of both of these philosophers of war that human behavior and foibles are random and unpredictable in any given situation or circumstance. Yet neither hesitated to draw firm, comparative conclusions of scale upon the basis of a substantial body of data. This is nowhere better demonstrated than in the following quotation from Clausewitz:

> *If we . . . strip the engagement of all the variables arising from its purpose and circumstances, and disregard [or strip out] the fighting value of the troops involved (which is a given quantity), we are left with the bare concept of the engagement . . . in which the only distinguishing factor is the number of troops on either side.*
>
> *These numbers, therefore, will determine victory. . . . Superiority of numbers in a given engagement is only one of the factors that determines victory [but] is the most important factor in the outcome of an engagement, so long as it is great enough to counterbalance all other contributing circumstances.*
>
> *This . . . would hold true for Greeks and Persians, for Englishmen and Mahrattas, for Frenchmen and Germans.**

In other places I have given much attention to the quantification of the variables that affect the outcomes of battles — and that also give insights into the patterns that can be discerned among the vagaries of human behavior in war and peace.† With the help of these quantifications it is possible to find reasonable, satisfactory, and undeniably logical answers to our questions. And with the help of these same quantifications, the process of the evolution of weapons and warfare — and the likely future significance of the trends discernible — becomes clear, or at least reasonable.

This does *not* mean that quantification will enable us to predict the future, or that quantitative relationships are in themselves

---

*Karl von Clausewitz, *On War*, Book 3, Chapter 8.

†See, for instance, *Numbers, Predictions, and War* (New York, op cit, 1979); the appendices of *A Genius for War, the German Army and General Staff: 1807–1905* (Englewood Cliffs, op cit, 1977), and *Elusive Victory; the Arab–Israeli Wars, 1947–1974* (New York: Harper & Row, 1978), and various articles in *Army, The Armed Forces Journal, National Defense,* and *History, Numbers, and War,* all by this author.

predictable — as the discredited geometricians came to believe. There has been no decrease in the uncertainty of future behavior since the time of Napoleon, and with human nature as it has been since the earliest records, no amount of study of the past will enable us to predict individual future events. We can project trends, we can use actuarial data to predict ranges of likely events and probable human performance, but discrete events and individual activities will always be inscrutable.

Bearing in mind, therefore, both the potentialities of and the limits to historical quantification, let us see what it can tell us about lethality, about trends in casualty rates, and about trends in all aspects of the evolution of weapons and warfare.

An approach to the quantification of lethality has already been mentioned earlier. The system applies to the characteristics of weapons a formula (that has been described elsewhere,*), with results as shown in Table 1 (p. 92). These numbers — Theoretical Lethality Indexes, or TLIs — represent consideration of such characteristics as rate of fire, number of potential targets per strike, relative incapacitating effect, effective range (or muzzle velocity), accuracy, reliability, battlefield mobility, radius of action, and vulnerability.

But in order to calculate actual lethality this theoretical lethality must be related to the battlefield density of the targets against which the weapons are employed. Table 6 shows historical patterns of ground force dispersion from antiquity through the 1973 October War. From this we can see that if a battle array of soldiers in antiquity had one man per 10 square meters — which is a reasonable approximation of what we know of ancient military formations — then in the October War troops were so dispersed that there was one man per every 40,000 square meters — a four-thousand-fold increase. And so it is necessary to divide the TLI shown for the weapons listed in Table 1 (see page 92) by the appropriate dispersion factor from Table 6 (see page 312). This gives a value called the Operational Lethality Index, showing relative battlefield values of weapons in different historical era. This calculation is shown in Table 7 (see page 313). The Operational Lethality Indexes (or OLIs) shown are also called "proving ground" values, because — while adjusted to contemporary dispersion patterns — the values are still ideal and optimum as far as the variable weapons-degrading influences of the battlefield are concerned; such influences as the effects of weather, terrain, defensive

---

*T. N. Dupuy, *Numbers, Predictions, and War* (New York, 1979).

posture, force mobility, force vulnerability, and so forth. Superimposed on the plot of weapon lethality in Figure 2 is a curve showing how dispersion has kept pace with lethality (pp. 288-89).

In fact, dispersion has actually increased more rapidly than lethality. On the average, for a combined-arms force of 100,000 men, lethality had increased from antiquity to the 1973 war by a factor of 2,000. (Of course, for many weapons it has been much more than that, but in a typical modern army more than half of the 100,000 men are truck drivers, or clerks, or cooks, or radio operators, whereas in the ancient armies all present were fighters). And while lethality for a large military formation has been increasing two-thousand-fold, dispersion has increased by a factor of 4,000.

Bearing that in mind, the table of casualty trends since the sixteenth century, as shown in Figure 3 (see page 314), is not surprising. Now we can see why it would be logical for casualty rates to decline, since the dispersion of soldiers has increased more rapidly than has weapon lethality per man. There are other considerations reflected in this graph, but the most important is the relationship of dispersion to lethality.

The same phenomenon is reflected in the statistical relationships of loss rates per year, and per day of active combat, shown in Table 8 (see page 315). There is much meaning packed into those comparative statistics. Let me just point out a few. Note how the daily casualty rate for division-sized units has declined to the range of about 2 percent per day for World War II and the more recent October War of 1973. Note the considerably higher loss rates of the Soviets in World War II in comparison with American and German losses. Note how, despite daily loss rates that were much lower in World War I than in the American Civil War, the grinding effect of long, drawn-out deadly battles in World War I produced a higher *annual* loss rate. Yet, in World War II, with daily loss rates somewhat lower than in World War I, the annual loss rates — despite battles that were also drawn-out and deadly — were much lower than in World War I. That statistical comparison demonstrates a significant phenomenon of warfare, to which I shall return.

Lethality and combat performance are often parallel in relationship, but not necessarily directly proportionate. Thus, the German Army and its supporting air arm in 1940 were so effective as to overrun France, Holland, and Belgium and force the British Expeditionary Forces off the Continent, all within a space of six weeks. Yet Allied dead in this vast, intensive series of battles totaled the surprisingly low figure of some 120,000.* In their great 1918 offensives, the Germans killed about 185,000 French troops, and killed, wounded, and captured 418,374 British; yet their offensives failed after gains measured in a few tens of miles.† Direct comparisons of this sort may be dangerously misleading unless parameters of comparison — including considerations of time, space, and numbers — are established in advance.

It must also be noted that high casualty figures reflect not only the lethality of the weapon inflicting them but also the tactics employed on both sides. In the first day of the Battle of the Somme in World War I the British advanced in lines more appropriate to the nineteenth than the twentieth century. At the end of that day they had lost nearly 60,000 men killed, wounded, or prisoners. One of their divisions in two hours lost 218 of 300 officers and 5,274 enlisted men of 8,500 who had attacked.** The Germans had similar losses in some of their attacks on Verdun. Therefore, in discussing the major advances in lethality of weapons, it is necessary to go on to discuss the tactics and organization that most successfully exploited their lethality, and thus were most effective in combat. It is also necessary to consider the tactics employed by the other side to counter the lethal effects of the weapons.

Advances in lethality must be considered primarily in terms of an informed judgment of the inherent capabilities of the weapon itself, rather than of the casualties it has inflicted. This approach seems justified, for example, because the relatively crude weapons of the American Civil War killed in action 21.3 men per 1,000 per year. The comparable figure for U.S. soldiers in World War I was 12.0, and World War II, 9.0.†† No one would argue, however, that the earlier weapons were more lethal; the difference in casualties lies in the adjustment of tactics to the inherent capabilities of contemporary weapons, dispersion being a major factor. Thus, after a century of obvious incompatibility, it would appear that in World War II weapons and tactics again were in general congruence.

---

*Ropp, *War in the Modern World*, p. 319.

†Winston S. Churchill, *The World Crisis*, one vol. ed. (New York: Scribner, 1949). Based on tables A, B, and II.

**Churchill, *The World Crisis*, p. 66.

††Beebe and DeBakey, Table 4B. By comparing deaths in action rather than total casualties, the question of unequal medical care is avoided.

TABLE 6
Historical Army Dispersion Patterns
(Army or Corps of 100,000 Troops)

	Antiquity	Napoleonic Wars	American Civil War	World War I	World War II	October War
Area Occupied by Deployed Force, 100,000 Strong (sq km)	1.00	20.12	25.75	248	2.750	4,000
Front (km)	6.67	8.05	8.58	14	48	57
Depth (km)	0.15	2.50	3.0	17	57	70
Men Per Sq Km	100,000	4,970	3,883	404	36	25
Square Meters/man	10.00	200	257.5	2,475	27,500	40,000

TABLE 7
Comparative Operational Lethality Indices

Weapons	TLI Values	Ancient or Medieval	17th Cent	18th Cent	Nap. Wars	Civil War	W.W. I	W.W. II	1975
Historical Period → Dispersion Factor		1	5	10	20	25	250	3.000	4.000
		(OLI Values)							
Hand-to-hand	23	23	4.6	2.3	1.1	0.9	0.09	0.007	0.006
Javelin	19	19							
Ordinary bow	21	21							
Longbow	36	36	7.2	3.6					
Crossbow	33	33	6.6						
Arquebus	10		2.0						
17th C musket	19		3.8						
18th C flintlock	43		8.6	4.3	2.2	1.7			
Early 19th C rifle	36			3.6	1.8	1.4			
Mid-19th C rifle	102					4.1			
Late 19th C rifle	153					6.1	0.61	0.05	
Springfield Model 1903 rifle	495						1.98	0.17	0.12
WW I machine gun	3.463						14.0	1.15	0.87
WW II machine gun	4.973							1.66	1.24
16th C 12-pdr cannon	43	43	8.6						
17th C 12-pdr cannon	224		45.0	22.0			—		
Gribeauval 12-pdr cannon	940			94.0	47.0	38.0			
French 75mm gun	386.530						1.546.	129.	97.
155mm GPF	912.428						3.650.	304.	228.
105mm Howitzer	637.215						—	219.	164.
155mm "Long Tom"	1.180.681						—	394.	295.
WW I tank	34.636						139.	12.	—
WW II medium tank	935.458							312.	234.
WW I fighter-bomber	31.909						128.	11.	—
WW II fighter-bomber	1.245.789							415.	311.
V-2 ballistic missile	3.338.370							1.113.	835.
20 KT nuclear airburst	49.086.000							16.362.	12.272.
One megaton nuclear airburst	695.385.000							231.795.	173.846.

314

FIGURE 3

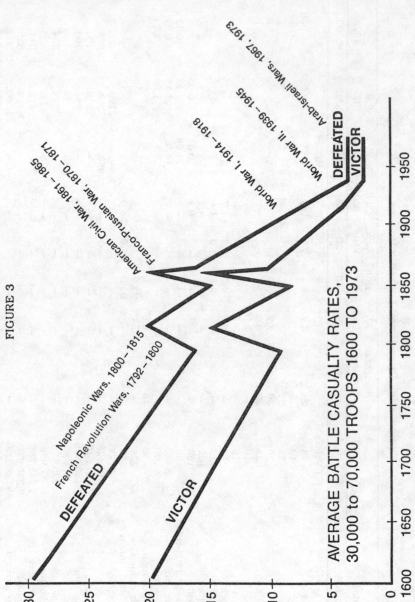

AVERAGE BATTLE CASUALTY RATES,
30,000 to 70,000 TROOPS 1600 TO 1973

TABLE 8
Selected Combat Casualty Statistics
(Approximate data)

CONFLICT	% COMBAT THEATER TROOPS/YEAR	REPRESENTATIVE ENGAGEMENT CASUALTIES % PER DAY	
US FORCES			
Mexican War	14.5	Antietam:	U — 17.7
Civil War	23.3		C — 28.9
		Gettysburg:	U — 9.8
			C — 12.5
Spanish-American War	1.0		
Philippine Insurrection	1.2		
World War I (six months)	51.0	av. per division	2.0
World War II	21.3	av. per division	0.9
Korea	17.3	av. per division	0.8
Vietnam	20.6		
Soviet Forces			
1944 (12 months)	82.0	Kursk ('43)	3.0
Middle East Wars	%/CONFLICT		
1967 Israel (6 days)	2.2	average	2.8
Egypt (3 days)	6.2	average	6.0
Jordan (3 days)	5.7	average	5.6
Syria (2 days)	3.0	average	4.0
1973 Israel (19 days)	3.9	average	1.8
Egypt (19 days)	8.0	average	2.6
Syria (17 days)	6.8	average	2.9

XXXI. Men and Ideas

Until the development of the atomic bomb and subsequently the hydrogen bomb, no weapon in the history of mankind, however great its potential lethality, has been as important for the winning of battles or wars as the men who controlled them. The application of sound, imaginative thinking to existing weapons has caused the great developments in military affairs and influenced international relations.

The importance of new or imaginative *ideas* in military affairs — as opposed simply to new *things* — can best be gauged by the fact that new ideas have often permitted inferior military forces to overcome forces that were larger and/or better equipped. Hannibal offers an outstanding example of this in antiquity. He had no new weapons (his elephants were relatively ineffective against the Romans), his troops were inferior in quality, training, and weapons. His amazing string of successes resulted from his ability to use combined arms, to improvise both strategically and tactically, and in particular to focus on maneuver. He has rightly been called the "father of strategy," and his imaginative thinking directly stimulated the development of the so-called Schlieffen Plan of World War I.

The successes of Genghis Khan were achieved in almost every instance against forces that were numerically superior and had similar or comparable weapons. Unlike Hannibal, Genghis invariably did enjoy superiority in training and discipline, but this alone could not explain the extent or nature of his conquests. The reason was an unexcelled genius for developing new ideas in organization and administration, combined with the same kind of imaginative tactical and strategical genius that Hannibal had displayed. New ideas, unexpected and unknown to his opponents, were the reasons for Genghis's success.

Equally relevant, although a different kind of example, is the way in which the Swiss used the long pike — almost identical to the Macedonian sarissa — to dominate European battlefields for a century at the end of the Middle Ages. Combining tactical mobility, speed of movement, surprise, and an unfailing offensive spirit, the unarmored Swiss, in dense columns not unlike the Macedonian phalanx, charged at the run to overwhelm heavily armored knights on horse or on foot, as well as all other varieties of medieval infantry. They were for several decades able to maintain an ascendancy over troops armed with early gunpowder weapons as well, either dashing through the beaten zones before enemy fire could do them serious harm, or else attacking by surprise from an unexpected direction before the clumsy existing systems of command and control could respond.

There is, of course, no better example of the impact of ideas on existing weapons than the military system developed by Gustavus

Adolphus. As we have seen, he not only modified weapons drastically, he combined them into a military system which, to some extent, has lasted to our own day.

Another example is the adaptation of the flintlock musket to linear tactics by the Prussians. They were not the only ones to do this, but Frederick William I and his grandson Frederick II succeeded by training and discipline in increasing the rate of fire of the Prussian infantry, even beyond any advantage provided by an iron ramrod, without in any way changing the weapon or its method of operation. Prussian training, discipline, and superior firepower — as well as his own imaginative genius — were then exploited by Frederick to make Prussia a great power and to change permanently the balance of power in Europe.

Napoleon introduced neither a new weapon nor a new tactical system. Although he was a tactician of genius, his principal impact on warfare was the injection of new and imaginative ideas into grand tactics and strategy — the most important of these being his concepts of mass and maneuver. One indication of the potential and actual lethality of ideas can be obtained from the comment of one of his enemies (Blücher, although the statement has also been attributed to Wellington), that Napoleon's mere presence in a battle or campaign was worth at least 40,000 men. The strategic concepts of Napoleon, novel at the time, are now commonplace as a result of the writings of Jomini and Clausewitz.

In World Wars I and II it was again demonstrated that the adoption of new ideas of tactics and doctrine can also give the introducing power the advantage of surprise. Twice within the lifetimes of men now living the German Army has scored stunning tactical surprises over its opponents — in 1918 and again in 1940 — yet in neither case did it use new weapons. Every item in the German arsenal was familiar, yet revolutionary use of these weapons came as a great surprise to Germany's enemies in both wars.

The Chinese Communists in Korea, who had no air support, little armor, relatively weak artillery, and were generally backward in terms of modern weapons and equipment, through a combination of initiative, determination, and imaginative exploitation of our previously unrecognized weaknesses, inflicted some sharp defeats on American forces. In different ways we, like the French before us, were exposed to similar lessons in Vietnam, where the guerrillas were able simply to use their enemies — us — as an arsenal.

Significant Tactical Changes since 1860

The dramatic impact of the introduction of the conoidal bullet in rifled musket about 1860 has been discussed earlier. (See p. 292.) In the next half-century the sudden imbalance between infantry and artillery weapons was slowly righted, and the cannon again became the most lethal weapon on the battlefield. But as of 1914 there had been no general impact on military practices from this greatly increased lethality of modern artillery (with recoil-system, breech-loading, rifling, and especially, high-explosive shell), of breech-loading, magazine infantry rifles, or, in particular, of the machine gun. The experiences of the Russo-Japanese War — which should have provided warning — were largely ignored. There were, however, some efforts to cope with the new weapons, and a wide disparity of practice existed. The German Army preferred a doctrine devised by the elder Moltke, based upon a combination of strategic offensive and tactical defensive. The latter made effective use of machine gun and high-explosive shell, but German organization, and tactics on the offensive, were still not very different from those of 1870. The British had not looked beyond providing a small force of superbly trained riflemen on the flank of the French Army. The French — imbued with a dedication to the moral value of the offensive — had completely misread the situation and made no adaptation of their infantry tactics to adjust to the lethal characteristics of automatic weapons and high-explosive shell, although they had devoted much attention to improving the quality of their artillery.

As a result of only partial recognition by the Germans of the defensive power of the combination of earthworks, machine guns, and high-explosive shell, and the even greater lack of comprehension by their Allied opponents, there was a tactical stalemate on the Western Front for three years. Political and strategic pressures interacted with this incomprehension to cause five major Allied offensives to the Germans' one; all relied primarily on frontal assault behind massive artillery barrages. Allied casualties were astronomical, with little to show for them, although German losses were also heavy.

Both sides sought ways to end the stalemate and to cut the cost of the unsuccessful efforts to break it. The Franco-British solution was at first simply mechanical: the tank. The decision-makers were willing to add the tank to their inventory, but not to change tactics, doctrine, or organization. The Germans decided to change tactics, organization, and doctrine, but missed the potential importance of the tank.

In fairly rapid succession the Germans introduced first the triangular division, and then combat teams built around a base of fire and a maneuvering element, and acting in tactical independence but strategic coordination. In using machine guns and mortars for an offensive base of fire, this system was the first fully to assimilate automatic weapons and high explosive. Using these tactics, in 1918, the Germans were able to overcome the Allied defenses and to make major breakthroughs — which, however, their logistics structure could not support. The importance of these new German tactical developments was recognized by the Allies, who applied them in turn — with the added advantage of the tank, which fitted perfectly with the new tactics.

The lessons of 1918 were subsequently examined by all great powers; but Germany, with a thorough general-staff research effort into past experience and current technological advances backed (after 1933) by adequate financial support from the Nazi government, made much more effective advances between the wars. Basing their new tactical system upon the infantry-combat-team concept they had developed in 1917–1918, the German military planners elaborated the concept by using armor in mass (while teaming subunits of armor with subunits of infantry), and by providing radically improved tactical air support to supplement and (if necessary in mobile warfare) supplant artillery. A flexible, decentralized, command system permitted taking full advantage of the diverse possibilities of such combinations. With this doctrine, the tank and the fighter-bomber may be said to have been fully assimilated into land warfare.

With the German innovations of 1918, infantry deployments opened up for the third time since the handgun first became an effective weapon on the battlefield. (The previous openings had been: the linear system of Gustavus Adolphus; and the gradual dispersal forced by firepower in the Civil War, Franco-Prussian War, and Russo-Japanese War, without, however, changing linear concepts.) The line was now replaced by small teams of men, combining firepower in terms of air and artillery support. Making full use of surprise, cover, and tactical mobility, the teams could saturate a small portion of the defense system with fire, exploiting the defense's problems of judgment and reaction time by a combination of mass (essentially massed firepower) and maneuver.

These new infantry concepts, pioneered by the Germans in 1918, and brought to full development by integration with armor and air in their blitzkrieg tactics of 1939–1940, were not materially changed during the course of World War II. They were embellished and modified to some extent in the two principal varieties of interservice task-force operations that contributed materially to final Allied victory in the war. The first of these was an Anglo-American adaptation of German pioneering airborne efforts. The second was the Anglo-American perfection of amphibious assault techniques. Fundamentally, however, despite a considerable amount of independent and parallel development, these interservice task-force concepts were technical adaptations of the basic German combat team tactics.

XXXII. Military History and Theory: The Laboratory of the Soldier

Napoleon and Military Theory

Military history has always been the laboratory of the soldier. A review of the experience of war from ancient times makes it clear that fighting men have built upon the experience of those who fought before them, adopting their weapons, adding new ones, and adapting their tactics and strategy in accordance with their own needs and abilities. Although much was written over the centuries about wars and how they were and should be fought, it was not until the nineteenth century that men tried to codify theories or to describe in orderly fashion the basic elements involved in combat and how best, in any battle anywhere, to conduct oneself and order one's forces.

The attempt to formulate theories about the art of war in modern times stems from Napoleon. Although he did not himself record his theories he did produce a number of maxims upon which others subsequently built. And his maxims, he made it clear, derived from those before him:

> Read and reread the campaigns of Alexander, Hannibal, Caesar, Gustavus, Turenne, Eugene, and Frederick. Make them your models. This is the only way to become a great general and to master the secrets of the art of war. With your own genius enlightened by this study, you will reject all maxims opposed to those of these great commanders.

To Napoleon it was obviously clear that there is a substantial theoretical basis for military operations. From his words, but to an even greater extent from his actions, there has been a steady intellectual progression toward the development of a theory of combat.

Theorists of the Nineteenth and Twentieth Centuries

Ten men have been outstanding in this intellectual progression from Napoleonic practice to theory. Through their efforts and others there appeared, over the course of approximately one century, the first conscious formulation of a theory of combat: the Principles of War.

Henri Jomini tried to explain the theoretical basis of Napoleon's operational genius, and he undoubtedly clearly understood what Napoleon had in mind. But in his many writings he was never able satisfactorily either to capture the philosophical aspects of Napoleon's thinking on war, or to distill the essence of the theory. The result was a somewhat mixed bag of discussion, rules, aphorisms and maxims.

Karl von Clausewitz, after Napoleon, was probably history's most profound thinker on war. He *was* able to capture Napoleon's philosophy, and to add to it some ideas of his own. But he found himself as baffled by the problems of distilling a theory out of this philosophy as Jomini had been. Like the Bible in theology, Clausewitz can be quoted in military affairs to support both sides of almost any sound or unsound concept that one might desire to document. This doesn't mean that Clausewitz was wishy-washy, or self-contradictory. It merely means that he is easy to quote out of context; and he never had a chance to edit a final, published version of his work.

Clausewitz is often quoted as ridiculing the idea that there could or should be any fixed set of principles of war. This is an example of quoting him out of context. In fact he devotes several chapters to a discussion of a theory of war, and he affirms that there are principles—he lists eight of the nine principles we usually accept. But he implicitly admits that the formulation of the theory would require an effort beyond that of *On War*, or possibly beyond the limits of what could be accomplished in his time in terms of scientific method. And he decries attempts to produce precise and mathematical rules for combat which, if followed by generals on the battlefield, would be the key to victory.

Dennis Hart Mahan was essentially a follower of Napoleon through Jomini. He was the first great American military theorist. He compiled his own maxims and rules which he thought relevant to military theory in America. But he never tried (as far as is evident from available writings) to produce a theory, as such.

Helmuth von Moltke was both an eminent historian and an

eminent military thinker. He was also a superb organizer and director of combat. His perceptive comment about the need to combine the tactical defensive with the strategic offensive was a major contribution. He was essentially a manifestation of the capabilities of an institution of genius — the Prussian General Staff; any of a number of his Prussian contemporaries could have done as well.

Charles J.J.J. Ardant du Picq was perhaps the most perceptive writer on the subject of moral forces — behavioral considerations — in war. His book *Battle Studies* is one of the handful of truly great military classics and one of the best of that handful. He was killed in battle (in the Franco-Prussian War) before his work could be incorporated into any kind of theoretical context, which was unfortunate for France.

Alfred Thayer Mahan was a military theorist in the style of Jomini, of his own father, and of Moltke. He was a profound and gifted thinker on military affairs — and especially the naval aspects of military affairs — who well understood the relevance of military history to the contemporary military problems of his time. He recognized and analytically employed principles, but never attempted a scientific approach to military theory.

Baron Colmar von der Goltz was one of a number of German military thinkers who emerged from the Prussian General Staff during its heyday, under Moltke and Schlieffen. He may not deserve to be included in the intellectual company on these pages, but his work had great influence in Germany, in France, and particularly in Britain.

Count Alfred von Schlieffen was another profound thinker on war who never attempted to distill precise or abstract theory from his obviously encyclopedic knowledge of military history and the warfare of his own time. As a soldier and a general he was probably superior to Moltke, but we shall never know. It seems likely, however, that if he had commanded the German armies in 1914, his plan would have succeeded, and subsequent history would have been very different.

Ferdinand Foch was a disciple both of Clausewitz and of Ardant du Picq, and one of the few theorists after Napoleon who rose to high command in the crucible of combat. He probably understood Clausewitz as well as anyone ever has — certainly better than most Germans. But — paradoxically — he misread his countryman, Ardant du Picq. He did try to think and write in scientific, theoretical terms, and there is much that is sound in his approach to military theory. But his influence, and his devotion to the moral significance of *l'offensive a l'outrance* (offensive to the utmost) came close to ruining the French Army at the outset of World War I.

John F. C. Fuller was the greatest military thinker of this century, and probably the most important since Clausewitz. It is interesting that in his earlier writings he tended to downgrade Clausewitz, but in later years he began to recognize that his own approach to military theory was essentially Clausewitzian. He was immodest enough to compare himself with Copernicus, Newton, and Darwin. He did not overstate the case. He was the first to codify the Principles of War as they have been known for most of this century. He was the first great armored tactician. Fuller knew that there should be more (both more content and more scientific rigor) to a theory of combat than just the Principles of War, but he never quite succeeded in formulating such a theory.*

These are the men whose not-very-well-coordinated efforts over a century produced the first manifestation of a theory of combat, the Principles of War.

The Principles of War

Listed following are the Principles of War, as they have been expressed in official U.S. Army Doctrine.† Modern military scholars are sharply divided in their reactions to and assessments of the Principles of War. However, this collection of concepts is as close as mankind has come to date to a formulation of a recognized theory of combat.

Objective. Every military operation must be directed toward a decisive, obtainable objective.

Offensive. Only offensive action achieves decisive results.

Simplicity. In combat everything is difficult; complexity fosters confusion, misunderstanding, and mistakes.

Unity of command. The decisive application of full combat power requires unity of command — which I prefer to call *Control*.

---

*Some readers may wonder why I have omitted Basil Liddell Hart from this list. I have been accused of prejudice against Liddell Hart, but I don't believe that I underrate him. It was by picking Fuller's brains that Liddell Hart was able to sell himself as a military theorist; in fact, Liddell Hart was a man of reasonable intelligence and brilliant writing skill who has no right on his own merits to be compared to any of these great military thinkers, as his poor biography of Foch amply demonstrates. The man who could write the historically inaccurate and analytically unsound assessment of Schlieffen and the Schlieffen plan that appears in his foreword to Gerhard Ritter's book on that subject, and who could describe Scipio Africanus as being greater than Napoleon, can never be considered a profound student of military genius or theory.

†Listed in the same sequence in which they appear in the *U.S. Field Manual*, FM 100–1, but the concepts are summarized in the words of the author.

Mass. Maximum available combat power must be applied at the point of decision; some prefer to identify this principle as *Concentration.*

Economy of forces. Forces not employed at the point of decision must be kept as small as possible, thus facilitating mass.

Maneuver. Forces must be disposed so as to maximize their effectiveness and minimize the combat power of the enemy.

Surprise. The enemy is forced to respond to the unexpected; surprise may be achieved in time, in place, or by method.

Security. Minimizes the possibility of being surprised, and the consequences if surprised.

The Principles are a good framework for a theory of combat. But what actually happens on a battlefield? How do the men and guns and weather and morale and leaders and all the other elements that are involved act and influence one another to produce victory or defeat? This is a problem that is currently of considerable interest to operations analysts and planners, and what better way is there to find out than to analyze battles of the past?

War Gaming and the Quantified Judgment Model

War games probably have been played almost as long as wars have been fought. The best-known, and perhaps the oldest still being played, is chess. (Although the Chinese *wei chie* — modified in Japan as *i go* — may be as old.) Military commanders for centuries have planned their battles, and one way or another diagrammed them before and after the event. Serious use of game boards for studying battle and for planning future operations is a fairly recent development, promoted particularly by the Prussian General Staff early in the nineteenth century. Invention and improvement of the computer in the era since World War II encouraged the development of war games as a basis for planning for all aspects of warfare and particularly for procurement of types and numbers of weapons. These games, mathematically sophisticated, are fed with numbers representing characteristics of weapons and various other factors, most of them derived from weapon test programs or from the output of other games.

Among games in current use only one derives its inputs entirely from experience and attempts to recognize all the factors that affect them in combat. Basically a lengthy but simple algebraic formula, the Quantified Judgment Model recognizes not only numbers of men and equipment but factors that work upon them to determine the development and outcome of combat on the battlefield. The model was developed from data relating to actual combat experience.

The QJM is not the whole answer, however, to the question of what combat really is, and although it quantifies many elements that are actually intangible, others and their influence are extremely difficult to identify. Toward developing an optimum understanding of combat, these unknowns are being explored. The search is on for a really inclusive theory of combat.

XXXIII. The Next War and the Timeless Verities of Combat

Attempting to Perceive Future Wars

Military establishments and military leaders have always been fair game for bright intellectuals. Journalists in particular take pleasure in exposing the stupidities of generals, the inflexibility of the so-called military mind, and the heedless regimentation of military procedures. Self-appointed critics of military affairs delight in such aphorisms as, "War is too important to be left to the generals," and, "Military leaders are always preparing to fight the last war."

To the extent that military men — including generals and lesser folk in uniform — are human beings, with all of the attendant fallibility, the criticisms usually have an element of truth. But essentially they are unfair. With due allowances for differences among individuals and national cultures, most successful military men are hard-working, intelligent professionals who do the best they can in attempting to master an extremely unruly and untractable discipline that is part art and part science.

Perhaps the most unfair of the common criticisms is that about preparing for the last war. A review of military journals in many languages over the past century will reveal that military professionals of all ages, backgrounds, and nationalities have conscientiously attempted to relate past military experience to current military technology in order to gain an understanding of how the next war is likely to be fought.

The longer the interval between wars, however, the more difficult it is to forecast how technological change may have invalidated the lessons of the previous war. It becomes easier for enthusiasts to get carried away by ideas that retain little relation to reality. One can find many examples of this in military professional journals published before the last two world wars. And it is interesting to see how such enthusiasts had a tendency to justify their unrealistic ideas by citing historical examples that were often wrong in facts, or interpretations, or perception.

This was particularly true in Europe in the decade before World War I, most significantly in France, where the study of military history was not taken as seriously as it was in Germany. As shown on earlier pages, it is clear from a review of the events of 1914 that neither side had predicted the nature of the next war very well during the prewar years, but the German perception was more objective, realistic, and logical than that of the French.

The Timeless Verities of Combat

Since no one can possibly know now what the next war will *really* be like, it behooves us to try at least to understand features that have made the operational aspects of warfare through the ages basically the same in war after war. Weapons and the characteristics of armies have changed, and with them the tactics employed on the battlefield. But the fundamental operational features, which I call the "timeless verities of combat," remain the same. I identify thirteen of these unchanging operational features or concepts.

1. *Offensive action is essential to positive combat results.* This is like saying, "A team can't score in football unless it has the ball." Although subsequent verities stress the strength, value, and importance of defense, this should not be allowed to obscure the essentiality of offensive action to ultimate combat success. Even in instances where a defensive strategy might conceivably assure a favorable war outcome — as was the case with the British against Napoleon, and the Confederacy in the American Civil War — selective employment of offensive tactics and offensive operations is required if the strategic defender is to have any chance of winning the war.

2. *Defensive strength is greater than offensive strength.* Clausewitz expressed this: "Defense is the stronger form of combat." It is possible to demonstrate by the qualitative comparison of many battles that Clausewitz is right and that posture has a multiplicative effect on the combat power of a military force that takes advantage of terrain and fortifications, whether hasty and rudimentary, or intricate and carefully prepared. There are many well-known examples of the need of an attacker for a preponderance of

strength in order to carry the day against a well-placed and fortified defender. One has only to recall Thermopylae, the Alamo, Antietam, Petersburg, and El Alamein to realize the advantage enjoyed by a defender with smaller forces, well placed, and well protected.*

3. *Defensive posture is necessary when successful offense is impossible.* Even though offensive action is essential to ultimate combat success, a combat commander opposed by a more powerful enemy has no choice but to assume a defensive posture. And since defensive posture automatically multiplies the strength of his force, the defending commander thus at least partially redresses the imbalance of forces. He is able — at a minimum — to slow down the advance of the attacking enemy, and possibly to beat him. In this way — through negative combat results — the defender may ultimately hope to wear down the attacker to the extent that his initial relative weakness is transformed into relative superiority, thus offering the possibility of eventually assuming the offensive and achieving positive combat results.

Portions of a numerically superior offensive force may also be required to assume a defensive posture, if the overall force commander has reduced the strengths of these portions in order to achieve decisive superiority for maximum impact on the enemy at some other critical point on the battlefield. A contingent thus reduced in strength may therefore be required to assume a defensive posture, even though the overall operational posture of the marginally superior force is offensive, and another contingent of the same forces is, in fact, attacking with the advantage of superior combat power.

4. *Flank or rear attack is more likely to succeed than frontal attack.* Among the many reasons for this are: there is greater opportunity for surprise by the attacker; the defender cannot be strong everywhere at once, and the front is the easiest focus for defensive effort; defensive morale tends to be shaken when the danger of encirclement is evident to the defenders. Again historical examples are legion. Any impression that the concept of envelopment or of a "strategy of indirect approach" has arisen either from the introduction of modern weapons of war or from the ruminations of a recent writer on military affairs is a grave mis-

---

*See also *Numbers, Predictions, and War,* pp. 12–15.

perception of history and underestimates earlier military thinkers.

"Seek the flanks" has been a military adage since antiquity. But its significance was tremendously enhanced when the breech-loading, rifled musket revolutionized warfare in the mid-nineteenth century. This led Moltke to his 1867 observation that the increased deadliness of firepower demanded that the strategic offensive be coupled with tactical defensive, an idea that depended upon envelopment for its accomplishment. Figure 4 shows the strategic application of Moltke's idea in the 1870 campaign in France; Figure 5 shows its tactical manifestations at

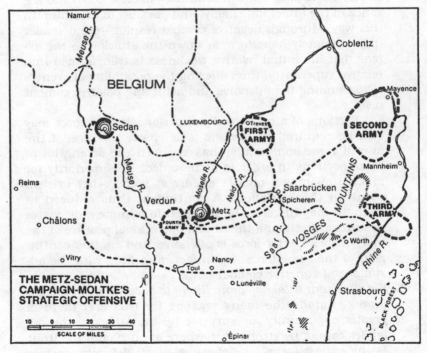

FIGURE 4.

Metz, where Bazaine — his line of communications to Paris cut by the German envelopment — was forced to attack, and be defeated.

5. *Initiative permits application of preponderant combat*

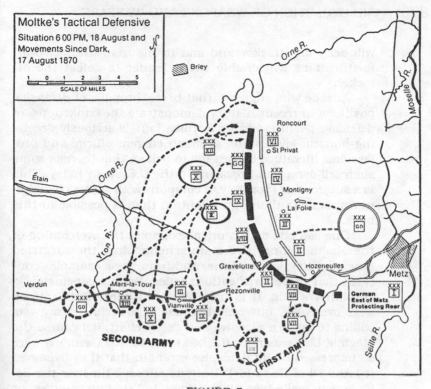

FIGURE 5.

power. This has been the secret of success of all of the great captains of history. It was as true of MacArthur as it was of Alexander; of Grant as of Napoleon. Some modern Soviet theorists have suggested that this is even more important in an era of high technology than formerly; they may be right. Certainly the importance of seizing and maintaining the initiative has not declined in our times, nor will it in the future.

6. *Defenders' chances of success are directly proportional to fortification strength.* To some modern military thinkers this is a truism needing no explanation or justification. Others have asserted that defenses are attractive traps to be avoided at all costs. Such assertions, however, either ignore or misread historical examples. History is so fickle that it is dangerous for historians to use such words as "always" or "never." Nevertheless, I offer a bold counterassertion: Never in history has a defense been weakened by the availability of fortifications; defensive works *always* enhance combat strength. At the very least, fortifications

will delay an attacker and add to his casualties; at best, fortifications will enable the defender to defeat the attacker.

Anyone who suggests that breakthroughs of defensive positions in recent history demonstrate the bankruptcy of defensive posture and/or fortifications is seriously deceiving himself. My reading of much current official and professional literature causes me to believe that there is some such self-deception prevalent in the U.S. Army today. This is a subject that (possibly in company with verities 8 and 9) warrants more thorough attention than is possible in this book.

One can cite as historical examples the overcoming of the Maginot Line, the Mannerheim Line, the Siegfried Line, and the Bar Lev Line, and from these examples conclude that those fortifications failed. Such a conclusion is absolutely wrong. It is true that all of these fortifications were overcome, but only because a powerful enemy was willing to make a massive and costly effort. (Of course the Maginot Line was not attacked in 1940; the Germans were so impressed by its defensive strength that they bypassed it.) And all of these fortifications afforded time for the defenders to make new dispositions, to bring up reserves, or to mobilize. All were intended to obstruct, to permit the defenders to punish the attackers, and above all to delay; all were successful in these respects. The Bar Lev Line, furthermore, saved Israel from disastrous defeat.

7. *An attacker willing to pay the price can always penetrate the strongest defenses.* No matter how alert the defender, no matter how skillful his dispositions to avoid or mitigate the effects of surprise or the effects of flank or rear attack, a skillful attacker can always achieve at least a temporary advantage for some time at a place he has selected. (This is one reason why Napoleon — and others — always endeavored to seize and retain the initiative.) In the great battles of 1864 and 1865 in Virginia, Lee was always able to exploit his defensive advantage to the utmost. But Grant equally was always able to achieve a temporary superiority when and where he wished. This did not always result in a Union victory — given Lee's defensive skill — but it invariably forced Lee to retreat until he could again impose a temporary stalemate with the assistance of powerful field fortifications.

8. *Successful defense requires depth and reserves.* It has

been asserted that outnumbered military forces cannot afford to withhold valuable firepower from operations and keep it idle in reserve posture. History demonstrates that this is specious logic, and that linear defense is disastrously vulnerable. Napoleon's crossing at the Po in his first campaign is perhaps the classic demonstration of the fallacy of linear defense.

The defender may have all of his firepower committed to the anticipated operational area, but the attacker's advantage in having the initiative can always render much of that defensive firepower useless. Anyone who suggests that modern technology will facilitate the shifting of engaged firepower in battle overlooks three considerations: (a) the attacker can inhibit or prevent such movement by both direct and indirect means; (b) a defender engaged in a fruitless firefight against limited attacks by numerically inferior attackers is neither physically nor psychologically attuned to make lateral movements (even if the enemy does not prevent or inhibit it); and (c) withdrawal of forces from the line (even if possible) provides an alert attacker with an opportunity for shifting the thrust of his offensive to the newly created gap in the defenses.

Napoleon recognized that hard-fought combat is usually won by the side committing the last reserves. Marengo, Borodino, and Ligny are typical examples of Napoleonic victories that demonstrated the importance of having resources available to tip the scales. And his two greatest defeats — Leipzig and Waterloo — were suffered because his enemies still had reserves after his were all committed. The importance of committing the last reserves was demonstrated with particular poignancy at Antietam in the American Civil War. And there is no better example than that of Kursk in World War II.

9. *Superior strength always wins.* In recent years two or three surveys of modern historical experience have led to such conclusions as that stated in one recent operations research report: "Comparing force-to-force ratios for determining the winner and loser in a . . . battle is inconclusive."

Table 9 (see page 335) is a list of ten battles of modern history, with numbers of men and weapons which would seem, at least superficially, to support the conclusion quoted above. Seven of these battles were won by the side with inferior numbers; in four of these, outnumbered attackers were successful. Table 10 (see page 336) lists these same battles in a format permitting an analysis of the circumstances of the battles and the opposing forces. If one takes into consideration surprise (when present), relative combat effectiveness, terrain features, and the advantage of defensive posture, quantifying their influence in some consistent fashion, as for instance it is done in the Quantified Judgment Model mentioned earlier, and modifying the original strength by these factors, in each case the strength of the successful side becomes greater. All other things being equal, God has always been on the side of the heaviest battalions, and always will be. This, of course, is what Clausewitz said in the quotation on page 326.

10. *Surprise substantially enhances combat power.* The importance of achieving surprise in combat has always been recognized, and many, including this writer and modern Soviet military planners, consider it more important today than ever. The quantification shown in Table 10 demonstrates how surprise increases the combat power of military forces in those engagements in which it was achieved. Surprise may be the most important of the Principles of War; it is at least as important as mass and maneuver.

11. *Firepower kills, disrupts, suppresses, and causes dispersion.* It is doubtful if any of the people who are today writing on the effect of technology on warfare would consciously disagree with this. Yet many of them translate it into a corollary that the more lethal the firepower, the more deaths, disruption, and suppression it will cause. As seen in Chapter XXX, this corollary is false. The personnel and tank loss rates of the 1973 war were quite similar to those of intensive battles of World War II. The common assertion that attrition rates of the 1973 war were much higher than those of World War II is wrong!

12. *Combat activities are slower, less productive, and less efficient than anticipated.* This is the phenomenon that Clausewitz called "friction in war." It is a direct result of the disruptive, suppressive, and dispersal effects of firepower. The significance of this is that it is a mistake to believe — as has been recently asserted by some writers on doctrine — that the results of field tests and training exercises, even highly realistic ones, will be directly reflected on the battlefield of the future. To be truly realistic,

our planning must reflect an interpretation of test and training results in the light of historical experience.
13. *Combat is too complex to be described in a single, simple aphorism.* This has been amply demonstrated by the preceding paragraphs. All writers on military affairs (including this one) need periodically to remind themselves of this. In military analysis it is often necessary to focus on some particular aspect of combat. But the results of such closely focused analyses must then be evaluated in the context of the brutal, multifarious, overlapping realities of war.

We have seen how technology has changed war dramatically in the past century and a half. Yet the thirteen "timeless verities" of combat have been as applicable and as true in the most recent war of these fifteen decades as they were in Napoleon's day — and as they were in the days of Alexander, Hannibal, Julius Caesar, Genghis Khan, Gustavus, and Frederick.

The reason for this, of course, is that, despite the many other changes, two essential characteristics of war have not changed. First, wars are fought by men, and there is no discernible difference in the fundamental nature of man over the past five thousand years of recorded history. And — as noted earlier — because the nature of man has not changed, neither has his basic objective when he turns to war: the employment of lethal instruments to force his will upon other men with opposing points of view.

Even if we cannot predict when or how future war will occur, or what its course will be, or how its individual battles will turn out, or how it will be affected by new technology or military materiel — we do know that the "timeless verities" will undoubtedly be applicable.

The Timeless Verities and NATO's Problems in the 1980s

As for Europe, for instance, a reading of the general popular press and of professional military publications can provide the careful reader with an appreciation of the characteristics and capabilities of the NATO and Warsaw Pact forces arrayed on opposite sides of the Iron Curtain, and of the general nature of the technology available to both sides. Obviously (as this book goes to press, in mid-1980) the NATO forces are in no position to assume the offensive, and there is no reason to believe that this can change over the next five years. Thus, if war breaks out in Europe, the Warsaw Pact will have the advantages of initiative, of the possibility of surprise, and of the various other benefits and limitations relating to offensive posture. At the same time, the advantages of defensive posture are at least theoretically available to NATO. To this analyst it would appear that the chances of a successful Warsaw Pact attack are far from overwhelming, *if NATO is adequately alerted, and has time to deploy its forces* and, above all, *to dig itself into strong defensive field fortifications before the assault is launched.*

There are many officials in and out of uniform in the NATO defense ministries who are convinced that modern means of electronic surveillance will assure adequate warning time for these preparations to be completed before the Pact forces can attack. However, a modern military historian remembers two things. First, the Israelis had equally valid reasons for being sure that they could not be caught by surprise by the Arabs in 1973; and in fact they had available to them — had they but realized it — all of the information necessary to predict the Arab attack, and to be adequately prepared for it. They were not prepared and, despite an elaborate system of fortifications and an overall combat effectiveness superiority, they were almost defeated.

Second, if there is one characteristic of modern Soviet warfare that has been particularly manifested on their battlefields, and which is probably emphasized more than anything else in current Soviet doctrine, it is surprise. It is my opinion that the Soviets — in the foreseeable future — *will not attack in Europe without surprise,* and it is my opinion that *they can achieve surprise* just as readily as did the Arabs in 1973. Thus (with the "timeless verities" in mind) since NATO does not have existing field fortifications, and does not (in my opinion) possess the same kind of combat effectiveness superiority that the Israelis enjoyed over the Arabs, I believe that *under the existing circumstances,* a Warsaw Pact surprise attack will be successful, and that we will lose a war in Europe.

TABLE 9
Selected Battle Statistics, 1805–1944

		Attacker[1]	Defender	N_A/N_D [2]	Victor	N_1/N_L [3]
Austerlitz	1805	French	Allies	0.84	A	0.84
Waterloo	1815	Allies	French	1.79	A	1.79
Antietam	1862	Union	Confed	1.77	D	0.56
Gettysburg	1863	Confed	Union	0.85	D	1.18
Peronne	1918	Germans	Allies	2.40	A	2.40
Montdidier	1918	Germans	Allies	1.20	D	0.83
Ukraine	1941	Germans	Soviets	0.88	A	0.88
Kursk-Oboyan	1943	Germans	Soviets	0.69	A	0.69
Anzio	1944	Germans	U.S.	2.05	D	0.49
Velletri	1944	U.S.	Germans	1.19	D	0.84

SUMMARY: In 10 battles — 5 Attackers, 5 Defenders successful

4 Numerically inferior attackers of these, three successful

3 Victors numerically superior (33%)

7 Victors numerically inferior (67%)

(1) Attacker shown was in attack posture etc.
(2) Ratio of numerical strength of attacker to defender
(3) Ratio of numerical strength of victor to loser

TABLE 10
QJM Analyses of Selected Battles, 1805–1944

		N_a/N_d [1]	W_a/W_d [1]	Basic Combat Power Ratio P_a/P_d [2]	Surprise Effects	Refined Ratio P_a/P_d [3]	Result [4]	Effective Ratio PR_a/PR_d [5]	CEV_a [6]
Austerlitz	1805	0.84	0.87	0.94	1.73	1.63	13.46	3.69	2.26
Waterloo	1815	1.79	1.97	1.86	2.82	5.25	11.67	3.33	0.63
Antietam	1862	1.77	1.78	1.16	—	1.16	−2.02	0.71	0.61
Gettysburg	1863	0.85	0.85	0.55	—	0.55	−4.15	0.55	1.00
Peronne	1918	2.40	2.55	1.33	1.12	1.47	8.20	2.64	1.77
Montdidier	1918	1.20	0.95	0.60	—	0.60	−1.61	0.76	1.27
Ukraine	1941	0.88	1.18	0.82	1.33	1.09	11.90	3.38	3.10
Kursk-Ohovan	1943	0.69	0.79	0.49	—	0.49	1.60	1.32	2.68
Anzio	1944	2.05	1.31	0.49	—	0.49	−3.47	0.59	1.21
Velletri	1944	1.19	2.18	1.59	0.60	0.95	−1.48	0.77	0.81

(1) Ratio of the total proving ground weapons values of attacker to those of defender.

(2) Combat power ratio of attacker to defender, considering all variable effects except behavioral and qualitative.

(3) Product of two previous columns.

(4) Quantified assessment of battle outcome; positive value means attacker success; negative value means defender success.

(5) Actual combat power ratio, based upon quantified battle outcome.

(6) Relative combat effectiveness of attacker with respect to defender; value less than 1.0 means that defender had greater combat effectiveness due to superiority in leadership, or training, or experience, or in some combination of intangible variables relating to combat effectiveness.

Appendix
Distillation

This appendix is an effort to distill wisdom from this book, to serve as a possible guide to research that might enable our republic both to promote and to control military excellence without danger to our essentially free society. Presented below, in the form of *Observations* and *Recommendations* are nuggets of wisdom that one military historian believes he has gleaned from the past, as a first step toward such research.

Observations

1. Prior to the development of nuclear weapons, there were three major advances in weapon lethality that created significant discontinuities in military tactics and organization: (a) the adoption of gunpowder weapons; (b) the introduction of the rifled musket with a cylindro-conoidal bullet; and (c) the combined impact of automatic weapons and high explosives on the battlefield.
2. The individual soldier has become increasingly independent in combat; this in turn has not only called for improved training, discipline, motivation, and coordination, it has also required fostering improvement in intelligence, initiative, and judgment on the part of each individual at lower levels.
3. The process of doctrinal assimilation of new weapons into compatible tactical and organizational systems has proved to be much more significant than invention of a weapon, or adoption of a prototype, regardless of the dimensions of the advance in lethality.
4. Assimilation of a significant increase in lethality has generally been marked (a) by dispersion, thus reducing the number of people exposed to the new weapon in the enemy's hands; (b) by giving greater freedom of maneuver; and (c) by improving cooperation among the different arms and services.
5. The pace of military invention in the last two centuries, in development of new and improved weapons, has generally followed the accelerating pace of the Industrial Revolution, with the result that the interval from conception of a new

or radically modified weapon to the time of adoption of a workable prototype has generally been growing shorter.

6. In modern times new and radically improved weapons have been appearing in "operations" some fifteen to twenty years after major wars; this time lag is partly due to budgetary and stockpile considerations; it is also due in large measure to the satisfaction of wartime leaders with the weapons and methods with which they became familiar in combat, with (save for a handful of exceptions) consequent lack of interest in new developments until a new generation of leaders appears. This has been true even though some of them became leaders because they were innovators.

7. In modern times — and to some extent in earlier eras — there has been an interval of approximately twenty years between introduction and assimilation of new weapons into compatible military systems; this time lag is in part due to the leadership problem noted before; it is significant that, despite the rising tempo of invention, this time lag remained relatively constant. This also applies to current efforts to assimilate tactical nuclear weapons into U.S. Army doctrine.

8. The criteria for judging the assimilation of new or greatly modified weapons are:
   a. Confident employment in accordance with a doctrine assuring compatible coordination with other weapons.
   b. Consistently effective, flexible use in offensive warfare, permitting full exploitation of advantages of superior leadership and/or resources.
   c. Doctrinal capability for dealing effectively with anticipated and unanticipated countermeasures.
   d. Decline in casualties for the employers of the weapon, often combined with a capability for inflicting disproportionately heavy losses on an enemy.

9. The preconditions for assimilation have been:
   a. Imaginative, competent, knowledgeable leadership.
   b. Effective coordination of a nation's economic, technological-scientific, and military resources.
   c. Opportunity for evaluation and analysis of battlefield experience.

10. For the mid- to late-twentieth century no way has yet been found to assure the first of the above preconditions, or (fortunately) to experiment realistically with battlefield conditions in peacetime. A nation's economic, technologi-

cal, scientific and military resources can be effectively coordinated, however, if the following institutional arrangements and policies exist:

    a. Industrial or developmental research institutions, basic research institutions, general and technical military staffs and their supporting agencies, together with administrative arrangements for linking these with one another and with the top decision-making echelons of government.

    b. Conduct of research, developmental and testing activities by these bodies through mutually familiar methods and procedures so that their personnel can communicate, can be mutually supporting, and can evaluate each other's results.

    c. Direction of the efforts of these institutions — in all matters relating to weaponry and doctrine — toward a common and clearly defined goal.

11. There are indications that the development of imaginative, competent, knowledgeable military leadership can be assured, or at least enhanced, by an intensive effort to analyze the causes and essential nature of military creativity, and to develop presumably achievable means for stimulating and enhancing such creativity and for elimination or suppression of the inhibitions to such creativity.

12. Consistent leadership in producing effective military innovations in the modern world is not an accident, not the reflection of some racial military aptitude, but is a function of a political administration that shares the rational and scientific outlook in common with supporting research and industrial institutions.

13. Prussian-German preeminence in military affairs during the century from 1848 to 1945 was due in large part to realization by Prussia and Germany, before other nations, that the Industrial Revolution required a systematic approach to assimilation of weapons and doctrine along the lines suggested by observations 9 and 10; this approach, built around their army's general staff, also permitted them to exploit fully and promptly their own battlefield experience and that of others; the results gave Germany significant, and in some instances decisive, military advantages over other nations, or numerically superior combinations of nations that had comparable or superior scientific and technical capabilities.

14. There is no indication that a technological breakthrough

can be expected in the near future that may permit — in peacetime — the equivalent of true battlefield testing essential for assimilation; thus the results of peacetime testing must be closely scrutinized in relation to historical experience, to assure the greatest possible realism in assessments and decisions relating to the changes.

15. Save for the recent significant exception of strategic nuclear weapons, there have been no historical instances in which new and more lethal weapons have, of themselves, altered the conduct of war or the balance of power until they have been incorporated into a new tactical system exploiting their lethality and permitting their coordination with other weapons; the full significance of this one exception is not yet clear, since the changes it has caused in warfare and the influence it has exerted on international relations have yet to be tested in war.

16. Until the present time, the application of sound, imaginative thinking to the problems of warfare (on either an individual or an institutional basis) has been more significant than any new weapon; such thinking is necessary to real assimilation of weaponry; it can also alter the course of human affairs without new weapons.

17. Theoretical, quantified, lethality indices, applicable to all weapons, can be derived by applying to the characteristics of a weapon such factors as rate of fire, number of targets per strike, relative incapacitating effect per strike, effective range, accuracy, reliability, battlefield mobility (where applicable), and fighting machine capability (where applicable).

18. Theoretical lethality indices appear to provide a basis for (a) selecting significant weapons developments in history for special analysis and (b) relating weapon lethality to tactical dispersion and mobility for analytical purposes.

19. There is a serious and major requirement for intensive collection, collation, and analysis of military statistics, to put to use the great mass of experimental data that has been generally neglected.

20. Relationships among lethality, dispersion, and the mobility of reserves, as demonstrated in historical combat, may prove useful in testing the possible battlefield viability of current or proposed organization and doctrine of tactical nuclear combat forces.

21. The assimilation of tactical nuclear weapons into a viable military doctrine poses unprecedented difficulties; but

three major human issues require the most urgent attention: morale, survivability, and leadership in the environment of a nuclear battlefield.

22. There is need for further investigation of psychological influences in wars of the past to provide insights relevant to likely military behavior of different national and ethnic groups in warfare of the future.

23. There is need for carefully developed educational programs to foster the understanding and transfer of ideas between the midrange personnel of the many specialized institutions and professions now concerned with preparation for war.

24. During most of military history there have been marked and observable imbalances between military efforts and military results, an imbalance particularly manifested by inconclusive battles and high combat casualties. More often than not this imbalance seems to be a reflection of incompatibility, or incongruence, between the weapons of warfare available and the means and/or tactics employing the weapons. In modern times the American Civil War and World War I have exemplified such imbalances and incongruities.

25. There have been six important tactical systems in military history in which weapons and tactics were in obvious congruence, and which were able to achieve decisive results at small casualty costs while inflicting disproportionate numbers of casualties. These systems were:

the Macedonian system of Alexander the Great, ca. 340 B.C.

the Roman system of Scipio and Flamininus, ca. 200 B.C.

the Mongol system of Genghis Khan, ca. A.D. 1200

the English system of Edward I, Edward III, and Henry V, ca. A.D. 1350

the French system of Napoleon, ca. 1800

the German blitzkrieg system, ca. 1940

26. Obviously the six systems listed above flourished in part because of the presence of military genius and other historical accidents. It should be noted, however, that these systems can be grouped in chronological sets of two, with about one hundred forty to one hundred fifty years between the systems in the sets, about fifteen hundred years between the midpoints of the first and second sets and about six hundred years between the midpoints of the second and third sets. The possible periodicity of these re-

lationships warrants further study in order to understand better how congruence of weapons and tactics has occurred in the past.

Recommendations

1. There should be a comprehensive review of present U.S. military methods, procedures, and organizations related to the development of tactics, organization, and doctrine for assimilation of new and prospective weapons. This review should focus on budgets, institutional arrangements, utilization of existing means, and the development of new means to assure the most adequate possible testing and evaluation in peace and in war.

2. Means of fostering military creativity should be explored.

3. The learning process in the armed forces should be critically examined, subjected to systems analysis, and arranged to ensure that it will continually acquire, process, store, retrieve, analyze, and publish data and conclusions relevant to combat effectiveness, and that this data will then be presented in timely fashion to the appropriate staffs and commanders at all levels.

4. Basic research in the related processes of the invention of weapons, their adoption, and their assimilation through changes in tactics, organization, and doctrine, is badly needed. Authoritative studies of the actual functioning of the German general staff, for example, are not to be found, yet it was a key factor in the development of modern military practices. Case histories in scholarly monograph form of significant tactical innovations and increases in lethality of weapons would provide material for analysis in depth and later recommendations in regard to U.S. policies and institutions.

5. The U.S. Army should encourage research into the history, economics, and sociology of military staffs and institutions in the same way it now encourages research in the natural sciences.

6. A research program should be undertaken leading to improved utilization of quantified or quantifiable military experience and statistics, and including exploration of new vistas and theories in quantification revealed in this study.

7. Studies should be made of the major human factors in fu-

ture war, with particular emphasis on the problems of morale, survivability, and leadership in the environment of the tactical nuclear battlefield.

8. Intensive interdisciplinary investigation of the cultural aspects of military behavior, and particularly the military effect of psychological influences on different national and ethnic groups, should be undertaken.

9. Educational programs should be prepared — if possible on an interservice national basis — to foster closer understanding and better transfer of ideas between midrange personnel of the many specialized institutions and professions — military and civilian — now concerned with preparation for war.

10. Forecasts of future wars should be produced through the collaboration of military historians and military planners based on reasonable interactions between new technology and the "timeless verities."

11. Historical studies should be made of the historical military systems that have been marked by congruence between weapons and tactics in order to ascertain the military and historical causes or occasions of such congruence, as a guide to achieving improved congruence of tactics and weapons in the short-term future.

Index